Historical Grammar of the Visual Arts

Historical Grammar of the Visual Arts

Aloïs Riegl

Translated by Jacqueline E. Jung

Foreword by Benjamin Binstock

ZONE BOOKS · NEW YORK

2004

Published with the assistance of the Getty Grant Program.

First paperback edition 2021
ISBN *978-1-890951-46-7*
First ebook edition 2021
ISBN *978-1-942130-XX-X*

Printed in the United States of America.

Distributed by Princeton University Press,
Princeton, New Jersey, and Woodstock, United Kingdom

Library of Congress Cataloging-in-Publication Data
Riegl, Aloïs.
    [Historische Grammatik der bildenden Künste.
English]
    Historical grammar of the visual arts / Aloïs Riegl;
translated by Jacqueline E. Jung; edited and foreword
by Benjamin Binstock.
        p.   cm.
    Includes bibliographical references and index.
    ISBN 1-890951-45-5 (cloth)
    1. Art—History. 2. Art—Philosophy. I. Binstock,
Benjamin. II. Title.

N5303.R513 2004
709—dc21

                                    2003053821

Contents

Second Version

Aloïs Riegl, Monumental Ruin

Why We Still Need to Read Historical Grammar of the Visual Arts

Benjamin Binstock

Art historians may come and art historians may go and never change your point of view; when I run dry, I stop awhile and think of Aloïs Riegl (1858–1905).[1] The intelligence, originality, and range of Riegl's writings remain unsurpassed in the history of art-historical scholarship. As a founder of his discipline and one of its most radical thinkers, Riegl represents a crucial precedent for the current reevaluation of the theory and practice of art history. The greatest representative of the Vienna school, Riegl pioneered analysis of evolving formal elements and modes of representation, their changing relation to the viewer, and the connection between "high" and "low" art or what would now be called visual culture. The legendary connoisseur Bernard Berenson is said to have displayed Riegl's *Spätrömische Kunstindustrie* on a lectern in his study as a "sacred text" of art history. More recently, the historian Andrea Giardina has invoked an "explosion of late antique" studies resulting from Riegl's invention of the term a century ago.[2] Several major art historians have sought to appropriate or to refute his arguments in order to establish their own systems, attempts I will argue were insufficient, bringing us back to Riegl's thought as the best possible albeit flawed foundation for the ongoing construction of the art-historical edifice. Although Riegl's texts are often outdated in their language and presentation, they involve crucial and potentially subversive ideas about art and art history, and he remains inadequately appreciated and read, particularly in the English-speaking world. As the translator of this volume Jacqueline Jung reminds us in her preface, the difficulty of Riegl's language also reflects the extraordinary profundity of his thought. In short, Riegl is both a colossus and antiquated, unsurpassable and inadequate, a monumental ruin (figure 22). *Historical Grammar of the Visual Arts* distills the diverse threads of his work and the essence of his distinct visual analysis in exceptionally accessible form as a primer or bible of formalism. If you are interested in art history, you should read this book and keep it, if not on a lectern in your study, on your shelf.

Riegl began his career at the Museum for Art and Industry of Vienna and wrote his first text on patterns in Oriental rugs, the origins of which he ingeniously traced to ancient Greek decorative motifs.[3] He extended his investigation of decorative patterns back to ancient Egypt in his following book, *Stilfragen*, or "Questions of Style," which a prominent scholar called "the one great book written about the history of ornament."[4] Appointed first *Extraordinarius* and then *Ordinarius*, or full professor, at the University of Vienna, Riegl quickly expanded his fields of expertise to include painting, sculpture, and architecture and took a leave of absence in 1897–1898 to compose his ambitious theoretical overview *Historical Grammar of the Visual Arts*. He elaborated on *Historical Grammar* in a lecture course the following year intended as a revision of his book but never finished his study, which was posthumously published by his students, although not, as here, with illustrations.[5] Instead, he developed some of its most profound insights into densely detailed, book-length *magna opera* on late Roman art and the Dutch group portrait.[6] After composing a few more brilliant essays, Riegl died at the age of forty-seven.

As the transition between his earlier, more narrowly "empirical" investigations and his mature interpretive studies, *Historical Grammar* can serve for those unfamiliar with Riegl's work as a succinct introduction to his ideas, and for Riegl adepts as a prime vista from which to assess his career as a whole. Because Riegl's study exists as two drafts, it provides unique insight into his evolving thought. In contrast to the exhaustive close readings of example after example in his other major texts, Riegl's *Historical Grammar* offers an unusual breadth of historical scope, illustrating an astounding range of expertise. His study integrates the different visual arts within a broad development related to the history of culture. Riegl follows a progression from the near view and tactile, static, volumetric, and symmetrical forms in Egyptian art, through the normal view and delicate balance of idealism and naturalism in classical Greek art, to the far view and optical, subjectively perceived, dynamic, and transient forms in Hellenistic and Roman art. This progression does not end with Antiquity, but proceeds with various modulations through the Middle Ages, Renaissance, and Baroque period up to our own day. We have included images primarily to remind Riegl's readers that his text is the living spirit of intellect rather than a dead object of antiquarian interest. The necessarily limited illustrations reflect some of his idiosyncratic, repeated references and the broader arc of his thought. But his insights are infinite in application and relevant to the entire span of the history of art.

The Will of Art

Riegl's most famous idea, and arguably the linchpin of all his thought, is *Kunstwollen*. Scholars cannot agree on an English translation of the term or what it means and often leave it in German as a transcendental signifier without a signified. *Kunstwollen* has previously been translated as "will to art," "will to form," "art-drive," "aesthetic urge," "that which wills art," "artistic volition," "art as will," "stylistic will," and "artistic will." All these translations err on the side of either a mystical (Hegelian) "spirit" acting through art or the given fact of the artist's intention or will. The most literal and, in my view, correct translation, adopted here, is "the will of art" (or art's will).[7] This translation accurately conveys that the principle at stake is not subsumed within an impersonal social or historical will, or limited to the intention or will of the artist, but rather grounded in art's evolving formal or visual elements or language. To adapt an infamous phrase of Woody Allen's: the art wants what it wants.

Riegl introduced his term in *Stilfragen* in the context of a debate with his contemporary Gottfried Semper (1803–1879), a major architect, artist, and theorist whose book *Der Stil* (Style) proposed that the style of an artwork was determined by function, material, and technique. Riegl acknowledged the importance of these factors but insisted on something prior and more crucial: "All art history manifests itself as a struggle with the material. Not the tool or technique has precedence in this struggle, but the creative artistic thought [*kunstschaffende Gedanke*], which wishes to widen its field of creation and intensify its formative power."[8] By the time of his book on late Roman art, Riegl had consolidated this and other terms such as "artistic thought" (*Kunstgedanke*) or "the purpose of art" (*Kunstzweck*) into *Kunstwollen*:

> In opposition to [Semper's] mechanistic conception of the character of the work of art, I advocated in *Stilfragen*, and as far as I know I was the first to do so, a teleological view according to which I saw in the work of art the result of a specific and consciously purposeful *Kunstwollen* that prevails in battle against function, raw material and technique.[9]

14

Margaret Olin has most carefully followed Riegl's use of *Kunstwollen* and similar terms. She believes Riegl initially "made no claim to originality" and ultimately "had no reason to claim priority for the concept" but instead "wished to resurrect" an earlier approach, citing prior emphasis on the artist's creative will and use of a related term, *künstlerisches Wollen*, by earlier art historians. In her view, "the very flexibility of the terminology suggests a more casual attitude toward the term *Kunstwollen* than the one that caused him to trumpet it as a newly developed 'teleological principle.'"[10] On the other hand, Olin posits a fundamental transformation in Riegl's outlook between the first and the second draft of *Historical Grammar*. "While the first merely struggles with the opposition between idealism and realism that troubled Riegl during the mid-1890's," she claims, "the second transforms Riegl's positivistic view of art as a quasi-scientific mode of description into a voluntaristic view of art as will."[11] Olin has read Riegl more closely than any scholar, and her points are well taken. Emphasis on the creative will of the artist dates back to the Renaissance and Antiquity. Nor did Riegl's concept spring forth fully formed at the outset of his career. Rather, he slowly elaborated on his idea, drawing progressively and cumulatively on different kinds of visual evidence, media, and historical periods and casting about for different terms, continually reformulating his thought, including the second draft of his *Historical Grammar*.

However, Olin, in my view, exaggerates the distinction between the two drafts of this text and underestimates the underlying coherence and originality of Riegl's idea. When, near the end of his career, Riegl refers back to his early use of the term *Kunstwollen* in *Stilfragen*, he is not misrepresenting himself but clarifying the development of his thought, as well as his concept. His teleological perspective involves a broader historical development derived from Hegel, yet Hegel's *Aesthetics* was not yet art history, since he subordinated art to Spirit and offered no specific methodology for reading visual art. Conversely, Semper turned too one-sidedly toward concrete factors of function, material, and technique. Riegl finds a middle ground between the unfolding of Spirit on the one hand and function or technique on the other in the formal elements of the work of art *as art*, the specifically visual character of its thought. He thereby saves art from being reduced to an illustration of history or a purely technical affair.

Riegl makes his argument explicit in *Historical Grammar*:

> Why does man create art? What is the purpose of the work of art? With these questions, we seem to have returned to the element of function, which played such a crucial role in Semper's empirical aesthetics. The kind of purpose Semper had in mind, however, was merely external.... We may now flesh out our definition: the creation of art is a contest with nature with the aim of bringing to expression a harmonious worldview.
>
> Herein resides the true purpose of art. All the external functions encountered thus far are merely welcome vehicles for the activation of art's supreme purpose. The drive to create art — that is, the human need for harmony — does not let any opportunity slip by without putting it to use. Thus each object arising from an external purpose is, more or less, a work of art. Yet external purpose must nevertheless be strictly distinguished from the purpose of art. The purpose of art coincides with conceptual purpose only when the conception is aimed directly at a harmonious worldview — for example, in Greek statues of gods, such as Jupiter Tonans [with the thunderbolt], or in the crucifix. One can accordingly recognize the fundamental mistake of Semper's theory, which stated that the creation of art originated with the practical purpose of utility. (Pp. 297, 300–301)

As an example, Riegl cites the earliest extant artifact, the arrow-head. This does not result simply from chipping at stone (technique) or the need to puncture an animal's flesh (function), for which other alternatives would suffice, but manifests harmony and symmetry (p. 351). The same principle applies in the case of the pyramids and onward through Greek and Roman temples, medieval cathedrals, and Baroque palaces. Riegl further complicates the "human need for harmony" by opposing what he calls "harmonism" within a historical dialectic to "Organism," terms that are roughly equivalent to "idealism" and "naturalism," "beauty" and "truth."

According to Riegl, art cannot be reduced to its practical, empirical function, but always manifests its own end or purpose, as art. He thus takes issue with the conventional view, still prevalent in art history today, that "art for art's sake" was an invention of the nineteenth century:

> One often hears the remark that the dichotomy between *industrial art* — that is, functional art — and *high art* — that is, art made for its own sake — is an exclusive characteristic of our own modern age and that earlier periods were blissfully unaware of the contrast. Our historical investigation of the developmental relationship between art and objective function clearly proves this notion to be false. Seventeenth-century Dutch seascapes were surely "high art"; but the same holds true for the Grimani reliefs and Roman Imperial portraits. (P. 122)[12]

Riegl therefore directs himself against the likewise prevailing emphasis in art history on the ostensible historical (religious or institutional) function of the artwork. He offers a humorously succinct objection to this outlook:

If an auction catalog labels each work first and foremost according to its functional intent, this is justifiable insofar as a potential buyer, *who need not be a particularly insightful or knowledgeable lover of art*, will principally want to know how he can put the thing to use. But it is questionable whether the discipline of art history should be satisfied with such a justification. (P. 121, my emphasis)

As opposed to the historian or other scholars, the art historian should be a particularly insightful and knowledgeable lover of art, one dare say, of the will of art.

Portraiture provides another example of the distinction between external practical function and art's inner purpose, or the will of art, as well as the dialectic of harmonism and Organism. In earlier times, portraiture embodied "the now-obsolete notion that a person is truly an individual entity," whereas today art

must depict not the individual, who no longer exists — or, more precisely, is a set of molecules too tiny to be depicted — but the universal connectedness of all natural phenomena. This art presents its subject not as a physically unified individual but as a complex of optical appearances that strike the beholder's eye instantaneously.

You might be thinking that this is just the exaggerated theory of a crazed hypermodern man. But you will see things differently if you trace the history of portrait painting back a few centuries. The precursors of modern Impressionism were the Dutch painters of the seventeenth century.... Now we must ask: What is the external purpose of a modern portrait? Portrayal of individuality; the patron, at least, still desires this. What is art's purpose? Portrayal of causal relationships in nature. Extrinsic purpose and art's purpose are thus two separate things; not only do they not correspond, but they even contradict each other. Today, the purpose of art predominates. One can predict the final result: art's purpose will completely subsume the

18

external purpose, and people will cease having their portraits made. (Pp. 361–62)

Art's purpose not only does not necessarily correspond to its external practical function but can even contradict this, hence the modern obsolescence of portraiture. The dissolution of the individual is further related to the shift from near view and tactile to far view and optical, or objective to subjective, yet Impressionism can also be traced back to seventeenth-century Dutch painters and, as Riegl explains elsewhere, late Antiquity (p. 388). The will of art as "a contest with nature with the aim of bringing to expression a harmonious worldview" is thereby given endless permutations and interconnections in close readings of visual elements of artworks throughout history, in a formalist fugue, or "Riegl variations."

The Reception of Riegl

Riegl's ideas have had a long journey to their current need for reevaluation. One of the earliest and most famous confrontations involved Erwin Panofsky (1892–1968), at that time a young pioneer of the iconological method who would go on to help establish the modern discipline of art history in America. In his 1920 essay "The Concept of *Kunstwollen*," Panofsky sought to defend Riegl's argument against mistaken interpretations, insisting that art "necessarily demand[s] consideration from other than a purely historical point of view." He specifically proposes to limit Riegl's concept to the objective "immanent meaning" of a single artwork, presenting his own method as an art-historical new covenant in relation to a Moses-like Riegl: "He himself could not recognize that he had justified a transcendental philosophy of art."[13] However, the distinction between their outlooks on this point is slight. Immanent or inherent meaning is another way of saying the meaning of art *as art*, that is, the will of art. Unfortunately, in the hands of Panofsky's acolytes, the iconographic method often amounts to precisely the opposite approach, an effort to reconstruct the function or objective message of an artwork for its audience, based on conventional thought of the period or, worse, a theological moral.[14] Riegl does not approach artworks as a means to convey a message (what), but interprets the cultural and historical content of formal or visual elements (how).

Whereas Panofsky addresses the meaning of a single artwork, Riegl is concerned with artworks inextricably embedded in a tradition and broader progression. Panofsky explicitly positioned himself in relation to the philosophy of Immanuel Kant and the neo-Kantian philosopher Ernst Cassirer, who approached art as a transhistorical phenomenon. Riegl's teleological or developmental scheme derives from Hegel, who historicized both art and Kantian aesthetics and thereby established the history of art. In attempting to found a transcendental philosophy of art, Panofskian art history, like Kantian philosophy, cannot address its own belated relation to history, or the history of art history. Following Hegel, Riegl recognized that the meaning of art is necessarily determined belatedly and subject to revision as part of an ongoing historiographical process.

Another major confrontation with Riegl involved Sir Ernst Gombrich (1909–2001), whose popular books have helped to shape public perception of art history throughout the world. Gombrich, who was originally from Vienna but did not identify with the Vienna school, vehemently rejected "attempts to rationalize the intuitive feeling that the various manifestations of an age are not random, but exhibit a common character, a common spirit." He "frequently criticized these rationalizations, particularly in their Hegelian versions," and offered an extended and specific critique of Riegl's book on late Roman art, *Spätrömische Kunstindustrie*:

A careful reader of the book will find, for instance, that Riegl sometimes rejected the evidence of coins found with the objects, because they suggested a date too early to suit his sequence. Moreover, some of the perceptual effects he so brilliantly analyzed as manifestations of a given phase in the evolution of the *Kunstwollen* are far from unique to this stylistic group. After all, there is no ornament that plays more teasingly with the switch between figure and ground than the Greek key pattern. A stroll through any collection of tribal art is also likely to produce intriguing parallels to Riegl's specimens. Some tribal artifacts may be explained as the results of diffusion and imitation, but with others there is no such possibility, and we would have to attribute to various remote regions the same perceptual development which we found in the Western world.

Riegl would have found difficulty in admitting such pluralism because, like his earlier *Stilfragen*, the *Spätrömische Kunstindustrie* has a polemical edge. The demonstration of the "synchronic" unities of artistic developments and of their intrinsic necessity was aimed — consciously or unconsciously — at the critics of modern developments who were trying in vain to stop the stars in their courses. Its message, popularized in Worringer's *Abstraction and Empathy*, was taken up by the revolutionary movements in the art of the early twentieth century, which strove to fashion a new art for the new age. The longing for such an escape from the stale round of historical styles inspired the movement of *Art Nouveau*, for which the unity of high and applied art was so vital a demand. No wonder that the study of style was colored by this quest for inner cohesion and unity. Its roots lie in the artistic situation of the nineteenth century.

Gombrich goes on to add, ironically: "Maybe a champion of Riegl's unitary theories would here object that our comparisons remained too close to the surface of the phenomena. If we dig deep enough we may still find the same *Kunstwollen* manifested in all of them."[15]

I would say Gombrich does not remain close enough to the surface of the phenomena, in the formal or visual qualities of artworks staring us in the face, or, as Riegl would say, in the differences between surface and depth, figure and ground, tactile and optical. Gombrich's other objections are just as easily refuted. His dubious claim that Riegl fudged evidence in relation to coins is irrelevant, since Riegl puts forward the same development in *Historical Grammar* without recourse to the objects whose dating Gombrich disputes. The figure-ground reversal in the Greek key pattern noted by Gombrich does not contradict but rather underscores the progression outlined by Riegl, which moves from such marginal patterns to whole mosaics or the interior of the Pantheon. Similar examples in tribal art are likewise no counterargument; these traditions either had their own, parallel development or were produced in an entirely different context, which is no refutation of the development articulated by Riegl. Nor is Riegl responsible for Wilhelm Worringer's arguments or Art Nouveau, which he possibly influenced. Gombrich's accusation that Riegl's argument derives from a polemic against stylistic pluralism in modern art is equally groundless. He never mentions stylistic pluralism, and in any case, as a historian, he is concerned with observing and explaining rather than opposing such developments. Riegl explicitly states, "There is one major deficiency in the modern era of art as compared with the two preceding ones, and this is that art has become the privilege of only a few social strata — namely, the cultivated elite" (p. 98).[16]

Gombrich was likely also reacting in part to the fate of Riegl's ideas in the hands of Hans Sedlmayr (1896–1984). Sedlmayr presented himself as a spokesman for "the quintessence of Riegl's thought," but he misrepresented *Kunstwollen* as simply another word for "style," a reductive interpretation that allowed him to introduce his own reactionary political and religious content.[17] Sedlmayr has been called Panofsky's "evil twin" and provides a curious parallel in his ambivalent reception of Riegl. The two younger scholars, fighting over Riegl's legacy or mantle, not only cannot improve on his term *Kunstwollen*, but manage to exclude the role of "art" in their interpretations of the concept, rending the mantle, so to speak, into the dichotomy of meaning and style. As the Nazi director of the art-historical institute of the University of Vienna during the war, Sedlmayr presided over the bankruptcy and dissolution of the Vienna school as Panofsky and Gombrich, among others, fled the Continent. After the war, until his death in 1984, the "rehabilitated" Sedlmayr continued to play a major role in German academic art history. Even if we leave aside the thorny problem of the relation of Sedlmayr's political activities to his scholarship and ideas, his ahistorical formalism was not Riegl's.[18]

Admittedly, Riegl makes off-putting references to racial groups. In *Historical Grammar*, he claims the Germanic peoples "had proved themselves at once possessed of an undoubted talent for ruling and little inclined, by virtue of their intrinsic good nature, to put the right of the stronger to . . . use" (p. 85). In Riegl's time, French art "is again having to surrender its erstwhile leadership to Germanic stock of purer racial consciousness" (p. 104). After the Holocaust, such pronouncements take on a macabre ring. Yet Riegl observes there is "no need to attribute any decisive role to the racial differences of the peoples in question. It seems obvious from the outset that the North would be less burdened by the heavy weight of tradition and that it consequently would, as a rule, represent the more progressive tendency" (p. 78). The issue here is neither the distinctions between the Germans and the French, which we recognize, nor their racial basis, which we do not recognize, but rather specific readings of particular formal elements of artworks in relation to these distinctions, which is Riegl's invaluable contribution. With all the excessive politically correct discourse in art history today, I personally find Riegl's outdated voice amusing, as when he observes: "We Teutons, with our deep emotional sensitivity, perceive the inner agitation of Italian Baroque figures as contrived and affected" (p. 168). On this score, we can all get in touch with the Teuton inside us.

Gombrich claims "it would be a pity if the immense value of Riegl's observations were obscured by certain weaknesses in his method," but Riegl's observations result directly from his method, whereas their value has been obscured by the objections of Gombrich and others, based on trivial points or misunderstandings.[19] Despite his methodological qualms, and like Panofsky before him, Gombrich furthermore ends up adopting many of Riegl's conclusions, presenting them in terms of his own commonsense formulas. Gombrich's famous dictum "Making comes before Matching" is merely a simplified version of Riegl's assertion on the first page of *Historical Grammar* that "the creation of visual art is a contest with nature, not a desire for interchangeability with nature" (p. 52).

More importantly, whereas Gombrich reduces the Western pictorial tradition to a monolithic (Hegelian) process of perfecting "illusion," Riegl sees competing or contrary representational aims at work. Hegel organized history into a totalizing system, with Greek sculpture as the pinnacle of artistic achievement in world culture, and proclaimed the end of art in his time as *aufgehoben*, or sublated, by philosophy as a vehicle of religious thought. By contrast, Riegl's close reading of the formal elements of artworks is predicated on cultural relativism: Greek art fits between Egyptian and Roman art within a broader progression involving different aims and achievements. Riegl also recognized that art in his time was developing different means and tasks, independent of religion. Adapting a Kantian formula, we might characterize Riegl's system as teleology without *telos* (goal).[20]

Riegl himself anticipates Gombrich's objections, distinguishes his outlook from Hegel's, and reminds us of the impossibility of escaping Hegel (another monumental ruin) in addressing the history of art when he objects to one scholar who

> seeks the principle of coherence not in the work of art itself but in the prevailing parallels with the development in politics and the spiritual life of different peoples.... This presumed coherence unquestionably exists, although it is frequently denied by pedants. In my opinion, this coherence is nothing less than the unconscious prerequisite of all historical thought.[21]

In short, Riegl acknowledges Hegel's essential insight into the connection between culture and history but opposes those who interpret art mechanically as an illustration of history, a mistake not limited to Hegelians. Nor is the principle of coherence to be sought in the supposed historical function of the work or the artist's intention or technique. Rather, the principle must be grounded in the work of art, its formal elements and visual qualities, or *Kunstwollen*, the will of art.

The Ruin of Art History

Art history as an academic discipline was founded or invented at German-speaking universities. Riegl's *Historical Grammar* could be called "the mother of all art-history surveys," as the first and most ambitious of its kind, succeeded by Gombrich's *Story of Art* and the lavishly illustrated tomes used to introduce undergraduates to art history in America. Riegl refers to his text as "elementary lessons in the visual arts" but warns that this is intended strictly for advanced study (p. 293). At the outset of his second draft, he places his enterprise in the context of the history of his discipline, telling the "story of art history" using an architectural metaphor, in a voice comparable to that of the Old Testament:

One hundred and fifty years have elapsed since the discipline of art history was born, since the structure of a history of art began to be built. In the beginning, Aesthetics was the master builder. She laid the foundations and sketched out the blueprints that would lead the whole project to its future completion. From that foundation three main sections would arise: a central building for architecture and two secondary wings for sculpture and painting. But soon it became apparent that many works of art did not fit into these categories. A fourth section was therefore added, a back wing to stand behind architecture, and it was called industrial art. Then all four parts were raised with speed and vigor into the heights.

But the higher the builders got, the more they were faced with the uncomfortable observation that they had rushed ahead too quickly in their initial zeal. The foundations proved weak, and the building materials, in many cases, poorly chosen and insufficiently prepared. All the blame, of course, was placed squarely on the master builder, Aesthetics, and she was promptly dismissed. The building, people discovered, had to be solid. This did not require a unified and consistent construction process; what mattered instead was to devote all attention and energy to the various wings independently. Here began the second phase of art-historical inquiry: the strengthening of the foundations and the elaboration of the materials — in other words, the phase of specialized investigation. Although the process of construction was not forgotten, it proceeded unevenly and without a plan, for it lacked steady leadership. Those working on one wing paid no attention to the progress of the others. As a result, although the four sections were indeed raised gradually into the heights, the connections between them progressively dissolved.

The problem could not remain unacknowledged for long. Today, the building is lacking connective corners, so that, for all its internal solidity, it still gives the impression of a ruin. It is time to create new connections among the four sections and to endow the fragmented whole with the impression of unity once more. This cannot be achieved without a plan; there needs to be a broad-sighted and consistent process of construction. Who shall be in charge? Once set aside, Aesthetics no longer exists; she has long been dead, and any effect she still possesses resides in the scattered auditoriums of academic philosophy. But she left behind an heiress. Although youthful and yet unnamed, she is present nonetheless. Already she has undertaken certain endeavors that hold much promise for the future, for they put to use the lessons of the history of art. Whereas the old aesthetics wanted to give instruction to the discipline of art history, her heiress — modern aesthetics, if you will — eagerly lets art history teach her. She recognizes that her very right to exist lies rooted in the history of art. (Pp. 287–88)

Like Gombrich, Riegl believes the structure created by the master builder Hegel was unsound, although not because of his unavoidable search for unities but because of his assumption that Spirit dictates to art. Hence the need for positivist art history and Riegl's integration of different media within a broader historical progression. In a slightly earlier essay from 1897 titled "A New Art History," Riegl compares the evolution of his discipline to the building of Saint Peter's in Rome. He equates the work of Johann Joachim Winckelmann and his successors with Donato Bramante's columns, which had to be "reinforced" by positivistic research in the nineteenth century, before the equivalent of Michelangelo and Giacomo della Porta's crowning cupola could be constructed in the form of a theoretical model encompassing all art history, to be supplied by Riegl himself.[22] In *Historical Grammar*, he asserts that "the actual crown of the whole, the clear recognition of the essence of the visual arts, can only become accessible through the developmental history of art's basic elements, dictated by the highest guiding factor of all artistic production" (p. 292). The highest guiding factor, the cupola or crown of the whole, is *Kunst-wollen*, the will of art. Another way of expressing the concept is "historical grammar of the visual arts":

> Language likewise has its proper elements, and we call the develop-mental history thereof the historical grammar of the language in question. Someone who merely wants to speak the language has no use for this grammar, nor does anyone who wants simply to under-stand it. But whoever wants to know why the language proceeded along this path and no other, whoever wants to grasp the position of the language within human culture in general — whoever, in a word, wants to comprehend the given language scientifically — cannot do without the historical grammar. (P. 292)

Several scholars have sought to relate Riegl's method to struc-turalism or semiotics, a connection underscored by the word "grammar" in the text published here.[23] Riegl's open-ended, post-Hegelian teleology could also be compared to post-structuralism, specifically the historically rigorous deconstruction of Jacques Derrida, who is reluctant to concede an "outside" to the text, language or representation.[24] In his late essay "The Modern Cult of Monuments," for example, Riegl observes that people create works of art "primarily to satisfy their own practical and ideal needs … without as a rule intending to leave testimony of their artistic and cultural life to later centuries." Accordingly, "when we call such works of art 'monuments' it is a subjective rather than an objective designation."[25] The same principle applies to art.

Not only the status but also the value of artworks is a dynamic cultural construction. Riegl distinguishes between what he calls "historical-value" and "art-value," corresponding roughly to a monument of a past age and a ruin in the present (figure 14). Either "a work of art possesses art-value insofar as it corresponds to a supposedly objective but never satisfactorily defined aesthetic," or "the art-value of a monument is established by the requirements of the modern *Kunstwollen*." Yet "these requirements are even less well defined and in the strictest sense can never be defined because they vary from subject to subject and moment to moment." Accordingly, "at the beginning of the twentieth century, most of us have come to the conclusion that there is no such absolute art-value."[26] Building on Riegl's idea, Walter Benjamin declared the artwork a ruin, having survived its historical context and existing only for its aesthetic truth, a notion elaborated by Derrida, who pronounces the artwork a ruin from the outset.[27]

Riegl's *Historical Grammar* is a survey of the will of art throughout Western art history, the crowning cupola of the art-historical edifice. Yet he also refers to this structure as a "ruin," or, more specifically, he invokes "the impression of a ruin," just as he looks forward to endowing "the fragmented whole with the impression of unity." He thereby calls attention to the potential undoing of his own construction, the ruin of his monument. This potential was concretely manifested in Riegl's career, since he never finished or published *Historical Grammar* but turned instead to his studies of late Roman and Dutch art. The ruin was also manifested through Riegl's reception, since Sedlmayr acted as della Porta to Riegl's Michelangelo in completing the Germanic cupola of the Vienna school, which was destroyed in the war, whereas Riegl's outlook was distorted for the English-speaking world through the well-meaning efforts of Panofsky and Gombrich. Riegl's *Historical Grammar* thus embodies the monumental ruin of German *Kunstwissenschaft*, the science of art history. And there is no going back.

One hundred years later, construction of the great edifice continues apace. Scholars have found that their predecessors "rushed ahead too quickly" and the foundations and building materials were "poorly chosen and insufficiently prepared." Further wings or sections have been added for photography, film, video, installation, and so on. Social historians, feminists, and scholars of gender, psychoanalysis, and cultural studies, among others, working on their own without regard for the other, consider themselves the unnamed young heiress of Aesthetics or, perhaps more accurately, the maidservant who usurped her place. For some, perhaps, not just aesthetics but the history of art has ceased to exist, although they may one day be criticized in turn for rushing ahead too quickly. I would agree with Riegl that art history's "right to exist lies rooted in the history of art," and conversely that there is no access to the history of art without the mediation of art-historical scholarship, whereas our explanations are necessarily elaborated within the history of art history. *Kunstwollen* is not the answer but the question, as close as anyone has come to naming our belated and ongoing effort to understand art as dynamic visual form, the great, unfinished project of art history. The answer must be sought "in the work of art itself," in its "immanent meaning," or the will of art, the best accounts art historians can come up with, an endless, cumulative process or story, *die unendliche Kunstgeschichte*.

Riegl's crucial distinction in *Historical Grammar* between practical external function and art's purpose, refined in his monument essay as "historical-value" and "art-value," is in this regard particularly relevant for his own work. In my view, too much emphasis has been placed on the historical context or function of Riegl's writings, which scholars influenced him, his supposed errors, or outdated elements of his text, as something preserved from the past, a monument. It is not what Riegl got wrong but what he got right that interests us. Far more significant is the value of his text for the present as a ruin, something we draw on for our own purposes, as Panofsky and Gombrich (and Sedlmayr) did before us.

Riegl accordingly has to be translated into English for those who do not read German; and even for those who do, reading Riegl in

English opens entirely new perspectives on his thought. At least in theory; Riegl has not been fortunate in translation. The titles of all three of his major studies published during his lifetime have been awkwardly rendered in English, signaling translations that are excessively literal or excessively loose.[28] Thank goodness, the title *Historical Grammar of the Visual Arts* is correct, as is appropriate for the only faithful and eloquent English translation of one of Riegl's major texts. This is no accident. The translator, Professor Jacqueline Jung, is a prizewinning art historian at the outset of her promising career who has translated Riegl with the exceptional intelligence and care he deserves, in a difficult labor of love. She will not regret her experience. My own effort to translate Riegl was the most rewarding experience of my career.[29] In theory, we should all translate Riegl, but reading Jung's Riegl is the next-best thing. Riegl's translation, in the literal and metaphoric sense, is part of the history of art history, and I think we are starting to get him right. As he himself said, "After all, it is the legacy of original sin that we must err in order to reach the truth."[30]

NOTES

1. The most important study of Riegl is Margaret Olin, *Forms of Representation in Alois Riegl's Theory of Art* (University Park: Pennsylvania State University Press, 1992). Other notable commentaries include Margaret Iversen, *Alois Riegl: Art History and Theory* (Cambridge, MA: MIT Press, 1993); and Michael Podro, *The Critical Historians of Art* (New Haven, CT: Yale University Press, 1982). Christopher Wood, ed., *The Vienna School Reader: Politics and Art Historical Method in the 1930s* (New York: Zone Books, 2000), includes a selection of fundamental texts by Riegl and other members of the Vienna school in English translation, with an excellent introduction and complete bibliographies. I thank Professors Olin, Wood, and Richard Brilliant for their insights. Working with the translator, Professor Jacqueline Jung, has been an effortless labor of love.

I happily acknowledge support from the National Endowment for the Humanities while a member at the Institute for Advanced Study in Princeton, New Jersey, where I wrote this introduction.

2. Andrea Giardina, "Esplosione di tardoantico," *Studi storici* 40 (1999). I thank Professor Glen Bowersock for this reference.

3. Aloïs Riegl, *Altorientalische Teppiche* (Leipzig: T.O. Weigel, 1891).

4. Aloïs Riegl, *Stilfragen: Grundlegungen zu einer Geschichte der Ornamentik* (Berlin: G. Siemens, 1893); Ernst Gombrich, *The Sense of Order: A Study in the Psychology of Decorative Art* (Ithaca, NY: Cornell University Press, 1979), p. 182.

5. Aloïs Riegl, *Historische Grammatik der bildenden Künste*, ed. Karl Swoboda and Otto Pächt (Graz: Böhlau,1966).

6. Aloïs Riegl, *Die Spätrömische Kunstindustrie nach dem Funden in Österreich-Ungarn* (Vienna: K.K. Hof- und Staatsdruckerei, 1901); Aloïs Riegl, "Das holländische Gruppenporträt," *Jahrbuch des allerhöchsten Kaiserhauses* 23 (1902), pp. 71–278; reprinted as Aloïs Riegl, *Das holländische Gruppenporträt* (Vienna: Österreichische Staatsdruckerei, 1931).

7. I previously put forward a brief argument for this translation and interpretation of *Kunstwollen* in Benjamin Binstock, "I've Got You Under My Skin: Riegl, Rembrandt, and the Will of Art History," in Richard Woodfield (ed.), *Framing Formalism: Riegl's Work* (Amsterdam: G+B Arts International, 2001), p. 232.

8. Riegl, *Stilfragen*, p. 24, as translated by Olin, *Riegl's Theory of Art*, p. 70. The passage is garbled in Aloïs Riegl, *Problems of Style: Foundations for a History of Ornament*, trans. Evelyn Kain (Princeton, NJ: Princeton University Press, 1992), p. 33: "All of art history presents itself as a continuous struggle with material; it is not the tool — which is determined by the technique — but the artistically creative idea that strives to expand its creative realm and increase its formal potential."

9. Riegl, *Spätrömische Kunstindustrie*, p. 9, as translated by Olin, *Riegl's Theory of Art*, p. 71.

10. Olin, *Riegl's Theory of Art*, pp. 71–72 and 208 n. 15. Olin even claims that "Semper's alleged reluctance to relinquish the idea of *Kunstwollen* stemmed

not from theory but from practical experience as an architect" (p. 72). She thus attributes Riegl's concept to his predecessor and primary opponent, which would eliminate the need to "resurrect" the idea at all.

11. *Ibid.*, p. 113.

12. Mathew Rampley, "Spectatorship and the Historicity of Art: Re-reading Alois Riegl's *Historical Grammar of the Fine Arts*," *Word and Image* 12.2 (1996), p. 209, claims that for Riegl, it is "only with Dutch painting that 'art' as a culturally autonomous activity first emerges, since all prior image making had consisted of the decorative manipulation of material to some external end." Rampley does not cite a specific passage to this effect. Although Riegl never makes the claim, Dutch paintings could be said to represent a new stage in that they do not serve any explicit function, whereas earlier instances of art as "an end in itself" contradicted their practical functions or used them as "welcome vehicles" or pretexts for their will of art.

13. Erwin Panofsky, "Der Begriff des Kunstwollens" (1920), in Hariolf Oberer and Egon Verheyen (eds.), *Aufsätze zu Grundfragen der Kunstwissenschaft* (Berlin: Hessling, 1964), pp. 38 and 41; Erwin Panofsky, "The Concept of Artistic Volition," trans. Kenneth J. Northcott and Joel Snyder, *Critical Inquiry* 8 (1981), pp. 25 and 30.

14. On this problem see Michael Ann Holly, *Panofsky and the Foundations of Art History* (Ithaca, NY: Cornell University Press, 1984).

15. Gombrich, *Sense of Order*, pp. 197, 199, 201–202.

16. Riegl's numerous points still relevant for modern art include his observation that "the chief endeavor of modern art is to celebrate the animated movement of the organic. It has not succeeded in eliminating the inorganic entirely, of course. Architecture continues to stave off such an attempt" (p. 183). Frank Lloyd Wright eventually proved Riegl wrong with the Guggenheim Museum, although Wright's achievement was later eliminated in turn by the barbaric appropriators of his building, the cultivated elite who inserted a large rectangular structure in its core, among other degradations: so long, Frank Lloyd Wright. On the other hand, this founding crime has ultimately benefited Wright's successor in this vein, Frank Gehry.

17. Hans Sedlmayr, "Die Quintessenz der Lehren Riegls," in Aloïs Riegl, *Gesammelte Aufsätze*, ed. Karl Swoboda (Vienna: Filser, 1929), pp. xii–xxxiv; Hans Sedlmayr, "The Quintessence of Riegl's Thought," in Woodfield, *Framing Formalism*, pp. 11–31. In his introduction to *The Vienna School Reader*, p. 10, Wood rashly adopts Sedlmayr's view that "the word *Kunstwollen* in Riegl can almost always be replaced by the word 'style,'" the inaccuracy of which is evident from every passage with the term cited here.

18. On Sedlmayr as Panofsky's "evil twin" and his Nazi activities, see Wood's introduction to *The Vienna School Reader*, pp. 36, 47. On Sedlmayr's relation to Riegl, see Benjamin Binstock, "Springtime for Sedlmayr? The Future of Nazi Art History," in *Wiener Schule und die Zukunft der Kunstgeschichte* (Vienna: Böhlau, 2004).

19. Gombrich, *Sense of Order*, p. 187. Wolfgang Kemp, "Aloïs Riegl," in Heinrich Dilly (ed.), *Altmeister moderner Kunstgeschichte* (Berlin: Reimer, 1990), pp. 40–41 and 54–55, likewise rejects Riegl's broader historical (Hegelian) claims, as opposed to his invaluable close readings: "The factors are available as endless antitheses: idealism-realism, monotheism-polytheism, anthropomorphism-transcendence, Germanic-Italian, etc., etc. Name the ingredients and the conceptual claptrapparatus [*Begriffsklapparatismus*] will continue to operate for some time.... One would hardly expect that the same author is among the most patient in our discipline at describing the nuance of formal elements." To the contrary, Riegl's close readings of formal elements are not simply the result of patience but predicated precisely on conceptual antitheses. Similar objections are raised by Henri van de Waal, "*The Syndics* and Their Legend," in *Steps Towards Rembrandt*, trans. Patricia Wardle and Alan Griffiths (Amsterdam: North-Holland, 1974), pp. 247–75, against Riegl's study of the Dutch group portrait, the ongoing relevance of which I defend in Benjamin Binstock, "Seeing Representations; or, The Hidden Master in Rembrandt's *Syndics*," *Representations* 83 (2003), pp. 1–37.

20. Rampley, "Spectatorship and the Historicity of Art," pp. 210–11, clearly sets out some of Riegl's connections with and differences from Hegel and Kant.

21. Aloïs Riegl, "Eine neue Kunstgeschichte" (1897), in *Gesammelte Aufsätze*, p. 49.

22. *Ibid.*, pp. 43–46.

23. Iversen, *Alois Riegl*, p. 70; Olin, *Riegl's Theory of Art*, p. 298; Mieke Bal and Norman Bryson, "Semiotics and Art History," *Art Bulletin* 73 (1991), p. 174. Norman Bryson, *Vision and Painting: The Logic of the Gaze* (New Haven, CT: Yale University Press, 1983), pp. xii–xiii, rejects Gombrich's "perceptualist account of art," in which "the viewer is as changeless as the anatomy of vision, and . . . [which] has in effect dehistoricised the relation of the viewer to the painting," yet he faults a semiotic view of art as too rigid, since this implies that "the meaning of the sign is defined only by formal means, as the product of oppositions among signs within an enclosed system." Neither problem applies to Riegl, who historicizes the viewer in terms of changing representations of perception.

24. For "nothing outside of the text," see Jacques Derrida, *Of Grammatology*, trans. Gayatri Spivak (Baltimore: Johns Hopkins University Press, 1976), p. 158.

25. Aloïs Riegl, "The Modern Cult of Monuments: Its Character and Its Origin," trans. Kurt Forster, *Oppositions* 25 (1982), p. 23; Aloïs Riegl, "Der Moderne Denkmalkultus, sein Wesen, seine Entstehung" (1903), in *Gesammelte Aufsätze*, pp. 147–48.

26. Riegl, "Modern Cult of Monuments," p. 23.

27. Walter Benjamin, *The Origin of German Tragic Drama*, trans. John Osborne (London: NLB, 1977), p. 182; Jacques Derrida, *Memoirs of the Blind: The Self-Portrait and Other Ruins*, trans. Pascale-Anne Brault and Michael Naas (Chicago: University of Chicago Press, 1993), pp. 68–69. See also Charles Rosen, "The Ruins of Walter Benjamin," in Gary Smith (ed.), *On Walter Benjamin: Critical Essays and Recollections* (Cambridge, MA: MIT Press, 1988), pp. 140–41 and 151.

28. Rolf Winkes's translation of what he called *Late Roman Art Industry* — the title is admittedly difficult to translate — is so literal it is unreadable. As the passages cited in n. 8 above and n. 30 below demonstrate, Evelyn Kain's translation of what she strangely calls *Problems of Style* is unsatisfactory; it is not simply a question (or problem) of style. The same can be said of what she together with a second translator/reviser bizarrely titled *The Group Portraiture of Holland*.

29. Aloïs Riegl, "Excerpts from *The Dutch Group Portrait*," trans. Benjamin

Binstock, *October* 27 (1995), pp. 3–35, and Aloïs Riegl, "The Main Characteristics of the Late Roman *Kunstwollen*," trans. Christopher Wood, in Wood, *Vienna School Reader*, pp. 87–103, are the next-best translations of Riegl in English and good introductions to his thought.

30. Riegl, *Stilfragen*, p. xix. *Ist es doch menschliche Erbsünde, nur durch Irrthum zur Wahrheit zu gelangen.* Compare Riegl, *Problems of Style*, p. 13: "Only through trial and error can one approach the truth."

Übersetzungsfragen

Form, Communication, and Questions of Translating Riegl

Jacqueline E. Jung

My esteemed colleague Benjamin Binstock refers to the activity of translating Riegl as "a difficult labor of love." This is a beautifully understated way of describing a task that for much of the last four years — through the slow process of first rendering Riegl's text into a rough and literal English, and then refining and re-refining the new versions that emerged — I have been more apt to term "arduous," "excruciating," "interminable." Yet for all the *Kopfzerbrechen* this translation has entailed, I am grateful for having had the opportunity to delve so deeply into this remarkable text and to help Riegl's astonishing thoughts become accessible to the many scholars who have neither the time nor the energy to sift through the difficult German original.

If this book — and all Riegl's writings — teaches us anything, it is that no communication can take place without a formal structure: indeed, that form is as crucial in determining meaning as the conceptual content it embodies, that it in fact determines how the content is perceived. Thus much of the frustration that accompanied this project derived not from Riegl's often convoluted sentences — they do contain a certain formal logic that makes the texture of his writing immensely rich — but from the formal editing that was required if the intelligence of the author's thought was to become evident. For one thing, the English language simply does not accommodate the lengthy chains of modifying clauses or the winding sentence constructions of which Riegl was so fond. The inevitable modification of sentence structures is of course a problem in any translation, but I found it especially troublesome in light of Riegl's own arguments for the supremacy of artistic form. In the following pages, I should like to explain how I approached this problem and why this translation takes the shape it does.

Riegl's dense and complicated syntax is well known to native German speakers and translators alike; but this book posed special problems because Riegl himself never revised these two drafts for publication. Even given the complexity of Viennese academic language at the turn of the twentieth century, one wonders whether a sentence such as the following would have made it past an editor's desk unchanged:

> Die dem Organischen streng zugewandten Holländer (und zu gleicher Zeit auch die Engländer) erblickten also schon mehr als hundert Jahre vor Canova in den schmückungs- und gebrauchszwecklichen Werken der römischen Antike die Natur, d.h. die den leiblich-zwecklichen Gebilden aus toter Materie allein gemässe anorganische unbewegte Grundform, bei diskreter Verwendung des Bewegten lediglich an organischen Motiven.

Translated literally, and following the original syntactic organization, this reads: "The turned-strictly-toward-the-organic Dutch (and at the same time also the English) glimpsed, then, already more than a hundred years before Canova, in the decorative and practical works of Roman Antiquity nature, that is, the physical-and-practical-constructions-of-dead-matter-alone-appropriate, inorganic, inert basic form, with discrete application of the mobile solely to organic motifs."

Even in the original German, this sentence is not easily compre-hended. But that does not mean, as some colleagues have suggested, that it is sloppily constructed — quite the contrary. Given his stress on the power of form, Riegl can scarcely have been unaware of what he was doing when he opted for an elevated tone and dense, wind-ing sentence constructions. I am inclined to think that this choice expresses Riegl's attempt to convey the kind of passionate engage-ment with his subject matter that we encounter more directly in the 1899 lecture notes, which are replete with frequent exclamations and quick, excited interjections. By constructing meandering sentences that build to a dramatic climax, Riegl infuses his book draft with a high level of intellectual vigor and energy; his surg-ing prose, with sentences that sweep the reader up mountains and down valleys of rhetoric, seems to me the verbal equivalent of the hand gestures and vocal inflections that must have enlivened his performances in the lecture hall. Formally, many such sentences also echo Riegl's own vision of art history as a dynamic, energized process of ebb and flow, and of art as an active force that continu-ally urges its practitioners forward and pulls them back again.

In the sentence cited above, Riegl has created a sense of mo-mentum that mirrors this schema of art-historical progress. An extended modifying clause introduces the primary and secondary subjects of the sentence — Dutch and English artists — whom we then learn perceived (*erblickten*) something new in something else. Our anticipation as to what the object of their discovery was builds with a piling on of modifiers, until finally, just as we are in danger of losing grasp of the conceptual thread, we are given our answer: it was *nature*, we are told, that these artists found in the works of Roman Antiquity. The importance of this object is then accentuated by a breathless, unpunctuated string of adjectival clauses, followed, at the end, by a denouement mentioning, in quick, simple syntax, the exception to the rule.

39

The English language does not allow for a full replication of that formal structure. I have tried nevertheless to retain something of the original sense of complexity and excitement by preserving the overall rhythm: "More than a century before Canova, the Dutch (as well as the English), with their strong affinity for the organic, found in ancient Roman decorative and practical works *nature* — that is, an underlying, immobile inorganic form singularly suited for the shaping of dead matter into physically purposeful constructions — while discretely applying a sense of movement to organic motifs alone" (p. 177).

Now, I would certainly not claim that this is a particularly elegant or easy sentence. But Riegl did not write an elegant or easy sentence. Here, and throughout the book, my goal has been to capture as much as possible Riegl's idiosyncratic — but nonetheless artfully constructed — voice, even while trimming down interjections and rearranging clauses. This voice is complicated and not always consistent, the kind we rarely find in scholarly discourse today: pompous, passionate, aggressive, deeply intelligent, bold, curious, and sometimes defensive, but never less than wholeheartedly engaged with the material. These qualities are to be found not only in the richly cadenced sentences of the early part of the book, but also in the clipped, staccato fragments that make their first appearance toward the end of the book draft (First Version, Chapter Six) and characterize much of the lecture notes (Second Version).[1] Whether speaking in a lofty, formal tone or a more casual one, this is not a voice aimed at readers who are not willing to confront the material with the same attentiveness as the author himself. Following the lead of Riegl, who at the beginning of his lecture series gently pointed novice students the way to the door, I have chosen not to direct my translation at readers who may be scanning the text "in sweatshirts and sneakers while working out on an exercise bike."[2] While an approach that aims for maximum accessibility and ease certainly works for some texts, it hardly seems appropriate for a volume so ambitious in intent, so bold in scope, and so deeply intellectual in spirit as this.

Let us take another example: the passage that introduces us, for the first time in this text, to Riegl's concept of *Kunstwollen*. Here, again, Riegl's rhetorical style builds up a sense of momentum that culminates in the concept of the *will of art* — a principle that is actually expressed twice, once explicitly and once implicitly, in this sentence:

> Das äusserlichste, unwesentlichste, unfassbarste am Naturding — dem damaligen Geschlechte gleich unfassbar wie die geistige Weltmacht, die hinter dem Naturding als sein eigentliches Wesen ausmachend angenommen wurde — seinen oberflächlichen Schein hat die altchristliche Kunst zum Ausdrucksmittel ihres intimsten Kunstwollens erkoren.

Again, the literal rendition: "The most external, most inessential, most intangible aspect of the nature-thing — to then-living tribes equally intangible as the spiritual world-power that behind the nature-thing was imagined as constituting its genuine essence — its superficial appearance Christian art chose to be the vehicle for expression of its most intimate *Kunstwollen*." Of course this will not do. Thus we have to dispense with the anticipatory buildup of the first three lines and move straight to the object for which Riegl makes us wait: "The outward appearance of a natural object — which is its most superficial, most inessential, and most incomprehensible aspect and was as ungraspable for those generations as the spiritual world-power they believed to underlie nature and constitute its true essence — this is what early Christian art embraced as the vehicle for expressing its own deepest will of art (*Kunstwollen*)" (pp. 154–55). Here I have tried to capture some of the momentum of the original by adding Riegl's commentary on outward appearances in the passage between the dashes, before getting to the real point of the sentence, which in both versions appears only at the end.

As Binstock suggests in his essay, the difficulty of translating Riegl lies not only in his use of language but also in the strangeness, to modern eyes, of his methods and ideas. We are simply no longer accustomed to seeing *art* as an active subject with its own specific motives and aims. But for Riegl it really is *Kunst*, not (or only rarely) *der Künstler*, that is in charge. And what art wants, according to this sentence, is what will best express its *Kunstwollen*. That this meaning makes the German sentence redundant (art chose something as the best expression of its will of art) is of little importance here, for Riegl's complicated writing is full of redundancies (note, for example, the repetition of the word *unfassbar* in the quotation above) and circular sentences. In this case, he wants to make clear that early Christian art grasped up the outward appearance of natural things because these brought to view most clearly its own will — the will of art.

Throughout the text, I have marked all related instances in which art plays an unexpectedly active role (for example, *Kunstabsicht*, the intent of art; or *Kunstzweck*, the purpose of art) by including the original German term in parentheses at its first appearance. English words or phrases in square brackets indicate my own interpolations, designed to flesh out confusingly incomplete sentences. Binstock explains in his introduction the conceptual underpinnings of Riegl's complex ideas about art and what it does, so I need not delve further into that issue here. What I should like to emphasize is that although this translation aims to make apparent the scope and intelligence of Riegl's ideas by making the sentences read fluidly in English, it does not seek to make these ideas appear familiar and unproblematic, as if Riegl were writing today. Brilliant and important as this book certainly is, it is also, like the art it describes, a product of a specific historical *Weltanschauung*; this is most blatantly apparent in the ethnic stereotypes with which it is peppered. The numerous discrepancies between the terms and concepts of periodization current at the turn of the twentieth century and those in use today are likewise important reminders of the ever-shifting ground on which the art-historical edifice has been constructed. So as to preserve the sense of Riegl's own historical perspective, I have retained his terms and definitions throughout, even in cases where clarity might demand more familiar ones; thus (to cite just three examples) in place of Classical and Hellenistic art we find "art produced before or after (the death of) Alexander the Great"; the thirteenth-century donor figures of Naumburg Cathedral, viewed today as the epitome of High Gothic sculpture, are categorized as Romanesque; and, as the book's original editors noted (p. 437 n.2), Riegl includes what is now called Mannerism in his definition of Baroque art.

The difference of Riegl's outlook from our own comes to view more subtly in the conceptual apparatus with which he presents works of art. In order that readers will understand this apparatus better, I should like at this point to indicate briefly how I have dealt with some key terms.

Art as Contest

When Riegl discusses art as a contest with nature, he uses the noun *das Wettschaffen* and the verb *wettschaffen*, and sometimes their related, more antiquated form, *um die Wette schaffen*. In English, these are rendered straightforwardly as "a contest or competition" and "to compete." In light of Riegl's arguments about human creative agency, however, it is important to note that the term includes the root *schaffen*, "to create," so that while idiomatically

43

the word means "to compete," its literal translation would be "to create for the sake of a prize." Riegl draws this connection himself in the parallel construction of his book's powerful second sentence: "Alles bildende Kunstschaffen des Menschen ist...im letzten Grunde nichts anderes als Wettschaffen mit der Natur." This pun, so crucial to the meaning of the argument as a whole, is, alas, necessarily lost in translation: "All human *art production* is therefore at heart nothing other than a *contest* with nature"(p. 51, my emphasis).

Again on the first page of his book draft, Riegl introduces another play on words that does not emerge in English. This has to do with the distinction between art's contest with nature and attempts to mimic or replicate nature exactly. Describing the latter activity, Riegl uses the words *Täuschung*, the illusory fabrication of natural appearances (which I have rendered simply as "illusion"), and *Fälschung*, the false creation of truthful appearances (which I have given as "counterfeit"). Though these terms seem to represent opposites, they in fact are used as synonyms. Here and throughout the course of Riegl's argument, art that seeks only to copy, not compete, is not art at all; as moments of deliberate deception, both *Täuschung* and *Fälschung*, in Riegl's view, are unworthy of consideration.

Purpose

The first "element of the work of art" to which Riegl devotes extended attention is function or purpose: *der Zweck*. Within this section of each draft, Riegl differentiates among *Schmückungs-zweck*, which I have translated as "decorative purpose," *Gebrauchs-zweck*, or "practical purpose," and *Vorstellungszweck*, or "conceptual purpose." Although Riegl employs the single noun *Zweck* throughout this section — rather than, say, *Funktion* — I have, with the exception of the word *Kunstzweck*, alternated between the words "purpose" and "function" simply to avoid excessive repetition. Riegl uses the word *Kunstzweck* as a purpose distinct from the three other "external" (*äusserliche*) purposes. In keeping with Riegl's ideas about *Kunstwollen*, which Binstock and I translate as "the will of art," it seems most appropriate to render *Kunstzweck* as "the purpose of art" or, where the flow of the sentence requires, "art's purpose." This expresses the idea of art's activity more forcefully than the alternative "artistic purpose," which seems too vague, almost dilettantish, for the importance Riegl attributes to this factor.

Motifs

In the chapters on motifs, Riegl draws an extended contrast between inorganic forms — best exemplified by the symmetrical, solid crystal — and their softer, looser counterparts, organic forms, and expands this contrast between real-world objects to general principles of artistic creation. Although "organicism" would be more appropriate in conveying Riegl's technical meaning of the noun *der Organismus*, which refers not to an organic creature (organism) but to the state of being organic, the word is too cumbersome to work here. I therefore, following Margaret Olin, translate it as "Organism," capitalized so as to distinguish it from our more familiar sense of the word.[3] The verb form, *organisieren*, appears, when a longer formulation such as "to make organic" is impossible, as "to Organize." The reverse of this, *anorganisieren*, which describes the process of making a form appear inorganic by applying the law of symmetry, presents greater difficulties; I translate it as either "to make inorganic" or the less wordy, though admittedly no less awkward, "to de-Organize." The conceptual opposite of Organism, *der Harmonismus*, will appear as "harmonism"; its verb, *harmonisieren*, as "to harmonize" or "to make harmonic."

Form and Surface

Throughout the chapters on form and surface, Riegl consistently uses the word *Form* to denote the three-dimensionality of a given object — not, as in the normal English sense, its general shape or contours. Where clarity requires, I will translate this as "three-dimensional form," "plastic form," or "sculpture." In cases where it is clearly being opposed to "surface" or "plane" and the connotation of volume is clear, I leave it simply as "form." Because his emphasis is on art as shaped matter rather than materials or technique, Riegl departs from conventional terminology in his discussion of art that is not freestanding. Thus he chooses the word *Halbform* — literally, "half form," or partially three-dimensional object — as a synonym for "relief," and employs *Riss*, which typically refers to a contour drawing or plan, to designate any strictly two-dimensional art, whether Greek vase painting, Roman mosaics, Italian frescoes, or Dutch still lifes. Because the Semperian argument for the primacy of materials, which substantially informs Riegl's presentation, is today no longer such a contested and hotly debated problem, I have reverted to the terms "relief" and "painting" where these are more clear; where Riegl really is speaking in general terms, I have retained the literal translation — "half form" and "two-dimensional arts" — as well. The opposite of form, *Fläche*, I have alternately rendered as "surface" or "plane," according to sense and to avoid repetition. (Riegl explains his terminology fairly late in the discussion, in Chapter Six, note 2, of the First Version, p. 440.)

Whereas in the book draft Riegl focuses on differentiating among form, objective surface (*die objektive Fläche*), and subjective surface (*die subjektive Fläche*), in the lecture notes he places more explicit emphasis on the viewer's share, distinguishing between optical and tactile varieties of sensory experience. Here he associates the subjective surface of a given three-dimensional form with the *Gesichtssinn*, which I have translated as either "optical sense" or "sense of sight," according to the flow of the sentence, and the objective surface with what he calls the *Tastsinn*, which I have given as either "sense of touch" or "tactile sense." Readers familiar with Riegl's later writings may miss the term "haptic" to designate such experience or such forms, but Riegl does not employ the term *haptisch* in this work. I have followed his lead by using the synonym "tactile," with its more explicit sense of hands-on materiality.

At this point, it gives me great pleasure to offer my gratitude to those who have helped this project along. For inviting me to take on this project back in September 1999 — and warning me candidly of the difficulties it would involve — I offer my first thanks to Jonathan Crary. At Zone Books, Meighan Gale was a model of patience as the process plodded on longer than anticipated, and I am grateful for her assistance and generous forbearance throughout this entire process. In the final stages, the superb copyediting of Ingrid Sterner significantly improved the text, and the diligent sleuthing of Amy Griffin and the researchers at Art Resource helped us enliven the text with images; for their patience, skill, and good humor, I offer them sincerest thanks. Over the last few years, many friends and colleagues cheerfully came to my rescue for matters pertaining to periods beyond by own area of expertise; for their ready assistance, I should like to single out Pieter Broucke, Christopher Hallett, Holger Klein, Andrew Stewart, and Alison Langmead, who put her remarkable facility in summoning up the most arcane architectural terms at my disposal many times. Finally, I should like to convey my thanks to Ben Binstock, the initiator of this project, who offered detailed and insightful comments on my various drafts, helped assemble the photographs that enrich this edition, and continually reminded me, especially as the process drew to completion, of the brilliance of Riegl's ideas beyond and within the dense tangle of words.

NOTES

1. The two-part format of the book, as well as the internal subdivisions, follow the 1966 edition by Pächt and Swoboda. Aside from adding pictures, the present volume does not alter the structure of that edition in any way.

2. Cf. the translator's note by Evelyn Kain in Aloïs Riegl, *Problems of Style: Foundations for a History of Ornament* (Princeton, NJ: Princeton University Press, 1992), p. xx.

3. See Margaret Olin, *Forms of Representation in Alois Riegl's Theory of Art* (University Park: Pennsylvania State University Press, 1992), p. 114.

First Version

Book Manuscript of 1897–1898

Introductory Remarks

The human hand fashions works from lifeless matter according to the same formal principles as nature does. All human art production (*Kunstschaffen*) is therefore at heart nothing other than a contest (*Wettschaffen*) with nature. The sense of delight with which a work of art fills us is commensurate with its human maker's capacity to bring to clear and convincing expression the respective formal laws of natural creation. In other words, it is in the recognition of the work of art's correspondence to the work of nature to which it refers that the source of all purely aesthetic pleasure lies. The history of art is the history of the creative human being's victories as he competes with nature.

Nature gives shape to raw matter according to the basic principle of crystallization, which is grounded in the law of symmetry: that is, the equal lateral distribution of even the tiniest molecules along an ideal central axis. Although it would seem that the forms of animate (that is, mobile) matter should follow other rules, this is not actually the case. The fundamental principle of symmetrical construction applies here as well — though it no longer manifests itself openly or straightforwardly because of the motor capacity that characterizes nature's animate products, whether in growth or in actual movement from place to place. The same holds true for works of visual art made by human beings. These are created to compete in part with the forms of dead matter, in part with animate forms of nature. Ultimately, however, they always proceed according to that same basic principle, even though it may be heavily concealed — revealing itself, perhaps, only in the frame that artificially contains the human work that competes with nature as a closed, integrated unit. We shall discuss this matter in depth in a later chapter on motifs.

The creation of visual art is a contest with nature, not a desire for interchangeability with nature. Man can never produce a perfect illusion (*Täuschung*) or counterfeit (*Fälschung*) of nature. This is true with regard not only to animate natural beings, whose life breath the human creator cannot infuse into dead matter, but even to the shapes of dead matter itself. If a crystal were to be artificially reproduced with the most meticulous accuracy, for example, microscopic investigation would still instantly reveal the arrangement of its most minuscule parts to be incompatible with those of a natural crystal. Even in those works of art that strive explicitly to mimic the superficial impression of natural appearances (Impressionist landscape paintings, for instance), the desire for illusion is not an end in itself. Rather, it is a means to accomplish the primary aesthetic goal: to demonstrate man's ability to conjure up a particular visual effect of nature. In so doing, the work of art does not seek to replicate actual nature — on the contrary; if the work were not immediately recognizable as a product of human hands, it would lose its entire purpose.

Behind every work of art, then, we must presuppose the presence of a work of nature (or several such) with which the work of art is designed to compete. It must be stressed that the human creator need not be conscious of that intent. The *motif* is what we shall call any work of nature to which the work of art corresponds. There is not only one possible manner of perceiving a given work of nature, but rather a variety of ways. More specifically, a person will perceive a work of nature with entirely different eyes according to his own relation to matter, that is, to works of nature in general. In considering any work of art, therefore, the crucial question — one more important than and even presupposing that of individual motifs — must have to do with the creator's particular attitude toward nature. In the next chapter, we shall attempt to construct the necessary basis for answering this question in any given case. In doing so, we intend, insofar as this is possible today, to arrive at a clear overall view of the historical development of the relation between visual art and nature.

Besides the question of "what?" (the motif), the following questions must be considered when evaluating a work of art: (1) For what purpose was it made? (2) From what? (3) Through what? (4) How? All these shall find responses in chapters on purposes, materials, techniques, and basic means of expression in the visual arts. We shall discuss purpose first, directly after the relationship between art and nature, for reasons of expediency alone and not for the sake of some inherent significance, such as has traditionally been attributed to it by art historians; motifs shall be considered only in a subsequent chapter. Questions of the significance of materials and technique will occupy us more briefly, because the value of these two factors has been greatly overestimated in the last half century. The historical development of these two elements, from which all works of visual art originate without exception, will be discussed in the final chapter, which deals with basic expressive means.

PART ONE

Worldview

Within knowable historical time, the understanding of man's relation to matter — which we simply call the "human worldview" — has undergone two substantial changes. The history of visual art can consequently be divided into three major periods, which correspond in essence to ages already long applied in the fields of human political and cultural history: Antiquity, the Middle Ages, and the modern era. The first period encompasses all Antiquity to the year 313 C.E., with the proclamation of Christianity as the official state religion in the Roman Empire. The second consists of the Middle Ages and Renaissance (strictly defined) up to 1520, with the death of Raphael and Pope Leo X [sic] and the expansion of the Reformation. Everything after that we ascribe to the third period.

It need hardly be stated explicitly that the two above-specified dates may not — and shall not — be held as absolute boundaries. Rather, within each age we may distinguish three subperiods: the first representing the development of the particular worldview, the second (usually the briefest) representing the worldview at the peak of perfection, and the third representing the process of its decline and eventual collapse. As a rule, this final subperiod provides as much insight into the subsequent worldview as that which it brings to a close. Conversely, no obsolete worldview, once overcome, vanishes instantly from the face of the earth. Although it might not persevere as a deep-rooted conviction, it can, thanks to the pressure of tradition, continue to reverberate for centuries in outer forms. These forms play the most important role in the visual arts.

CHAPTER ONE

First Period

Art as Improvement of Nature Through Physical Beauty

The conception of artistic creation as an improved version of natural creation requires that man consider himself superior to nature. Although that condition certainly obtained in the era of mature Antiquity, this should not lead us to conclude that it was so from the very beginnings of human history. On the contrary, a certain rudimentary quality of works created by otherwise culturally advanced peoples gives us good reason to suppose that ancient humanity devoted itself to rougher, more imperfect ideas and mental images (*Vorstellungen*). Everything in nature that moved, grew, and died without the agency — or even against the will — of man seemed superior to him for its very autonomy of existence and will. Everything in nature was therefore a god; and so we might aptly designate this most primitive worldview "infinite polytheism." Whether it is possible, in light of man's oppressively timorous attitude toward nature, to speak of any sort of contest with that force is problematic at best. But the question cannot be categorically answered in the negative, since not a single uncivilized people on earth (even the wildest) has survived in that primal state utterly unchanged. The one foolproof means of determining an answer therefore lies irretrievably out of reach.[1]

The crucial moment for man's progress to a loftier conception of his relation to surrounding matter occurred when he began to confine his apprehension to those individual phenomena of nature that struck him as particularly powerful or frightening. This moment was decisive because then man came to recognize his own superiority over other natural beings. With that shift, we find ourselves standing in the very first period of history: the first opportunity has opened up to activate desired improvements of nature. This process reached its natural conclusion when man perceived his superiority over all other creatures of nature. At the same time, he still had to acknowledge behind every natural phenomenon the presence of a driving, animating force far removed from human perception or control. A person can cut down a tree but cannot at his own discretion make one grow. A distinction thus came to be drawn between sensorially perceptible phenomena of nature and invisible natural forces — a distinction yet unknown to primitive peoples, who ascribed an autonomous will to everything in nature. Thus man reached the point when he recognized his superiority over the things of nature while at the same time acknowledging his inferiority to the forces that conceived and animated them. Although these forces were openly present, they remained out of reach of human visual faculties. For that reason, man strove to reconstruct them in his imagination, and because in his naive way of thinking he could only grasp them sensually, he inevitably endowed them with sensible form. Once man had gained insight into his superiority over all other natural creations, there is no doubt as to the one possible shape this could take: only human form could appear worthy of a force superior to human beings. Thus was born anthropomorphic polytheism, which the Greeks would bring to its fullest perfection. Forces of nature have thenceforth been [envisioned as] human beings like us — but without our shortcomings in physical beauty and without our mortality.

How did art approach its contest with nature under these conditions? If natural phenomena reveal to the human eye only those aspects that are inessential, random, and transitory, then art must create for them the essential, the meaningful, the eternal parts. Thus did antique man improve nature through art. So long as this was the aim of all visual art, the following two basic principles rightfully and unconditionally obtained:

a. Only the perfect is entitled to exist in art. As in antique man's daily life, so in his art, the right of the strongest prevailed. The person in power could allow himself anything, whereas the weak had to tolerate all; although the latter might beg the conqueror for clemency, the right to be spared was not his. This was the natural order of things. In art, too, only the strong, the victorious, the beautiful counted as worthy of representation; only exceptionally did the weak, the oppressed, the ugly gain admittance, and then as a foil against which the victor's glory was amplified.

b. This perfection can only be perceived through the senses; it pertains to body, not soul. Spiritual perfection divorced from physicality remained unknown to antique culture. No essential distinction was drawn between religious and profane art in Antiquity because there was no division between phenomena of nature and the natural forces that underlay them. Those powers of nature were themselves sensual phenomena, even if they remained invisible to mortals. Man's spiritual functions were inextricably bound up with his bodily ones. Inside a beautiful body a beautiful soul was thought to reside — although the latter term was proper only to more advanced stages of antique development.

We can discern three subdivisions within this general picture of the earliest period of visual art when man sought to improve nature. In keeping with nature itself, these represent the growth, summit, and decline of the governing principles.

Growth

The phase of growth occurred primarily in ancient Egyptian art.[2] Monuments of this art still betray numerous vestiges of an earlier animal cult and thus form a link in the chain leading us back to the primitive period of infinite polytheism. In cases where fully human figures were employed to personify natural forces, these display only a negligible degree of corporeal individualization and none spiritual at all. The heads produced during the same time span are so similar as to be nearly interchangeable.[3] This accords with the fact that the Egyptians extended the deification of human beings much further than any other people. Whereas the Greeks presented their heroes as intermediate creatures — Herodotus, for example, conceded that it was only his sixteenth ancestor who had been a god — the Egyptians considered every king predestined to be divine and to take his place among the gods immediately after death.

Summit

The summit consists of Greek art before Alexander the Great. The embers of primitive attitudes that still clung to the Egyptians glow here only dimly; yet the seeds of future decay seem already planted. Although physical perfection — that is, the beautiful — remained art's main postulate, gradually and subtly the process of individualization began to take hold. At first, to be sure, this individualization applied only to concrete bodily qualities: thus Zeus was shown as a bearded man in the prime of life, Aphrodite as a young woman with her sensual charms in full bloom, and so on. But we begin to notice an accidental quality added to the mixture that runs contrary to the notion of the absolute and perfect, the generalized and typical, the eternal. The contemplative expression characterizing the heads of most Attic deity statues already contains the seeds of an impending process of spiritual individualization. This individualization would ultimately pose a threat to that other major postulate of the antique worldview, absolute unity of matter and spirit, for the act of contemplation is itself contingent, accidental. On the other hand, it represents the least momentary of all possible facial expressions, which is why the Greeks unconsciously made it their symbol of the spiritual and the eternal.

Decline

Decline occurred in Hellenistic and Roman art prior to Constantine the Great.[4] For Mediterranean people of antique culture, anthropomorphic polytheism had constituted the official way of looking at the world for the more than six centuries after the death of Alexander the Great. Countless statues honoring the twelve ancient gods were chiseled in traditional formats, countless temples constructed according to long-standing schemata. When we survey the great mass of extant artworks from this long stretch of time, our general impression is still powerfully governed by that struggle for the physically perfect, the beautiful, which expressed the nature-improving aim of all antique art. At the same time, individual details betray aspects that deviate from that aim.

The *Laocoön* group in particular has aroused much interest in this regard, even back when the discipline of art history, still young now, was just taking its baby steps (figure 1). The glorification of suffering humanity embodied in this group is indeed unprecedented in the history of Greek art. If, after all, the hero's downfall was supposed to appear as the god's triumph, then that victorious god would have to be included in the depiction; indeed, he would have to be the dominant figure within the group. In the statues of Laocoön and his sons, however, the theme of suffering — and hence imperfection — is presented as worthy of artistic representation for its own sake and not just as a foil. In this respect, the sculpture stands as a direct precursor of Christian art.

To all appearances, the *Laocoön* seems to represent a more or less isolated phenomenon. But several newly emergent genres of art bear witness to a still more remarkable deviation from the principles that previously shaped both man's attitude toward nature and the artistic creations it conditioned. This can be seen, above all, in the art of portraiture, with its extremely high degree of physical individualization. It is also apparent in the refined and veristic portrayal of animals with no particular significance, such as the lamb and lion in the reliefs of the Grimani fountain (now in the Vienna Hofmuseum) or, even more striking, the deer, lobster, and other such things in the Vatican Museum's Sala degli Animali (figures 2 and 3). Here we see an obvious interest in the imperfect, transitory, naturalistic appearances of humans and animals for their own sake. One must inquire, however, how that interest could be reconciled with the postulate that only the perfect, the essential, and the generalized were worthy of representation while the imperfect was, at best, a necessary and unavoidable evil.

Finally, the facial expression of interior conditions received increasing attention at this point. Even in its period of decline, antique art behaved with the greatest restraint in this domain. Interior spiritual states are by definition incapable of representation; they can be given expression only through the depiction of certain concomitant or subsequent effects in the physical realm — a person's gestures, for example. Such signals were excluded from classical art because of their accidental and transitory quality. In Roman art, human figures likewise tend to retain their contemplative — that is, generalized and pensive — character for precisely this reason. But in cases where this quality was needed to fulfill a specific conceptual purpose — for example, in the figure of Darius in the *Alexander Mosaic* at Pompeii (figure 4) — the attendant external signs of interior spiritual agitation received a considerably

62

more dramatic character than in previous ages; again we might recall the *Laocoön* at this point (figure 1).

So: suffering in place of triumph and imperfection in place of perfection — both qualities, it should be added, represented for their own sake and not for any particular conceptual purpose. We witness, moreover, spiritual states and accidental contingencies conceived as increasingly desirable supplements to the purely physical realm, which in earlier times had to absorb them without a trace. These three symptoms of late antique art plainly manifest the inception of a profound and far-reaching change in people's view of their relation to material nature. This relation found its most direct expression in cultic activities; as noted earlier, an-thropomorphic polytheism continued to dominate this arena until the end of the period. This worldview persisted in a form seem-ingly as impervious to outside attack as that of the desire to im-prove nature, which we believe remained the fundamental driving force for visual art up to the end of the era. On closer exami-nation, we encounter symptoms of decline in the field of cult as well, symptoms as unmistakable as those we detected in Hel-lenistic and Roman art. Noteworthy is the sudden introduction of deities meant to embody sensorially inaccessible concepts, such as Kairos (Opportunity). We might also draw attention to the increasing penetration of Eastern deities from the conceptual sphere of Semitic peoples, who historically possessed a deep incli-nation toward abstract speculation — a point to which we will return later. But what was truly decisive was the increasing indif-ference of educated people to their ancient, long-inherited deity cults. In essence, polytheism had already become paganism back when Christianity still stood far from its future triumph. The state — that is, the collective representation of educated men — none-theless clung fiercely to its ancient deity cults because the entire state apparatus was established on these. It was not Christian beliefs that so upset the Roman heads of state but the uncertainty as to whether Christians would fulfill their civic duty of sacrificing to the state's gods. Politics, religious cult, and art in the ancient world — especially the Roman Empire — were thus intimately enmeshed. To a certain extent, they formed a single entity. The separation of political and cultic realms demanded by Christ ("Render therefore unto Caesar the things which are Caesar's; and unto God the things that are God's") was something the ancients could never allow. As the threat of such a division gradually — and despite much resistance — grew imminent, Constantine the Great opted to replace the cult rather than disrupt that unity. Following the same lines, art and cult would likewise have had to pursue separate courses. All those portraits and animal pictures already indicate the emergence of a fascination with profane art that was originally foreign to the antique period.

It was only logical, therefore, that the heirs of the Roman Imperial system should strive to reinstate the unity they held to be necessary, even indispensable, within the sphere of art. The result was Byzantine art, which has survived, along with other astoundingly outdated traces of antique civic, social, and caste life, into the present day as an art of both state and religious cult. These groundbreaking changes gradually unfolded from the moment of the establishment of the Roman Empire and the appearance of Christ — though certainly the older forms appeared to persist, at least superficially. The majority of educated men in the empire now had only to proclaim affiliation with the Christian faith as representative of their new worldview, and the old anthropomorphic guises of natural forces vanished (though not without their influence continuing to resonate for many more centuries).

Did antique art disappear at that moment too? Hardly! On the eastern Mediterranean, where it was born, it was able to salvage as much of its essence as was compatible with the Christian view of man's relation to matter and bring that with it into the new era. Here more than anywhere, tradition, which plays such an important role throughout the history of art, demonstrated the full extent of its power, successfully bridging the deep chasm that divided two distinct ways of viewing the world. The Semites were of a far different mind from the Romans of Greek nationality and culture regarding monotheistic art's capacity to accommodate pagan attempts to improve nature. But on one point Byzantine and Islamic art shared common ground: in both, the antique right of the stronger continued to prevail. Strictly speaking, then, both art forms should be treated as an appendix to antique art, even though they emerged and flourished after Constantine and even though their existence extends well into the modern period, indeed up to our own day. In these arts, the impact of the new monotheistic worldview manifests itself in a mostly negative way. To understand them, however, we must first examine the essence of the new worldview and the relation between art-producing man and nature that it engendered. For practical reasons, we will therefore subsume these arts into our second great period, into which they chronologically fall.

Second Period

Art as Improvement of Nature Through Spiritual Beauty

Whereas infinite polytheism presupposed a corresponding number of autonomous forces underlying the diverse phenomena of nature, reformed polytheism perceived numerous natural phenomena as embodiments of one and the same power. Monotheism brought this refinement process to its culmination by establishing a single force as the original agent of all natural phenomena. This solitary power could not, strictly speaking, allow itself to be grasped in sensual form; indeed, so immeasurably huge and so perfect was it that even humanity nearly vanished by comparison, as did all other animate and inanimate matter. This supersensory God alone was perfect, whereas all matter, including mankind, was imperfect and transitory. If an art governed by the monotheistic worldview was to compete with nature, it would be obligated to represent the supersensory, the spiritual and intellectual, the properties of the soul. Because the elements of this realm cannot be apprehended by the senses, however, they cannot be depicted in visual art, and consequently the human artist should have to forfeit his contest with nature. In this sense, strict monotheism must be intrinsically hostile to art, and indeed it has always been so.

Relatively early, peoples of Semitic race recognized monotheism more or less explicitly as the ultimate end of all theosophical speculation. That not everyone reached this conclusion at once is probably due to the worldly interests that drew specific groups away from speculative thought: military interests for the Meso-potamians, commercial ones for the Phoenicians, and so on. As far as we can tell, only the Jewish people enjoyed the contemplative leisure time necessary for intensive and lucid reflection on the monotheistic notion of God. And it was the Jews who adopted a decidedly negative attitude toward art in Antiquity, at the very moment when neighboring peoples, especially the standard-setting Greeks, elevated visual art to their most important and valuable expression of life.

The at once formidable and utterly incomprehensible Jewish God, however, having yet to make any inroads among other Semitic tribes, could expect even less luck among Western peoples, who were already little inclined toward theosophical speculation and deeply devoted to sensual presentations. If monotheism wanted to replace state-sanctioned polytheism — which, in the eyes of the educated elite, had already become a formula devoid of meaning — it would have to be adapted to the capacities for thought and feeling of non-Jewish peoples. Concessions to the demand for sensual rep-resentations of God were therefore inevitable from the outset, and Christ located them by positing a tripartite nature of the one God. The peoples of Oriental culture, long predisposed toward mono-theism, could be easily satisfied with that notion. But the conquest of the Greco-Roman West required something more than a reli-gious system that simply mediated between monotheistic ideas of God and sensual representations of him. The new teachings needed to bolster themselves with an additional element that Western peoples would find fully liberating and redeeming. This ultimately lay in the social aspects of Christ's message: the struggle against the exclusive right of the stronger and the establishment of an existen-tial right for even the weak, the suffering, and the vanquished.

Christ's lesson consisted of two parts. Although meant to be applied equally and universally, these parts split down the middle to plant themselves, with respective advantages, on the two main constituencies of the Roman Empire. The effects were already apparent during the apostolic era. On one side, we see the formerly Jewish Christians. For them, the notion of monotheism was of utmost importance, and they tried to transpose as much as possible of their terrible, vengeful, superhuman Yahweh onto the triune Christ-God, immersing themselves for centuries in speculation on the nature of the Trinity. On the other side, we see the formerly pagan Christians, who were chiefly interested in the social core of Christ's message. The former group combated the (originally non-antique) human interest in imperfect, transitory, material nature and instead held fast to the antique right of the stronger; the latter fought against the right of the stronger above all else, pushing into the background any hostility toward or mistrust of nature. The first group did not so much turn their backs on Antiquity as return to its initial conceptual position that nature must never be represented in its accidental, contingent appearances. The second group had necessarily to extend to the imperfect phenomena of nature the tolerance they preached toward all imperfect beings. The first trend led to Byzantium and Islam, the second to Roman Catholicism.

Further Developments of Art That Improves Physical Nature

Byzantine Art

When the emperor Constantine transplanted his residence from Rome to Byzantium, it was not because of any threat the barbarians posed to the earlier capital; after all, they resided much closer to the Bosporus than to central Italy. Rather, it was clear to the

69

emperor that the conditions necessary for the construction of a future empire were more readily available in the Orient than in the western Mediterranean provinces. A universal empire into which every element could be custom-made to fit neatly was, from the very outset, an abstraction better suited to the more speculative Orientals than to the Romans and Romance peoples, whose attention was dispersed among a thousand living forces. As a result, the emperor's headquarters were moved not into the Orient itself but to its gateway, the point where Greek and Semitic worlds conjoined. Because the Greeks occupied an intermediate position, both culturally and geographically, between West and East, they seemed perfectly primed to assume the leading role in both directions.

The very property that had allowed the Roman Empire to expand to such enormous size and near-exclusive dominance over all peoples — that is, the absolute discipline and orderliness of its administrative apparatus down to the smallest detail of daily life — could now be cultivated to its fullest potential. This strict regulating structure controlled all aspects of the Byzantine state: politics, religion, art, social life. An endless hierarchy culminated at a single peak with the emperor-pope. Here we have the right of the stronger hardened into unbreakable and, wherever possible, perpetually binding laws. All mundane tasks of any consequence were meticulously regulated through precise ceremonial acts. So ambitious a state system could certainly not have neglected the visual arts. On the contrary: in place of the universalizing art of Rome, we find a Byzantine art that possesses an almost equally universal, uniform character, an art obviously sustained through a similar process of mass production in state-run workshops. Visual art always being a contest with nature, however, the time has come to examine how Byzantine people comprehended that force.

Because, in faithful adherence to antique culture, the Byzan-

tine state system was based on the right of the stronger, it comes
as no surprise that it applied this principle to the visual arts as
well. Monotheistic religion proclaimed only the spiritually perfect or inwardly beautiful to be worthy of depiction, but these
qualities were by definition incapable of being represented. To
render them in the body's various accidental concomitant manifestations would have meant attempting to reproduce the perfect
by means of the imperfect. The Byzantines never considered
seeking such a solution to the artistic problem, just as they had
stayed content with an externalized and highly formal ceremonial
system in the realm of religious cult. In faithful continuation of
Antiquity, they apprehended visual art simply as a physically beautiful and hence improved version of nature. Monotheism influenced this position only negatively, in that anything of Roman
Antiquity that displayed interest in the imperfect forms of nature
for their own sake, such as the art of portraiture or delight in the
nude figure, was abandoned.[1] The Byzantines wanted to resurrect
Antiquity in a pure state while rejecting any form whose anthro-
pomorphism might imply pagan origins. They therefore reached
backward, both in principle and in specific details, to earlier
stages in antique art's development, especially Greek art before
Alexander.[2] In contrast to late Roman examples, which, as we
shall see, seem often to have deliberately sought out ugly features,
their portrayals of the human figure were dignified and beautiful.
Later we will examine in closer detail how the Byzantines used
their dependence on pre-Alexander Greek art to avoid an excessively literal contest with nature. The task of eradicating the danger of slipping from an "improved" depiction of nature toward
the increasingly accurate reproduction of nature's imperfect transitory appearances fell to the panacea of Byzantine culture, the
regimented state system. A canon of legally permitted motifs was
established for the visual arts, and any depiction of nature that

strayed beyond its bounds was threatened with legal prosecution. Byzantine art of state and cult was thus able to persevere until the collapse of the Byzantine Empire; indeed, it has survived to this very day in the Orient and in remote regions of eastern Europe.[3]

The character of Byzantine art, as we have sketched it here, reached its purest expression in the course of a lengthy development, in part only after the Iconoclastic Controversy. In the first centuries of its existence, we find numerous manifestations that do not tally with its later character, such as thoroughly "naturalistic" juxtaposed with wholly "stylized" configurations of fruit on capitals. Here we witness the conjunction of extremes; but these prove that the Roman antique tradition managed to preserve well into the Byzantine Middle Ages that very contest with nature's imperfect appearances that strict monotheism so despised. One would hardly err in crediting this achievement to the Greeks, who were the most Western of Byzantine peoples, and perhaps more specifically to their court circles. Certainly it could not have been agreeable to Oriental tastes, and this latent conflict would become palpable when, thanks to their withdrawal from worldly concerns, a small Semitic people again found the leisure time to develop a monotheistic religious system of the strictest kind. Not only did broad regions of the Byzantine Orient capitulate to Islam at its first appearance, but even those provinces that were at least temporarily protected erupted into the Iconoclastic Controversy. This conflict rendered the final, fatal blow to the legalistic regulation of Byzantine arts of state and cult.

Art of Islam
Islamic art is a Byzantine art; it took the latter as a direct starting point while extracting from it anything that suggested unperfected manifestations of nature. In its reconstitution of Antiquity in the purest form, Islam reached even beyond the Greek art made

before Alexander to seize ultimately on the art of the ancient Near East. By substantially curtailing the right of the stronger in the visual arts, on the other hand, Islam moved more decisively away from antique polytheism.[4] This right still existed in Islam, to be sure, but the monotheistic system allowed its application to one being alone. In the all-encompassing universe, this was the single God and, in the world of believers, the single caliph; the system never included any hierarchical structure of demigods or lesser administrative officials. Islam recognized no hierarchy between the masses and the emperor-pope, and, by extension, no state-governed cult. Despite their common antique aversion to depicting the transitory forms of nature, Byzantine and Islamic art thus stood in direct opposition to each other, Byzantium admitting only religious and no profane art, Islam recognizing only profane and no religious art. It was a further outcome of Islam's stringently monotheistic worldview that the internal components of its art betray no hierarchy, no distinction between strong and weak, no degrees of perfection. In profane art serving private purposes, everything was shown on equal terms and without variations of rank. How this quality manifested itself in art's formal character — for example, in the relation between pattern and ground — is something we will examine more closely at a later point.

Further developments in the realm of Islam proceeded in the exactly reverse direction from those in Byzantium. The Islamic monotheistic observance gradually forfeited ever more of its severity, so that art drew increasingly close to Byzantine and even Western art (rococo). As we have seen, Byzantine art took the opposite path, moving from relative freedom to greater rigidity. At the same time that aristocratic intermediaries — for example, the Mamluks — found their way into the caliphal state, the Byzantine state sank gradually into a mere Asiatic sultanate. It is small wonder, therefore, that after an abrupt initial divergence, the respective strands of visual art eventually drew as closely back together as possible. Byzantine decoration came to gain a fully Arabic character, while the mosques of the Islamic Turks adopted the design of Byzantine churches.

The Actual Course of the Second Period in the West

The monotheistic system was thus in no position to remove the visual arts once and for all from the overarching influence of the antique mind-set. It is worth noting that the two varieties of Oriental monotheism manifested the more rigorous adherence to that worldview. The future could only belong to a way of thinking that would set the contest with nature decisively onto a new basis, one that would not simply rest content with either loosened or more regimented efforts to improve physical nature but attempt instead to transplant those improvements firmly into the spiritual realm. Even Western Christianity, which ultimately acknowledged the bishop of Rome as its visible head, did not deem nature in all its transitory appearances worthy of depiction. At the same time, Roman Christians in the West wanted to see tangible embodiments of nature's newly discovered essential property, the spiritually perfect. Unperfected nature was indispensable as the sole possible visible bearer of the spiritual. Its imperfection proved to be a less significant stumbling block for Western Christians than it was for Oriental people, for the former used every means possible to emancipate themselves from the right of the stronger and therefore exercised greater forbearance toward the imperfect whenever they encountered it. And yet, as before, the danger of regarding physically improved nature as representing nature's true essence had to be evaded at all costs. This dilemma gave rise to the following early Christian postulate: Away with the physical improvement of nature, with its superficial beautification and idealization! Forms that are imperfect in nature will be made

74

to look even more so in art; thus these can be exalted all the more as precious vessels of art! This attitude explains the striking decline of a sense of beauty in late Roman Imperial art. Some commentators have described this phenomenon as "barbarism," meaning that protracted contact with barbarian peoples had sapped the late Romans of their previous refinement of artistic sensibility. Others have correctly recognized the true motivation by holding the Christian religion responsible, but again under the false assumption that early Christians were hostile to art. This presupposition is rooted in the biased notion that visual art is synonymous with physically beautified nature. This notion, however, applies unconditionally only to classical Antiquity and perhaps the Renaissance; surely the contest with nature could manifest itself in different, no less justifiable ways. Such an alternative was employed by early Christians.

No period of art is less familiar today than that of the fourth and fifth centuries of the modern era. Although it launched the first phase of our second major period, which we designate the phase of growth, its own fundamental importance prompts us to treat it separately, as an introduction. If one wished to endow this starting point of our first major phase with a title, one could formulate it as "Ugly nature as vehicle of spiritual beauty." One of the factors responsible for what has hitherto been an utter disregard or disdain for late Roman art is the cult of ugliness perceptible in many of its figural works. Another is its multitude of completely contradictory visual forms, for example, the simultaneous employment of very high and very low relief elements. This inconsistency makes it difficult, if not impossible, to obtain clear recognition and definition of the total character of this period, at least so long as people misunderstand the driving forces behind a process so dominated by brash extremes. The best path toward a deeper understanding is by way of the craft industry of the late Roman period. On this ground, the struggle against the right of the stronger materialized most openly and decisively; and just at this time, the image of the crucified Christ, that flagrantly anti-antique celebration of suffering, transitory humanity, began, at least tentatively, to emerge in Christian art.

Later, in a different context, we will have the opportunity to shed more light on this singular art-historical phenomenon. For now, let a few words suffice as to the way spiritual perfection came to be expressed in its natural vehicle, the human figure. At the inception of this new period, people refrained from character-izing spiritual beauty in a truly artistic way; the Western Roman Christians were at first too heavily overpowered by the influence of antique tradition to accept and incorporate incidental, contin-gent appearances into their art. Intangible inner perfection and spiritual beauty within the human figure — for example, in saints and pious laypeople — were straightforwardly signified, if the nar-rative content did not already make them obvious, by an attribute or written caption; in neither case was there any dramatic spiritu-alization of heads or gestures. With regard to the demands placed on the physical body as vehicle of spiritual expression, early Christian art thus marked a regression beyond even that of pre-Alexander Greece. However, the sharpest divergence of Christian art from the art of pagan Antiquity can be seen in the image that would soon become the dominant symbol of the Christian faith: the crucifix. Antique tradition had long guarded itself against any kind of physical representation or embodiment of this particular ideal of spiritual beauty, the sacrifice of one's own corporeal self, while the Byzantines had always conceived it strictly as a neces-sary evil. The Roman Christians alone never tired of erecting this image on every road and hanging or painting it on every wall; to them, it signified eternal comfort against the suffering, no matter how extreme and violent, inevitably entailed in their struggle against the right of the stronger. It is fully understandable, conversely, that Byzantine people could never establish their abstract extension of the ancient Roman universal state on the foundation of such attitudes. Throughout Western history, these attitudes have repeatedly arisen as a curtailing force whenever a religious institution has sought to establish itself as an exclusive and comprehensive political power. This can be observed from the time of Gregory VII, who reduced the formidable position of Roman Emperor of the German Nation to a mere shadow figure, to that of Savonarola, who dealt the death blow to the Medici art-state. Early Roman Christianity thus provided the crucial factor that gave rise to a new art, distinct from antique art not only in a few superficial expressive means but at its very core: it proclaimed transitory nature worthy of representation, even if not yet for its own sake. In the long run, the artistic form early Christians gave nature could be really satisfactory only to religious zealots. While natural objects were deliberately distorted, and thus appeared just as inaccurate as the physically perfected nature of Antiquity, spiritual qualities found expression purely through thought-stimulating devices that made demands not so much on the observer's imagination as on his intellectual faculties.

As soon as any immediate danger of a return to paganism had been removed and the rigidly uncompromising attitude of early Christianity could relax somewhat, the path of development opened out in two directions. On one side, it guided people toward naturalistic accuracy in their portrayal of transitory nature, and, on the other, it allowed them to portray spiritual qualities through means more genuinely artistic than simple explanatory inscriptions or extrinsic attributes. The latter demand could be met only through the incorporation of incidental appearances in bodily expression, and this in turn prompted yet another heightening of naturalistic accuracy in depictions of nature. A normal progression would have to be directed toward an equivalent advancement in the contest with transitory nature — this time, a nature animated by spiritual impulses. But this progress was continually disrupted and hindered by the regular reappearance of the antique conception, in principle obsolete, of art as physical improvement and perfection of nature. This tendency pitted itself against both the contest with the physically transitory and the search for accidental, thus imperfect, manifestations of spiritual impulses.

The battle between these two impulses — a progressive one aiming for naturalistic accuracy and spiritual animation, and a retrospective, retarding one drawn toward the physically perfect and spiritually vacant — dominated the entire Middle Ages. That it ran separate courses north and south of the Alps can be simply explained with reference to the varying degrees of intensity with which the backward-looking, classicizing tendency made itself felt respectively in the ancient cultures of the South and among the younger and comparatively impervious Northern peoples. There is therefore no need to attribute any decisive role to the racial differences of the peoples in question. It seems obvious from the outset that the North would be less burdened by the heavy weight of tradition and that it consequently would, as a rule, represent the more progressive tendency throughout the Middle Ages. It will come as no surprise that by 1520, the year in which this period comes to a close, German and Netherlandish art had moved closer to replicating transitory nature in all its forms, the imperfect external *habitus* as well as the incidental bodily appearances that accompany momentary spiritual impulses, than was ever done previously. But we would be remiss in neglecting to observe the slower development unfolding concurrently in the South. There, works were being created at the end of this period that hold a lofty position alongside products of the Attic golden age in having excited the unanimous wonderment of the entire world. Such works have received the honorary title "classic," for in them everything that has ever stirred up pleasure in human beings, in art and in nature alike, finds a harmonious balance.

Italy

THE GROWTH OF NATURE-SPIRITUALIZING ART IN ITALY

When referring to art-historical developments in the South, we are thinking exclusively of Italy. Although the romanized populations in Spain and southern France were barely more infused with Germanic influence than was the case in, say, Tuscany, various extrinsic, and perhaps also intrinsic, circumstances led those two regions to depend heavily on artistic developments in Germanic lands. While the medieval products of these regions certainly hold considerable interest as instructive art-historical episodes, they possess no real significance for the development of art as a whole.

Not every region of Italy was destined to become a hotbed of new developments. In Rome, the mighty dual traditions of Antiquity and early Christianity stamped out any attempts at innovation throughout most of the Middle Ages. In northern Italy and the Adriatic as far as Aquileia, Byzantium maintained the decisive impact during the same period. With Rome, northern Italy, and the East standing as centers of retrogressive tendencies, adhering to indigenous as well as imported (Byzantine) traditions, art not only was incapable of proceeding beyond its early Christian forms but actually regressed further into the direction of Antiquity. Byzantinism, almost by definition, exemplifies this impulse most thoroughly. In contrast, an energetic thrust toward future developments occurred relatively early, at least since the eleventh century, in Lombardy, the single part of Italy into which the great migrations had brought a high concentration of Germanic tribes.

But the overwhelming influence of the antique tradition would soon assert itself there as well. After a promising start, Lombard art drew to a standstill as early as the twelfth century, without having come close to achieving the kind of success that Northern countries such as France and Germany enjoyed. It can hardly be fortuitous that this stagnation of Lombard art coincided chronologically with the forward leap of another Italian region. Even in its geographic location, this one occupied the middle ground between tradition-steeped Rome and innovative southern Italy, where art was beginning to surge forward by imbuing transitory nature with spiritual qualities. We are speaking of the political and intellectual efflorescence of Tuscany since the days of Gregory VII.

Here, too, various influences clashed violently until a clear champion finally emerged. In Pisa, the antique concept of improving nature grabbed people's attention, while in Siena people sided with the Byzantine cult of beauty. Only in Florence did anyone venture with conviction onto the track of the future; though even there, it took until the end of the thirteenth century for the successful approach to be apprehended unambiguously.

It should be clear that in Italy this developmental phase, which regarded art as spiritually perfected nature, did not proceed as a gradual and consistent progression from muddled groping to lucid consciousness of the final goal. The initial and most consequential impetus was given in the fourth and fifth centuries; this has been discussed in greater detail above. For centuries afterward, Christian art in Italy was confined to rather feebly warding off some influences that were retrogressive and classicizing, others that were Byzantinizing and hostile to spiritual elements. It required renewed motivation to push central Italian art in the direction of spiritualization, that basic postulate of all Western Christian art. This was provided by the appearance of Saint Francis of Assisi, whose character was so vividly bound up with early

Christian social sensibilities. In voluntarily depriving himself of worldly possessions, Francis asserted anew the inherent worthlessness of transitory matter. This conviction led him not to take some egoistic, Oriental flight from the world, however, but to embrace passionately the very deficiencies of imperfect things and to strive vigorously to alleviate the sufferings of the infirm and the oppressed.

The newly awakened attention to the spiritual in art received rich and salubrious nourishment from another side as well. This time it came from Saint Dominic and his order, especially Saint Thomas Aquinas, who took it upon themselves systematically to fortify and to renovate the Christian worldview. It was characteristic of the art of this order, whose philosophy was based so firmly on Plato and Aristotle, that it resuscitated more extensively the primary representational vehicle of classical antique art, personification — though the Dominicans employed only personifications of intellectual or spiritual concepts and processes (allegories), not of natural or sensorially perceptible phenomena.

The Summit of Nature-Spiritualizing Art in Fourteenth-Century Italy

Vasari was right to praise Giotto and his immediate predecessors as the liberators of art from its Byzantine yoke. Giotto was destined to guide Italian art decisively onto the path toward both spiritualization and the measured approximation of nature's transitory appearances, all the while rigorously avoiding any unnecessary incidental details. Indeed, Giotto supremely epitomizes that basic characteristic of high medieval art and culture in Florence: lofty, stern solemnity (figure 5). While his figures' gravity still allows for little individualization, these figures bear no traces of either the contented contemplation — or, more apt, the indifferent staring — of antique statuary or the morosely ceremonial dignity of Byzantine saints. The physical receives equally scant individualization in Giotto's work. Rather, there exists a common Giottesque *type*, which again leans not toward the perfected nature of Antiquity and Byzantium but toward a version made ugly. To see that this was not fortuitous, one need only compare the figures of Giotto with the preciously sweet types favored by the Sienese. The minimal incorporation of incidental details into Giotto's depictions of physical and spiritual activity would have made it impossible for the master to bring adequately to view the lofty sentiments he wished to convey without relying on written inscriptions. Hence his communication of complex stories by means of densely packed figural groups, whose carefully balanced compositions betray the continued impact of the antique tradition, though it is probable that Giotto himself remained unconscious of it. A relative abundance of scenic accessories was introduced for the same purpose, though these secondary details never exceeded the barest degree of necessity and rarely went beyond mere allusion in their representational function. It is self-evident that allegory would come to play a tremendously important role in an art so energetically focused on rendering the supersensible in tangible, visible form. The art of Giotto and his followers approximated the ideal of a purely Catholic art more closely than anything before or since.

THE DECLINE OF NATURE-SPIRITUALIZING ART IN THE RENAISSANCE

The least obvious but nonetheless definitive characteristic of Giotto's art is its confident grasp of transitory nature. Herein lay the enduring appeal that would manifest itself with renewed vigor once the somber outlook of the Florentine trecento had yielded to a more optimistic and life-affirming mood. This was accomplished at the outset of the new century by Masaccio, who introduced something seemingly casually that would reappear in mature and perfected form three generations later. This was an equal balance between an interest in rendering the truthful appearances of transitory nature on the one hand and the endowment of nature with an almost individualized spiritual animation on the other; the transitory aspects were still, however, confined to a minimum. After Masaccio, the task of capturing the true external appearances of transitory nature became the overriding goal of Florentine art. Once people recognized the extant remnants of Roman Antiquity as possessing an analogous character, these provided a convenient means to this end. For the most part, the new works were still imprinted with the stamp of ecclesiastical authority, so that the unity of art and nature appeared to remain firmly in place, at least superficially. But by mid-century, Botticelli had already begun painting mythological pictures for the Medici which vividly demonstrate that, as at the time of the Grimani fountain reliefs, a new, private art, revealing different understandings of man's relation to nature, was beginning to assert itself alongside the official, public manifestations of those relations. The art of portraiture was likewise yielding individual personalities utterly different from those Sienese field marshals of the previous century. Running parallel to this trend was a steadily increasing delight in the secondary details of interiors, as well as in landscapes. We begin to see the ultimate direction of this development in works made shortly after the middle of the quattrocento, and we find its culmination in the High Renaissance of the early sixteenth century. Insofar as transitory aspects of nature were demanded, these were mastered by artists over the course of the fifteenth century; artists now began to filter out anything superfluous or inessential and to place exclusive emphasis on the physically beautiful and spiritually perfect. Leonardo's *Last Supper* can justifiably be regarded as the preeminent representative of this harmonious balancing in art of antique pagan and Christian monotheistic views of nature. Raphael, who came closest to Leonardo's achievements, moved too far toward the side of the physically perfect; it is surely no accident that he was a professional collector of antiquities, objects that were teaching people to appreciate not so much the approximation of true natural appearances as a supreme degree of regularity or, in other words, physical perfection.

Nearly all the greatest creations of these masters, from Masaccio to Raphael, belong to the sphere of religious, that is, Church-sanctioned, art. But are they truly religious? That is, do they continue to be stamped with the view of man's relation to nature officially sanctioned by Roman Catholicism? Certainly the Italians believed this was so, or at least they claimed to. The German Catholics, on the other hand, following the slightly earlier lead of the Florentine monk Savonarola, aggressively denied it. With the death of Raphael, another era appeared to end; and, as had been the case more than a thousand years, and again just three centuries, before, the cry resounded for a deeper understanding of man's relation to matter. This cry, which also echoed in the South, came initially from the North. What shape had art taken there?

Germanic Peoples

THE GROWTH OF NATURE-SPIRITUALIZING ART AMONG GERMANIC PEOPLES

The emperor Constantine foresaw it accurately: in the western half of the Mediterranean provinces, the abstract universal system of the late Roman and Byzantine state proved in the long run to be untenable. This was due not so much to the barbarians' superior military strength as to the laxity with which peoples of Western culture warded them off. Neither emancipation from the right of

84

the stronger, desired so deeply by Westerners, nor the practical fulfillment of Christianity's theoretical promises and demands was to be expected on the part of the Roman state, which continued to cling tightly to its antique foundations. This conviction, at least vaguely sensed if not overtly acknowledged, crippled any defensive action in the West that did not spring directly from the emperor. With justified pride in their ancient civilization, the cultured peoples of Gaul, Spain, and Italy peered contemptuously down their noses at the ignorant barbarians. The latter, however, had proved themselves at once possessed of an undoubted talent for ruling and little inclined, by virtue of their intrinsic good nature, to put the right of the stronger to the kind of use that antique people would have regarded as only just and fitting. In this respect, it is easy to understand how the Germanic tribes rose so quickly to uncontested leadership in far-ranging territories, even those in which they made up only a small minority of the population, and consequently were able to mingle and merge completely with the local inhabitants in language and customs within just a few centuries. This was particularly the case in Spain and southern France but also in Burgundy in northern France, where it happened more gradually. Although the rift separating the Germanic rulers from their romanized subjects may have run deepest in Lombardy, even the Langobards eventually surrendered to the process of romanization — later, perhaps, than the Franks in northern France had done, but all the more thoroughly for that. In contrast to these Romano-Germanic hybrid peoples, whom we fittingly designate "Romance" (*romanisch*), the state systems in present-day Germany, England, and Scandinavia represent the element within medieval Europe that remained essentially Germanic.

Germanic peoples found themselves from the very beginning in a relation with their peers of Roman heritage that was partially advantageous and partially disadvantageous as far as art was concerned.

The advantage lay in the fact that the two determining factors for artistic production — the perception of nature and the most appropriate means for competing with nature — were passed on to them from outside and could therefore develop freely, with no resistance from the historical burden of potentially conflicting attitudes. That is to say, Germanic peoples had no indigenous artistic tradition founded on the right of the stronger and aimed at improving physical nature, which they had to overcome with force as the late Romans did. Because, in contrast to the Semites, they lacked any deep-rooted inclination toward abstract speculation, their understanding of nature as expressed in their conception of the gods was barely developed at all. The pagan Germanic belief system could not resist Christianity and its clear ethical statutes for long, however, and the way was soon paved for the adoption of Roman Christian art. But the path leading to such art was not obstructed by extrinsic or artificial factors.

This lack of history also acted to the disadvantage of Germanic groups. Above all, it made them incapable of understanding the deepest essence of the highly refined art of late Rome. Certainly the Teutons, with their naive and unpolished artistic sensibility, found those ugly human forms pleasing, believing themselves to be witnessing the human figure as a pure result of the contest with nature. This would of course mean that they fundamentally misconstrued the intentions of early Christian art. If Germanic people wanted to take up the heritage of the Romans culturally as well as politically, they had first to familiarize themselves with certain aspects of antique culture. Although their initial lack of contact with the outmoded principles of antique art was certainly advantageous in this respect, this advantage could become fruitful only after Germanic peoples learned to appreciate those achievements of antique art that were of long-term validity, achievements with which the new Christian art also had to reckon.

86

The accuracy of these conclusions is confirmed by the later progress of medieval art history. Germanic peoples managed far earlier than the Tuscans to produce an art fundamentally distinct from that of Antiquity. But it is noteworthy that, among themselves, the decisive successes were accomplished by neither the least intermixed populations, such as the Scandinavians, nor the most thoroughly romanized, such as the western Goths in Spain. Rather, they were made by the Franks and Burgundians in what is currently France, followed by people in the Rhineland, and then the Langobards — though the latter soon reverted to the direction of the Tuscans and consequently fall out of our discussion. All this will emerge more clearly in the finer points of the development, whose definitive phases we shall now sketch out.

THE FIRST IMPACT OF LATE ROMAN (AND BYZANTINE) ART ON GERMANIC PEOPLES

What we are calling the "first impact" refers to art of the Great-Migration period, which lasted until 768 c.e. Although Teutonic peoples had gained superficial familiarity with late Roman decoration, they did not fully understand it, and as a result they refashioned it according to their own tastes. This shall concern us, for now, only with regard to what it reveals about the primitive Germanic attitude toward nature. This attitude manifested itself most vividly in the transmutation of band interlace into zoomorphic patterns. Although the kind of complete filling of surfaces or blank spaces that late Roman artists accomplished with their *entrelacs* greatly appealed to Teutonic peoples, the simpleminded-ness of the latter did not allow them to comprehend the refined and abstracted equalizing tendency that underlay those antique patterns. Rather, in their longing to apprehend some intelligible subject, they transformed into snakes those abstract intertwining shapes that the late Romans had deliberately stripped of any recognizable natural referent. In this way, the uniform covering of a surface, so at odds with the right of the stronger, was made to conform with Germanic predilections. In contrast, the suppression of the sensorially perceptible aspects of nature that arose from Semitic monotheism was not so appealing.

To compete with transitory nature was the chief objective of Teutonic peoples from the outset. Although their tendency toward perfectionism manifested itself chiefly in the symmetrical distribution of interlace patterns, the oldest datable products of Germanic art often brought this to view in a way very different from their Roman models. This state of affairs has crucial implications for our understanding of all subsequent artistic creations of Teutonic peoples. Symmetry was typically absolute in Roman prototypes, but Germanic artists employed a form of symmetry that was either ruptured — for example, in diagonals — or applied only to groupings. In the latter case, the symmetrical organization becomes apparent only in a larger overview, after the various complicated sections are pulled together perceptually. Harmony was present in both instances, but those aspects that in Antiquity shone forth lucid and unimpaired appeared in Germanic art in a way that was veiled and obscured. And yet here, too, we see evidence of the contest with nature, for in its organic creations nature likewise allows the universally prevailing principles of harmony to emerge only in shrouded and splintered form. Just as the Teutons, being a primitive people, had to acknowledge the right of the stronger to some extent, so they eventually succumbed to the urge to perfect physical nature. Both concessions, however, were made to a significantly lesser degree than in Antiquity. In each case, ample room remained for free play within the necessary order and regularity, which seemed to stave off the impression of any external compulsion. In each, however, the mitigating factor was a spiritual one. This was bound up, in part, with the right of the stronger. The subordinate relation of the Germanic liege to his lord was rooted neither in inherent respect attained through physical force nor in passive submission to the dictates of some supersensory fate; it lay, rather, in the spiritually noble sentiment of loyalty. We encounter this characteristically Teutonic version of the right of the stronger continually in the sphere of visual art as well. Here the physical perfection of the transitory world neither constituted an absolute postulate, as in Byzantium, nor dissolved, through its spiritual refinement, into something fundamentally and supremely abstract, as in Islam. Soulless beauty ran just as counter to Germanic tastes as the disembodied idea. For Teutonic man, the perfecting of the transitory was always motivated by spiritual factors.

Spiritual motivation also lies at the heart of the second issue, the concealment of symmetry in medieval Germanic art. Hidden symmetry is the primary characteristic of organic — that is, animated — nature as opposed to inorganic nature, where symmetry appears unveiled and open to view. Movement, on the other hand, is the physical manifestation of an internal spiritual impulse, that is, an impulse of the will. The loveliest rock crystal displays nothing but pure bodily existence; it is dead matter. But the plant, which moves through growth, and the animal, which moves through translocation, follow impulses that cannot be sufficiently explained through their own purely physical existence. Whereas the antique worldview had vigorously ignored the distinction altogether, the Christian worldview presented this impulse in spiritual terms, as the expression of the will of a boundless, supersensory God. Germanic art initially sought to perfect the transitory world in a restrained and concealed manner. Once Christianized, it came to present this process of perfection openly as an infusion of nature with spirit, sanctioned and demanded by the Church.

CAROLINGIAN AND OTTONIAN ART

The prospects for a fruitful rivalry between this incipient Germanic Christian art and its late Roman and Byzantine counterparts at first were slight indeed. Germanic arts were threatened above all by their excessive delight in unperfected forms of nature; one thinks, for example, of the twisted masses of interlaced snakes with human heads most liberally cultivated by Viking art before it succumbed to stagnation. Here again Charlemagne intervened, this time forcibly mandating instruction in Byzantine art. It is possible today to accept as valid a point long and stubbornly combated back when the technical-material theory of artistic production prevailed — namely, that the essential characteristics of Carolingian and Ottonian art emerged under Byzantine influence. But what Germanic people were really seeking — transitory naturalism, veiled perfection, and spiritual expressiveness — lay on a different path. Byzantine art taught them how to improve nature in the most physically harmonious form but with no spiritual expression. Despite this, Charlemagne's intention was well placed, the training necessary, and the discipline gained thereby salutary. It marked the first time since they began creating art that Germanic peoples were exposed to a form of art that, in its aim to improve nature, was intrinsically foreign to their own. As always, they threw themselves into the new with deep devotion and full, fiery rigor. They sought to learn first how to imitate it respectfully, then how to filter out and preserve those aspects useful to them while discarding everything else, even if this included its essential features. Alongside Byzantinizing works propagated by secular courts and ecclesiastical circles, numerous manuscript illuminations now appeared that, with their often convulsive attempts at spiritual expressiveness and inclusion of incidental traits in their depiction of the physical world, kept alive a tendency unique to Germanic Christian art.

THE PHASE OF ROMANESQUE ART

Germanic peoples grew progressively more conscious of the direction of their own artistic impulses after the eleventh century. In the forms they inherited from Byzantine art — not, or only to a minimal degree, from the Roman tradition (this was also the case in France, for which reason the term "Romanesque" is woefully inappropriate) — they began to seek out only those aspects that revealed transitory appearances and accidental bodily expressions of the spiritual. As soon as aspects connected to physical perfection were also discarded, Teutonic artists quickly realized that Byzantine forms offered virtually nothing useful for their own needs. This explains the extraordinarily rapid development, especially in Germany, of an indigenous Northern art. With the thirteenth-century donor figures at Naumburg (figure 6), a point was reached in the contest with physically and spiritually accidental forms that even much later artists would barely surpass, at least with respect to the characterization of the independent figure. This change manifested itself most drastically, however, in the realm of ornament. While we encounter Byzantine foliate ornament (*folia graeca*) constantly in eleventh-century art, we observe in art of the thirteenth century ornamental forms that much more closely approximate the appearances of local flora — in other words, transitory nature. We notice this shift in tracery as well, a new invention that arose from a spiritualized conception of architectural form.

As we could for Italy, we can distinguish several discrete phases in the progress of Germanic Christian art. These, to be sure, do not represent a smooth upsurge from seedling to full blossom. Rather, they reveal in the middle a rupture, whose motivation was the same in the North and the South: it came from art that seeks to improve the physical forms of nature. In the North, this setback was the prerequisite for any productive future development. In numerous Viking artifacts, we possess horrifying testimony as to what would have happened to Germanic art had it been left to run its own course. But, having passed through their Byzantine training, artists in Germany, France, and Lombardy turned resolutely toward the direction most appropriate to a Germanic Christian art. In examining the results of this progress, we shall consider only France and Germany, for reasons already discussed. Although Germany could boast more radical accomplishments, victory belonged to the French, not only in the Germanic Christian world but also beyond.

The Summit of Germanic Christian Art in the Thirteenth and Fourteenth Centuries

Twelfth-century Frenchmen enjoyed the advantage of possessing a drop of antique blood. Whereas the Germans rushed headlong and recklessly into extremes, the French halted a step earlier to create an "Ideal," for the first time since classical Antiquity. This Ideal, to be sure, was fundamentally nonclassical. In place of stable and self-contained physical presence, it introduced restless bending and swaying, that is, movement; instead of beautiful, spiritually disengaged contemplation, it altered facial proportions so as to produce a spiritually nuanced, thus accidental, expression of sweetness. This Ideal was emphatically Germanic; but even as an Ideal, it never denied that its origins lay in the antique search for perfection and desire for regularity. This is the "moderation" that has always distinguished French art from the purely Germanic; this is the "system" that the French have always endeavored to pluck from the stream of random appearances. This system has entered the scene whenever the inventive capacities of Germanic art elsewhere have waned, as in the age of Louis XIV, and has retreated as soon as they have begun to stir up, as in the fifteenth century. The French system had intruded onto German land as early as the thirteenth century, however, and at that time the foreign Ideal proved more powerful than the indigenous predilection for portraying the outright transitory. By the fourteenth century, it had come to dominate Germany thoroughly, although in both northern and southern Germany certain symptoms were simultaneously accumulating that clearly indicated a forthcoming change of direction. It is, nonetheless, surely no accident that the Gothic period is once again lauded in our own century as the ideal form of Germanic Christian art, just as Giotto's works are regarded as the ideal of Italian Christian art.

The Decline of Germanic Christian Art

With Jan van Eyck — and, in Burgundy, Claus Sluter — Germanic Christian art abandoned the Ideal and turned with heightened energy to the unmediated portrayal of the transitory as bearer of spiritual beauty. This new movement reached its peak in the works of Albrecht Dürer and ended with his death. No earlier Germanic artist had mastered imperfect and natural physicality as thoroughly as Dürer did — as proof, see his own sketched nature studies — while simultaneously imbuing it with so much spiritual content. The art with which he became acquainted when he visited Italy was useful for him primarily in a technical sense. The thought of consciously improving nature, in the manner of Raphael, or of formulating an ideal, as did Leonardo, was very far from Dürer's mind. It is thus understandable that, precisely because he was a convinced and solemn Germanic Christian, Dürer had to be sympathetic to Martin Luther's Reformation, for he still believed in the possibility of cohesion between a Christian worldview and visual art. That this unity was deeply threatened by the form Italian culture took at this historical moment appeared obvious to most Northerners. But that the particular forms of Italian art in the age of Julius II and Leo X had caused this threat to grow imminent

seems not to have been apparent in Germany, where Dürer's contemporaries were fervently seeking to acquaint themselves with
Italian art; everyone at the time wanted to see "antique art" in
Germany. Herein lies an apparent contradiction, but one that
is easily resolved. Although they traveled by different routes, the
visual arts in Germany — and France as well — had arrived at exactly the same end point as those in Italy. Northern people were
also looking at religious images, which still constituted the vast
majority of paintings, not so much for their intellectual or spiritual content as for the degree to which they, as pictures, succeeded
in actively competing with nature. Dürer was deluded to trust that
the unity between conceptions of nature and the Christian worldview could be sustained in art. The guardians of religious interests
were of a different, and ultimately [more] correct, opinion. The
Reformers, by dispensing with ecclesiastical art, and the popes, by
giving free rein to the new idea of nature, respectively affirmed, if
only silently, the gulf dividing faith and knowledge, and religious
and profane art. In so doing, they rescued the possibility of the
Church's presiding over a more popular art.

CHAPTER THREE

Third Period

Art as Reproduction of Transitory Nature

The Renaissance presents much the same picture as the Hellenistic-Roman period in several respects. In both cases, works of art appeared that, by suggesting a contest with transitory nature, contrasted with the prevailing worldview, which deemed only a physically or spiritually improved nature worthy of representation. And in both instances, we witness the same unmistakable emergence and development of the underlying basis of that phenomenon: profound interest in transitory matter for its own sake, manifested above all in the vigorous pursuit of natural-scientific research.

As far as religion was concerned, people in the age of the Diadochi and in Imperial Rome let the study of nature quietly run its own course. This approach took its toll when the belief in pagan gods subsided as a consequence. Christianity took care to avoid this mistake. It seemed unfeasible simply to put a stop to the new investigation of nature; one had, rather, to find some way of coming to terms with it, for this interest in nature had gained a powerful hold on every cultivated circle. A natural-scientific worldview quickly took shape, which sought to explain the appearances of the material world by tracing the laws of physics as far as possible. This led to some obvious successes. And whether they wanted to or not, artists now had to take this worldview into account. Dürer, though completely steeped in this attitude, still thought of himself as maintaining a conceptual adherence to revealed faith. He was mistaken; revealed faith regards matter as merely the visible manifestation of the will of a divine spiritual power, but Dürer took a greater interest in matter itself than in the spiritual cause that had presumably given it shape. Revealed faith and natural science diverged from each other more sharply than this artist, with his deeply religious sensibility, could have imagined. When he finally became conscious of this latent split, there was no question as to which route the artist would follow. It was not that of revealed faith but that of natural science, which alone corresponded to the current views that art would soon express.

The danger that art would grow completely alienated from, and perhaps even do damage to, the Christian worldview — a danger that had been imminent since the fifteenth century — was actualized following the deaths of Raphael and Dürer. The German Reformers turned flippantly to the easy solution, reminiscent of that taken by Muhammad, of abolishing all ecclesiastical art. As in Islam, in the world of Reformed Christianity only profane art was acceptable — at least in principle — but it was allowed to devote itself freely to the natural-scientific worldview. The fate of revealed faith was thus rendered independent of the change in attitudes toward nature evinced in the artistic sphere.

This new rule was easier to mandate than to enforce. As in the Byzantine Empire, in Protestant lands iconoclastic movements erupted repeatedly well into the seventeenth century. This was due in part to the masses' continued reliance on tradition, in part to the fact that the cultivated elite wished not to dispense with aesthetic enjoyment of spiritual content, which seemed present only in pictures associated with the conceptual domain of the Church. Thus it happened that a Protestant artist, Rembrandt, enriched the legacy of Germanic Christian art most brilliantly in modern times. Rembrandt's art was not ecclesiastical, however: his pictures were meant not for the edification of faithful communities in religious houses but for the private aesthetic enjoyment of his art-starved compatriots.

The Catholic Church pursued a different course. It did not wish either to acknowledge any conflict between revealed faith and natural-scientific inquiry or to relinquish the agitating tool that was popular art, to which the spirits of Romance people were still exceptionally receptive. At this point, the Church advanced the following argument: The material world obeys physical laws to a certain extent, and to investigate these is not forbidden; indeed, in certain practical instances, such as for medicinal purposes, it is even commendable to do so. But beyond that point, human faculties fail, and there the final cause of all things, proclaimed by revealed faith, takes over. From here on, faith and science coincide perfectly. There is consequently no reason to forbid artistic creation grounded in a natural-scientific worldview or to banish from the Church existing works of art based thereon. This argument implies that all art, whether profane or religious, is free to compete with transitory nature. At the same time, of course, the Church directed artists toward the spiritual all the more fervently in an effort to extract as much autonomous significance as possible from transitory matter. And yet it was clear that what would henceforth matter most, even to Catholic artists, was the contest with transitory nature, whether this was manifested in the reproduction of physical appearances or in the expression of spiritual impulses.

What had only begun to suggest itself during the Roman Imperial period emerged after the sixteenth century as the self-conscious aim of all Western art: in place of physically or spiritually perfected nature, the artist now competed with the material world in all its unabashed transience and imperfection. Just as proponents of the post-1520 worldview held even the most modest object of nature to be worthy of attention, studied its inner workings, and searched relentlessly for its correspondence to the basic laws of their own existence, they shunned no natural subject on principle alone in their artistic contest. It cannot be denied that thanks to the weight of tradition, earlier stages of development, especially the religious art of the second major period, maintained their influence for centuries — and that they even continue to resonate today, when the visual arts have learned to capture even the most fleeting and momentary impressions of the transitory world. Nor should this be especially surprising, for artistic progress advances not in a regular sequence but in fits and starts and with repeated setbacks. This was doubtless also the case in earlier periods; and although we lack the means of closely tracking those developments step-by-step, an abundance of documentary sources allows us to do so for more recent centuries. Before examining this progress in detail, we must first investigate the consequences of this broader transformation.

Did the visual arts gain anything through the change we have just described? Once art was freed from a restrictive approach to nature, did it finally achieve true perfection? By relinquishing its claims to superiority over the material world and taking an equal place alongside it, did art increase its own significance for humanity? These questions are difficult to address for us who live in the midst of this period. We should probably answer them all in the affirmative. Yet there is one symptom that could give us pause: namely, that so many of us are dissatisfied with what has become of modern art.[1] All things considered, there is one major deficiency in the modern era of art as compared with the two preceding ones, and this is that art has become the privilege of only a few social strata — namely, the cultivated elite. To comprehend this shift clearly, one need only recall the popular quality of much of the art of fifteenth-century Florence or Nuremberg. In such places, the whole population seems to have been breathlessly engaged in artistic issues — and we are already dealing here with the historical moment of transition to modern art. The bonds between visual art and people of all classes were tighter still during the Attic golden age. The artist of that time was really an artisan or philistine; firmly planted in the ground of tradition, he created nothing more than what everyone already knew. It was no different with those Germanic Christian or Giottesque masters who produced art for the glory of God.

Today's artist, on the other hand, is a distinguished gentleman churning out pieces to satisfy the dilettantish predilections of other grand and wealthy men, be these private individuals or institutions such as the state or the Church. Now that a stable norm for observing nature no longer exists, every artist looks at it with different eyes. To "understand" the artist's private vision requires special schooling and a hobbyist's enthusiasm — things, of course, accessible not to the greater mass of the populace but only to members of the privileged classes. In a word, art has lost its immediate significance for the life of modern humanity. It has become the object of aesthetic "appreciation," to which one must be first initiated and then educated. From this viewpoint, one might say that with the dawning of the new era, the golden age of the visual arts has passed away; the illusionism of the Renaissance signaled its farewell gleam. The naive hunger of the larger mass of humanity for fulfillment of its inner "emptiness" seeks sustenance in a different art form, one that relies not on the sense of sight but on the sense of hearing, one that does not reproduce matter but rather "improves" time: that is, music. It was a perfect foreshadowing of things to come that at the very moment Luther snatched visual art away from the Reformed Church, he offered it song as a substitute.

In the realm of song and music, of course, we also find artists and connoisseurs standing side by side with "natural" singers and musicians and audiences with simpler tastes. But the fact that the latter are as good as extinct in the field of visual art lends this sphere its particular current stamp, as well as a Hippocratic quality.

To apply a threefold division into stages of growth, summit, and decline to art of the modern era is intrinsically impossible because we, living through this third period ourselves, cannot regard it with the requisite historical and critical distance. If certain signs, especially having to do with societal life, do not deceive, it seems we find ourselves approaching a peak — without, however, being able to discern clearly where the path is leading. We shall therefore attempt nothing further here than briefly to sketch out the preceding phases of development.

Once again, the progress appears to run distinct courses north and south of the Alps. We encounter it in most unified and uninterrupted form in Italy, and therefore we shall begin there.

Even after 1520, Italian art did not adapt to the new contest with transitory nature in a straightforward way; only in recent years has it begun to do so. Is this reluctance due to the continued resonance of a long tradition of improving nature that goes back to ancient Italian peoples? Or is it attributable to the influence of the highest Church authority, who, as the predominant patron of Italian art for over two centuries, was overwhelmingly responsible for its greatest masterworks? We should probably opt for the latter suggestion, for if adherence to physical perfection were an inherited racial trait, it makes little sense that in our own days we find this tendency transformed into its opposite.

What was perceived around 1520 as Italian art's great flaw was its suppression of the spiritual by the physically perfect, especially evident in the works of Raphael. In the North, the Reformation demanded spiritual absorption, something that existing religious art was felt to be unable to accommodate. The Counter-Reformation held a different opinion. But even earlier, before Counter-Reformation tendencies were integrated deliberately into Italian art, one artist intuitively discerned the successive goal and independently tried to grasp it. This, of course, was Michelangelo.

a. Michelangelo approached the old Christian problem of spiritualizing transitory nature in an utterly unique way. In this, no one has ever followed him, and only a genius of equally extraordinary gifts will ever be able to do so. Michelangelo sought to reproduce the spiritual in the physical, but not, as in classical Antiquity, through beautification of the physical body or, as in Germanic art, through accidental gestures. Although this artist realized that it was impossible to avoid the physical and sensual domain in art, he employed it as a vehicle for making the supersensory realm visible. Therefore, he endowed the physical body with supernatural shape (figure 7). Of course, exceptional artistic powers were required to prevent figures from looking either unnatural or grotesque. Michelangelo succeeded in doing this: his figures appear at once daimonic and convincing.

b. The works of Michelangelo's numerous imitators make it instantly apparent that the trail he blazed could not be traveled successfully by another. Other artists therefore rushed back onto the natural path that art north of the Alps had forged so fretfully long ago: the portrayal of the spiritual through accidental aspects either belonging to or following from the physical. Herein lies the true essence of Roman Baroque art.[2] Of course, this goal would never have been attainable without some concession to transitory physical forms. But Roman Baroque art maintained the utmost restraint here too, struggling to preserve as much physical perfection as it could. In this approach, there lies a certain incomplete or contradictory quality: hence the rather unsatisfying impression that Baroque works leave on the modern Germanic beholder.

c. Around the middle of the seventeenth century, after the seal-ing of the Peace of Westphalia, the agitated mood that had sparked both Reformation and Counter-Reformation finally quieted — and in Italy, so did the demand for the spiritualization of the work of art. This postulate, with which Roman artists had been engaged for over a century, was now abandoned; it was replaced by a desire for physical perfection, which in the rest of Italy had remained in effect since the Middle Ages. But this was accompanied now by a heightening of transitory natural appearances; no period, except-ing perhaps the most recent, took perspectival illusionism further than the late Baroque (for example, Pozzo). What was the purpose of the lively transitory movements that accompanied the still over-whelmingly religious art in Italy after Michelangelo, if they were not based on perceptible spiritual impulses? It was only natural that the aim of representing the transitory physical world would fall away once the aim of representing spiritual expression did.

d. This shift triggered a retrogressive process that culminated, in the second half of the eighteenth century, with the art of Anto-nio Canova. This phenomenon would not have been feasible in a genuinely Christian art. Canova sought to reproduce precisely what early Christian art had struggled so vigorously to avoid. We must also keep in mind that his artistic production lies in the Enlightenment, a time when religious sensibilities were slacker than ever. What is remarkable is that the most classicizing reac-tion occurred in the name of nature. Suddenly the fleeting move-ments portrayed by late Baroque masters looked unnatural; as in Antiquity before Alexander, a worldview took shape in which only the enduring, the serene, and the eternal were regarded as nature's truest expressions. What was a matter of deep religious conviction for every cultured people over a thousand years ago became, during the last century, merely the pet scholarly or aes-thetic idea of the cultivated classes.

Our picture of this progress in the North is more variegated if not more confused. Initially, the new awareness of the cleft between revealed faith and the natural-scientific worldview had a retarding effect here. The Germans lacked the levity that allowed the Italians to move so easily beyond the problem. It took until our own day for Germans of both Catholic and Protestant confessions to recover from the embarrassment of that conflict; indeed, until very recently it seemed that any genuinely creative progress would be completely denied to the Germans after the deaths of Dürer and Holbein.

Only two small populations originating in the low countries managed to expand on the work of their great northern German forebears after the Reformation. The Flemish masters of the sixteenth century may well have shared with Dürer a conviction that visual art could continue to radiate around the Church as it had always done, just as theology maintained its status as the noblest of academic fields. But after the iconoclastic movements and, even more, at the beginning of the seventeenth century, they began to see things more clearly. It was decisive for Flemish art that its most brilliant representative was able to acquaint himself at leisure with those features of Italian Baroque art that agreed both with his personal style and with Flemish art more generally. Flemish art was thus able to develop into a predominantly religious Baroque art, but without Roman Baroque's distracting obsession with physical perfection.

At the same time, the Frisian Dutch, having emerged victorious in their battle for independence, gained the courage to build an art exclusively on the natural-scientific worldview and to discard any consideration for revealed faith. It is characteristic nonetheless that this art, whose sole aim was to compete with transitory physical forms — either for their own sake or in order to give sensual form to spiritual impulses — would last barely longer than fifty years and would ultimately give way to a lengthy reaction on the nature-improving side. Even the great Rembrandt, who was as intellectually profound as a Germanic artist had ever been and peerless in the confidence with which he grasped the transitory appearances of the physical world, grew obsolete during his own lifetime. As soon as the strict puritanical zeal of the war years had passed, his genuine early-Christian-Protestant contempt for the physically perfect — for beauty — ran up against opposition.

By around 1650, then, the time had again become ripe for the hegemony of French art. Only after the sometimes overwrought obsession with spiritual expression had finally subsided in Italy, after the Rubens school had become trivial in Antwerp and even the Dutch craved the visualization of physically perfected forms — only then was the path free once more for the advancement of French art, with its predilection for measure and balance, an art as far removed from an excessive desire for the transitory as from a desire for the spiritual. French art has dominated Western Europe for the last two centuries. It has never solved any problems, for these will impose themselves only on extremes; nor has it produced a truly captivating master. But with its technical confidence and uniformly appealing mode of presentation, French art has been able to maintain a consistent position of categorical respect. Today, however, this art is again having to surrender its erstwhile leadership to Germanic stock of purer racial consciousness.

The most remarkable advances in modern art have been displayed by people of the Iberian Peninsula. Their artistic progress during this latest period has paralleled that of Germanic peoples — on occasion, it has even rushed ahead of these. The Italianate Mannerism of sixteenth-century Spanish artists took a very similar form to that of their Flemish contemporaries. At the time of Rubens and Rembrandt, however, we witness the activity of Velázquez and Murillo in Spain, both of whom were fierce competitors with transitory nature. And in an age when the selective whims of artists and connoisseurs in the rest of Europe were soaking in the rejuvenating baths of classicism, Goya emerged in Spain. Thus the deepest and most complete adherence to the natural-scientific worldview in art occurred in the very land whose leaders had striven with fire and sword and at all costs to preserve the unity between faith and knowledge.

PART TWO

Elements of the Work of Art

CHAPTER FOUR

Purpose

All works of visual art are created to fulfill some function. The purpose of any work of art must therefore be sharply distinguished from its artistic *habitus*. The relation between these aspects is not fixed and immutable and is thus subject to historical investigation. By its very nature, this relation operates within a broad playing field bounded by two opposing extremes. On the one side stands a complete preponderance of functionality, next to which any aesthetic effects seem to arise spontaneously and without conscious consideration — as with a simply hewn rectangular beam or a stone chipped into a triangular arrowhead. On the other side is the total supremacy of the intent of art (*Kunstabsicht*), next to which a work's functional intent merely provides a pretext for its existence — as in cabinet painting.

The term "function" or "purpose" denotes the intention to satisfy some basic human need. Human needs are partially bodily and partially spiritual. The bodily needs, those of our five senses, can be divided into two main categories:

1. needs that arise from our sense of sight exclusively; in these cases, we can speak of *decorative purpose*; and

2. those that arise from other senses; here we can speak of *practical purpose* in the broadest sense of the word. Shelter, for

instance, appeals to the sense of touch; a saltshaker to the sense of taste; a container for smelling salts to the sense of smell; a musical instrument to the sense of hearing.

Spiritual or intellectual functions seek to arouse certain mental images and associations of ideas, and we therefore feel justified in referring to these as the *conceptual purpose*. The most important imaginative concepts for visual art concern man's relation to superhuman powers, be these forces of nature or moral forces.

The need for decoration originates in the eye — the same organ through which we perceive visual art, critically evaluating how well a given work succeeds in giving expression to its contest with nature. This is probably why visual art and decoration are so often held to be identical. Certainly decoration and art are both pleasing to human beings. But man also finds pleasure in the successful awakening of spiritual ideas, and in these cases we can speak of art but not decoration. There is no decoration without art; but art does exist that does not seek to be decorative. From its very inception, decoration has been nothing more than the filling of a void. Only when, in man's struggle to banish his *horror vacui*, some internal drive urged him to compete with nature — did decoration become a work of art.

Practical needs tend to be directed toward senses other than that of sight. Yet the sense of sight inevitably encounters the things human hands create to satisfy those needs. It naturally follows that wherever a practical necessity makes itself felt, a void emerges for the eye and the decorative function cries out to be addressed. The same holds true for imaginative or conceptual needs.[1] The degree to which the decorative purpose has been taken into account in relation to the others has likewise varied in different time periods and is therefore no less open to historical inquiry.

It must be emphasized that in any given period of art, not excluding Islamic, no one of the three functions can be singled out as the solitary focus of attention. The very question as to which one first entered human artistic practice cannot be answered with any certainty. Although observation of surviving primitive races suggests the decorative purpose as most ancient and elemental — for example, in the form of tattooing — no people presently on earth is completely oblivious to practical and conceptual functions. In so-called prehistoric art and art of the oldest historical period, ancient Egypt, artists were always concerned with all three purposes equally.

Let us now turn to the relations between purpose and art as they developed during each of our three major eras.[2]

First Period: Art Perfects Nature

Ancient Egyptian Art
In this first phase, every work of art is distinctly stamped by one of the three purposes. The division between function and art is revealed most unambiguously in works of conceptual purpose. All figures look nearly identical in outward appearance, and extra-artistic mediating devices such as attributes or hieroglyphic inscriptions were required to bring the desired aim to light.

Greek Art Before Alexander the Great
Here a balance was struck between function as the sole impetus for artistic creation and the increasingly compelling desire to compete with nature. Decoration was no longer simply stretched across every available surface, as in tattoos or on the outer walls of Egyptian temples; it began, rather, to respond to certain natural conditions of the work of art — what we now call the tectonic. Decorative elements served to distinguish and focus attention on discrete segments of a whole, for example, head, neck, and hands. Because in nature these elements are differentiated only

imperfectly, man could improve their respective distinction as he competed with nature. Even vases were divided into neck and foot. Still, no work of art arose that was not designed to accommodate a specific objective function beyond the contest with nature. This fact, which obtains for all art made before Alexander, is what scholars have in mind when they claim that the Greeks did not distinguish between industrial arts and high art.

Antiquity from Alexander to Constantine the Great

At this point, art became an end in itself. We need only recall here the Grimani reliefs and various other animal figures discussed above at page 62 (figures 2 and 3). What purpose did those animals serve? Certainly not a conceptual one, for they fell outside the circle of creatures that classical artists typically employed to embody supersensory ideas. Even less could they have served any practical purpose. Their function was solely decorative. But this, too, was no more than a pretext; the real justification for these works lay in the contest they initiated with transitory matter. That contest elevated art to an end in itself. Even works that were unquestionably produced to fulfill a practical function were soon conceived in terms not only of that function but also, and more important, of how far they could push the contest with nature.

Second Period: Art Spiritualizes Nature

All monotheistic observances must fight with special fervor against the contest with transitory nature. Islam did so most fiercely. Realizing that the conceptual purpose posed the most imminent threat that transitory nature would be esteemed for its own sake, Islam prohibited its adherents from pursuing that purpose at all. Of course, circumventions of this law were never entirely absent, especially in Persia but also in Egypt during the Mamluk period.[3] Strictly speaking, Islamic art retained only decorative and practical

112

functions. Byzantine art admitted the conceptual purpose, at least within certain rigorously defined boundaries; but this purpose was given unimpeded free rein only in Western Christianity, so long as it took as its object only invisible spiritual forces and their perceptible manifestations on earth. Islam's mistrust proved well founded in the end, for Western Christian art took far less time than had been needed in earlier Antiquity to make the contest with transitory nature for its own sake into the supreme goal of all artistic activity.

a. The early Middle Ages until the twelfth century demonstrated both a desire to compete with transitory nature and a strong affinity for improving physical nature, but always for the sake of some practical purpose. The most eloquent proof resides in the attributes and explanatory captions often attached to conceptually meaningful figures.

b. The Gothic or Giottesque phase struck a mediating balance between art and purpose during the period governed by the Christian worldview. In northern and southern Europe alike, we witness heightened efforts to reconcile purpose and artistic design. In Northern art, examples are pointed arches and tracery; in Southern art, the allegorical treatment of conceptual principles.

c. The art of the van Eycks in the North and the Renaissance in the South reveal clearly the renewed joy with which man took up the contest with transitory nature in art. In Italy, the question was no longer "Which architectural form is best suited to an ecclesiastical function?" but "What is the most artistic form for a temple?" In other words, people sought the form that best corresponded to the nature of the building as they understood it. In this way, they were able to abandon the long-sanctioned basilican system of ancient Rome and move on toward the centralized plan. Eyckian oil painting likewise signaled nothing less than the abandonment of fresco painting, which hitherto had been the most practical medium for decorating church interiors, in favor of a technique better equipped to compete with transitory nature; the winged altarpiece would never have supplanted the monumental fresco simply on its own merits.[4] The artistry evident in Dürer's *Martyrdom of the Ten Thousand* is no less an end in itself than in his self-portraits; that in Raphael's Madonnas is no less striking than in his *Galatea*.

Third Period: Art Competes with Nature for Its Own Sake

The emancipation of visual art to an end in itself was not adversely affected by the renewed intensification of revealed faith during the Reformation and Counter-Reformation, as it had been at the end of Antiquity by the triumph of Christianity. On the contrary: for reasons outlined in Part One, only at this time was such emancipation possible. What throughout post-Alexander Antiquity and the Renaissance remained contraband, so to speak, was legitimized after 1520 when art truly became an end in itself, and continues to predominate today, perhaps more strongly than ever. To attempt to subdivide the four centuries of art history that have since elapsed on the basis of the ever-shifting relations between artistic form and function appears hardly feasible at this writing. But we can say this much with justification: in a future, more farseeing survey of art history, the sixteenth through nineteenth centuries will be pulled together to form a single phase, and the beginning of a new period will be set in this, our own day.

The reasoning runs as follows. From the moment art, as an end in itself, could proceed freely, the danger arose that art's liberation would do harm to its erstwhile motivators and determinants, the three functions. That this threat was not actualized all at once may be ascribed solely to the restraining influence of tradition. Rembrandt himself painted history pictures, albeit with strong genre inflections, even though Dutch Protestant art had fundamentally repudiated any religious conceptual purpose. Italians held the embodiment of the religious conceptual function to be the primary responsibility of art well into the eighteenth century, even though after Michelangelo this too was merely a bare pretext. But after classicism, when, urged on by purely artistic factors — the drive to return to nature, we are explicitly assured[5] — artists took the (for Western art) unprecedented plunge into the contest with perfected nature, it became evident that purposeful art, art not geared exclusively toward aesthetic tastes, would be shaken to its very core.

The result was that desperate and clumsy attempt to reinvigorate the functional role of art by latching onto earlier periods that had been more attentive to art's practical objectives; we see this in history painting since Carstens and in the so-called reform movement of industrial arts. For a time, all art that was an end in itself was anathematized. Because, however, this movement proceeded from the purely aesthetic considerations of the cultivated classes rather than from a deep spiritual need of modern humanity, it did not survive long. Today, the trend is as good as entirely vanquished, and art has again become no less an end in itself than it was a century ago.

What shall become of purposeful arts in the future? Man may, perhaps, easily dispense with history painting, which seems to be nearing extinction in any case, and likewise with any embodiment of conceptual principles. With increased intellectual and spiritual capacities, man may also be able to dismiss his need for decoration as merely an animalistic urge. Still, the practical function, whose task is to supply people with habitation and the hourly satisfaction of a thousand needs, persists. In a later chapter on motifs, we shall discuss what seems to be the only solution for this unquestionably urgent state of affairs.

A given work's purpose offers the opportunity for historically investigating not only its relation to artistry but also, as we argued earlier (p. 109), its relation to the other purposes embodied in the work and of these to one another. Although all three purposes have been active throughout each art-historical period, they have not always claimed the same relative status. The practical function has sustained the least injury from its competitors, for the obvious reason that the practical demands of a given moment do not readily tolerate restrictions.[6] The relation between decorative and conceptual functions, by contrast, is considerably more variable: either the former is absorbed into the latter or vice versa. In all periods wherein purpose prevails, the conceptual function, if it plays any role at all, will always dominate the decorative. Only when the conceptual purpose recedes does the decorative purpose assert itself again. Let us now examine our three periods in terms of this rule.

As noted earlier, the question as to whether human artistic activity originated in the need to fulfill a decorative function remains open. Certainly the naked savage does not wait to create decoration until he has obtained some handmade apparatus to serve as a substratum; he tattoos his own body, which is fashioned by nature itself. But it is not entirely certain that tattooing did not originally possess some intrinsic conceptual — perhaps apotropaic — significance. Ethnologists such as Grosse, and scholars of prehistoric eras such as Hoernes, tend to regard the conceptual function as the earliest and argue that its various embodiments only gradually became "ornamental."

But let us return to historical ground. Ancient Egyptian art challenged its decorative requirements by incorporating conceptually meaningful motifs: figures of gods, the uraeus, the scarab, lotus plants, and so on. Attic vases manifest most vividly the proclivities of Greek art after Alexander. While the primary decorative

motif continues to be heroic battles and the like — that is, conceptually meaningful narratives — true "ornament" does appear in
certain specifically designated places. Just as we found art of this
period making efforts to establish equilibrium between function
and artistry, we also find it seeking to create balance among the
purposes. For Antiquity after Alexander, we need only cite Pompeii; neither on walls nor in household appliances did people of
the Italian Renaissance display such a tremendous profusion of
decoration as the Pompeians did. Motifs that had previously served
conceptual functions were now applied in abundance, with the
simple intent to decorate. Once art became an end in itself, everything that conceptually meaningful art had accumulated over the
centuries became a welcome repository of decoration. Although
Pompeian art (especially Mau's Second and Third Styles) might
accurately be termed decorative, the majority of its motifs were
inherited from earlier periods. How all this would have progressed
during the Roman Imperial era we cannot know, because of the
sudden intrusion of the social movement of monotheism, which
introduced a new worldview and, with that, a new art.

If one were to conclude on the basis of Pompeii that decorative
art could flourish only after art had become an end in itself, one
would be instantly confounded by the fact that decoration played
a highly significant role in early Christian art of the fourth and
fifth centuries, a period in which any autonomous art was regarded with the utmost hostility. This art, however, had a Janus
face; having assumed its place in history, it could not free itself
from its antecedents all at once. It therefore learned to accept and
absorb these insofar as they conformed to the new conception of
the relation between man and matter. Because late Roman decorative art of the fourth and fifth centuries maintained a strict
distinction between spiritual or intellectual purposes and decoration, it is understandable that during this growth period the

conceptual function never overwhelmed the decorative as thoroughly as it had done in the earlier, though otherwise parallel, case of ancient Egyptian art. Islam, for its part, was merely taking the logical last step by freeing the decorative function almost entirely from competition with the conceptual. Byzantine art sought to balance the two in a manner reminiscent of Greek art made before Alexander.

The so-called Migration style created by Germanic peoples in the sixth and seventh centuries reveals the true character of a decorative art divorced from any conceptual function. This style grew directly out of late Roman decorative art and eventually incorporated Byzantine details. Irish art is particularly instructive as to how even consciously conceptual representations could be adapted to decorative art's demands for comfort. Western Christian art remained markedly conceptual until the end of the Giottesque-Gothic period. The early Christian dichotomy between decorative and conceptual functions seems to have been set aside in North and South alike since at least the ninth century. Because all artistic works at this time were created for the greater glory of God, the conceptual purpose gained supremacy over the decorative. With the Gothic phase came a certain rehabilitation of the decorative function. But the full transformation occurred only during the period of decline as art once again grew into an end in itself.

Fifteenth-century Italian art did not have the abundance of conceptually significant motifs at its disposal that Antiquity did after Alexander; inasmuch as Christian art produced such motifs, they remained a *noli me tangere* as a result of the Christian worldview's exclusively spiritual character. Hence the enthusiasm with which people latched onto the antique ornamental forms and mythological motifs that had survived from the Imperial age, and the no less profound impression these Italianate forms went on to exert in the North. Once again we witness the emancipation of art as an end in itself leading to an upsurge of decorative art.

Of crucial importance for the formation of the relationship between conceptual and decorative purposes in the final period (after 1520) was the fact, noted earlier, that now, when art was an end in itself, extrinsic decorative or conceptual functions suffered. In the Southern Baroque period, the conceptual purpose stood firmly in the foreground, at least as a pretext, and this resulted in a fierce suppression of the decorative. A slight increase in decorative activity accompanied the waning of late Baroque art's supposed affinity for the conceptual function. Classicism greedily snatched up antique ornamental forms but did not know how to manipulate them as independently and creatively as the Renaissance had done, contenting itself instead with merely copying the outer forms. This provides good evidence that the naive sense for decorative production had gone astray and explains why the reform movement of industrial art had to establish schools, where techniques that had once arisen from the spontaneous impulses of fantasy could be systematically taught and comprehended.

In the North, the temporal coincidence of the Reformation with the introduction of ornamental forms from Renaissance Italy yielded the result that suddenly, for the only time in the history of Germanic art before the nineteenth century, a patently decorative art emerged in Germany: this was the so-called German Renaissance. It is no accident that its capitals stood in Protestant lands, for here the relinquishment of conceptually purposeful ecclesiastical arts led to both an enthusiastic cultivation of decorative functions and an embracing of many now-inoffensive ornamental forms from the South. In Catholic regions, it is more apt to speak of an "Italian Renaissance in Germany" than of a true German Renaissance, for here the conceptual function continued to be nurtured in Church art even as this was placed thoroughly under Italian influence. In Protestant areas, German art remained chiefly decorative until the middle of the eighteenth century, even though this was fundamentally at odds with the prevailing intellectual proclivities. Only classicism was able to draw this art nearer to the great international artistic movements. Indeed, in Germany the consequences of a centuries-old cultivation of art as an end in itself were sensed with special acuteness, certainly more so than in lands where people had not been steeped in the decorative so deeply or for so long.

In other countries with Germanic populations, the decorative function did not play the same role as in Protestant Germany: not in Flanders, where Baroque art after Rubens nearly suffocated under an over-weighty cloak of ostensibly conceptual motifs; or in Holland, during whose own golden age decoration was treated almost puritanically; or even in England, which belongs to our most modern phase, having attained an independent position in the history of art only in the days of the positive classicist reaction to nature. French art has likewise striven to maintain a proper balance in the relations between decorative and conceptual purposes and did succeed in this, to a certain extent, until the end of the eighteenth century. But after classicism, which found its most brilliant embodiment there, the decorative spirit sputtered out in France as well. In keeping with its basic proclivity toward moderation, modern French art has sought neither to join enthusiastically in retrospective attempts at reform nor to assert its place at the zenith of extreme innovators; for the moment, therefore, it has had to relinquish to others its leading position in the progress of European art.

In conclusion, let us offer a few comments on the significance of purpose for evaluating a work of art. Of course, a work's purpose must always and unconditionally be taken into account. But it is quite a different matter to ascribe excessive significance to purpose when making judgments, as when the previous century's aesthetic system established it as the basis for categorizing all art — architecture, sculpture, painting, and, later, industrial arts. If an auction catalog labels each work first and foremost according to its functional intent, this is justifiable insofar as a potential buyer, who need not be a particularly insightful or knowledgeable lover of art, will principally want to know how he can put the thing to use. But it is questionable whether the discipline of art history should be satisfied with such a justification.

Certainly, as we affirmed earlier, every work of art is created to serve a particular purpose; but with some artworks, the objective function merely provides a pretext. A picture might be created to fulfill some conceptual purpose but might also be made as an end in itself. Even though, from the standpoint of the auction catalog, such a picture could still be described as a panel-shaped object meant to hang on a wall, is the discipline of art history well served by this kind of broad designation? Even a modern catalog would hardly categorize the Grimani reliefs as "wall fillers" or the like, but would simply call them "reliefs" (figure 2). This would, quite appropriately, make plain that what is most definitive about these works, as ends in themselves, is their basic artistic medium, the means by which the contest with transitory nature is played out — in this case, the relief form.

As a result, there exist many works of art whose functional determination offers no absolute and singular defining quality. Once this is accepted, a scientific history of art will no longer be able to use purpose as the primary criterion for assessing a given work. Another must be found, one that comes closer to grasping the true essence of any work of art, the contest with nature, than objective purpose. We shall have occasion to return to this problem in our ongoing search for a more useful criterion, especially in the final chapter.

One last misconception shall now be put to rest. One often hears the remark that the dichotomy between *industrial art* — that is, functional art — and *high art* — that is, art made for its own sake — is an exclusive characteristic of our own modern age and that earlier periods were blissfully unaware of the contrast. Our historical investigation of the developmental relationship between art and objective function clearly proves this notion to be false. Seventeenth-century Dutch seascapes were surely "high art"; but the same holds true for the Grimani reliefs and Roman Imperial portraits. Modern art is hardly the first to find purpose simply in its contest with nature — though it has expressed this tendency most brashly and has cast off any pretense of objective purposefulness most recklessly. Today's religious art tends merely to churn out copies of works from earlier, more propitious periods; even when it does try to devise something genuinely modern, it is unable to transcend a genre character. Thus in this respect, too, we feel justified in believing that with modern art we have reached the central peak of the third period of art, which began in 1520.

CHAPTER FIVE

Motifs

Because motifs in visual art are designed to compete with nature, they can only be taken from nature. Every natural being is either inorganic or organic — that is, either inert, as with minerals, or capable of motion, as with flora and fauna, including human beings. Movement manifests itself either as a combination of locomotion and physical growth, as with humans and animals, or as simple growth, as with plants. By the same token, motifs in visual art must be either organic or inorganic.

Man creates inorganic motifs from the mineral mass known as dead matter. Nature has shaped this dead matter into crystals, bodies bounded by regular planar surfaces that conjoin at angles. The special property of the crystal is that its main body can be split along an ever-present, if only ideal, central axis into two equal halves, with each adjacent surface likewise being divisible into halves along its own central axis. The characteristics of crystallinity are thus (a) delimitation by regular surfaces conjoined at angles and (b) absolute stereometric and planimetric symmetry. In certain cases — in a regular polyhedron, for example — this symmetry can be multiplied on all sides: the dividing line need not first transect the linear central axis; rather, any line cut through the middle point will yield two congruent halves.

Once man feels the urge to create some decorative or conceptually meaningful work from dead matter, he naturally employs the same laws by which nature shapes dead matter: the laws of crystallinity. Because the crystalline motif obeys natural laws most perfectly, it is the only intrinsically appropriate and justifiable motif for human artistic creation. Art, after all, deals exclusively with inorganic matter, including once-organic materials, such as wood and bone, that become lifeless after losing their growth capacity. Whenever primitive man prepared to fashion a decorative or practical object, he unavoidably, if only unconsciously, posed the question as to how nature would approach the task. A basic symmetrical form, delimitation by regular surfaces that abut each other at angles, and inertia, the restful state of being — these properties are inherently and naturally given for any human creation produced from inorganic matter. Man could not imagine devising an organic form for an object that was itself incapable of exercising organic functions. Herein lies the fundamental significance of inorganic motifs for all human artistic activity.

So long as man's contest with nature involved predominantly decorative or practical aims, it could not fix its view on anything but inorganic nature. Hence — to underscore once and for all the significance of this point for art history — the stubborn tenacity with which the basic formal principles of inorganic nature, such as absolute symmetry in lines and planes, have continued to assert themselves in human artistic production up to the present day. Only in the design of inorganic forms does man stand on equal ground with nature, for here he creates purely out of inner compulsion and uses no external models. The moment man oversteps this boundary and begins to reproduce organic things, he slips into external reliance on nature; then his creative act loses its autonomy and becomes imitative.

An extreme artistic purist could feel justified in wanting all artistic activity to proceed using exclusively crystalline forms. Although no one would be so bold as to raise such a radical demand today, in light of man's successes in creating organic forms artistically, a more moderate version of this demand has repeatedly been made. We need only recall the attitude of one ardently admired critical writer of an era only halfway gone, Jakob Burckhardt. This author believed unconditionally that he had discovered the law of crystallization to be a constant in architecture and at least the compositional structure of painting. In this light, we can also understand why other scholars, such as Gottfried Semper, have ascribed to certain primitive nature-peoples a purer and loftier aesthetic taste than most European artists possess. Whereas the primitives, with unselfconscious confidence, create inorganic designs of eternal effectiveness and relevance, cultivated men generate chiefly organic works whose relevance is limited to only certain tastes.

How did people come to abandon inorganic methods of design, which were inherently most natural, in favor of reproducing organic beings in dead matter? We probably need to seek the impetus for this move outside the domain of art proper: it must have emerged from some function. Neither practical nor decorative needs offered the opportunity to stray from inorganic artistry, but the conceptual purpose did. Because it was the liveliness and movement of superhuman forces in nature that so impressed human beings, these could only be conceived as animate and organically mobile. If man, to satisfy his obscure desire for a lucid visualization of the invisible powers that either threatened or protected him, wished to reproduce those powers in bodily form, he could only do so by means of organic constructions. He began by choosing the most complex creatures of nature: first animals and eventually human beings. It cannot have happened otherwise: conceptual needs brought organic motifs to art.

It is necessary at this point to stave off one possible misunderstanding. The foregoing account might seem to presuppose that inorganic motifs appeared first for decorative and practical reasons, with organic motifs being introduced only at a more mature stage of development and in response to conceptual needs. However, as we stressed above, there are no adequate grounds for ascribing priority to any of the three functions. Ethnologists and scholars of prehistory could very well be correct in arguing that the copying of organic motifs antedated the "Geometric Style." In an earlier work (*Problems of Style*, pp. 28ff.), I myself spoke out in favor of this view, which I justified on the basis of the finds in Dordogne. Now, however, I must emphatically refute the further conclusion that those carved reindeer figures I summoned as proof were created as an incipient expression of an unconstrained contest with nature for its own sake. They were, rather, dictated by conceptual requirements, and in this sense they correspond fully to the general outlook of a hunting people. The confident accuracy in portraying accidental features in many of these figures will surely and justifiably continue to arouse wonder and admiration. But for all their inorganic character, ancient Egyptian animal figures reveal similar accidental traits. Clearly these accidentals seem extraneous only to us; to the figures' original makers, they may have appeared essential.

It is possible, then, that human artistic activity began as a contest with organic nature aimed at satisfying some conceptual need. This would, admittedly, presuppose a people possessing a downright animalistic lack of bodily requirements but substantial spiritual and intellectual needs. This strikes me as contradictory in the highest degree; today I find it more likely that the use of inorganic motifs to fulfill decorative and practical requirements did come first. But even accepting the first scenario, we must acknowledge that it remains both decisive and in accordance with art-historical findings (which we point out here only briefly) that the earliest stages of art from which monuments survive reveal inorganic "stylization" to be the most basic elemental property, even in organic motifs. To gain insight into this vitally important point, we must first understand the difference between inorganic and organic forms as they appear in nature.

What distinguishes organic from inorganic things, in essence, is the capacity for movement in the former, which manifests itself either in simple growth or in volitional translocation. Running parallel with this difference in being is a perceptible difference in form. A tree or a quadruped, when viewed from the side, at first glance reveals no crystalline aspects; these things lack both stark symmetry and a closed demarcation of equal planes. The right and left masses of these organic bodies are not distributed evenly, and the bounding surfaces are rounded off, thus eradicating any clear sense of closure. Such, in any case, is our first impression.

Looking more carefully, however, we recognize that the basic principles of crystallinity are not entirely absent in these organic bodies. We discover them, for example, in the tree's cells, in its annual rings, in the structure of its leaves, indeed in its very struc-ture—but everywhere they are veiled, hidden, and brought only incompletely to expression. This also holds true for four-legged animals. Through the efforts of a skilled anatomist, a quadruped can be split along a central axis into two halves with identical outer contours. Here, too, the material principle of symmetry is present, but overlaid and thus partially obscured by competing principles.

What are these other principles that prevent the formal law of crystallization from enjoying absolute sovereignty in organic nature? They are, first of all, the laws of motion, which are unique to organic beings. These compel the continuous rearrangement of molecules, which permits them to coalesce into a symmetrical structure only during pauses in the process of motion. A second component is the relationship with surrounding forces of nature. The immobile crystal, being vulnerable and completely at the mercy of those forces, is found relatively rarely in nature. Far more often, we encounter mineral masses in an amorphic state, which either is natural to them or is one to which they have been transformed through the destructive power of the elements. Thanks to their capacity for motion, organic beings can defend themselves against those hostile natural forces — though this defense triggers an elastic rearrangement of their molecular composition away from a symmetrical, crystalline structure. The principal cause of the characteristic curvature of most organic things is to be sought in this point.

Thus man found himself faced with the task of reproducing an organic natural being in dead matter. We must keep firmly in mind that this called not for imitation or literal portrayal but for competition. If conceptual requirements demanded a depiction of a four-legged creature, the primitive artist was not compelled to portray a specific individual or, even less, an accidental attitude of that individual. He needed instead to depict a representative of the given species with no intent to individualize. He therefore endowed it, as much as possible, with the prescribed form that was both demanded by the dead material with which he was working and latent in the creature itself when motionless. It was only natural, in other words, for artists to adopt principles of inorganic nature in their initial efforts to compete with organic nature.

Even through close examination of the wildest nature-people, it is difficult to form an adequate picture of this early process of making inorganic — or, as we call it today, stylization. A wooden post hewn into a rectangular shape, with two points at the upper end to signify the idol's eyes, would already be a likeness of an organic thing, a human being. But it is designed in accordance with principles of inorganic nature, using corporeal symmetry with no curvature or sense of movement. As both the Dordogne finds and the oldest Egyptian monuments make plain, this very modest suggestion of organic physicality was surpassed early. Individual components gradually managed to extricate themselves from the closed and self-contained crystalline mass to attain, in the end, the curvature characteristic of organic life. But absolute symmetry and immobility were still preserved. We see this, for example, in those seated figures of Egyptian deities whose legs are pulled close together and arms are pressed tightly against the sides.

Once movement was deemed acceptable, transitory and accidental qualities entered art. This was a moment of great consequence for artistic production, even more important, perhaps, than the introduction of organic motifs, for so long as those motifs were trapped in rigid symmetry and immobility, they occupied the same level as inorganic motifs and were distinguishable from the latter only in their curves — an element that, for reasons we will examine later, inorganic forms swiftly learned to accommodate. Egyptian artists of the Old Kingdom also brought movement to their animal figures. But so long as conceptual needs did not dictate otherwise, this was generally confined to a calm forward step. Even this limited movement meant the loss of absolute symmetry; thus asymmetry came to accompany curvature. What, if anything, remained of the inorganic? Although it was no longer so plainly apparent, it was still substantially present.

In a given form, movement is designed in such a way that the absence of absolute symmetry will be minimally apparent. But any symmetry displayed by the individual parts of the animate natural model will receive vigorous emphasis in man's artistic contest with nature, even if it appears only in veiled form; this applies especially to the human face. In other words, organically rounded or mobile features are shown only when they are necessary for bringing some conceptual point to view, whereas features that are closed, inorganic, and symmetrical are amplified as much as they can be without effacing the underlying organic referent of the motif. Thus artists endowed mobile organic forms with inorganic harmony solely by means of symmetry and a closed and uniform treatment of surfaces.

To assist in this effort at making inorganic, a second principle was introduced. This law, while especially pertinent to organic things, is just as integral to inorganic motifs as symmetry: proportion. Just as symmetry determines the relationship between right and left sides, proportion governs that between bottom and top. But whereas symmetry presents an absolute relationship expressible in strict mathematical formulas, proportion enjoys much more room for play. One example can demonstrate this with sufficient clarity.

A pyramidal crystal bisected along its vertical axis yields two equal halves. But when cut along a central horizontal line, it splits into two quite dissimilar portions: a smaller pyramid above and a broad support below. Proportion lies in the relation between these upper and lower parts. Not all crystals develop proportionally. A regular polyhedron, and all crystals that produce two equal halves when cut down the middle, has the same shape on every side. Like a sphere, it possesses neither top nor bottom. The pyramid, on the other hand, consists of a broad base and a pointed peak. The former component represents the pull of gravity toward the earth's core, which we might call structural stability, the latter the attempt to break free from that pull, which we might call the most solid or controlled form of upward motion. The relation between the width of the base and the distance of the peak from the base (the height of the pyramid) is designated the pyramid's proportion. Although there is no corresponding mathematical formula, this relation is bound to certain limits; a pyramid may be neither excessively squat nor excessively tall and thin.

If the law of proportion accommodates a variety of sizes in inorganic nature, it does so all the more in organic nature. Although the norms are more difficult to ascertain in this realm, certain outer limits do apply; when a thing of nature refuses to conform to them, we describe it as ugly. A person's face might exhibit the most punctilious symmetry, but if the forehead is too low, the cheeks too broad, or the nose too long, we call the whole thing unattractive without there being the slightest possibility of disagreement. Differences in opinion can be posited only if the boundaries are either just barely reached or just barely overstepped; in such cases, a harsh critique can easily lead to exaggeration of the lack of proportion, a milder one to its underestimation.

As was the case with symmetry, proportion reveals itself most clearly and systematically in inorganic objects. It seems only natural, therefore, that in the earliest stages of its contest with organic nature, art applied not only the inorganic law of symmetry but also the equally inorganic principle of proportion as extensively as possible. A difference still remains, but this will be better explicated later by reference to a concrete example.

We have finally reached the point where we can comprehend the essence of art's improvement of nature, which, as we argued earlier (pp. 57–59ff.), characterized all ancient artistic production because of the basic prevailing worldview. The organic in nature appears mobile, and movement veils and obscures its immutable underlying formal principles, that is, symmetry and proportion — or, to put it more generally, harmony. This is why all organic forms look imperfect and accidental. The same laws, on the other hand, appear pure and unconcealed in inorganic motifs: these are the perfect, eternal forms. To make organic motifs inorganic or harmonious thus means to perfect, to improve, to beautify them.

This was art's sole mission as it competed with nature in classical Antiquity, a period when man was fully confident of his dominion over nature. As man engaged in a creative contest with nature, knowing he had the upper hand, he reproduced not transitory, accidental, or imperfect qualities of things but only those aspects that were eternal and perfect and as immutable as the dead matter itself from which he fashioned the work of art.

Did this approach succeed in subordinating the organic properties of curvature and movement completely and permanently? Or did it throw open the doors to rebellious elements that would one day, under more favorable conditions, fight for emancipation and autonomy? These questions concern us next. If there was one unruly element in the process of making inorganic — an element that people struggled to banish at all costs but could not dispense with once organic nature was admitted into the artistic contest — it was motion. As hard as people tried to squeeze all the latent manifestations of harmony from a work of nature and to construct a work of art from these, the movement inherent especially in animal motifs seemed to pose an obstacle to complete success. After all, if no suggestions of movement were present, the conceptual objective would not be met. But once people succumbed and allowed organic motifs to introduce fleeting motions, a new factor entered man's artistic activity: illusion. This is what gives such importance to this historical moment.

Up to this point, art had been truthful and cohesive. A restful statue of a seated Egyptian deity, though it is an imitation of a natural being rather than a purely human fabrication, betrays no disruptive fissure between nature and art; the immobile posture of the figure is in full accordance with the immobility of the dead material. As soon as a human figure is shown stepping forward, a rift begins to gape open. Now the figure appears to stride ahead through its own will, even though the dead material does not permit another step. When art makes us believe in a figure's movement, it is producing an illusion. This consequential step was taken by artists of Old Kingdom Egypt. Try as they might to cancel out, through the strictest rules of harmonization, any imperfect and momentary qualities that might have been introduced by the figure's movement, illusionism had entered human artistic production. All its consequences would be felt from that moment on; indeed, they would affect those who learned from the Egyptians even more profoundly than they did the Egyptians themselves.

The end of this process is easy to predict. First, there was an increasing desire — initially unintentional, perhaps even unwilling — to create the illusion of movement. Then came a more enthusiastic engagement with the problem, until, in the end, it overwhelmed any other factors and became the dominant motivating force of artistic creation. It would nevertheless be mistaken to see illusionism as the true essence of the visual arts in general, as some scholars have done. The converse is more accurate: so long as art gave primacy to function, it shunned illusionism. Art consciously strove for illusion only after it became an end in itself — though this, in turn, would lead once again to the destruction of illusionism.

The second characteristic of organic things is their curvature or roundedness. In natural creatures, the projecting corners and hard edges of the crystalline world appear worn away through the struggle for survival. Curvature and crystallization are intrinsically disparate qualities; in certain respects, they are diametrically opposed. To be sure, they are linked in an abstract mathematical sense; the sphere is merely a polyhedron with an infinite number of sides. But this does not explain why, as early as predynastic Egypt, organic curvature was soon extended to works of art that, in themselves, had nothing to do with organic motifs, that is, those made to satisfy decorative or practical aims. The Geometric style incorporated circles, and the oldest Egyptian ceramics also contained rounded forms. This is especially striking because the introduction of curvature caused one crucial postulate of antique art, which we shall examine more closely later, to fall away: the absolute clarity, firm definition, and closed unity of crystalline form. This may explain why for so long — at least until Alexander the Great — people dared attach curves only to small practical objects of utility and not to furniture or architectural constructions. Although that final victory was achieved in times when art was an end in itself, the use of curved walls in buildings and furnishings would remain a fleeting phenomenon. Crystallinity continues to dominate in these domains up to the present day, in the form of straight wall surfaces that conjoin at regular angles.

The reason for the remarkably early application of curvature to inorganic motifs lies in the Egyptians' recognition that this property provided art — which seeks to create according to inorganic principles while also drawing on organic nature — with the proper means to strike a balance between the two extremes. In practice, a useful object such as a vase can be fashioned in full accordance with harmonious inorganic principles and with no suggestion of organic nature, yet still be endowed with curvature. But the vase's roundedness brings movement to the inorganic, not a momentary motion but one closed, eternal, and continuously turning back on itself — all of which, of course, the modest dimensions of a vase or decorative knickknack make it easy to overlook. This factor can only reach its full significance in an art, such as that of pre-Alexander Greece, that rests on a harmonious balance between those previously essential factors of creation. An art permeated with these aims had to make the bent or curved line the principal element of its artistic productions. In the end, the Greeks recognized and embraced the curve as the true line of beauty. The Egyptians came close to resolving this ornamental problem — whose eventual solution has been in effect ever since — but the Greeks of the Mycenaean age were the first to discover the undulating tendril.

The transference of organic curvature onto the inorganic motifs of decorative and practical arts signifies a clear victory for the organic. This primarily affected the formal treatment of motifs, and it was followed by an equally consequential advancement involving the motifs themselves.

Let us imagine a conceptual purpose that has introduced animate organic nature into art and, alongside it, a decorative and practical art that obeys only the principles of inorganic nature — art of the Geometric style, for instance. Perhaps for a time these two strands lay side by side, discrete and separate; but the crucial next step could not be avoided in the long run. This was the application of conceptually meaningful organic designs to decorative works of art. Works designed to serve conceptual purposes were also works of art and, as such, pleasure-giving things. But the filling of blank space with pleasing forms is what the decorative function craves. It is therefore understandable that conceptually purposeful organic motifs would be carried over into the decorative arts. The advantage gained thereby was twofold: these motifs were pleasing as decoration, and they awakened certain desired mental images or concepts. They thus recommended themselves over purely inorganic designs, which now receded in importance.

Although we already observed a preponderance of organic motifs in ancient Egyptian art, these always served some conceptual purpose: figures of gods, scarabs, the uraeus, the lotus, the papyrus, and so on. Freedom to choose among organic natural objects with a view toward reproducing them in visual art was unknown before the Hellenistic age.[1] On the contrary: as soon as man began to employ conceptually significant organic motifs for decorative purposes, he sought to curb their active, organic character as much as possible and to impress on them inorganic harmony — or, as one says today, to stylize them. The more stylized and inorganic, the more pleasing was the organic motif, for it struck the eye as correspondingly harmonious. In decorative art, organic motifs were often so thoroughly transformed into inorganic ones that we have difficulty today discerning their original organic referents.

This gave rise to another point of deepest consequence for all subsequent development. An organic motif that may have been utilized — and, in the process, de-Organized — by one people to serve a specific conceptual purpose had the capacity to give pleasure to other people as well. These new groups were likely to be ignorant of the motif's original conceptual significance. Thus it happened that the Greeks adopted the stylized lotus blossom and palmette as decorative motifs over strictly geometric motifs, and clung to these well into the Hellenistic period as nearly their only decorative vegetal design. And thus it happened that all Mediterranean peoples could employ the animal types prevalent in ancient Near Eastern and Egyptian art well into the early Greek period. Not only the ancient Egyptians, then, never thought to pick their decorative motifs at whim from organic nature and instead employed the same few motifs, formerly introduced for conceptual purposes, over thousands of years. Many other peoples — even peoples of artistic abilities far superior to the Egyptians' — never looked to organic nature for artistic motifs.

This leads us to an empirical principle of great consequence: in every period of art in which purpose predominates, decorative or ornamental motifs are governed by tradition. The reason lies in the fact that during such periods the source of the pleasure engendered by a work of art is not the organic motif itself; rather, it is the inorganic quality that has been extracted from the organic motif through the artistic process. Any motif is as well suited to this end as the next; and if through some artistic accident (deriving from the conceptual purpose) one particular motif happened to be selected and worked up, there was no compelling reason to comb nature for another. An artist could hope to do no more with a second motif than what was already accomplished with the first. Thus the Greeks before Alexander borrowed the Egyptian lotus blossom, mediated to them through imported objects, as something that suited their needs; to make it conform to their own tastes, they further harmonized it until it reached its full perfection.[2]

The oldest Egyptian monuments make plain that men were already availing themselves of the immense field of organic nature in their artistic contest with nature over five millennia ago and that they sometimes sought, in the process, to create the illusory impression of spontaneous movement. Even so, for thousands of years it never occurred to artists to put that immeasurable domain to adequate (or even just extensive) use or to exceed the barest degree of necessity in their efforts to produce the illusion of motion.

It should be evident from the foregoing discussion that man's artistic activity, insofar as it concerns motifs, continually fluctuates between two poles: the *harmonic*, which strives to bring the immutable formal law of crystallinity to view in all motifs, including organic ones; and the *organic*, whose supreme goal is to represent organic motifs in all their accidental and transitory momentary appearances. If we consider this rule in conjunction with the other primary determinants in the development of visual art — that is, worldview and purpose — we arrive at the following observations.

a. Any worldview that values natural things only in physically improved form will generally be predisposed toward the harmonic, for physical beauty is equal to harmony, that is, symmetry and proportion. Conversely, a worldview that strives exclusively for the spiritual improvement of nature without regard for its physical *habitus* — or that simply tolerates the transitory appearances of nature as such — will be intrinsically inclined toward the organic.

b. In periods when utilitarian purpose constitutes a work of art's sole reason for being, people always prefer to make motifs as harmonic as possible, or, as we shall call it here, to *harmonize* them (*harmonisieren*); conversely, during times when art is an end in itself, people tend to make them organic, or to *Organize* them (*organisieren*). It must be kept in mind that the contest with nature for its own sake is not necessarily concerned with transitory nature. Although this typically is the focus of the contest in periods when art is an end in itself, there have been times when the contest centered on improved, that is, harmonized, nature (as in classicism). As for the particular purposes, the harmonic generally corresponds better to the decorative and practical functions, while the conceptual purpose naturally tends to require organic solutions.

c. We discovered a third primary principle while examining the relation between organic and inorganic motifs but shall articulate it again in accordance with its significance: harmonism leads to dependence on tradition, Organism to the generation of new motifs. We must, however, take care not to accord the harmonic a position inferior to the organic, as scholars and laypeople alike tend to do. Harmonism no more implies stasis than Organism does. By the same token, reliance on tradition does not imply rote imitation of other artworks, for this would be no different from copying things in nature. Rather, as the development of vegetal ornament from the ancient Egyptians to the time of Alexander the Great makes plain, it involves a constant struggle to improve and perfect. Even classicism was hardly a cool imitation of Antiquity; no informed person would ever mistake an Empire acanthus tendril for an Attic or Roman Imperial example. One could even pose the question as to whether harmonism or Organism — or, in modern terminology, idealism (stylization) or naturalism (illusionism) — was more propitious for the visual arts and gave worthier expression to man's contest with nature.

If one wants to do justice to both sides, one need only survey the course of art history to clearly recognize which role the organic has played. The periods in which organic tendencies prevailed were relatively brief; these tendencies were quickly displaced by harmonizing reactions, which lasted considerably longer than the revolutionary surges of Organism. But the very fact that the latter continued to erupt every so often proves that they were crucial. Their necessity lies in the fact that changes in cultural attitudes or modes — which, especially in recent times, tend to occur in swift succession — demand corresponding changes in the artistic motifs bound to them by tradition. Because harmonism, steeped so heavily in a tradition of its own, actively opposes this process, forceful intervention on the part of Organism is required to counter that resistance; this is the case today more than ever. As soon as Organism clears the path for its motifs, harmonism can take over, turning rote imitation into a contest with nature worthy of man. Thus our examination of the course of art history yields a picture of a fiercely progressive Organism continually reined in and steered along by harmonism.

It now remains to substantiate these principles with reference to the art-historical periods defined in Part One in terms of their respective worldviews. Because close engagement with the superabundance of individual motifs is out of the question in an essay that aims for grammatical conciseness, we will content ourselves with establishing the general character of these principles, touching on specific details only when these are necessary for removing potential misunderstandings.

The Nature-Beautifying Period

From its first discernible traces in ancient Egypt until the reign of
Constantine, all antique art stood under the sign of harmonism.
Just as anthropomorphic polytheism and the postulate of functionality remained prerequisites for any work of art, the endeavor
to harmonize organic forms persisted as a fundamental element
until the very end — although, to be sure, these factors weakened
somewhat during the final phase. No informed person would ever
confuse even a very late antique work with one of more modern
times. If we were to ask what it is that ultimately makes the difference, we would always return to harmonic criteria as the unmistakable signs of the work's antique origin.

Ancient Egyptian Art

Egyptian art, which includes the oldest monuments made by man,
helped us earlier as we tried to draw conclusions about the initial
stages of development during the primitive period of infinite polytheism — a period for which contemporary ethnology, with its
unreliable sources, leaves us stranded. The characteristics of the
treatment of motifs in ancient Egyptian art have therefore already
been discussed. Surely some progress occurred during the two
millennia following those stiffly seated or modestly striding figures of the Old Kingdom. If our account is correct thus far, this
development must have entailed a shift from the strictest harmonism to an increasingly loose handling of organic forms. But
we also find certain phenomena that could tempt us to imagine
the opposite course; these seem in fact to have led some commentators astray. Considering the important place that the problem of
the lack of change in Egyptian art holds for the history of art in
general, we must engage more closely with these phenomena and
offer some explanation for them.

Statues of historical personages have been recovered from Old

Kingdom tombs that reveal accidental, portrait-like features in both stance and bodily structure, whereas kingly figures of later times, especially the numerous extant Ramesside sculptures, are designed more harmonically, more "beautifully." We further encounter on the walls of these tombs depictions of agrarian labor, hunts, and other industrial activities. Because these images display individualized traits, one feels justified in viewing them as slices of real life and in attributing to their makers the intent to create a kind of genre art. Portraits and genre pictures, however, are artistic categories that seem utterly at odds with strict harmonism. Because this "naturalistic" character disappeared in later statues and was replaced by "beautification," and because eventually those "genre scenes" gave way to countless generic images of sacrifice, one could easily come away with the impression that ancient Egyptian art began with "naturalism" and grew into "idealism" only in the course of its development.

It cannot be denied that some statues of historical personages, such as the *Seated Scribe* at the Louvre or the *Village Headman* in the Giza Museum [today, Egyptian Museum, Cairo], exhibit the highest degree of "realism" achieved before the Hellenistic period (figures 8 and 9). This realistic quality, however, inheres not so much in the artistic presentation as in the motif as such. In each case, the subject was undoubtedly an actual individual. But the motivation for his reproduction in art was not the intent to produce a portrait; this would presuppose Egyptian art's already being engaged in the contest with nature as an end in itself. Rather, there was a specific conceptual objective. In accordance with the general outlook of the ancient Egyptians, in which we may discover remnants of a rudimentary animism, the display of a person's own counterfeit within his tomb, along with the pictorial depiction of the labors his slaves would perform on his behalf or personifications of his estates presenting their yields, was enough

141

to confirm his continued enjoyment of these goods after his bodily death. The statue thus functioned as an alter ego of the living individual, and this conceptual aim, not artistic whimsy, resulted in the statue's endowment with the individualized features of the living person. No portrait, no contest with organic nature, was intended, but rather a straightforward imitation of the living model for a concrete and wholly nonartistic purpose. Thus the *Scribe* is seated cross-legged on the ground in a deliberate effort to prevent him, were he enthroned, from blasphemously calling to mind the "ideal" figures of deities. Thus, too, the *Village Headman* was equipped with the well-fed face and potbelly that had prompted the Arabs to name him *Sheikh el-Beled* (Village headman). The same conceptual purpose engendered those supposedly genre "slices of life."[3]

Once the "realism" of the figures is understood in this way, the normal course of development is instantly reestablished for ancient Egyptian art, for these individualized figures exhibit a far more inorganic treatment of details than the Ramesside statues do. A possible cause of confusion is the relative ugliness of the older figures when compared with the general beauty of the more recent ones. But in this respect, the harmonism of the Ramesside era marks an advancement over Old Kingdom art in the direction of the organically rounded. In older likenesses of individuals, transitions among broad planes still appear relatively hard and angular. This clearly betrays the struggle to display the most closed, unitary, and sharply defined – in other words, crystalline – planes possible, even in organic motifs. Such awkward transitions – which are not, as one might mistakenly think, natural and individualized but unnatural and quite clumsy – are eliminated in Ramesside statues, which consequently produce a much more naturalistic and organic impression. One must not be fooled on this point by the portrait-like quality of the older figures.

142

The succeeding development moves directly and unmistakably toward Greek art. This conforms to what we know of Egyptian art's subsequent development. Works of the Saite period capture our attention with their extraordinary softness of contours and perfect flow of lines. With these features, the Egyptians were already approaching the Greeks' recognition of the curve as the quintessential line of beauty. But, as in so many other artistic matters, here, too, they did not take that final step.

Let us now say a word about proportion in ancient Egyptian art. As we saw earlier, the laws of proportion cannot be grasped with the same mathematical precision as the laws of symmetry. Whereas symmetry meant the same thing to the Greeks as to the South Sea Islanders, the definition of proportion varied because it was determined by each people's respective racial outlook. To be sure, a growing emancipation from the influence of customary views of nature and a movement toward a purer and more regularized conception were not only possible but even, if the evidence does not deceive, actualized in Greek art. If modern Greeks in fact descend from the ancient Hellenes and exhibit the physical features of that race — and most evidence favors this assumption — then one must admit that, with only rare exceptions, the ideal physical type represented in Greek art does not correspond to reality at all. This suggests that the Greeks before Alexander endowed human figures in their art with different, "more beautiful" proportions than those they observed as normative among themselves.

A similar partial emancipation from "national" proportions can also be noticed in the Egyptians' Ramesside statues, though these did retain such typical features of the Egyptian race as the prominent pursed lips. On the other hand, if we find the proportions of Old Kingdom statues designed less purely, we should not therefore understand the advances of the Ramesside period to consist of a backward movement from Organism to harmonism.

On the contrary, this progression simply conforms to the normal course of development in which proportion, with its less sharply formulated rules, requires a longer time to gain a well-defined place in man's artistic production. Proportion — the establishment of balance between top and bottom; between base, crown, and intermediary connector; between legs, head, and trunk; and so forth — thus fitted quite comfortably into the life sphere of pre-Alexandrian Greek art; and there it found its most perfect formation and most thoroughgoing use.

Because for the purposes of this book it suffices merely to establish the main points of development, we shall refrain from engaging more closely with arts of the ancient Near East. In their relation between harmonism and Organism, these occupy a middle ground between Egyptian and Greek art before Alexander. This may account for the distinctive appearance of ancient Asiatic arts.

Greek Art Before Alexander the Great

What Greek art before Alexander set out to do — and ultimately accomplished — can be best appreciated by comparison with the achievements of its forerunner in the Nile valley. Greeks of the Attic golden age were unacquainted with idols as rigid as the *Colossi of Memnon* or with portrait figures as realistic as the *Sheikh el-Beled* (figure 9). Greek artists endowed the human subject with far freer movements and hence a more organic appearance than the Egyptians ever did, while also granting it the proportional limbs and harmonious facial features required by the inorganic law of crystallinity. Moreover, in comparison with the Egyptians, the Greeks significantly curtailed the number of motifs drawn from organic nature, particularly in the animal realm. The conceptual aims that Egyptian artists, still partially entrenched in animal cults, had bound to their organic artistic creations simply did not exist for their Greek counterparts. The Greeks made enduring use only of those motifs that, once stylized into inorganic form, were well suited to decorative purposes. Thus, by the time of the Attic golden age, they had expanded the role of various plant types and reduced the number of Asiatic animals. Furthermore, the Greeks gave a more inorganic form to Egyptian foliate columns and discarded caryatids almost entirely. Here again we discover the Greek mission to reconcile the oppositions that ancient Near Eastern arts displayed. Whereas Egyptian art reveals a division between stark crystallinity and slavish imitation of organic nature, Greek art displays a balance of the two. This was achieved first by means of an organic rounding off of inorganic forms, and then by an inorganic reconfiguration of organic forms.

The contrast between Egyptian and pre-Alexander Greek art is most striking in works that brought to view a conceptual point through narrations of historical events. Thus on one Egyptian pylon we see depicted the battle of Ramses II against the Hittites (figure 10). The artist took pains to incorporate the maximum number of figures and to characterize the enemies in an organic and natural way — both emphatically organicizing traits. Nonetheless, the disparity in size between the king and the hostile armies, the spatially incongruous juxtaposition and overlapping of the figures, and, finally, the fixed and inorganic arrangement of individual forms all strike us as distinctly unnatural elements. In contrast, Greek art during its classical flowering shunned the portrayal of contemporary battles, opting instead to visualize those battles through the struggles of heroes, which by their very nature demanded a lesser degree of Organism. Greek art never went as far as Egyptian in distinguishing foreign races (Aegina sculptures [figure 11]). Moreover, it substantially reduced the number of fighters and arranged these few according to the laws of symmetry. These are thoroughly harmonic elements; they offer a contrast with the art of the Egyptians, who conceived no more of harmonizing conceptually purposeful organic motifs during the New Kingdom than they had during the Old (see pp. 142–44). On the other hand, the treatment of individual body parts in Greek art is incomparably more freely dynamic and therefore more organically true to life than in Egyptian reliefs. But the Greeks' most important accomplishment lay in composition.

Composition is nothing more than the transposition of the basic principles of harmonism — symmetry and proportion — from the single figure to the group. The most severe composition is absolute symmetry, with or without proportion. The Egyptians were already familiar with this basic form and typically employed it when adapting organic motifs to decorative functions, for example, in confronted rams; this is also characteristic of Mesopotamian art. But they found this rigidly inorganic schema excessively unnatural for rendering a multi-figured scene and were incapable of solving the problem except by relinquishing harmonism entirely in the arrangement of motifs. Once again, then, we find that oscillation between extremes — on the one hand, a very severe compositional arrangement and, on the other, a near-complete absence of restraint — that was so characteristic of Egyptian art. Although the Assyrians did not fully understand how to give artistic structure to incoherent organic shapes, they were more successful in doing so than the Egyptians. In this domain, too, the Greeks were the first to discover a happy medium, avoiding both a bustling chaos of crowds of figures and rigid symmetry in the disposition of the few figures they did include. To do this, they devised a symmetry lightly veiled by subtle contrasts. Proportion was observed solely within the individual figure; only during the Renaissance was it transferred to the larger pictorial structure. Although antique artists designed the single figure proportionally, they did not hesitate to compose groups according to the principle of symmetry. After Alexander, proportion did enter into groups — witness the *Alexander Mosaic* (figure 4) — as did a concomitant loosening of symmetry that extended to the balancing out of masses. But for reasons we will enumerate later, the distinctive conical composition with a peaked crown surmounting a broad base was devised only during the Renaissance. So profoundly does composition express the specifically Greek artistic spirit that one could regard its step-by-step development as the single thread through which the history of all art made before Alexander can be traced. This has recently been undertaken with great success for the circumscribed sphere of vase painting (see Theodor Schreiber, *Die Wandbilder des Polygnotos*, volume 17 in the series Abhandlungen der philologisch-historischen Klasse der Sächsischen Gesellschaft der Wissenschaften).

Antiquity After Alexander the Great
Until recently, all antique art produced after Alexander the Great was regarded as a corrupted version of classical art. Today people seem more inclined toward the opposite extreme, placing a barricade between Greek and Roman art and proclaiming the latter fundamentally distinct in spirit from the former. As misguided as our forefathers' views may have been on this point, it would mean throwing out the baby with the bathwater if one were to wrench late antique art out of Antiquity completely. There is something about, say, the Grimani reliefs (figure 2) — or even the deer, lobster, and so forth in the Vatican Sala degli Animali (figure 3) — that calls to mind more readily images of the Attic golden age than anything made during the cinquecento or seicento. As unmistakably as the contest with transitory organic nature guided the chisel in those works, a breath of harmonism still lingers over the whole that would have been unattainable in any age but that of anthropomorphic polytheism.

On the other hand, this latest phase of antique art was able to achieve a truly distinctive character due to the following circumstances: first, anthropomorphic polytheism underwent a visible decline; second, ostensibly functional works of art now arose that clearly originated more in the pure delight in competing with nature than in any intended purpose; and, finally, organic motifs were introduced into artistic creation, posing a threat to inorganic forms in even their traditional mainstay of decorative and practical arts. Even the walls of massive stone buildings such as the Pantheon were pressed inward to form a circle, and their inner surfaces were embellished with airy vegetal designs interspersed with zoomorphic creatures.

In dealing with human subjects, artists drew their motifs from the ample stock of organic motifs amassed by the conceptual needs of foregoing periods, especially the legends of gods and heroes. Even plants and animals that never possessed conceptual significance were portrayed with meticulous adherence to their transitory organic appearances. Still, any attempt to catalog the whole array of organic motifs compiled during the early Imperial age would yield a rather modest number, which were furthermore connected by a common thread. Among plants, the grapevine appeared most often; the number of other identifiable flora barely exceeds a dozen. As for figural motifs, cupids were employed with particular regularity as decoration. This was due not so much to any mythological significance they may once have possessed as to their special appropriateness for harmonic art. The child was seen less an individual person than a conceptual category — an attitude familiar to the Renaissance and Baroque periods as well, both of which also set out to unite Organism and harmonism. In murals and floor mosaics, human figures tended to be shown floating: again, we find organic motifs shown moving in an ideal rather than natural way. The selection of subjects from the vast storehouse of available organic motifs thus seems to have been governed by a specific intent, whose goal was more to idealize or to de-Organize the organic than to engage in a contest with it.

Thus we come away with a picture of post-Alexander Antiquity far removed from that of the Renaissance, not to mention of modern times or even the seicento. Alongside the new organic motifs the ancient tradition from before Alexander continued to persevere, with its rich array of harmonized inorganic motifs. Organic fruit garlands constitute but a small fraction of motifs compared with the old egg-and-dart patterns, dentil motifs, acanthus friezes, and so forth. We might assign to the creators of the former motifs a position comparable to that of those earlier schools of philosophy that renounced any belief in anthropomorphic gods. Both exemplify the spiritual and intellectual currents of their respective times, but in extreme forms that would reach full acceptance and resonance only in later periods.

The Nature-Spiritualizing Period

Western monotheism, whose triumph ushered in our second period, spurns inorganic and organic nature alike. If nature is regarded as contemptible on principle, then the act of competing with it has neither value nor sense. But fragile earthly man cannot dispense entirely with creative activity. His bodily needs must seek fulfillment through practical objects of utility, and his sense of sight cannot accustom itself to an absolute void. In consequence, even the strictest monotheism was forced to retain a remnant of visual art, at least for the sake of decorative and practical functions. The conceptual purpose, on the other hand, was no longer sensed to be urgently necessary. This was especially the case in the Orient, where people were accustomed to speculative thought detached from concrete mental images. Islam therefore discarded the conceptual purpose entirely.

In the West, the demands of the "inner senses" for sensual

ideas of the divine could not be fully suppressed. If Christianity wanted to secure its dominant position, it could do so only through calculated toleration: thus the conceptual purpose was granted freely to art. This brings to view another difference between East and West: whereas the Byzantines gave free rein to the conceptual function in principle but restricted its actual use in art to the barest level of necessity, Westerners ceded it complete freedom in practice as well. Thus of all the guises assumed by art after Alexander, monotheism excluded only one on principle: the contest with nature for its own sake.

This gave rise to the attitude toward motifs that would be adopted by the art of all monotheistic cultures. In Islam, the confinement of art to exclusively decorative and practical functions was itself advantageous for inorganic forms. Arabic people invented no new motifs of this kind but simply adopted those transmitted to them through history. Of these, they preferred minimally organic motifs, such as band interlace, and deprived these of organic roundedness by cracking their curves into crystalline angles. The *entrelacs* published by Jules Bourgoin in *Les Eléments de l'art arabe* represent Islamic art at its most severe.

Alongside this tendency ran a more moderate strand. This sought to retain the antique vegetal tendril ornament — a motif of organic origin — as a practical tool but stripped it far more rigorously of any organic qualities than late Roman and Byzantine harmonism had done. Thus arose the arabesque, which was eventually fused with the broken band-interlace patterns. Whenever animal figures or, exceptionally, human figures were strewn into decoration — for example, in silk textiles — no efforts were spared to strip away their organic significance and expose with maximum clarity their inorganic decorative character. Artists accomplished this with special success by "patterning" the individual surface components of the animal's body with tendril ornament.

But still the Arabs refused to render their Supreme Power in sensual form or to employ art to satisfy conceptual needs — a stance Muslim people have maintained to the present day, notwithstanding a few concessions to figuration (see pp. 73–74). In obedience to tradition, they possessed for their Supreme Being only a symbol, and this was, significantly, a stone: the Kaaba. Can a more appropriate and eloquent symbol exist for a worldview and a people whose art adhered to the principles of inorganic creation more steadfastly than any other in human history?

The inevitable outcome of Islamic art's combination of a fundamentally inorganic character with the elimination of conceptual functions was that it stayed enmeshed more firmly in tradition than any other art. The "conservatism" of "Oriental" art has by now become proverbial.

So much for the selection and treatment of motifs in Islamic art. In our discussion of motifs in late antique and early Christian art, we shall examine the peculiar application of these motifs, which best reveals the true essence of Islamic art.

The Byzantine attitude toward motifs is characterized by a clash between a firm adherence to the Roman state ideal founded on the right of the stronger, on the one hand, and the social core of Christian doctrine, on the other. This opposition accounts for the extreme appearances of Byzantine art just after Constantine. The semi-inorganic band-interlace patterns of the late Roman early Christians are found side by side with harmonized vegetal tendrils that are almost identical with Greek versions from before Alexander. We also find accurate imitations of organic natural objects that betray echoes of the contest with nature for its own sake — for example, Turkish grape clusters and figs on the capitals in Spalato. Only gradually did this equivocation cease: the Roman state ideal proved mightier, and after the Iconoclast Controversy the inorganic side acquired unmitigated supremacy. The newly regimented conceptual purpose now generated human figures that bore no less palpably the stamp of harmonic beautification.

The natural outcome of Byzantine art's slow formation was that it likewise came to stagnate in tradition — perhaps even more so than Islamic art, which, in any event, Byzantine art increasingly resembled. Although modern observers do an injustice to the inorganic tradition when they sweepingly dismiss it as a fetter to artistic progress — at least with reference to antique art (see our comments at p. 150) — such an assessment comes close to being justified with regard to Byzantine art after Iconoclasm.

Thus the future belonged to Western Christianity. At this point, we might expect the conceptual purpose this culture tolerated to have reciprocally introduced organic motifs to the other two functions, as in the early stages of antique art. But the preconditions for such a move had changed profoundly. Anthropomorphic polytheism had given art the task of physically improving those organic motifs it accepted in order to fulfill conceptual purposes; once improved, the motifs were instantly available to art's other purposes. Spiritual monotheism, by contrast, strove to improve the spiritual content of a given motif; this could be accomplished only by the addition of external signs, such as written labels or attributes, meant to trigger conceptual associations. The problem was thus an inherently nonartistic one. How could it be solved in a way that would satisfy decorative and practical demands, which required motifs unconditionally, even if these were necessarily starkly inorganic?

This state of affairs was rooted in the very essence of monotheism and therefore remained untouched by any of the dogmatic and ethical changes that would later transpire within Christianity. Art of the Christian West could never again expect to reap anything from the field that had provided antique art with its most fruitful motifs, the religious conceptual purpose. This point illuminates most vividly the disadvantageous position into which the visual arts had slipped since the downfall of polytheism. Still, decorative and practical functions continued to demand motifs. When this requirement found itself unable to gain satisfaction from conceptual purposes in Christian art, only one alternative remained: art had to become an end in itself. This is the second foundational point to which the essence of Christian monotheism gave rise. The emancipation of art into an end in itself — and, parallel to that, an overt and irreconcilable divorce between religious and profane arts — had to be achieved by Christian people in a relatively brief span of time, before the fanatical one-sided views of early Christianity had been put to rest. As a result, profane art aimed at satisfying decorative and practical needs had to gather its motifs from different sources from conceptually purposeful religious art. We shall again consider North and South separately.

Art in Italy

THE EARLY CHRISTIAN PERIOD

Art of the early Christian period was equally hostile to organic and inorganic nature. For reasons just discussed, this attitude took different forms with regard to conceptual and decorative or practical purposes.

To satisfy conceptual purposes, early Christian art had to accept organic motifs, above all the human figure. It did this in such a way that figures would appear neither organic enough to compete with transitory nature nor harmonic enough to compete with physically perfected nature (as in Byzantine art). This art was equally indifferent to both options; as a means of avoiding both, it endowed its figures with a transitory but intentionally ugly quality. Only a fanatical age, however, could stay satisfied with that solution. Therefore in Italy, too, presumably under the influence of Byzantine art, the process of making ugly gradually became a process of making inorganic, albeit a very restrained one. This was the solution best suited to the strictly functional character of early Christian art.

If in this essential making ugly of the human figure we can distinguish a unicum in the history of art, we encounter another in the decorative arts of early Christian Rome in the fourth and fifth centuries. From the outset, artists selected only those motifs that possessed the slightest organic significance, such as band interlace or spiraling tendrils, from the vast array at their disposal. But early Christians also did not wish to bring any inorganic (that is, nature-improving) meaning to view, for they regarded this as no less abhorrent than organic significance. Thus their task lay in simultaneously employing a motif and suppressing its *habitus* as a motif. This was accomplished by giving as much autonomous significance as possible to the ground against which the motifs stood out.

As we shall see again later, the clear articulation of motifs against a neutral ground was a fundamental principle of antique art; it might even be understood as a visual manifestation of the right of the stronger. In late antique and early Christian art, on the other hand, ground was manipulated into independent configurations, generating uncertainty as to where we in fact see ground and where pattern. This — and here is the main point — causes the observer's eyes to pay attention neither to the organic significance of the motifs nor to their inorganic harmonization but to the regular flickering of adjacent areas of light and dark (in the case of reliefs) or of various colors (in the case of paintings). Harmony resides not in bodies and lines but in highlights and shadows or colors, and motifs become a mere means to an end. The outward appearance of a natural object — which is its most superficial, most inessential, and most incomprehensible aspect and was as ungraspable for those generations as the spiritual world-power they believed to underlie nature and constitute its true essence — this is what early Christian art embraced as the vehicle for expressing its own deepest will of art (*Kunstwollen*). This art was thus able at once to give the purest conceivable expression to its monotheistic hostility toward everything in both organic and inorganic nature and to satisfy its social proclivities with unsurpassable success. In coloristic harmony, there exists no "stronger" element against which a "weaker" merely serves as a foil; the eyes simply perceive a multifaceted whole in which no single element predominates.

In Italy, this coloristic principle barely outlasted the fifth century. Its traces lingered for a while in Byzantine art, at least during the initial, richly varied phases before Iconoclasm. But its final and most enduring refuge was found in the art of Islam. Indeed, since Gottfried Semper and Owen Jones most scholars have held this coloristic principle — the law of coordinating forms and colors — to be the foundational postulate of all "Oriental" art. When one compares Islamic works with related monuments of late Roman and early Christian art, however, it becomes instantly apparent that this view goes too far. Although Islamic decoration may certainly have suppressed the organic significance of motifs, it also took visible pleasure in inorganic harmonism. Moreover, Islamic works rarely fail to include a dominant element that lifts itself out of the uniform harmony. The element emerges not as a multifaceted, meaningful pattern against a neutral ground but as a continually repeated form within a colorful and densely patterned ground. Two coloristic systems thus appear overlaid, though one of them inarguably dominates by pulling the eye back to itself. This dominant element represents the stronger, which exerts a natural right of lordship over the weaker. But in this culture, the stronger is neither an aristocracy composed of many members nor a bureaucratic hierarchy of which the monarch constitutes the pinnacle, but rather the single absolute power of the caliph. And the weaker is not the dull mass of obscure folk but the entire, highly variegated society, from palace administrators to beggars, which occupies a lower plane relative to the supreme power holder.

This characteristic was but poorly developed in the early stages of Islamic culture, when the Arabs needed to forge tight social cohesion simply because of their military activity. (Example of works of practical purpose: the older form of the mosque; of decorative purpose: the stucco decoration in the Ibn Tulun Mosque, where the kinship with late Roman coloristic decoration is also most readily visible.) Over time, the absolute right of the stronger attained increasingly terse expression, as we see in the later mosque-type derived from madrasas as well as in Persian rugs, tiles, intarsias, window hangings, and so forth. As a result, Islam adopted the kind of coloristic harmony established by late Roman early Christianity only insofar as this helped suppress the organic significance of motifs. But Islam shied away from creating complete equality, the embodiment of Christian social values, and instead developed a new way of arranging the relations between pattern (the dominant motif) and ground (the subordinate motif) that was better suited to this religion's understanding of the right of the stronger. In this solution the true essence, as well as the unique contribution, of Islamic art rests. It was not coloristic harmony, which the Muslims neither invented nor developed to its fullest capacity; the early Christians in Rome had already accomplished both. Nor was it harmonization of the organic motifs inherited from Antiquity; the Byzantines had surpassed them long before in this domain.

Let us return to the fate of early Christian art in Italy. The intensification of coloristic harmony in decorative art to an extreme level led to a dead end. The one exit was found only when the Muslims reestablished the principle of subordination (the right of the stronger) in their own unique way. For reasons already discussed, enrichment by new motifs was not to be expected in the conceptual realm. So long as the driving force of the new worldview — the spiritual — was communicated solely by means of the nonartistic language of labels and attributes, and so long as both harmonic beautification and truth to accidental natural appearances were banished in equal measure from figural arts, the development of organic forms in conceptually purposeful art could proceed no further. It is our good fortune that the loosening of early Christianity's stricter observances ultimately allowed the influence of antique traditions, especially the Byzantine, to assume relevance in Italy. To be sure, these influences could spur no further advancements; indeed, they could by their very nature only work against the normal artistic progress of the Christian West. But they helped that art escape stagnation and thereby paved the way for the balancing mission that Italian art would eventually bring to its glorious fruition.

THE GIOTTESQUE PHASE
Giotto's great contribution was to free conceptually purposeful art from the nonartistic language of written labels and attributes, on the one hand, and the soulless, harmonic figural types of Byzantine art, on the other (figure 5). He did this by introducing accidental and momentary qualities into figures' gestural language and, at the same time, allowing for the narrative depiction of current events. But Giotto's art never forgot that its sole task was to proclaim the glory of God; it existed only to glorify a supreme, supersensory, spiritual power. In consequence, it never exceeded the bare minimum of necessity in its inclusion of accidental details, while the modern events it portrayed were exclusively those with strong spiritual significance, such as the life of Saint Francis. Giotto's art thus represents both a zenith and a moment

of balance within the broader domain of Italian Christian art in the second major period. It admitted the organic, but only in order to endow the spiritual with sensual form. Any excess of Organism was tempered by the proven means of the inorganic.

So deeply was this art rooted in the conceptual function that it had little left over for the remaining two purposes. This accounts for the remarkable fact that at the same time conceptually purposeful arts were experiencing this tremendous upsurge, the fields of architecture and decoration were met with utter passivity. As much as the Italians felt that this conflicted with their own creative genius, they opened their doors, reluctantly if not unwillingly, to Northern Gothic. In the field of decoration, they simply helped themselves to motifs passed down from the earlier phase.

The Renaissance

The stern, grave Guelf sensibility of fourteenth-century Tuscans loosened considerably during the subsequent age of humanism. This is instantly and concretely apparent in art of the time.

Now, as in the past, conceptually purposeful art maintained a dominant position. But in this case, it becomes especially clear how right Muhammad had been to forbid any competition with organic nature, whose aim was to give sensual form to things spiritual. Once the physical world gains primacy in art, its concomitant accidental qualities will inevitably win supremacy over the shapeless spiritual. This is exactly what happened in fifteenth-century Italy. Although pictures with religious subject matter continued to be painted almost exclusively, this content increasingly formed a mere pretext for portraying contemporary objects and actions. Even if the episodes took place in Old Testament times, the main characters would be clad in fifteenth-century costume and the events transplanted into the streets of quattrocento Florence. To be sure, we still encounter in Masaccio the grave and lofty sensibility of a Giotto; he, too, was just as concerned with spiritual conceptual purposes as with the accurate natural appearances of figures. But the joy in reproducing accidentals was already gaining dominance among his closest successors; we see this especially in Gozzoli. Thus artists came to depict modern life in Florence without originally having set out to do so. Once things proceeded thus far, it must have been instantly apparent that art was on its way to becoming an end in itself. And there is no contradiction in the fact that, despite all efforts to reproduce the organic and accidental ever more faithfully, a mitigating tendency toward harmonism remained in force. Perhaps this was an unshakable hereditary trait of the Tuscan race as it had taken shape in Antiquity. But it was augmented by a second factor: the unmediated stimulus of monuments of the very art for which harmonization of the organic had been a guiding principle — that is, art of Antiquity. To properly assess this phenomenon properly — which, indeed, gives us the opportunity to speak of a renaissance in the true sense of the word — we must leave off discussing the conceptual operations of Renaissance art and turn to its activity in the decorative and practical realms.

Certainly the embodiment of conceptual purposes — alongside the emphatic emancipation of organic and accidental qualities that, as we have seen, characterized the Renaissance — could benefit the remaining two functions more readily now than during the exclusively Christian phases of Western art. But these functions were not disposed to wait passively for that to happen. From the first moment that the appeal of the accidental for conceptual purposes began to increase at the expense of the spiritual, the other functions, determined to retrieve what they had neglected for centuries, started to gather motifs from any source that suited their needs. These included the ruined monuments of antique art strewn in such abundance across Italian soil.

What was the incipient Renaissance seeking for its decorative and practical needs that it believed to have discovered in antique monuments? It desired an accidental and natural quality for its motifs, but in a much higher degree than the Byzantinizing motifs of earlier phases of Italian Christian art had allowed. At the same time, it wanted a harmonized version of accidentals; this was due as much to the innate proclivities of the Tuscan race as to the suitability of these features for the traditional conditions of the given purposes. Both were discovered in the antique monuments of the Roman Imperial age.

That the imitation of these monuments was merely a means to an end becomes clear when one compares this phenomenon with the way Tuscan artists handled conceptually purposeful art. While no one thought to copy any of the numerous surviving figural reliefs of Imperial Rome, artists faithfully replicated acanthus friezes, fruit garlands, foliate pilasters, and vases — in other words, motifs of decorative and practical utility. Likewise, it is no accident that the preferred models came exclusively from the Roman Imperial age and not, say, the Attic golden age, for the Renaissance craved the extensive deployment of accidentals found in Imperial art and not the strongly harmonized treatment of these in Attic art, which artists endeavored to overcome through Byzantinizing approaches. Still, this renewed interest in antique monuments could not avoid having some impact on conceptually purposeful creation. This led not to the mechanical copying of antique figural monuments but to a liberal reuse of their conceptually significant motifs. Thus Botticelli painted for a Medici villa those mythological pictures whose progeny would for the next three centuries constitute the noblest task of Italian masters next to religious art. Such paintings bring to view most dazzlingly the twofold change that occurred during the Renaissance.

1. They indicate a contest with a physically but not spiritually

perfected nature. This would have been impossible during the time of Giotto; it signals that a profane art, which dispenses with any spiritual motivation for improving nature, was fast approaching in every domain.

2. Because this was accomplished by Christian artists and, consequently, did not involve any pagan intent, only one conclusion is possible: the contest had become an end in itself and was frankly acknowledged as such.

The separation of religious and profane arts, and the legitimization of art as an end in itself, thus emerged *ipso facto* as real phenomena. But the fiction that this was not the case lingered until around 1520. This view was necessary if Italian art was to preserve the naive confidence that would allow it to generate the works characteristic of the age of Julius II and Leo X.

Germanic Christian Art

THE PERIOD OF GROWTH TO THE TWELFTH CENTURY
We can subdivide this period into three distinct phases.

EARLY ORIGINS FROM 476 TO 768 C.E.
Most of the motifs first available to Germanic peoples stemmed from late Roman and early Christian art; only later were these joined by Byzantine motifs. The Teutons were not mature enough to understand the coloristic harmony of the late Roman ornamental system. In the earliest Germanic monuments, one observes how people struggled to make sense of those subtly occluded and veiled motifs. After the sixth century, under the impact of Byzantium, band-interlace patterns began to appear, which Germanic artists were able to transform into snakes by simply zoomorphizing them while, with the rarest exceptions, eliminating entirely the harmonized tendril motifs of late Roman art.

All these were works of practical utility. But the conceptual purpose was hardly unwelcome to Germanic artists. On the contrary,
we notice these artists quite readily reproducing human figures in
full or even in part. As crude as their efforts turned out to be,
they are characteristic of Germanic art's basic inclination to compete with organic nature.

CAROLINGIAN-OTTONIAN PERIOD

With regard to motifs employed for decorative ends, the Carolingian-Ottonian period is inarguably dependent on Byzantine art.
As for conceptually purposeful motifs, it is entirely possible that
many were inherited from late Roman artistic traditions and perhaps developed further by Romance people in Merovingian France;
but Byzantine influence is directly demonstrable in many areas of
this realm too. Of particular interest are monuments that clearly
betray how the Germanic copyist, finding the early Christian or
Byzantine figural model indifferent to his given task, assiduously
helped it along by exaggerating the gestures into caricatures. No
less revealing is the earnest care with which Germanic copyists
transplanted into their manuscripts genre scenes, which were
originally made for their own sake and which tradition allowed
to persist here and there — for example, in the embellishment of
canon tables or in decorative borders.

ROMANESQUE PERIOD

The Romanesque period relied on borrowed motifs in all artistic
domains but always employed them with remarkable independence. By the thirteenth century, it had therefore become able to
give exceptionally vivid artistic expression to the Germanic Christian worldview.

In conceptually purposeful arts, the momentary quality of
gestures was resolutely sought out. If this characteristic does not

often come to view with sufficient clarity, we must place the blame on borrowed motifs that possess a basic harmonic tendency, which appear crude and stilted when measured (as is typically done) against the standard of fully harmonic art. Finally, works of this period are characterized by their competition with the organic, which is evident not only in the motifs themselves but also in their formal treatment both individually and in groups (see the Naumburg sculptures [figure 6]).

We thus witness Romanesque artists in northern Europe (and Lombardy) striving for something that Tuscan artists would approach assertively only toward the end of the thirteenth century. The leading position of Germanic peoples was not only temporal but also material, in two respects. First, unencumbered by retrospective harmonizing scruples, they confidently grasped organic nature in all its accidental appearances. Second, with regard to their decorative and practical requirements, they neither waited passively for motifs to be gradually handed over from the conceptual sphere nor pretended to be content with motifs passed down through tradition. Rather, they worked to produce an entirely new version of art better suited to Germanic Christian tastes. Because this process involved manipulating dead matter to satisfy specific bodily needs, Germanic people called on inorganic creative principles, even going so far as to crack the rounded forms of Roman and Byzantine art into crystalline planes. From these same structuring elements, Romanesque art began to develop the inorganic decorative motif that would reach its formal culmination in the Gothic period.

The Summit of Germanic Christian Art
While the unleashing of Germanic creativity during the Romanesque period led to manifold and quite disparate efforts and results, the triumph of one of these — the French solution — re-

established unity. Earlier we noted that the French solution was in no way the most extreme. Rather, it was both the most measured and the most thoroughly self-contained solution and therefore, in the end, the most perfect. At this moment in history, it became evident for the first time that radical advances in Organism (as in the Naumburg sculptures) were incapable of further development; they were always succeeded by a reaction toward the inorganic. As different as the French ideal was from its antique counterpart, it, too, triumphed over German art's unbounded Organism. Thus Northern Gothic signaled at once a pinnacle and a moment of equilibrium in Germanic Christian art, just as Giottesque art did concurrently in Italy.

In works of conceptual purpose, Organism was held in check by the preference for a delicate, charming aspect in gestures and proportions. Gothic works of practical function in France continued to exhibit organic rudiments of periods temporally closer to Antiquity, such as columns and foliate capitals, whereas the more radical German Gothic cultivated its basic inorganic motif more systematically and consistently. In decorative arts, tracery designs brought to fruition the process of generating an inorganic motif that, when applied to works of practical function, would simply repeat the basic inorganic motif on a smaller scale. A parallel phenomenon is the organic reworking of motifs borrowed from Byzantium (*folia graeca*). As their counterparts in post-Alexander Antiquity had done with the acanthus, thirteenth-century artists took pains to overlay older motifs with natural organic significance (as in grape leaves, oak leaves, and such).

THE DECLINE OF GERMANIC CHRISTIAN ART

Around the year 1400, first in northern Germany and soon afterward in the South, artists recovered the thread that had been dropped during the thirteenth century. A vigorous contest was initiated anew with the accidental and organic, though still for the sake of spiritual conceptual purposes. We observed the same trend in quattrocento Tuscany; however, despite the common basic inclination of Northern and Southern art in this period, few things are more instructive than their differences. Whereas Germanic artists moved toward both extremes — on the one hand the accidental and organic, on the other the spiritual — the Italians gravitated toward a balanced middle ground.

Northern Germans were determined to illustrate sacred stories according to the values and appearances of modern times, though they still attached to them a Giottesque gravity. The spiritual did not merely provide a pretext for these works but was really their whole point; whether its visual embodiment was cloaked in outmoded early Christian garb or familiar modern attire was therefore inconsequential. Because, in keeping with the deep seriousness of their conceptual aims, people wanted to communicate these ideas with real urgency, the contemporary guise recommended itself with special strength. It appears incorporated everywhere: in the figural motifs of a given picture (the portrait), in the setting (landscape), in interiors, accessories, and so forth. Italian artists' harmonic improvement of the physical world, which helped them maintain their happy medium, remained foreign to their Northern counterparts. It was neither received through racial tradition nor suggested by the direct study of antique monuments.

Despite such disparities, by 1520 Northern and Southern art had arrived at the same point: a flagrant divorce of ecclesiastical and profane art even in the conceptual sphere. This resulted not from any conscious efforts on the part of Germanic artists but simply from the nature of the circumstances. Just as interest in the transitory appearances of natural things necessitated a reversal of the prevailing worldview, delight in the artistic depiction of accidentals could only lead to satisfaction of that pleasure for its own sake. By the time of the van Eyck brothers, the portrait had already detached itself from ecclesiastical art to become something fashioned not in honor of God but for the sheer delight in the individual personality. Artists portrayed current events as deeds of men, not, as in the Carolingian palace at Ingelheim, as deeds of God enacted through men. Genre pictures brought to view slices of contemporary reality rather than, as in earlier times, imitating antique scenes of everyday life. One can trace Germanic people's affinity for this approach to the very beginnings of their documented history. Nor did the desire to visualize nature awaken abruptly and for the first time in the fifteenth century. It was only at this point, rather, that it became a cultural imperative, and this pressed people closer to resolving the question of whether the contest with nature was acceptable only for God's sake or for its own. Although for a full hundred years people believed they could ignore that question, the Reformation forced them to confront it. With that, Northern Germanic art also came to an end.

What, we might ask, accompanied this shift in the decorative and practical fields? Surely the new interest in the accidental and organic could not remain without effects, even if the generally inorganic character of Gothic left little room for these qualities. In practical works of the late Gothic period, goldsmiths and other such artists were able to endow motifs with as much movement as the inorganic nature of these strictly purpose-oriented objects, made of dead matter, would tolerate.

It was possible to go further with decorative motifs. The sense of movement brought into tracery designs grew so heightened as to seem wholly incompatible with the basically inorganic motif. This gave artists the opportunity to transform that inorganic motif into an organic one, as in the overlapping "tree branches" of late Gothic traceries. The late Gothic ivy vine represents the last Organizing adaptation of the acanthus tendril, an ornamental motif of Byzantine origin that had never fallen entirely out of favor. With the breaking away from tradition in the decorative domain as well, the final step was attained. Artists plucked motifs from transitory organic nature and filled empty space with their likenesses. Antique monuments, which in any case were not at the disposal of Northern artists, were unnecessary for this step; works of conceptually purposeful art had already conditioned people's eyes to attend to even the tiniest details. Thus strawberries, flowers, insects, and other such things sprang up in the margins of prayer books, especially in Burgundy.

The Period Since 1520

Italy

After the Italian High Renaissance, with its balancing of harmonism and Organism, the future could only belong to an art that would engage confidently in the contest with transitory organic nature, at least in the conceptual sphere. In keeping with their racial tradition, the Italians were unable to pursue this course with any resolve. Thus they surrendered the leading role that around 1520 seemed destined to fall to them; indeed, in terms of wider significance for the progress of art, they fell into second place. One should not, however, underestimate Italian art made after 1520. Not only did it continue to transmit crucial stimuli to the North in the conceptual realm (Rubens!), but it also brought about the only truly consequential achievement for the practical purpose since 1520, which possessed a corresponding significance for the decorative sphere.

Italian art continued to hold harmony up as its supreme principle, for single motifs as well as their relationships with one another. Such art preferred to ignore accidentals entirely. This sensibility led Michelangelo to undertake a superhuman task by attempting to express spiritual movement through an inorganic presentation of the human body rather than through accidental traits (figure 7). Although his followers needed to bring accidental elements into gestures, these were never more than a necessary evil, something added superficially to the harmonized motif. Hence the reason we Teutons, with our deep emotional sensitivity, perceive the inner agitation of Italian Baroque figures as contrived and affected. In all fairness, however, we must not forget that Italian patrons did not want things any other way. Visualizations of profane conceptual purposes — or, more apt, works made as ends in themselves — appeal more to our tastes. These are works with mythological subject matter, which involves an unequivocal presentation of perfected nature, particularly in the form of the nude human body. Realistic arts such as genre painting and landscapes, insofar as these concerned the Italians at all, had to fulfill the same basic intention. This is why we miss a sense of mood in Italian landscape paintings; an Italian patron, on the other hand, would not have known what to make of a landscape that was atmospherically rich.

The principle of composition still determined the arrangement of motifs. The conical structure of the *sacra conversazione* was sensed to be excessively inorganic, and artists struggled to veil its symmetry more successfully. Caravaggio, for example, designed the main triangle of his Vatican *Entombment* as a right angle. While symmetry was no less present here, it was concealed almost by half; the regularity of the lines does not allow this to escape notice. Tintoretto's contrapposti are likewise cases of displaced symmetry. Although these appear quite rousing at first glance, the beholder's senses are calmed as soon as he realizes that, despite all the contrasts, he has before him merely an elegantly composed picture. In this respect, it is instructive to look at the accidental motifs favored by Italian Baroque artists. On the ceilings of large rooms, for example, the state of floating was often visualized in a deliberately naturalistic manner. Although the painted figures float around up there in much the same way an ordinary person would do, real people do not concern themselves with flying through the air. We encountered this same predilection among the Roman Imperial ancestors of these Baroque painters.

The contributions of Italian Baroque art to the decorative and practical fields, while universally important, held special significance for Germanic peoples. From Antiquity until 1520, Germanic peoples had been responsible for the only truly original achievements in these areas; with Gothic, they really did establish what earlier terminology deemed a "new building style." For all its timeless value, what the Italians produced during the quattrocento cannot be described as a "new building style," strictly speaking. Italian artists were committed above all to balancing harmonism and Organism; this task had already been perfected in Imperial Rome, and monuments of that time presented themselves as ready models. The real contribution of the Italian Renaissance thus lay in creating a happy medium using foreign tools rather than in independently inventing new ones, as Romanesque and Gothic art had done in Germanic countries. Only after 1520 did Italians approach the problem that Northern artists had put to rest long before. From the outset, it was taken for granted that the formal language of Antiquity was not to be disrupted in harmonized elements. This demand on the part of the Italian harmonic tradition made it impossible for piers, arches, and other architectural features to be separated from their function as either supporting or supported elements, as occurred in Gothic art. Something new had to be introduced, and there was no doubt as to what that would be. So forcefully was everything in art driving toward the accidental and mobile that the conceptual function in Italy had to tolerate it, if only superficially. There was likewise no other option in works made to satisfy bodily needs. Late Gothic art in Germanic territories had already recognized and submitted to this tendency. But because this art always wanted to stay "truthful," never exceeding the barest degree of illusionism, it came to stagnate and by the seventeenth century had faded away. Italian art did not share these scruples. It was determined to simulate the movement of inorganic masses; in its figures, it convincingly — even at times exaggeratedly — emphasized accidental manifestations of the spiritual. Yet this all remained superficial, in works of practical and decorative purpose no less than in conceptually meaningful figures.

In this domain, too, Michelangelo took the first steps and again ultimately claimed an exceptional position. But the characteristics sketched out above are plainly visible in the work of his successors, above all in church architecture. Instead of the whole building being set into motion, as would be natural for any unified body, this was attempted on only one part, the facade. Everything else remained hidden. (How differently Gothic artists proceeded!) While a great burst of movement sweeps across the facade, no movement is perceptible within the building. Thus there is almost no correspondence between the interior and the movement on the exterior — another factor that manifests this architecture's contrast with Gothic.

This did not satisfy artists in Baroque's second phase. By ridding movement on the exterior of whatever spiritual motivation it had once at least pretended to possess, designers intensified that movement to a degree hitherto unimaginable: thus began the dramatic undulation of facades. When Roman art had made use of rounded walls, those were evenly curved all the way around; the cylinder of the Pantheon is simply a prism with an infinite number of sides. The curves of late Baroque architecture, by contrast, are irrational. Yet harmony continued to hover over this wild mobilization of inorganic elements as the supreme intent of art

(*Kunstabsicht*). Proportions were still safely observed; symmetry was still suggested, often with drastic and illusory means; and an overall harmonic appearance was still held in special esteem.

It was only natural that the creation of new practically purposeful motifs should be joined by new decorative motifs as well, in the way Gothic architecture was accompanied by tracery. Like Gothic tracery, Baroque ornament arose from the structurally organic motifs of practical art. But whereas tracery had as its core form the semi-crystalline rounded or pointed arch, Baroque ornament was based on an element with an incomparably greater capacity for movement: the volute. This had initially grown out of the vegetal tendril but was mediated to Baroque ornamentation by architectural components such as consoles and gables. Its development thenceforth parallels that of practically purposeful motifs. Artists quickly abandoned molding profiles with regular curves and, especially during the second phase of Baroque art, piled up layers of irrational curves until the underlying inorganic motif threatened to vanish entirely (for example, in frames).

Here people felt they had to stop. Italian art could proceed no further once harmonism began to suffer. The endowment of inherently immobile inorganic forms with movement was now perceived as contradictory and unnatural; so, too, were human figures floating across a ceiling. The tendency of modern German critics simply to appropriate the shift in public opinion that occurred in Italy at the middle of the eighteenth century entails their falling prey once again to the old errors of aesthetics. One must not forget that men are not bound to proceed the same way nature does. If nature appears incapable of setting inorganic things into motion, man is not prevented from doing so in his art; the ancient Egyptians certainly exploited this allowance — for example, in their ceramics. If people for a full century could apprehend the most mobile inorganic form as the highest expression of artistic

sensibility, then perhaps this understanding of the relation between nature and art can assert itself once more. We should not
want to make impossible an impartial assessment of such a change
because of our own one-sided allegiances and aesthetic prejudices.

On the other hand, by recognizing the general character of Italy's
harmonically inclined artistic spirit, we can understand how the
imitation of classical Antiquity by Canova and others in the middle
of the last century was lauded as an emancipation from the unnatural and a return to organic nature. In fact, despite their more
tangible harmonism and more placid appearance, the most somber
classicist acanthus tendrils are incomparably more organic than
the most exuberant Baroque curves.

People of Germanic Roots
At the same moment the Reformation was wrenching open a
spiritual gap between North and South, Germanic people became
acquainted with Italian Renaissance art; this gave them their first
inkling of the significance of harmonism for the visual arts. The
resulting paradox found its first clear expression in the art of
Germany. As it took shape since the van Eycks, the normal progress of Germanic art, which involved competing with organic
nature while adhering to a spiritual, intellectualized intent, was
sharply interrupted by the new acquaintance with Italian art and
the beautified physical world presented therein. Dürer had still
been able to resist the temptations of external harmonism. Holbein, on the other hand, plunged wholeheartedly into the new
options, and he did so in the very domains for which inorganic
forms were best suited: the decorative and the practical. The
Gothic style and its tracery forms appeared flimsy and weak when
held up against the formal richness of the Italian Renaissance. In
upper and lower Germany alike, works of practical and decorative purpose were cloaked in the harmonized organic forms of the

Renaissance. These works are brought together under the rubric "German Renaissance." Running parallel to this were a Netherlandish, a French, an English, and a Spanish Renaissance.

There still remained the Germanic insistence that a work of art provide spiritual stimulation, a demand Italian art could not adequately fulfill. This requirement had previously been satisfied by ecclesiastical art, with its sensual presentation of omnipotent spiritual power through transitory organic motifs. But the Reformation was putting a halt to any naive continuation of this custom. It is significant that church art still persisted in the newly Protestant lands and that iconoclastic outbursts were necessary to stifle the practice for good. In the end, ecclesiastical art was retained only in Catholic territories. Even here, however, the naive medieval outlook was no longer in effect; in keeping with Counter-Reformation attitudes, images in churches came to be regarded principally as an external means for giving sacred space a worthy decorative embellishment. Religious painting thus sacrificed the aspect that Germanic peoples had always cherished most deeply, its spiritual conceptual purpose. As for the remaining decorative function, everyone recognized that the Italians had found the better, more beautiful solution. It was therefore inevitable that Germanic religious art, insofar as it was not actually produced by Italian masters, dissolved into mere imitations of Italian harmonic art — that is, into the so-called German (and Netherlandish and French and so on) Renaissance.

The conceptual requirements innately crucial to Germanic people thus remained unfulfilled. In visual art and literature alike, these people began to fix their attention on worldly things to a far greater extent than others had done since the second half of the fifteenth century. These included worldly wisdom, as expressed in poems on folly; the joys of earthly life, manifested in banquets and hunts; the mundane events of everyday life, displayed in market scenes; and, finally, the appearances of man's natural surroundings (landscape). This series of steps reveals how the conceptual function gradually dissolved into thin air, moving from the embodiment of philosophical ideas to the depiction of first active, then passive, expressions of human life and activity, until, in landscapes, there remained only the purpose of art as an end in itself. This autonomous function of art offered Germanic people a substitute for the conceptual function, since the mood such art elicited was no less spiritual than any conceptual meaning.

The specifically Germanic artistic spirit [*Kunstgeist*] proclaimed itself in such works at the same time that Italian harmonism was exercising its foreign dominion in decorative and practical art as well as in works of religious conceptual purpose. How deeply this art impressed the Germans is evident in their seldom daring to clothe manifestations of their own national artistic spirit in the lofty expressive mode associated with oil painting. The vast majority of such works they left to the graphic arts, though, to be sure, this transposition guaranteed these works a more popular character. This is a point of deepest significance. The Germans seem here to have sensed that the new direction in which the shift in worldviews was taking visual art would necessarily lead to art's isolation from the common folk, to whom it had belonged in the Middle Ages. There was no better means of preventing art from becoming the special privilege of the cultivated classes than graphic art. If this medium no longer entices in the same way today, this only seems to prove that in the current cultural climate there will be no stop to the aristocratization of art.

Just as Germany accommodated two confessions at once, it maintained this artistic duality until the middle of the eighteenth century. This lengthy stagnation — this dissolution of once rich talent into sheer mediocrity — is often blamed on the disruptive impact of the Thirty Years War. But that event was no more devastating than the War of Independence in Holland, which in no way hindered the incomparable flowering of art there during the seventeenth century. It was not the Thirty Years War as such that prevented a break from stagnation; it was, rather, that war's undecided outcome. Because neither confession could claim victory and hence sole authority, the rift already present among German people stayed in place for a full century after 1648. Only after eighteenth-century rationalism raised to a fundamental matter of principle the divide between faith and knowledge, which had lain latent ever since humanism, did German art enjoy free rein to pursue its own paths.

Post-Reformation conditions were considerably more favorable in the Netherlands than in Germany. In the Low Countries, the opposition between the two outlooks sharpened so quickly that an open confrontation such as Germany would first experience during the Thirty Years War erupted as early as the sixteenth century. The affluent denizens of Flemish cities, probably swayed further by their mixture of Frankish and Latin blood, were not disposed to let the Reformation hinder their enjoyment of harmonized Italianate works of religious art — hence iconoclasm. The thoroughly Germanic Dutch, by contrast, were from the very start inclined toward stricter observances from the very start. It was no coincidence that the Spanish armies won over the southern Netherlands for Catholicism while the northerners fought to practice the Protestant religion. This division was to be the salvation of artistic progress.

Flemish art worked vigorously to institute balance between the organic, spiritualized approach of the North and the harmonic methods of the South. This required a major artistic force, which was found, at just the right moment, in Rubens. As in Italy, ecclesiastical art held the leading role; but Rubens employed it in the opposite way from his Italian counterparts. Rather than devising a beautiful motif and adding a spontaneous gesture or an accidental light source from outside, Rubens would choose an organic motif with a fleeting pose or attitude, then harmonize the secondary components such as costume, coloration, or illumination. Thus he achieved convincingly lifelike appearances even when jumbling together contemporary and mythological characters. Caravaggio's shabby figures, by contrast, always give the impression of having been deliberately invented. Rubens's ability to balance harmonism and Organism not only remained undiminished over time but even increased. This was because he never neglected realistic subjects or categories alongside his conceptually based projects such as religious and mythological paintings. This allowed him and his whole school to become a more powerful mirror for the worldview of the age than was hitherto possible. Conversely, Rubens's most gifted pupil, Van Dyck, distanced himself from Germanic artistic sensibilities by clinging to Italian methods, such as the expression of accidentals through gestures and academic compositions, but without ever attaining a truly Italian sensibility. This is especially apparent when one compares portraits from both sides.

A shift in Flemish practical and decorative artistic activity ran parallel with this phenomenon. The Netherlandish Renaissance was quickly supplanted by closer conformity to Italian Baroque models.

The Dutch, by contrast, were the first people to attempt to construct an art solely on the foundation of Germanic Protestantism. Motifs and everything associated with them had to be organic and had to arouse some kind of thought in the beholder, if only an indefinite emotional state (*Stimmung*). Harmonization was banished on principle.[4] The countless artists that that tiny country produced in such a short time attests to the entire population's engagement with the problem. This was the last time Germanic art gave expression to the soul of an entire people, and it did not endure long. Early in his career, well before he had reached the peak of his development, Rembrandt had to combat the harmonic predilections of Amsterdam's aesthetes. These tendencies gradually found their way into all of Holland's cultivated circles, signaling the end of this first essentially anti-harmonic art (fifteenth-century art was not deliberately un-harmonic). As Flemish art slowly relinquished its livelier impulses, the path was opened for French art. Like Flemish art, French art attended equally to harmonism and Organism, but in its own distinctive way.

Before we examine this development, let us take a glance at how the Dutch dealt with practical and decorative functions during their brief artistic flowering. In these areas, the connection to the Gothic period was severed by the Netherlandish Renaissance; but the harmonized motifs of Italian Baroque ran contrary to the whole national outlook. The question is thus of paramount art-historical interest as to which motifs the Dutch, who already showed themselves predisposed to the organic in conceptually oriented art, would choose for works of the two practical functions. The result sounded in favor of Roman Antiquity, as theorists had reconstructed it in books and objects in the days of Raphael and his followers. More than a century before Canova, the Dutch (as well as the English), with their strong affinity for the organic, found in ancient Roman decorative and practical works *nature* — that is, an underlying, immobile inorganic form singularly suited for the shaping of dead matter into physically purposeful constructions — while discretely applying a sense of movement to organic motifs alone. Motifs were either designed in strict crystalline fashion with no movement, as in residential constructions, or given organic shape and thus moderate movement, as in bundles of fruit or acanthus tendrils. But any movement in inorganic forms was regarded as unnatural and was therefore typically rejected in works of larger scale. Herein lay the "truthfulness" of this strictly Germanic art, which thus, for the first time since the Gothic period, rediscovered its own essence.

Although sixteenth-century French art experienced the same influences as its German and Netherlandish counterparts, we observe with little difficulty a return to the Gothic ideal in French Renaissance art's distinct predilection for slender and charming figures. French art assumed broader significance for the Germanic world only in the seventeenth century, when it embraced the heritage of its closest relation, Flemish art. French art also drew primarily on organic motifs, though never in an unmediated state. Among the characteristic external features that Le Brun and his crowd shared with Rubens were lively gazes and the reckless commingling of the real and the allegorical. However, the French dispensed with the superhuman endowment of the limbs by which Rubens, following Michelangelo, gave harmony to the vigorous motions of his figures. They replaced this with the old ideal of precious courtly elegance, which eighteenth-century masters such as Watteau would further cultivate through their choice of motifs. In decorative and practical domains, such painters tended to bring motion to the inorganic, as their Italian and Flemish counterparts did, but they employed greater restraint than their forerunners. Although French artists followed Italians during the first half of the eighteenth century, when the mobilizing of inorganic forms (volutes) reached its furthest extreme, they still felt compelled to undergird it with an element of Organism. (This is similar to the late Gothic transmutation of mobilized traceries into networks of branches.) Significantly, these artists opted for the mussel shell, whose shape, being regular yet asymmetrical, stood squarely between the organic and the inorganic. The return to natural (inorganic) forms did not occur as abruptly in France as in Italy, for the

Louis XVI style allowed for a smooth transition to the more severe classicism of Empire style. In this transition, the French proved how congenial Roman Antiquity was to their own artistic sensibility. Only the Russians would abandon themselves to this style with equal freedom; they, too, discovered in Roman Imperial Antiquity the historical style that most closely approximated their Byzantine union of state and cult.

Postmedieval Spanish art, influenced first by French and then by Flemish art, did not pursue the harmonic route of the Italians but rather chose the organic path of the Germans. The shift from French to Flemish models suggests that French Organism struck the Spanish as excessively restrained and that the spirit of Spanish art (*der spanische Kunstgeist*) desired stricter adherence to the accidental and organic. Spanish works of the seventeenth century reveal with special clarity the specific will of art in Spain. The Spanish not only competed with the Dutch in their organic treatment of motifs but even surpassed them. These parties, however, approached the problem from opposing sides: whereas the Dutch aimed to create a Protestant art, the Spanish worked toward a Catholic art that would include nothing that was incompatible with the most rigid form of revealed faith. In consequence, art made for its own sake, with its pantheistically colored moods, was automatically excluded; whenever we encounter Spanish works with realistic subjects, their functional, usually decorative purpose is made so obvious that any sense of mood or atmosphere disappears. In religious art — which includes the entire gamut of seventeenth-century Spanish art — the Spaniards put into practice what contemporary Italians regarded as a mere pretext for their cult of beauty: now the single conceptual objective was the glorification of God's spiritual omnipotence. Only one other realistic subject was taken seriously for its own sake: the portrait. In this domain, artists reproduced the organic motif as accurately as any

Dutch painter had done, in some cases even more so. But they added a harmonic element that was esteemed just as highly by the Spanish as elegance was by the French: *grandezza*.

The progress of seventeenth-century Spanish art further resembled contemporaneous developments in Holland in that all its inventive energies were expended in conceptual activity, with none left over for practical or decorative purposes. In this respect, the Spanish differed from the still partially Latin French, who considered their primary task (and, cleverly enough, also the primary means) for achieving artistic hegemony in Europe to be the harmonic balancing of the various artistic functions. Although the Spanish found no reason to hold the same disapproving attitude toward Italian Baroque as their Dutch counterparts did, it is noteworthy that the great masters and arrangers of organic motifs gave a considerably more severe appearance to Italian Baroque motifs. Only after that great era passed did the so-called Churrigueresque style develop (parallel with the late Baroque in Italy), with its extravagant mobilization of inorganic volutes. But as soon as classicism urged artists in the practical and decorative domains to return to nature, conceptually purposeful Spanish art witnessed in Goya the emergence of a master who would surpass even Velázquez in his treatment of accidental organic appearances.

But it was the Dutch who, in the seventeenth century, stepped decisively onto the path to which the future of art after 1520 belonged. Even this radical advancement was unable to establish a strong foothold at first. The previous worldview, rooted in revealed faith, still weighed far too heavily on people's souls for artistic activity to extricate itself swiftly. Only the rationalist movement of the eighteenth century — specifically the new, scientifically grounded epistemologies of Kant, Laplace, Goethe, and others — cleared the path for an art based purely on the natural sciences. One might guess that during the nineteenth century, art would throw itself into the infinite abundance of organic motifs; but at first it did the opposite. At the very moment all obstructions to accepting the contest with nature for its own sake seemed to have vanished, people suddenly remembered that no earlier period knew such purposelessness in art. They therefore tried diligently to reestablish some functionality in artistic production. This is most evident in the so-called reform movement of industrial arts, whose most important endeavor was the rehabilitation of the inorganic. Inorganic form was now regarded as a necessary outcome of material and technical factors — a conclusion that our analysis of the actual historical development has clearly proved erroneous. In so-called high art, on the other hand, the conceptual purpose was pulled once again to the foreground. This whole episode was, of course, just a case of swimming against the current, as is obvious in the way artists uncritically recycled motifs from earlier periods. The empire style represented the initial stage of this route. Artists could not adhere to one single period, for none possessed the qualities that would fully satisfy contemporary needs. By the time artists reached Velázquez and Rembrandt, however, the blinders had fallen from their eyes, and they quickly steered themselves back onto the course that had been staked out after 1520 but then abandoned.

Let us pause now to consider the unprecedented phenomenon of an art that sought motifs neither in nature nor in some past art that seemed to portray nature with special acuity, but rather in other obsolete artistic periods that displayed a wide variety of attitudes toward nature and its artistic reproduction. This would seem to undermine a cardinal point of our analysis: namely, that all artistic creation depends directly on the respective worldview. The problem is only illusory, however, for modern artistic activity regards the older monuments it takes as models as nothing more than ends in themselves. What interest does a quattrocento painting of some saint hold for the modern collector? Surely not the spiritual conceptual purpose it was designed to fulfill, but rather the contest with nature it embodies, its degree of resemblance to organic appearances and the naïveté with which the artist disregarded many aspects thereof. Although we call this method of observation, which has been current in the last several decades, art-historical, we would be equally justified in describing it as natural-historical. That art-historical knowledge is judged imperative for understanding modern artworks in terms of these older paradigms proves yet again how alienated the modern visual arts have grown from the wider masses.

Today it is taken for granted that the contest with organic nature, in whatever form, will be conducted for its own sake. The old conceptual purposes are deemed anachronistic.[5] Some artists contrive pantheistic fantasies set in more or less atmospherically charged natural environments; or, if the picture is meant to express some specific intellectual content, they enshroud it in a mystical haze, whose very obscurity creates a surprising sense of mood. (This is done most often in Germany.) In such works, both organic nature and man's contest with it serve merely to give substance to abstract concepts. This, of course, represents the opposite extreme from the earliest antique art, which sought and represented the bodily world alone. Thus art made for its own sake is once again generating purposeful creative activity; but its current function does not pertain to any bodily or spiritual needs — the latter having always, so to speak, been simply disguised versions of bodily ones. Rather, it concerns the truly transcendental desire we might most aptly describe as the presentiment of a world spirit.

Modern art has also declared the contest with organic nature to be an end in itself in the decorative and practical domains. If all antique art strove, in varying degrees, to de-Organize its motifs, if medieval art moved backward by treating motifs with increasing severity, if recent art has finally advanced again by imbuing the inorganic with movement, then the chief endeavor of modern art is to celebrate the animated movement of the organic. It has not succeeded in eliminating the inorganic entirely, of course. Architecture continues to stave off such an attempt; nor has anyone in the furniture industry yet succeeded in "making a chest of drawers from a pumpkin," as an old practitioner of the now-obsolete reform movement once mockingly ordered. Is this due to the weight of tradition, which continues to cripple invention in these areas (though it may disappear tomorrow, as happened long ago in the fields of jewelry and ceramics)? Or is there a boundary here that man can never transgress when composing with forms and surfaces? We are still awaiting a reliable answer, and historical experience urges us in the meantime to refrain from excessive speculation. But on one point we must be clear: if the emancipation of practical and decorative activity is really to dominate art in the future, this will require a radical transformation of the economic conditions of production.

Earlier we made the point that the distinction between artist and artisan was unknown to strictly purpose-oriented periods. This distinction was only fully accepted with the development of an autonomous art directed at dilettantes, which occurred after a series of transitional stages. If in the future the decorative and practical realms are likewise to become absorbed into the idea of art as an end in itself, they, too, must move from the hands of ignorant artisans into the hands of artists. Because of both decorative and practical art's adherence to tradition until the nineteenth century, which resulted from their restriction to a very few formal types and chiefly inorganic motifs, artisans are capable only of tradition-bound and non-inventive creation. Should the contest with the transitory appearances of organic motifs be made available to these functions as well, traditional creative methods would have to come to an end. Because earlier methods no longer satisfy decorative and practical purposes, these, too, must be taken up by the hands of artists. This would require an extreme division of labor, with the artist being exclusively responsible for invention and the craftsman for manual labor and mass production. In a few fields, such as textiles, this process has long been in effect. But any further development in this direction would entail even the most skilled tasks of the so-called art industry eventually falling prey to mechanical operations.

Art enjoyed its fullest independence from and equality with nature for as long as man faced natural forces and their causal laws blindly and without comprehension. Man worked up dead matter according to the same principles as nature did but fashioned genuinely creative products that were free from any organic model. But his intuition of nature's spiritual aspect quickly began to rattle his confidence in his own dominance. As soon as ideas of the spiritual prompted him to begin reproducing organic motifs, man submitted, for the first time, to dependence on nature. Because he still sensed his own superiority, his art presented an improved version of organic nature. This sense was increasingly confounded when, beginning in the age of the Diadochi, interest in the natural sciences progressively intensified. At that point, artists began to devote ever more attention to the accidental appearances of the organic world, a domain for which the triumph of the Christian worldview initiated a new phase but not a fundamental change in attitude.

Today we face nature with knowledge and understanding; we have a good command of its causal laws and are not stupefied by natural phenomena. But at the same time that we have conquered nature intellectually, we have sunk to increasingly slavish dependence on it in our art. If antique art only deigned to depict nature in perfected form and Christian art regarded it merely as a vehicle for visualizing spiritual powers, contemporary art has surrendered itself to nature's most transient appearances. Let us no longer delude ourselves about something artists have long been unwilling to admit: that for us today, in diametric opposition to Antiquity, nature is an improved form of art. Art today is nothing more than a means of mediating and amplifying the simple enjoyment of nature that characterizes modern culture. A snippet of nature framed between two trees or visible in a circle formed by thumb and index finger yields the same effect as a likeness of that view in a rectangular frame (if not a better one). If a desired mood arises more readily from a picture than from the actual bit of nature, this is due to the picture's greater isolation from secondary distractions. The artist's unilateral emphasis, even exaggeration, of discrete transitory qualities such as lighting and color, which is often described as his "subjective vision" and extolled as the chief source of pleasure in modern painting, in no way establishes his superiority over nature (which this is ostensibly meant to convey). At the moment exaggeration borders on unreality, the picture loses any ephemeral value. This attitude is already fading; and another, which regards nature as a passive mediator or translator of the world spirit, is gaining more ground. But it is obvious that organic nature is its own best interpreter, while art simply forms a welcome surrogate for those who want to enjoy woodland solitude in their cozy sitting rooms. The more closely the artist approximates the transitory appearance of a bit of forest, the more easily he reaches that goal.

The beginning and the end of the development of motifs in the visual arts can be summarized as follows: The earliest worldview conceived natural things simply as transitory embodied beings but elevated them in art to eternal beings by couching them in inorganic forms. Today's worldview conceives the things of nature as tangible manifestations of an eternal world spirit but degrades them in art to transitory ones by couching them in the most drastically organic forms. This explains why in the past a formal type might remain valid for hundreds or even thousands of years, whereas today the prevailing mode generates new artistic forms daily. These two poles, directly between which the medieval Christian attitude lies, bracket the development of all human artistic activity to the present day.

Form and Surface

All things in nature possess form; that is, they extend themselves in the three dimensions of height, width, and depth. The sense of touch alone offers unmediated confirmation of this fact. Paradoxically, the sense of sight, that very faculty whose chief purpose is to allow us to absorb impressions of objects outside ourselves, tends more often to deceive us about the three-dimensionality of what we see. Lacking the capacity to penetrate solid bodies, our visual organs can perceive only one side of a body at a time, and this in turn presents itself to the eye as a two-dimensional surface. Only by drawing on previous tactile experiences do we mentally flesh out into three-dimensional form the two-dimensional surface that our eyes actually perceive. This process is naturally performed more quickly the more readily certain aspects of the observed object call to mind experiences of touch. What might appear from a distance as a patch of light or color of a certain size may from a closer standpoint prove to be a series of alternating illuminated and shaded areas; this immediately signals the presence of convexities — modeling — and thus the third dimension. This effect is naturally amplified the closer the beholder stands to the natural thing, until finally his memories of tactile experience have won the upper hand so unequivocally that he is no longer aware of the illusion caused by his visual organs. If the process is taken to an extreme, however — that is, if the eye is pressed right up against the object — the effect swings back to the opposite pole: no longer able to survey as a whole those aspects that recall tactile experience, the eye apprehends only a surface.

These reflections allow us to recognize the significance of the distance at which the visual faculties apprehend a natural thing for the viewer's internal comprehension of that thing and, by extension, for man's contest with such objects in art. If eye and object are placed in direct proximity to each other — we shall call this the *near view* — the viewer obtains the impression of purely two-dimensional surface extension.[1] If the viewer backs away somewhat, the eye is able to observe certain aspects of the object that recall tactile experience. This potential increases with growing distance from the object, to a point where the modeling appears most distinct and the impression of three-dimensionality is therefore most convincing and unmitigated. To avoid wordy explanations in the future, we shall call this simply the *normal view*. When the distance between eye and object exceeds the normal view, an inversion of the process occurs: modeling gradually disappears behind the increasingly dense wall of intervening air until only a solid surface of light or color meets the retina. We shall designate this the *distant view*.

We have now become acquainted with an alternating process of ascent and descent, which culminates in the normal view and whose beginning and ending points seem to be identical. But the fact that the normal view represents a balance between two contrasting extremes suggests that the beginning and ending points are really diametrically opposed. If a distant view leads us to see a flat plane where in reality a modeled, three-dimensional surface exists, there is no doubt that this is a sensory deception. Because this surface owes its appearance principally to the inadequacies of the human visual apparatus, we shall henceforth call it the *subjective surface*. On the other hand, the surface whose impression we obtain from the near view is no illusion; it actually exists and, to distinguish it from its subjective counterpart, may be designated the *objective surface*. All three-dimensional bodies are bounded on all sides by two-dimensional surfaces. The surface that the eye reports back to the internal senses when viewing an object at close range is therefore a factually existent part of that body, of which, in this case, the eye perceives no more than a small flat surface. Observing this part — surface — while ignoring the body as a whole — form — entails certain restrictions, to be sure, but involves no illusion. The objective surface of a thing in nature exists no less than does its form, of which that surface constitutes an inextricable part.

For any given thing, we have thus to distinguish three elements: (1) *form*, which is fundamental to the object; (2) *objective surface*, which, being an intrinsic component of form, is equally fundamental to the whole; and (3) *subjective surface*, which is a mere illusion of the visual faculties.

In principle, the two surfaces coincide. The illusion lies only in the deceptively unified two-dimensionality exhibited by the subjective surface; the objective surface crumbles into surface fragments that lie more or less sharply adjacent to one another on different planes. In other words, while the individual surface pieces are in fact two-dimensional, the whole outer surface of an object apprehensible with a single glance is not. Which of these three components did the earliest art privilege in its efforts to improve nature? Undoubtedly the two essential elements: the three-dimensional form and the objective surface composed of two-dimensional surface parts. This art must at first have concertedly ignored the illusory and insubstantial subjective surface. Because the objective surface proclaims itself through the modeling of its surface fragments, the earliest nature-improving art must have emphasized and worked through the surface components of the three-dimensional motif with special fervor.

In the previous chapter, we learned that all artistic creativity is governed by the opposition of inorganic and organic motifs. Now we must investigate how the split between three-dimensional form and objective surface (individual surface fragments) is reflected in that opposition. We find this disjunction at its most severe in purely inorganic motifs. In crystals, a rigidly symmetrical configuration and crisply delineated borders allow each surface part to lie as a self-contained unit extending along strictly two-dimensional planes. The surface components of organic motifs, by contrast, typically flow into one another through curves and bulges and thus appear asymmetrical and unclearly defined; at the same time, their rounded volumes rescue them from complete two-dimensionality, which is generally limited to the very smallest bits of surface. Thus we see that inorganic motifs, whose overt harmonism gave them a dominant role in the early stages of man's artistic activity, also brought most perfectly to view the requisite distinction between overall form and surface fragment. As noted above, man soon found himself compelled to compete with animate organic nature. But just as he struggled to give clearest possible expression to the harmonic principles of inorganic nature, man's efforts to highlight the division between an overall form and its surface pieces had to be no less diligent. This postulate emerged from the nature-improving impulse so fundamental to ancient art. So long as this motivation took precedence, artistic approaches to natural motifs had to comply with prevailing attitudes toward form and objective surface parts. Although ancient art did stay bound to a closed handling of form and surface pieces, we will see numerous symptoms emerge during the phase of decline that suggest an incipient loosening of the rule.

The separation of surface pieces from one another in organic motifs — especially pronounced in Egyptian Old Kingdom statuary — derives essentially from tactile experience and appears in blatant contradiction to the experience of sight. Because the optical sense plays the primary and most indispensable role in man's perception of nature and art alike, it makes sense that ancient man, when studying the natural motif with which he would creatively compete in art, initially chose the manner of viewing that allowed him simultaneously to activate the sense of touch. This could be neither the distant view nor even, at first, the normal view; it could only be the near view. Anyone who carefully examines ancient Egyptian images will recognize that they were conceived for strictly near viewing. With even the slightest movement beyond a near viewpoint, all modeling vanishes, and they become like flat mirages.

In addition to this, there is a second result: the only kind of contest appropriate for nature-improving art is that involving a form bounded by surfaces — that is, sculpture in the round — portrayed in the normal view. Neither the close presentation of a natural motif as one aspect of a larger three-dimensional form (which we call half form, or relief) nor a distant view of the same subject portrayed as a two-dimensional subjective surface (any two-dimensional medium, or painting in the broadest sense) is reconcilable with an art that aims at capturing the essential, the perfect, the self-contained. Nevertheless, we encounter both phenomena in certain monuments of Old Kingdom Egypt. Even at this early stage, something must have compelled the makers of nature-improving art occasionally to grant visual expression to the subjective surface — that is, to the transient and illusory appearance of things.

First Period: Nature-Improving Art

Egypt

Before we trace these motivating factors, we must investigate how the earliest Egyptian art approached subjective surfaces. What do we learn from close examination of ancient Egyptian reliefs and wall paintings?

These reveal, first of all, that ancient Egyptian artists handled the necessary evil of illusory views in the same way they did the necessary evil of organic motifs. Just as they worked to improve the latter by maximally subordinating them to the harmonic principles of inorganic nature, they sought to apply the rules of organic near viewing to subjective vision. Egyptian reliefs and wall paintings, in other words, are meant to be viewed at close range; as with freestanding sculptures, one must observe them close-up to appreciate the proper objective of their contest with nature. In its efforts to improve nature, this art sought to bring to view the underlying essence of things, even though all that was visible was their transitory, subjective superficial appearance. Conversely, any element that betrayed the slightest intent to reproduce these fleeting appearances was stringently suppressed. This appears most unambiguously in Egyptian wall paintings, which dispense with modeling entirely and thus consist almost exclusively of silhouettes (figure 12). With the observer well aware that he was looking at a flat surface, Egyptian artists wanted not merely to avoid sparking any illusion that he was beholding a three-dimensional form but also to stifle in advance such illusions as were implicitly present. If an arbor had to be shown, for example, the artist would first draw the ground plan, and then add the trees in profile and the enclosing fence flat against the ground, rendering everything head-on as objective surfaces (near view). Ancient Egyptian reliefs likewise never exceeded the minimum projection necessary to give the impression of a three-dimensional object viewed from one side. Artists did not aim to model all sides of a given motif evenly, to undercut its edges deeply, or to introduce any of the other means through which their counterparts in later periods would suggest the continued roundness of the invisible back side of the projecting motif.

Thus subjective surface made its way into the visual arts through the media of relief and painting. Until now, relief has typically been discussed in conjunction with objective form, that is, the plastic arts or sculpture in the round. This is probably because it does not entirely dispense with three-dimensionality, that defining characteristic of form. Although relief occupies the middle ground between sculpture and painting, it has always stood closer to the latter than to the former. We can therefore pose a contrast between relief and painting, as works of subjective surface, and works of three-dimensional form bounded by objective surfaces. What relief and painting share is their purely flat and planar ground.[2]

Independent sculpture has no ground because, to naive observers and in the near view, every object is completely contained in three dimensions; it exists autonomously in empty space. Today we know that ostensibly empty space is in fact filled with air, but ancient people would still have chosen to ignore this inherently intangible phenomenon even if they had precise and readily accessible knowledge thereof. This began to change with introduction of the normal view. Here, the object that pressed itself outward toward the observer was bordered on either side by a flat surface, from which, when viewed from a certain distance, other bodies began to jump out as well. Once the normal view progresses into the distant view, all projecting bodies merge with their surroundings to form a single surface.

Every relief and every painting must have ground, which presents itself as empty matter. The beholder's eye accepts this easily, being accustomed to seeing blank surfaces on either side of a given body. But we must inquire whether the ground in relief and painting was really intended to represent the flat surroundings of objective bodies perceived at normal and distant ranges. If this were the case, it would mean that art was admitting illusory appearances in place of the essential, which accommodates only the three-dimensional body in empty space. Art based solely on the near view would therefore have to struggle vigorously to make the ground appear not as that illusory ground visible from distant standpoints but as the unavoidable material complement of the motif, something that separates the various figures rather than binding them together. Once again, this endeavor manifests itself most directly in the art of ancient Egypt.

The oldest relief carvings — from Naqada, currently in the Egyptian Museum — are sunken reliefs with diagonally beveled edges; other monuments were fashioned at the same time in true sunken relief, with the outer edges of motifs cut perpendicular to the relief surface. In both instances, the ground is higher than the projections of the actual motifs (or at least the greater part of these), making plain that this is not the flat apparent ground of the normal view, which in nature extends farther around the edges of a three-dimensional motif when viewed from one side. In early art, we do find alongside these varieties the sort of relief that would later be adopted in Greece: that is, projecting reliefs with receding ground, typically made of wood and meant to remain unpainted. It is revealing that even though the Egyptians employed all three types of relief concurrently until the final decline of their art (evidently for hieratic rather than artistic reasons), the Greeks never adopted either variety of Egyptian sunken relief, though they were surely familiar with both.

Observation of Egyptian wall painting leads to the same conclusion. Each figure is delineated by a solid contour line and is thus displayed as a self-contained entity, while the surrounding ground asserts itself as a necessary evil.

Thus everywhere in ancient Egyptian art, ground is pushed back, and the significance that it would naturally accrue in normal or distant views is diminished further by artificial means. It is curious, therefore, that people did not simply limit their artistic activity to independent sculpture, which, as we have noted, was the medium best suited both to the improvement of nature and to near viewing. The invention of relief and of painting could only have been spurred by such external factors as the need to fill blank space. A necessary concomitant of three-dimensional form was objective surface. Such surfaces had to be filled in whenever they were expansive enough to call attention to themselves as voids; this could only be accomplished with reliefs or paintings. The most obvious example can be found in the broad outer surfaces of Egyptian temple walls. Although the decorative purpose may have provided the initial impetus, it did not take long for conceptual functions to step in. These were certainly the driving force behind the mural pictures inside the mastaba tombs, which predate any extant temple walls (figure 13). This medium yielded an advantage that a stubborn adherence to independent sculpture could never have brought about. The visualization of certain conceptual purposes demanded not just one motif but many (human figures in particular, but other subjects as well); an example would be the pictorial depiction of a deceased person presented with various earthly enjoyments. To render such scenes using sculpture in the round, one would have to fashion multi-figural groups with complex and shifting internal relationships — a notion wholly at odds with the basic Egyptian conception of the work of art as a static and self-contained unit. People evidently perceived disruptions of this basic principle of figural autonomy and self-containment as less drastic when it occurred in reliefs or paintings. In these media, any closed, consistent three-dimensionality was always patently illusory, no matter how resolutely artists struggled to deny it.

The conceptual purpose, which, as we saw earlier (pp. 135–36), paved the way for the adoption of animate organic motifs, also introduced the subjective surface to art. And just as the contest with organic nature eventually led to the illusion of movement despite early resistance and even outright opposition, it was inevitable that with the entry of the subjective surface, artists would gravitate toward the illusion of the fleeting appearances of the physical world.

As soon as multiple motifs could be shown juxtaposed on a common plane, two new relationships emerged that would be deeply consequential for all subsequent artistic production. These were, first, the relation of individual motifs to one another and, second, their collective relation to the ground.

Under no circumstances could the interrelation of motifs receive stronger emphasis than the conceptual purpose demanded. Any neglect of accepted boundaries, as in a human figure breaking out of his proper sphere, unavoidably produced the impression of the momentary, the accidental, and the mobile, and thus ran counter to the basic inclination of nature-improving art. This is why Egyptian two-dimensional arts show each individual figure as starkly isolated, both in placement and in pose or gesture.[3] We need not further emphasize that there was no question of spiritual engagement in this art. It is no accident, of course, that so many inscriptions extend across Egyptian reliefs; a pictorial language capable of exercising so little impact on its own must naturally call on verbal language for assistance. Moreover, every motif, indeed every figure, is rendered just as the artist perceived it, in the near view. Secondary attributes extraneous to the given conceptual purpose were assiduously avoided because of the complete and utter functionality of this nature-improving art, which aimed solely at grasping the essential and the perfect.

Likewise, ancient Egyptian art had no place for the free development of the relation between motifs and ground, which in the field of decorative art we call the relation between pattern and ground. Ground was regarded as a necessary evil that served to divide motifs from one another, not a factor entitled to independent, even if subordinate, existence; it could therefore never hope for explicit acknowledgment. This is especially evident in Ramesside battle reliefs, where the absence of visible ground amid the tumult of figures upsets the clarity otherwise deeply desired (figure 10). One might even say that ancient Egyptian two-dimensional arts sought to present only pattern and no ground at all and that instances when they did not succeed were due only to difficulties encountered in the actual execution. Ground is more apparent in Old Kingdom tomb paintings (figure 12), because alongside the figures there had to be rendered flowers, vases, hieroglyphs, and other such things, which allowed for sharper distinctions among the various objects. The primeval human need for the unfettered filling of empty space may also have played a role in this basic negation of ground. In the end, however, the death knell of this negation was sounded by reformed polytheism's demand for the utmost clarity and self-containment of individual motifs, which the Greeks later adopted and implemented with great resolve. Just as the Egyptians never managed to gain full understanding of reformed polytheism but rather stayed closely tied to the remnants of an earlier, though obsolete, animal cult, they also arrived at a premature standstill with regard to the artistic ramifications of the reformed polytheistic worldview. And as was the case with respect to relations between inorganic and organic, between three-dimensional form and objective surface, so too with respect to the relation between pattern and ground these artists became trapped inescapably in the conflict between old and new, thus leaving room for the Greeks to fulfill their balancing mission.

Once even limited access was granted to the subjective surface, something else had to push its way into the visual arts: color. It must have been obvious from the start that color is similarly rooted in an illusion of the optical faculties, simply because it cannot be grasped with the tactile senses. As an inessential property, color does not need to be taken into consideration by an art that seeks principally to improve nature. We should therefore not be surprised to discover many early artifacts from ancient Egypt that were never painted. Strictly crystalline rules of creation require no coloration whatsoever, but Egyptian artists frequently also let organic motifs remain colorless. Alongside these, however, we also encounter numerous more or less polychromatic works of art. This indicates some concession to organic appearances, much like curves or suggestions of movement. But, like those factors, color was also muted and veiled as much as possible by overall harmonization.

First, color was presented not as a superficial quality but, in keeping with the near view, as something essential and no less intrinsic to three-dimensional form than the objective surface. It always seems to permeate the form deeply rather than just adhere to it superficially. Used this way, color proved itself a boon to nature-improving art by bringing into sharper focus its closure and self-containment, whether as an overarching form or as an assembly of distinct and varied parts. Second, it was never terribly important that coloristic tones be reproduced exactly as they appeared in the natural object that supplied the motif. They were confined, rather, to strictly median values. After all, an art whose aim is to improve nature cannot take into account the countless nuances a colored object displays under direct or reflected light; even in its latest phases, ancient art did so only to a small degree.

Moreover, the Egyptians introduced these median coloristic values only when they would not conflict with the sense of harmony. It is well known that this sense of coloristic harmony — grounded, like the drive to produce harmonic, crystalline forms, in the physiological foundation of human beings — often expresses itself in a preference for complementary colors. For modern man, the notion of this color choice as important and necessary has faded along with the impulse to produce crystalline forms, which may be bound inextricably with the former notion in man's physiological makeup. But this idea impressed itself with tremendous force on the Egyptians and all later ancient peoples, the Greeks in particular; even the very latest works of Antiquity, Egyptian textiles composed in patterns of strong red and green, purple and raw-linen yellow, bear striking witness to this.

Such coloration, known as polychromy, is defined as possessing the following characteristics: first, solid, unmodulated coloration of individual formal components; and, second, the subordination of a color's subjective median tone to the harmonic postulate of complementary color choices. These features apply to the polychromy of not only sculpture in the round but also reliefs and paintings. As with corporality, with coloration the near view was transposed even to objects perceived at normal or distant range.

Thus far we have examined the ancient Egyptians' treatment of form and surface in organic motifs. Now we must consider the way these two factors were handled in inorganic motifs. The most important and most noble of these motifs finds expression in architecture.

Ancient Egyptian art is alone in boasting a purely crystalline building type. Our surviving examples, the pyramids, also happen to be the most ancient architectural monuments of all humanity. Here, clearly defined forms are composed of clearly defined parts, which exhibit absolute symmetry and the most elemental proportionality: expansive divergence in the direction of gravity and a counterbalancing sharp convergence in the opposite direction. Man, being an organic creature, however, has the specifically organic need for movement, and a purely crystalline form could only be appropriate when he himself had become an inorganic mass, that is, the dust of a corpse. Rooms in which living human beings circulate must be wide-open spaces full of air and light, not simply a chamber for a sarcophagus with extremely narrow corridors leading to it. Although no remnants of ancient Egyptian homes have survived,[4] experts are undoubtedly correct in imagining these as not essentially different from the mud huts of contemporary fellahin: a pyramidal base with graded walls unbroken by windows. This same basic form is also displayed by the New Kingdom temple, which will be the basis for our further discussion of ancient Egyptian architecture.

The semimystical cult of a still barely reformed Egyptian polytheism required numerous discrete, enclosed spaces that had to constitute a cohesive whole. People therefore strung together as many pyramidal supports, built on either quadratic or oblong ground-plans, as were required to serve that purpose. Thus already in the Ramesside era, we encounter the massed structure, though without the slightest effort to present the overall mass as unified and coherent, in the way Roman and especially Byzantine massed structures would successfully do. Approaching from afar, the observer always sees a simple trapezoidal surface, which, he knows, yields a pyramidal form when combined with three like planes. Once again, we are dealing with an objective, two-dimensional surface that is clearly bounded on each side, and we draw on our tactile experience to flesh it out into three-dimensional form. In themselves, however, form and surface still remain sharply distinct. This division makes itself especially evident in the way that surfaces are completely covered with figural reliefs, which freely extend themselves as decoration across the whole plane without this filling of the blank surface ever serving to make the surface appear part of a larger whole. To put it another way, we are missing that quality which in classical art we call the tectonic: the consideration of inner structure and "the spiritual." Here, form and surface are kept wholly discrete and not made to cohere.

There is one element of the exterior walls of Egyptian temples that anticipates subsequent developments. The line serving as support for the pyramid signals a gaping cut that is at odds with the self-containment of all natural things. An artificial termination had to be devised, and this took the form of the cavetto. The rows of standing leaves often painted thereon are proof that the cavetto had an organic model, perhaps a palm tree's crowning frond, which descends in a similarly concave shape, or an upright feathered headdress. Certainly the foremost function of the Egyptian cavetto was to provide a crowning terminal. But when viewed in tandem with the roll molding that it first expands in the opposite direction (swinging back outward) and then terminates, it arouses suspicion that behind the planar surface there lies a form capable of movement. This suggestion of latent movement also stems from the cavetto's curved profile, which generates a play of shadows. An organic motif, curved lines, movement, shadow effects, and the resultant illusion of plastic form: these were all new things entering into an originally crystalline and inorganic architecture. The contrast between these elements and the smooth, unshaped wall surface stretching out beneath them is thus all the more jarring, for this surface, through its unconstrained concealment with relief images, continuously threatens to obscure the three-dimensional form for whose sake it was created in the first place.

Were it not for the crowning cavetto and roll moldings that

temper the trapezoidal shape of the walls, one might assume that ancient Egyptian three-dimensional art sought to give expression only to surfaces while wholly suppressing form, at least on a building's exterior. But examination of interior spaces proves this conclusion to be false. Here, where one would expect four flat walls, one finds every measure taken to conceal the four wall surfaces and to present the eye with three-dimensional forms; this is especially the case in those interior spaces that are completely closed on all sides, such as the covered arcaded halls at Karnak (figure 14). Here the whole interior becomes a forest of pillars, with each columnar support constituting a self-contained entity — but again we encounter a fundamental division between form and surface. Pictorial motifs and hieroglyphs cover the column shaft on all sides, just as they did the exterior surface of the walls surrounding the temple and with just as little consideration for the shaft's overall shape. Thus the treatment of the closed interior space reveals that form and objective surface, though regarded as equally essential, were conceived independently and without mutual reference.

We must now say a few words about those organically shaped pillars (ceiling supports) in New Kingdom temples, which were designed to compete with the forms of plants (palm trees) or human beings (deities). We still find crystalline pillars in older tombs such as that at Beni Hasan. The transformation of these into organic forms in New Kingdom temples through a rounding off of their angular edges may strike us as simply a natural development, since Old Kingdom ceramics, for example, had already adopted some organic curvature. The aim to compete openly with specific organic species must appear remarkable in itself. It is important, however, to recall that the conceptual purpose responsible for introducing organic motifs into artistic creation gained heightened significance in New Kingdom art, thanks to the growing influence of the priestly class.

Greek Art Before Alexander the Great

In Greece, the artistic corollary of the right of the stronger — that necessary companion and offspring of the polytheistic worldview — was the principle of subordination. The weak was to be not simply negated, as it was for the Egyptians, but put into the service of — made subordinate to — the stronger. According to this principle, form and surface could no longer coexist as equals. The fiction that the objective surface was an essential and autonomous entity — a fiction without which the Egyptians would never have admitted this surface into art — was relinquished. Instead, the objective surface was assigned the role that naturally suited it best: it became a subservient component of three-dimensional form. This latter, in turn, became the indisputably dominant force — though without the subordinate surfaces, of course, it could not exist at all.

At this point, art could no longer remain bound to a strict near view. The eye had to pull away far enough away from the motif to escape the overwhelming dominance of the diverse surface parts and gain an adequate overview of the form as a whole. Whoever wants fully to appreciate the art of pre-Alexander Greece must stand one or two paces farther away from the work than he would when viewing an Egyptian piece. Of course, Greek art did not all appear at a single stroke; the Aegina figures must be viewed at considerably closer range than the Parthenon sculptures (figure 11). Nor can one declare that art before Alexander simply substituted the normal view for the near view. This happened only after Alexander the Great, when the high point in Greek art's progression toward balance was already surpassed. A full normal view signals something more than the slight concession to form necessary for expressing form's dominance over objective surfaces. Standing firmly outside the domain of tactile experience, the complete normal view also grants validity to subjective surfaces. This explains why Attic art, in which the equilibrium Greek artists always sought found supreme expression, could move beyond near-view perception but not yet immerse itself thoroughly in the normal view.

Based on what we have learned from so-called Mycenaean monuments, we can claim one thing with certainty: from its very origins, at least as far back as we can trace them, Greek art aimed to give concrete expression to the polytheistic worldview in a way that was rigorous but that would also bring any conflicting opposites into harmonious balance. Because this goal appears fully achieved in works of the Attic golden age, these must be the basis of our discussion of the relation between form and surface in Greek art prior to Alexander. In general, this relation can be expressed in terms of a suppression of objective surface in favor of form, but not to such an extent that the impression of subjective surface emerges.

ORGANIC MOTIFS

The human figure, which played a more significant role in Greek art before Alexander than in that of any other period, took precedence over all other organic motifs. It is important to distinguish between nude and draped figures.

In the nude figure, transitions appear considerably smoother, with surface parts gliding into one another along those semicircular lines and curving surfaces that manifest so beautifully the Greek balance between organic and inorganic. But even while maintaining an independent existence and self-containment, these surface parts have multiplied. For example, the forehead, which in Egyptian art consisted of a single broad surface, is now internally divided through a series of creases. Although in nature such creases are accidental features, in art the harmony of the furrows and their often rigorously symmetrical disposition give them the impression of something necessary and essential. Hair on the head, which in

Egyptian art was conceived as a compact, bulging mass with a smooth surface, in Greek art was likewise internally articulated into wavy strands or clumps. Even though the hair formation of, say, the *Hermes* of Praxiteles would rarely be found in real life, the beholder is never conscious of its strangeness; this is due, once again, to a felicitous combination of organic accidentals in the motif and inorganic determinants in the formal treatment. The multiplication of surface parts, which instantly distinguishes pre-Alexander Greek figures from their Egyptian counterparts, is nothing other than a multiplication of internal articulations. At the most basic level, this multiplication is synonymous with movement, which is why the Egyptians restricted its use to the absolute minimum. The Greeks, on the other hand, felt that they no longer needed to fear a richer and freer arrangement of internal parts, because these were now held firmly together by the larger, visually dominant form. This likewise explains why we now observe figures that display exceedingly active stances and postures, without feeling any twinge of embarrassment that their movement does not follow through. Despite the clearly momentary stance of the *Discus Thrower*, no one can perceive this figure as an organic being suddenly frozen in place, because no one would wish to see it break out of a pose so perfectly harmonious. The formula that pertains to all classical art is also relevant here: what is interesting and important is not the motif as such, dictated by some conceptual purpose, but its harmonic rendering as part of the creative contest with nature.

Nature-improving art had to resist applying draperies to the human figure for two reasons: first, because this represented a transitory element and, second, because it obscured the form. But art could not avoid it forever. Man's primitive sense of shame prompted him to wrap at least his female figures in some kind of covering. Even the Egyptians had done so, though here too they could not escape stark contrasts. Where draperies appeared, they took the shape of broad planes that thrust themselves forth independent of the human form, which in turn disappeared behind them. Egyptian plastic arts dispensed with internal pleating almost entirely.

The Greeks, on the other hand, used the accidental folds disdained by Egyptians to strike a dual balance. First, folds allowed these artists to break up the broad plane of the draperies; second, by arranging the folds harmoniously, they could imbue the transitory with the character of the essential. Drapery as a whole, however, they employed as a subservient element that would make visible and reinforce the impact of the primary subject, the shape of the underlying human figure; this, too, contrasts strikingly with the approach of Egyptian art. The drapery folds of Archaic statues appear utterly flat, as if pleated and ironed, so as to avoid shadows; here folds articulated the drapery surface while leaving unimpaired its effect as a cohesive unit. Although body and draperies were still kept separate and the near view was not significantly overstepped, the inclination toward such a shift was already unmistakably present.

The process appears complete in the sculptured figures of the Attic golden age. Here folds were often deeply cut into the drapery mass so as to generate heavy shadows, a highly significant innovation. Gone is the symmetry of Archaic fold arrangements; at first glance, the internal folds now appear randomly distributed and devoid of a governing pattern. But at a deeper level, they are arrayed to enhance through their flowing accompaniment the figure's volumetric effects. The folds stretch horizontally across the torso and the broad arc of the chest, while below, at the hips, they fall vertically downward like fluted channels. It would occur to no one who stands before the statue that an arrangement of folds so carefully weighted would be unlikely in real life; this, again, is the secret of organic harmonization. How brash and unnatural looks the conical funnel formed by the drapery stretching across the loins and legs of the Ti figure, one of those realistic Egyptian portraits from the Old Kingdom tombs! And yet the draperies of Ti may correspond better to natural appearances than, say, those of the Eirene of Scopas. The real — that is, what is natural in nature — need not be identical with what appears natural in art.

Finally, Greek art was no longer averse to establishing relationships between and among three-dimensional figures, a step that led ultimately to the composition of groups — even though in art before Alexander we cannot yet speak of groups created for normal or distant views. We refer, rather, to the pediment sculptures of Greek temples. Each pediment contains numerous sculptured figures of men and deities, which collectively bring to view some conceptually purposeful narrative. None of the figures is strictly self-contained; on the contrary, many display no in depen dent justification for existence except as part of a larger whole. The overall composition, however, is meant to be perceived not in a normal view but as a series of discrete components. Thus the parts retain their own particular integrity within the whole, even though they are clearly subordinate to it. That Greek art before Alexander had yet to arrive fully at the normal view can hardly be demonstrated more clearly. Moreover, the figures all stand together on the same plane, as in Egyptian reliefs, and the stark composition, organized symmetrically around a central peak, finishes the process of harmonizing what was, in itself, organic and accidental.

With the limited materials available today, it is difficult to ascertain with any precision the extent to which the Greeks' mission of creating balance concerned itself with polychromy. It is noteworthy that the heads of sculptures, with the exception of hair, eyebrows, and lips, were typically left in the natural hue of the stone block, with draperies alone receiving artificial coloration. The Egyptians had inverted these relations, painting in the flesh portions while leaving clothing the natural white of the limestone. A conception seems to be emerging that color is not intrinsic to the overall form but something applied from the outside, something purely superficial.

The move away from the near view is most evident in half-form or relief art. This is perfectly understandable, because planar representation fundamentally corresponds to the normal view, toward which the entire progress of Greek art before Alexander was ultimately directed. Reliefs of the Attic golden age present themselves neither as the flat, planar reliefs of the Egyptians nor as the very high reliefs of Hellenistic or Roman times. Even when multiple figures were brought together as a group, each figure was still conceived independently. This does not yet agree with the normal view, but no longer conforms to the near view either.

Lacking any large-scale works of painting, we can monitor how this relation played itself out in two-dimensional art only on the basis of monochromatic vase paintings. Black-figure paintings, with their silhouette impressions, are strongly reminiscent of Egyptian wall paintings — though, when observed more closely, the former display a significant move toward subjective planarity. This advancement reveals itself even more distinctly in red-figure vase paintings.

Here, too, the seeds of further growth already lay latent in Egyptian art. In their surface-bound arts (relief and painting), the Egyptians always constructed figures in profile so as to circumvent the foreshortenings, and the concomitant illusion of depth, that were unavoidable in *en face* representations; such frontal views posed special problems for painted images — for example, in depicting the nose. Even in profile figures, artists did their best to eliminate any subjective or superficial impression and to maintain an objective surface devoid of depth. But even the Egyptians could not simply stop with pure silhouettes. Although the chest was always presented *en face*, with both arms occupying a single plane, every beholder was well aware that hair hangs straight down from the temples and that eyes lie in front of the nose. When two-dimensional depictions showed all these features aligned on a single plane, they were bringing things that in reality lie at various depths onto one and the same subjective plane. This illusion becomes even more palpable in draped figures.

Once again, the Greeks entered into a development already in progress by deeming the simulation of a spatial dimension acceptable in two-dimensional art, as a necessary evil if not an intrinsically worthwhile goal. But they used other artistic measures, especially the principle of harmonization, to render it as innocuous as possible.

Thus we encounter in figures of Greek vase painting before Alexander a modeling of bones and muscles along with substantial indications of drapery folds. Modeling is suggested exclusively by internal lines, which define the boundaries of the various planar components of the larger form. These are not meant to suggest shadows, for that would have led to the concealment and denial of the objective surface.

Once artists had proceeded thus far, it makes sense that they no longer shied away from depicting bodies *en face*, which the Egyptians dared represent only in profile. This was especially the case with the human figure. In red-figure vases, we observe numerous instances of foreshortening, particularly in the face, hands, and feet. But this foreshortening never exceeded the barest degree of necessity. No thought was given in all Antiquity to the exaggerated sort of foreshortening that would characterize, say, Italian art between 1480 and 1580. This was not even possible, for in a purposeful art that seeks to improve nature, an accidental moment could never form the principal goal of artistic intention [*der künstlerischen Absicht*]. For Greek artists both before and after

Alexander, foreshortening was nothing more than an unavoidable means of satisfying specific conceptual purposes. This becomes most clear when we examine how this art handled interrelations of figures within a single cohesive narrative in two-dimensional representations.

We find many depictions in vase painting before Alexander of figures grouped around an objective center point in space. Although this provided opportunity for pictorially distinguishing figures in the foreground from those in the background, and thereby creating an illusion of spatial depth, this was never actually done; instead, figures were simply divided into upper and lower registers. Occlusion of one figure by another, and the lack of clarity this entailed, was avoided as much as possible, though partial overlappings were sometimes inevitable. This makes clear that in the subjective surface, the illusion of spatial depth, admissible in the individual figure only as a necessary evil, was in no way transposed to the group. The viewer was expected to back away far enough from a near view that he could easily apprehend the entire form of an individual figure beyond its objective surface parts, but not so far that he could survey several figures simultaneously. Despite the varied spiritual or intellectual relationships that linked figures conceptually, each figure remained artistically isolated. The third element, which would bind them together physically, was still missing. This could be nothing other than artistic space; with regard specifically to painting and relief art, it is surface. So long as the surface between two figures in these two-dimensional arts was solely material ground, there could be no thought of perception in the normal view. The next step was therefore the visualization of space. Although this goal was not achieved during the period before Alexander, the requisite seeds were already well in place. In order to give sensory expression to a specific conceptual purpose with maximum clarity, artists again called on a host of secondary accessories. Such accessories often presupposed a specially defined space: a bed, for example, would indicate a self-contained interior room. This spatial condition was initially perceived as a simple product of the intellectual or conceptual associations the accessories called to mind. But the process seems to have introduced the means for establishing the spatial cohesion of multiple figures once the deliberate shift was made to the normal view.

Based on the foregoing account, it will not be difficult to determine the relation between motif and ground in pre-Alexander Greece: it is identical with that between form and surface. Although the motif remains the crucial component, ground is treated as equally indispensable, even in its subordinate role as foil. Enough ground must always be available so that the motif will stand out as crisply and distinctly as possible. We must not, however, delude ourselves into thinking that this acknowledgment of ground formed the decisive prelude to future developments, at least where conceptually purposeful images were concerned. Once ground was no longer considered merely a necessary evil that one could deny or negate, as it was by the Egyptians, and once it assumed significance as a material surface, it inevitably signified the airy space surrounding figures on both sides. The "ungrounded" tumult of figures observable in Ramesside battle reliefs would have been inconceivable to the Greeks (figure 10).

INORGANIC MOTIFS

Let us begin again with architecture, the most important basis for the development of inorganic motifs. Examples of temple construction are all that have come down to us, and because of the incomplete preservation of their interior components we can envisage only their exteriors. Nevertheless, there is good reason to suppose that the interior space of a Greek temple was treated as secondary in importance. This does not necessarily mean that the Greeks dispensed altogether with an artistic handling of their interior spaces; it is just that no comparable monuments have survived. In the temple, the exterior was clearly the definitive component. This can be sufficiently explained by the special characteristics of the cult.

With regard to the exterior structure, it is not certain that the temple offers the clearest picture of the more general architectural aims of pre-Alexander Greece. The Greek temple departs perceptibly from a purely crystalline form, betraying in certain details the unmistakable remnants of timber hut structures. It is most likely, then, that it was solely for the sake of tradition — more precisely, for the sake of specific conceptual religious considerations — that until the Attic golden age the Greeks retained an architectural form that they probably would not have chosen had they been able to decide freely and according to their own aesthetic desires. In this view, the Greek temple in no way represents that pure architectural ideal that people since the Neoclassical period have thought it to be. Nonetheless, the temple brings clearly to view the approach of Greek art before Alexander to the relation between form and surface.

We have already recognized the supremacy of form over still distinctly acknowledged surface to be the basic principle of Greek formal design before Alexander the Great. At the same time, we find surfaces consistently multiplied, and form thus articulated more richly. Whereas the Egyptian temple displayed on its exterior only a trapezoidal wall surface topped by a cavetto with no indication of the uppermost termination (the ceiling), the Greek temple clearly distinguished between lateral enclosures (walls) and the primary enclosure (the roof) (figure 15). From a strictly aesthetic standpoint, the pitched roof represents a rather dubious form of embellishment for the building's flanks, for while its broad sloping surfaces could be maximally neutralized — that is, their planar extension made nearly invisible — through their upward inclination, these surfaces could never be wholly suppressed. On the short sides of the temple, by contrast, the pediment formed a crown of impeccable harmonism. But the chief advantage of retaining the visibly diagonal roof planes surely lay in the opportunity this presented for minimizing the lateral wall surfaces. The long sides of the Archaic temple *in antis* were still bounded by smooth, uninterrupted walls, whose monotonous planarity destroyed the overall impression of three-dimensional form despite the building's pitched roof. These walls could not simply be eliminated, for they were as crucial as the objective surface itself for establishing the comprehensive form. For that reason, they were retained in principle but were supplanted with rows of freestanding columns on which the roof came to rest, so that the eye now fell on nothing but three-dimensional forms. These columns were neither covered with pictorial images, like their Egyptian counterparts, nor treated as thoroughly plastic entities, as in Baroque architecture, but rather were embellished with neutral fluting. Form and surface thus remained discrete, as in Egypt, but both were equally and simultaneously perceptible, and the impression of three-dimensional form now predominated. The near view continued to prevail, because the columns were completely freestanding and not merely simulated by semicylindrical forms attached to the wall (engaged columns); likewise, the figures placed in front of, and thus enlivening, the pediment were no longer reliefs but sculptures in the round. But, as was the case with organic motifs, the overt repression of the objective surface again led to the impression of subjective planarity. This is best illustrated by the following scenario: When observing a peripteral structure from a great distance, one feels that one is simply seeing responds attached to walls. Only when one stands at a distance just slightly removed from the near view can one recognize the spatial divide between the independently formed columns and the wall surface behind them. Only then is the Attic artist's intention with regard to the beholder perfectly fulfilled.

The other art whose basic form was based on an inorganic motif (or several such) exhibits a relation between form and surface similar to that observable in architecture. We need only recall here the earliest and finest Attic vases. These display the following properties: more complex articulation into foot, belly, neck, and lip, but with each part slipping smoothly into the next in arcing curves to yield a closed and unified form; accompanying ornamentation of the parts, which both encompasses them individually and reinforces their coherence; and independent adornment of the larger surfaces, especially the main body, with pictures. It was clearly important to give as much weight to the ornamentation that separates as to that which connects. This reveals most dramatically the Greeks' divergence from Egyptian art, which, because it struggled against complex articulations, tended to eschew such ornamentation. Even the mural reliefs in Egyptian temples appear bounded by the edges of the walls rather than by discrete borders, which would have at once isolated them and integrated them into the three-dimensional form. As noted earlier, form and surface were sharply divided in Egyptian art. For the Greeks, on the other hand, the distinction between an internal field and its borders became as much a basic postulate as the harmonious equilibrium of pattern and ground. This surely resulted from the same characteristic desire for clarity in nature-improving art that also conditioned the creative expressions of the Egyptians. But the latter struggled to sustain this clarity by clinging to starkly inorganic forms, whereas the Greeks engaged far more boldly with the problem of expressing clarity in diversity.

Antiquity After Alexander the Great

Earlier, we noted that after Alexander certain attitudes came to prevail among ancient Mediterranean peoples that were no longer compatible with a strictly polytheistic worldview. From these new views we observed the emergence of works of art in which the overwhelmingly purposeful character of all art made before Alexander diminished perceptibly in importance, and we witnessed the introduction of artistic motifs that revealed an unprecedented interest in the transitory appearances of organic nature. At the same time, we insisted that for each case it would be a mistake to ascribe too much importance to these changes. The process ought to be understood, rather, in the following terms: until the reign of Constantine, the prevailing laws of both the general worldview and of art experienced progressive loosening and increasingly frequent transgression without ever being formally modified. One should not understand this to mean that those laws became dead formulas. We need only recall here the persecutions of Christians, the most ferocious of which occurred immediately prior to the final collapse of the state-sanctioned polytheistic cult. If the pagan state-cult could continue to assert itself so forcefully even under Diocletian, one must assume that the same held true for the art which arose from that cult. Let us put this a different way. Prior to Constantine, when the improvement of nature formed the supreme law of art, art's most adequate vehicle of perception and expression, the near view, likewise prevailed. This law was transgressed countless times after the Hellenistic period, when artists were tempted with increasing frequency to move toward normal and even distant views. Yet on careful inspection, the beholder is always aware that, regardless of how he apprehends the work, the near view still remains foundational to the work as a whole and that the artist yielded to the seductions of subjective surface appearances only in individual details.

Before we investigate the treatment of motifs in art after Alexander, let us acquaint ourselves with those elements that are especially well suited to impart the impression of subjective surface, that is, the illusion of spatial depth, to a given work. We shall begin by considering only works that are inherently bound to the subjective surface — which, as a group, are often called planar works and which include both relief and painting. Of these, we shall pay special attention to strictly two-dimensional arts such as painting. As we will see, at a further stage subjective-planar elements will also be transposed onto three-dimensional form, supplanting the objective surface with the subjective.

LINEAR PERSPECTIVE

As noted earlier, the objective and subjective surfaces of a given object in fact coincide, but only at their edges; surface content tends to be greater on the objective plane than on the subjective. That is, the objective surface parts of a given thing do not all lie on a single plane but rather bend outward and inward. When viewed from a distance, the surface parts that lie within these bent or curved sections remain unacknowledged. Even at normal viewing range, where all the bends and curves of the surface can be surveyed easily and precisely, the eye does not perceive these internal components in their actual size. This has to do with a special property of our visual apparatus; according to this sense, surfaces — and the bodies they form — become smaller in all three dimensions the farther they move from the human eye at a given position (the vantage point). A surface in the shape of a regular parallelogram, which, in itself, allows for no sense of spatial depth, will look like a trapezoid if its height or breadth exceeds a certain measure. The diminution of surfaces and the forced convergence of their contours become even more tangible when the extension of these surfaces into space comes into play.

The foreshortening of the relatively small human figure in breadth is so slight as to barely require treatment in art. Foreshortening in height assumes value only when a very high or a very low vantage point is used; it is revealing that this was emphatically avoided in Antiquity. There was no place in the purpose-oriented, nature-improving art of Antiquity for either the highly refined kind of art that dominated for over a century between Melozzo da Forlì and Andrea dal Pozzo or the modest attempts at lowered vantage points evident in the Adam of the Ghent Altarpiece. The foreshortening of the human figure in depth, on the other hand, is so strong, and so immediately striking, that we modern observers find it exceedingly disruptive if a work of art fails to observe it; our sense of discomfort increases the more ambitious and richly articulated a composition is. The standard according to which we moderns assess the contest with nature was not, however, that used in Antiquity.

In Antiquity, the natural objects with which art creatively competed were observed in the fundamentally tactile domain of the near view. Whatever was visually perceptible in these objects was relevant only insofar as it could be substantiated by the sense of touch. Because purely optical illusions contradicted both tactile experience and the experience of near views that derived from tactile sensation, there was no reason to consider introducing these. As we saw before, this is precisely what happened in Egypt. The Greeks, too, initially avoided any foreshortening; a powerful move toward more intimate observation of transitory natural appearances must have occurred in their cultural life more generally for the Greeks to have brought foreshortening, and the concomitant impression of subjective surfaces, into their representational art. Even then, they admitted only the most obvious kind of foreshortening, foreshortening in depth, and this only partially. Neither the Greeks nor the Romans elevated linear perspective to a fundamental principle. Although both were willing to engage with it, they did so hesitantly and without vigor, clearly with at least the vague awareness that to embrace it fully would conflict with their traditional artistic principles.

One need only recall red-figure vases to perceive the validity of this point. While foreshortening in depth does occur here in individual figures, the composition as a whole treats each figure independently, presenting it in an almost purely near view. Although we know that a row of figures placed above another is meant to indicate a group located farther back in space, this is a conventional means of communication, not an artistic one. Hellenistic artists quickly learned to portray figures in front of or behind one another; the *Alexander Mosaic*, for example, includes many figures that are largely occluded by others in the foreground (figure 4). This highly consequential step presupposed a change in the conception of ground — a change, as noted earlier, already latent during the Attic golden age. From this point on, the ground of a two-dimensional work — whether relief or painting — was grasped no longer as a necessary evil, a material that separated figures, but as a space that could unify them. As this space was subsequently filled with accessories that served to make the conceptual purpose more intelligible — though always, of course, playing a secondary role to the principal subject, the active human figure — the artistic device of background was born.

The successive arrangement of figures in depth, the conception of the material surface as space, the introduction of a background — these are all innovations that presuppose at least some artistic acknowledgment of the subjective appearance of surfaces. The eye, on its own, can take in a multitude of real bodies simultaneously, along with the space they fill; here the tactile sense is not effective. The artist must therefore remove himself several steps from a group he means to depict until he can survey it in something close to a normal view. This did not happen during the entire ancient era. No single relief or painting from Antiquity adhered rigorously to a unitary vantage point (figure 16). The primary postulate of the near view was never relinquished. Linear perspective was regarded as a forbidden fruit. Although people had fewer reservations about nibbling this fruit as the bonds of religious laws and convictions loosened, in no case did an ancient artist arrive at a deep or thoroughgoing acceptance of the normal view. If one had, it would not have been possible for modern viewers to overlook the "painterly" character of art made after Alexander (as compared with that of classical Antiquity) until Wickhoff's so recent rediscovery of it. Even in Roman Imperial art, that "painterly" character represented the exception, not the rule. Classical archaeologists naturally beheld in Roman Antiquity only the tendency to improve nature, but this emerged as a kind of haziness that they could only understand as indicative of collapse or decay. Only someone attempting to evaluate Roman art with the awareness of recent artistic developments firmly in mind can recognize this blurriness as a richly consequential innovation. One should not be surprised if modern investigators are inclined — like earlier classical scholars, but in the opposite direction — to blindly overestimate what is new, what stands much closer to them. That Roman Imperial art never proceeded beyond a sort of groping experimentation in its use of linear perspective, however, is a fact that Wickhoff himself explicitly recognized. In doing so, he hinted at the reason he felt to be most decisive — namely, that observation of linear perspective did not allow itself to be "held to unbending rules." In Antiquity, the "unbending rules" for which he so yearned were to be found only in the tactile domain of the near view.

Light and Shadow

Nature-improving art regarded solid bodies as independent entities, without concerning itself with the surrounding space. But
once this rigid conception loosened, so that, at least in reliefs and
paintings, the ground-plane could assume significance as a space
that binds together individual figures, the things that fill space in
the real world — namely, air and light — could likewise be taken
into account. Of course, neither atmospheric air nor its various
movements possess sufficient corporeal existence for ancient
artists to have employed them as motifs. If we consider optical
experience over that of the tactile senses, however, it is clear that
both elements effect certain visible changes in objects. Although
the earlier principles on which nature-improving ancient art was
based left no room for these optical changes, they were able to
take their place in art from the moment artists began (even if
reluctantly and incompletely) to take account of subjective surface
appearances. The most important such changes were the visual
transformations of objects by light; these also manifested themselves in near viewing and even in the sphere of tactile experience,
even though the tactile sense proved them to be inessential because transitory.

At extreme levels, light and shadow not only are inessential to
natural objects but indeed contradict the primary postulate of
nature-improving art: absolute clarity and self-containment. Bright
light causes outlines to lose their definition and dissolve, while
deep shadows can not only obscure but even obliterate motifs —
for what is invisible ceases to exist. Consequently, dark-toned
painting was unknown to ancient artists, and the thought of making such paintings for their own sakes, as the Caravaggisti would
later do, was inconceivable. But painting with light effects was
also foreign to ancient artists, if the essence of such painting lies
in the careful depiction of bodies in full, natural daylight. Of

course, the motifs through which these artists engaged in their contest with nature were meant to appear bright; however, this was due not to the artists' desire to show the play of transient natural light on objects but to their deep yearning for clarity, attainable only through the avoidance of anything dark.

This was the rule, in any case. But it, too, was broken many times during the period after Alexander. While such instances are significant in themselves, one must beware of overestimating their importance and drawing too many generalizations from them. In a Pompeian mural showing the Trojan horse, for example, we find an effort to represent moonlight illumination, that is, the introduction of a sharp stream of light that loosens the overall clarity and cohesiveness of the forms. But it can hardly be fortuitous that such instances are exceptional within the larger mass of Pompeian frescoes. Let us imagine a seventeenth-century Dutch town buried by a volcanic eruption and unearthed again in our own time. In the pictures that would emerge, we would discover everywhere the very pictorial elements that appeared as isolated exceptions in Pompeii.

Cast shadows were introduced far earlier — for example, in the Lateran mosaic of the "unswept floor" (figure 17). Again, the conceptual purpose gave rise to these, though in this case it overlapped with the impulse to create art as an end in itself. There was no better way of calling attention to the floor — the convincing representation of which was, after all, the very point of the image — than by means of the shadows thrown by morsels of food upon its surface.

Symptomatic as these instances may be of the changes in art and in man's attitude toward nature following the death of Alexander, they represent exceptions introduced every so often by conceptual purposes. Such thoroughgoing concessions to conceptual demands would have been impossible in the arts of pre-

Alexander Greece and, even more, of Egypt. Yet alongside these exceptional cases, shadows had a more vital role to play in art after Alexander — though only to a modest extent and with rather muted intensity.

As noted earlier, in the normal view the modeling of a given body's objective surface parts becomes visible chiefly through the shadows that interrupt the seemingly unified subjective surface. Greek artists after Alexander could certainly have taken these shadows into account as they began to move beyond strictly near-view presentations. However, they still adhered too firmly to the postulate requiring them to portray only the essential to justify the existence of shadows in artistic representation. They therefore created a sense of modeling through contour lines that suggest the palpable boundaries of the surface parts. That people were not oblivious to the significance of shadows for modeling forms is evident in the use of deep drapery folds, especially around the lower hems. These make plain that artists after Alexander did admit shadows as a more general means of modeling, at least in the case of independent figures; eventually they would also dispense with the solid lines around the periphery of the figure.

People clearly perceived the following circumstance as posing an intolerable contradiction: they had to allow for the freest organic movements, including instances of moderate foreshortening, while retaining a form of linear modeling that corresponded only to tactile experience in its narrowest sense. It is impossible, of course, to find a single painting from Imperial Rome in which modeling with light and shade was sought as zealously as was done in works by quattrocento masters such as Mantegna or Verrocchio. Indeed, the lack of relief effects apparent in Imperial polychromatic painting could lead one to conclude that art had already proceeded from normal to distant perception. But this would be an error caused by a confusion of objective with subjective surfaces. Things in Roman Imperial frescoes appear flat when compared with, say, Mantegna's figures not because the ancient artists were seeking to capture subjective appearances more fervently than their quattrocento counterparts. On the contrary, it is because the former adhered stubbornly to objective planarity and fundamentally avoided any attempt to produce an illusion of spatial depth.

AERIAL PERSPECTIVE

Experience teaches us that bodies whose volumes appear diminished by compression and other such factors stand out all the more sharply in their contours and coloration. One would also expect this to be true in cases where the dimensions of bodies and planes look smaller with increased distance from the eye. Although this phenomenon seems explicable with reference to the organization of the human visual apparatus, the opposite is really the case. The farther away from the vantage point a given body and its bounding surfaces move, the vaguer their contours, the blurrier their colors, the more uncertain the distinctions between light and shadow grow. Any clear definition within the form gradually disappears, and only a fleck of color or light remains, until, in the end, even this vanishes. This cannot be explained as resulting from the arrangement of the human visual apparatus. It is based, rather, on an external impediment to optical powers: atmospheric air. This air inserts itself like a barricade between the eye and the observed object, and sooner or later, depending on the respective strength or weakness of the object's illumination, it effects the slow obscuration and eventual disappearance of the object. This phenomenon is herewith designated aerial perspective.

If nature-improving art apprehends the physical as the essential component in natural phenomena and reproduces it as such, then this art must not only disregard aerial perspective but also

make a concerted effort to avoid it. The closed outline is a requirement of all nature-improving ancient art. Even when this
does not consist of a firmly articulated line but rather is implied
by a chromatic boundary, the ancient work of art leaves no doubt
as to where the motif ends and the surrounding space begins. The
form remains delineated as sharply as if it could be physically
touched; never does it dissolve into flecks of light or color, as in
seventeenth-century Dutch art. As a result, it may seem that
ancient art — even during its final phase of decline — could reserve
no room either for aerial perspective or for the distant-view perception that this required. Yet we encounter in the colored paintings of Imperial Rome certain features that are only attributable
to the observation of aerial perspective. These involve neither
dissolution of contours — for which, as we have seen, there was no
place in Antiquity — nor a blurring together of light and shadow.
Rather, we find an equalization of color tones, which was not
prompted solely by the distant view but had already begun to
emerge with an attentive near view. This signals a fundamental
shift in the basic conception of the function of color in art.

The earliest art, that of Egypt, employed color the same way
in two-dimensional works as in sculpture and relief. It conceived
color as something fused with form but not really essential to it.
Greeks before Alexander regarded color as something even less
intrinsic to art — though because we possess no examples of polychromatic painting from that period, we cannot verify this with
certainty. After Alexander, people must have come to recognize
color as something that merely adheres to the surface of things.
We must presume this at least in those cases where a body was
modeled in light and shadow, for if the color of flesh displays a
lighter nuance here and a darker one there, it must be obvious
that this chromatic shift is based on an optical illusion; the tactile
form remains the same whether it is illuminated or in shadow.

Careful observation of the color of an object's surface reveals that what often appears to be tonally uniform when viewed from a distance actually contains many chromatic nuances and that a seemingly uniform coloration is thus merely the end result of the interaction of a larger variety of colors. This phenomenon is grounded only partially in aerial perspective; it arises to a much greater extent from other physical laws, above all optical ones. To discuss these in detail would lead us too far afield and in any case is unnecessary for our current purposes. But one thing does link this phenomenon to aerial perspective: that its impact likewise depends on the distance of the eye from the object perceived. This distance cannot be so small that the eye can clearly distinguish the individual flecks of color; the eye must be able to apprehend these in their final, unified appearance. However, the effect does not necessarily require the distant view or even the normal view, least of all in the portrait heads and still lifes that Roman Imperial artists rendered on the basis of their observations in two-dimensional art. It is surely no coincidence that late antique artists chose precisely these domains for experimenting with their observations of coloristic phenomena. In both portrait and still life, after all, the accurate recording of transitory natural appearances was an end in itself. Nonetheless, even the portraits of Imperial-age Egypt or the pictures of fruit at Pompeii retain such great harmonism and such strong form that one would neither mistake them for the work of Hals or de Heem nor puzzle over their inclusion among the great treasures of Antiquity. Even the most progressive Roman artists, in any case, never moved beyond the single figure in their equalization of color tones. As the most important characteristic of ancient painting, alongside its early experimental treatment of linear perspective, Wickhoff cited its lack of attention to reflections, by which he doubtless meant not only reflections of light but also, and just as important, of color.

225

The three new elements just discussed, which stamp art made after Alexander with the appearance of leaving behind the old and moving toward new goals, found their most tangible expression in painting. These elements must also have left their mark on relief and ultimately on fully three-dimensional monuments. We shall now briefly investigate these.

In reliefs, the forward-moving influence was expressed in two main ways: first, the increasing projection of individual motifs from the ground; and, second, the distribution of motifs on multiple overlapping planes.

Greek artists of the Hellenistic period (for instance, in the Pergamon Altar) clearly aimed to proceed more decisively beyond the near view than their predecessors had done during the Attic golden age. Neighboring figures, though tightly connected with one another, still occupied a single plane; the ground surface had not yet become space. But this element soon made its appearance, as demonstrated by the well-known reliefs on the Arch of Titus (figure 18). Here we have several tiers of figures that are meant to be perceived at correspondingly varied levels, though this in fact happens only to a modest extent. In general, figures in the background receive the same kind of observation, midway between near and normal views, as those in the foreground, even if the level of outward projection is stronger in the latter. Linear perspective thus seems to be applied just as "gropingly" in reliefs as in painting.

Thanks to this increasingly strong projection of motifs on multiple planes, a sharper contrast of light and shadow, totally unknown to Egyptian art, also entered reliefs. But as the shadows cast by the projecting motif now fell on the ground, they called attention to the fact that this was indeed still ground and not yet the space artists had sought since the Hellenistic period. If people wanted to approximate reality more closely, they had to reject the ground surface completely and replace it with something that gave the impression of empty space. This was the very last phase of Roman Imperial art: motifs — for example, of foliage — were undercut in such a way that the shadows within the deep crevices, not those on the blank surfaces surrounding the motif, would be interpreted as empty space. Once artists actually broke through that ground, they ended up again with three-dimensional sculpture. The independent sculpture in the round tended toward the objective surface no less than the deeply undercut reliefs did. Simultaneously, and running parallel with this phenomenon, the progressive heightening of surface projections increased. Most of the figures on the porphyry sarcophagi from Santa Costanza (now at the Vatican), which represent the culmination of this trend, look more like independent sculptures attached to an outer surface than they do reliefs.

Relief originated as a barely discernible projection from the ground, meant to suggest the objective surface of an object oriented toward the viewer. The zenith of the medium's development was reached in Rome during the final phases of the pagan Imperial age, with the highest possible projection of the motif from the ground, on the one hand, and the full denial of ground, on the other. In such works, the eye no longer apprehends objective surfaces separately from the overall impression of form. At this point, the relation between ground and motif also underwent a critical change. Egyptian artists had treated ground as a necessary evil and therefore had sharply distinguished it from motifs (see p. 197), and Greek artists before Alexander had granted it a freer, if still subservient, status, but now ground was liberated completely. This liberation at first appears to be a negation; however, when we encounter works wherein the ground forms a distinct pattern, this can only indicate that it earned itself a place equal to that of the motif. To be sure, this phenomenon only became widespread during the early Christian period (fourth and fifth centuries). So long as the polytheistic worldview prevailed, with its right of the stronger, there was no place for equality or the emancipation of the subservient. But we can already discern the trend taking shape after Augustus: the apparent breaking away [of relief forms from the underlying surface] characteristic of Imperial art is nothing less than an acknowledgment of ground. The impact of a motif that appears to have been broken through resides nearly as much in its empty intermediate spaces as in the pattern discernible between them.

The three elements of subjective surface had the least destructive effect on form. One would be hard-pressed to find a statue from even the very last days of pagan Rome whose ancient origins would ever be in doubt. Although the repression of objective surface parts in favor of overall form was taken further here than during the Attic golden age, no artist after Alexander aimed for the appearance of subjective surfaces alone, such as we find in Bernini's Baroque works, with their sophisticated foreshortenings and meticulous framing devices. Form remained oriented toward the near view that could be tested against the tactile senses, not toward the subjective planar effects of the distant view. Parts that would be struck more directly by light were worked up with corresponding care, whereas those that would fall into shadow were treated more negligently — but artists never went so far as to pull large areas of the objective surface away from view. No artist polished marble works, as Bernini would later do, so as to soften both the transitions between surface parts and the overall modeling in the round. The relatively frequent use of bronze, however, suggests that the natural sheen of this material made it particularly well suited to the production of such transitions.

Three-dimensional art transgressed the limits of nature-improving art most tangibly when it came to the unification of multiple figures into a group. Judging from our observations in the field of painting, it should come as no surprise that Hellenistic art advanced well beyond the conception that had prevailed during the Attic golden age. Multiple figures were now combined into a genuine group, at least physically. This required the observer to back away from a strictly near view if the resulting entity was to be perceived as a cohesive whole. Nonetheless, all the figures in the group remained bound to a common plane; this is the case, for example, in the *Laocoön*, which, like the Pergamon Altar, presents itself as a relief freed from ground (figure 1). Even in cases such as the *Farnese Bull*, where planar unity could no longer be so rigorously sustained, composition provided the strongest substitute (figure 19). In the Vatican *Nile*, by contrast, the main figure appears too dominant for us to be able to apprehend the whole as a truly independent group. It is most revealing that the Romans, for all their progress toward subjective planarity, advanced no further along the route forged by the Hellenistic Greeks. This path would have led to the fully free group, such as was created in the sixteenth century by Guido Mazzoni and Antonio Begarelli. There was no place for such things in a nature-improving art that accommodated only the near view.

It only remains for us to examine the changes that polychromy wrought on three-dimensional sculpture in the period after Alexander. That such changes were unavoidable was due, first, to shifts in the treatment of color in painting and, second, to the natural, even if modest, affinity of three-dimensional form for subjective planarity. We already discovered the prerequisite for all further changes in polychromy to be the conception of color as attached externally to a given surface rather than as integral to a form. In painting, this shift in attitude led directly to colorism, that is, a striving toward equilibrium and mood. It is therefore to be expected that artists would also make the transition from polychromy to colorism in sculpture.

The relative importance of our regrettable inability to demonstrate this transition on the basis of surviving artifacts should not be overestimated. In the whole history of art, there is no example of an artist's seeking a completely coloristic treatment of sculpture. Artists engaged with such an approach to a certain extent; they might, for example, give the cheeks of a figure a pinkish hue, as in the imperial clay busts from Egyptian tombs. But neither in Antiquity nor in the modern age up to the present day was the goal to create a total appearance of reality. This was sought especially seldom in life-size figures, though somewhat more readily in small ones; the very format of the latter eliminated any possible illusion that they were something other than a human creation. The reason for this reluctance lies in the fact that art always seeks to compete with nature but not to replicate its creations. Things that nature forms in three dimensions, man wants to reproduce, as if by magic, in two; even if he accomplishes this with the utmost accuracy, no observer will doubt whether it is a human work or a work of nature. The coloristic painting of life-size statues brings with it the danger that the sense of confusion or interchangeability with nature that art always strives to avoid will arise. This explains the low regard in which art lovers hold painted wax figures. We can thus conclude that (1) the painting of sculpture (as well as reliefs) can never extend far beyond the basic rules of polychromy; and (2) art that is no longer compatible with the basic rules of polychromy must distance itself from any kind of painted sculpture. This is all the more true if other means to a successful contest with transitory organic nature are abundant.

If Wickhoff could conclude, despite the paucity of extant evidence, that the painting of sculpture and relief still enjoyed widespread — indeed, in his opinion, universal and unconditional — acceptance in early Roman Imperial art, this in no way implies that such art was fundamentally inclined toward the appearance of subjective planarity. Surviving remnants exhibit a more poly-chromatic than coloristic treatment. Artists now obeyed the limits imposed by the natural motif in their selection of colors, whereas earlier people had followed the arbitrary dictates of the decorative purpose (as in the preference for complementary colors). One can also point to the fact that in the late Imperial age, just as reliefs were being fashioned with deeply undercut (apparently broken-through) ground, the painting of sculpture was almost entirely for-saken. This is evident in the treatment of the eyes in late Roman heads, where the pupil is articulated no longer through paint but through the activity of the chisel. One can scarcely imagine anything that illuminates more dramatically the contrast with the basic prin-ciples of ancient Egyptian art. In Egyptian painting, all modeling was suppressed and all form reduced to a flat silhouette. In late Roman statuary, even the pupil was not treated as an objective surface but was brought to view by means of three-dimensional form. Why should polychromy be necessary when form itself was capable of supplanting color?

Let us now test the model we posited for organic motifs — gradual suppression of objective surface and amplification of overall form until a partial sense of subjective planarity emerges — against the relation between form and surface in the inorganic motifs of art produced after Alexander.

For reasons already discussed, the transmitted type of the Greek temple was not the most propitious field for the uncon-strained expression of mature Greek art's aesthetic demands. Our knowledge of the temple's development after Alexander is all too fragmentary to give us a clear idea of what this was like. But enough has come to our attention that we can determine at least the basic progression of inorganic motifs in the three-dimensional arts of Antiquity after Alexander. The most important point is that

231

within the overall form of the temple, the peripteral columns — independently formed surface components — were pulled back and attached to the closed wall as responds (pseudo peripteros). Because these rounded responds produced a dissonance with the straight wall, they were replaced with pilasters in nearly all mature Hellenistic architecture (with whose temple designs we are, admittedly, not very familiar). These pilasters now supported the ceiling just as freestanding columns had done earlier. The intermediary wall surfaces, which remained unembellished, assumed the status of surface fragments subordinate to the dominant pilaster forms. The result can be described as follows: the freestanding supports, once pulled back and incorporated into the walls, make the overall form of the building more compact and imposing, whereas the pilasters, which present themselves as fully rounded piers that support the ceiling, even though they are really only reliefs, create a subjective planar impression. The late Roman temple, about which we know far too little, seems to have moved even further in this direction; see, for example, the temple of Venus and Roma in the Forum. These cases make clear that the traditional peristyle building type had been abandoned completely, something that was possible only once art was conceived, at least to some extent, as an end in itself. Other architectural works from Imperial Rome offer more instructive examples of this kind of original invention than do the fragmentary remains of temples.

In the period after Alexander, new building requirements allowed people to pose the question as to the most practical kind of form freely and without recourse to tradition; theaters and baths opened themselves particularly well to such investigation. The solution could only fall on the side of centralized crystalline form. But because crystallinity always privileged surface parts over the form as a whole, and also because of its severity in general, it no longer corresponded to post-Alexander tastes, which preferred heightened expressions of organic movement. The sharp edges of the centralized crystalline prism were therefore smoothed over, and thus the cylindrical wall was born. If this design were found only in Roman theaters, we might be able to justify the conclusion that practical requirements gave rise to centralized form — though this would do little to explain why the centralized structure assumed a specifically circular shape. But any such motivation must be set aside with regard to the Pantheon, a building that could just as well have served as a bathhouse or other such purpose. The rotunda form of the Pantheon sprang from aesthetic considerations alone (figures 20 and 21).

Thus the curve, which was introduced early in small-scale works of practical function, finally broke into the last bulwark of absolute crystallinity, architecture. Ever since the earliest Egyptian dynasties, the wall was not conceived as anything but a flat, regular surface, whereas now it was bent into an arc, with all its surface parts smoothed into a single continuous form. This had important consequences for the ceiling, which traditionally consisted of an entablature surmounted by roof rafters. Not content to adhere even to this convention, artists granted curves to the ceiling as well, shaping it into a centralized domed calotte.

External form was the definitive factor of artistic intent in all antique architecture. On the outside, the Pantheon appears as a compact form bounded by curves both in height and in depth; only its lateral boundaries consist of straight vertical lines (figure 20). The impression of a cohesive form triumphing over discrete parts is disrupted only once, in the cornice dividing the upper rim of the cylinder from the lower edge of the domed calotte. This exemplifies the principal way of articulating form handed down by Greek temple construction; the load of the ceiling is distinguished in the same way from the supporting walls as the load of the straight roof was distinguished from the supporting pilasters. It is therefore

supposed correctly that the currently smooth brick cylinder originally was overlaid with marble pilasters or responds.[5] This would
mean that the system of the straight wall articulated by half-
rounded (relief) forms, which we encountered first in the Hellenistic pseudo peripteros, was now transplanted onto a curved
wall. One wonders whether such transposition was acceptable in
itself. We know that the system was devised to bring to view the
vertical support of a horizontal load. Like the round arch, however, the dome exerts parabolic rather than horizontal pressure, or
what is called lateral thrust. Let us assume for the time being that
although the Romans were well aware of this fact, they did not
believe that they needed, or ought, to take it into consideration.

In the end, we can only surmise the relation between form and
surface that originally confronted beholders on the exterior of the
Pantheon. Other circular structures, which dispensed with marble embellishments from the very beginning because of the appeal
of these to potential looters, have retained their exteriors intact.
To be sure, these buildings — theaters — differ from the Pantheon
in two key respects. First, their walls did not need to support a
solid ceiling; second, they did not have to create the kind of absolute lateral closure for the interior space that had been necessary in the Pantheon, which, being unfenestrated, was illuminated
solely by means of an oculus in the dome. When we discover the
Hellenistic respond system applied to the Colosseum, it can only
have been as a decorative device for articulating the wall and not
as a support for a (nonexistent) ceiling (figure 22). And when we
find, in contrast to the Pantheon, the cylindrical wall punctured
by numerous openings, we must bear in mind that it would be
difficult to discover another building purpose that tolerated this
kind of fragmented external enclosure. Nonetheless, it is possible
to discern two characteristic features of the new spirit of art (*des
neuen Kunstgeistes*). First, this art deemed acceptable the employ-

ment of a serious structural-symbolic system for purely decorative purposes, even in cases where the essential preconditions for its existence were manifestly absent. Second, this art eagerly took advantage of the rare opportunity to puncture the external form in many places. In other words, people devoted ever more zeal to simulating fully three-dimensional form by means of partial forms (reliefs), and they strove to eliminate any ground that remained between these partial forms by punching it through. We encountered both phenomena earlier in organic motifs.

It is worthwhile to examine more closely the exterior of the Colosseum. To attach a single row of engaged supports around the massive wall cylinder would have required outrageous dimensions for the responds as well as the cornice: hence the subdivision of the wall into four stories. In the three main levels, the system comprises responds (the cylindrical wall would not have accommodated pilasters), which, in conjunction with the continuous cornice, appear to support the next story. The respond shafts are not fluted; too deeply was the artist's concentration focused on the overall form for him to divert his attention to a finer handling of individual smaller forms and surface parts. The portion of the cylinder between the responds is punctured by round arches, which attract the eye no less powerfully than the wall surfaces between them. When taken in conjunction with the dominant form of the cylinder around which they rhythmically march and with the responds that flank them, these arches establish that marvelous impression of movement that the gigantic mass of travertine continues to arouse in beholders.

Let us pause for a moment with these round arches. We can look at them in two main ways: first, as an interruption or puncture and, second, as an arched shape. In both respects, they represent an innovation in the development traced thus far.

Since we are fully accustomed to the puncturing of wall surfaces by windows, it is difficult for us to see the arched openings on the Colosseum as anything but windows. Monumental buildings of classical Antiquity, however, did not include windows because these would have compromised the closed unity and clarity of the overall form. Neither the ancient Egyptian temple nor the Greek peristyle building accommodated fenestration; the Hellenistic system of walls articulated by pilasters was no different. As soon as a window breaks into a surface part, this part assumes an independent structural significance that runs counter to the basic logic of the system. It would indeed be astonishing if a principle so basic and fundamental to all nature-improving art should, as early as the time of the Flavian emperors, be not only transgressed but even overthrown completely.

If one looks more closely at the Colosseum, one notices, first, that the straight jambs of the arches come to rest on the cornices — that is, on a ground — and, second, that the arches fill nearly the whole space between each pair of responds. This makes plain that the round-arched openings are not windows at all but doors — in other words, intercolumniations similar to those in peripteral structures. At this point, we must ask why the Romans did not simply continue using the peripteral system, with a straight architrave resting on columns. Evidently, the obstacle lay in a technical difficulty. If the columns were distributed proportionately, the distance between them would have to be so wide (which indeed it currently is) that the architrave would be unable to bear the load. This leads us to the critical point: the round arches that appear to be windows are really the structural supports of the levels immediately above them (and thus the roof as well, if one existed). The round arches are in fact what the responds pretend to be. Naturally being well aware of this, Roman builders extended relieving arches around the brick cylinder of the Pantheon; because the Pantheon was not meant to contain windows, however, their openings had to be walled up. In the Colosseum, then, we encounter the same phenomenon we noticed earlier in the Pantheon: just as in the latter case the weight of the domed ceiling appeared to be bearing down vertically, in the former the lateral thrust of the round arches seems to be replaced by the vertical pressure of the horizontal cornice on the columns. Let us examine more closely why this happened.

It was certainly not due to aesthetic restraint. Any child or simpleton knows that he can create an opening by placing a horizontal beam across two vertical posts and that the one will exert a downward pressure on the others. An arch, by contrast, is constructed by means of a complicated assemblage of parts; the point where the arch bears weight resides not where one would expect it to — namely, on the imposts of the arch-bearing supports — but in the keystone at the apex of the arch. Understanding the interplay of pressure in arch-based architecture requires more than the naive mentality of the child who builds up his house of cards according to the laws of crystallinity. Artists had already reached that point by the time of the Flavian emperors; domes and round arches were accepted no less openly than curving walls, and for the same reasons. We must therefore ask why artists hesitated to take the next step and plant the arch directly on top of the supports (to form an arcade) and instead disguised the arch as a subordinate puncture (to form a window). This was surely because any overt acknowledgment of the arch would have entailed the aesthetic rehabilitation of the wall surface, and this would have run contrary to an essentially nature-improving art. Here, too, we witness the same phenomenon we encountered so often in organic motifs: artists let themselves be enticed onto paths that deviated from established principles but could not, in the end, summon up the courage to abandon those principles for good. Only just before Constantine officially swept away those old laws do the first true arcades appear on the exterior of a large-scale building (Spalato). The triangular spandrels carefully squeezed between (and indeed almost smothered by) the responds on the Colosseum, the entablature, and the arches arrayed as if they were horizontal beams could now expand into independent, unconstrained subjective surfaces oriented toward the distant view. At this point, we have exceeded the boundaries of nature-improving ancient art. It remains for us to study one more side of three-dimensional arts after Alexander, and this is the handling of architectural interiors.

In the closed interior of a building, the beholder gains no impression of overall form. One observes an endless sequence of adjoining wall surfaces all around, but one cannot see the bounding edge of a solid mass against the air. However, nature-improving art craves the comforting containment of form within stable boundaries. Egyptian art satisfied this desire by filling the entire interior space with three-dimensional forms, which fragmented the wall surfaces all around and thereby neutralized their impact: witness, for example, the hypostyle hall (figure 14). In the closed interior of an Egyptian temple, the same thing happens as in a Greek peripteral structure: the beholder's view of the solid outer wall is obstructed by the columns aligned in front of that wall. While the fragmentary remains of Greek monuments made before Alexander do not allow us to determine precisely how artists achieved the balance they sought throughout their interior spaces, buildings produced after Alexander offer some, if only elementary, insights. Let us turn once again to the Pantheon (figure 21). Although the current state of the interior hardly represents the original arrangement in its details, two features must have been both planned and executed from the start. These were, first, the elimination of all independent three-dimensional forms in the interior and, second, the alternating disposition of niches and projecting aediculae in the lower part of the wall cylinder.

The removal of all discrete three-dimensional forms indicates the extreme position to which this art had moved with respect to its ancient Egyptian forebears. The earlier architecture admitted the appearance of forms only if their surfaces were forced into invisibility, whereas here surfaces were wholly embraced. The new acceptance of surface probably arose from the conviction that this was the surest way to awaken the beholder's memory of the over-all external form. This was a dangerous path. From a modern perspective, it seems to point straight toward unmitigated subjective planarity, but it actually led to a successful solution in the simple rotunda. The lowest parts of the wall, where the objective surface would have leaped too forcefully out at the beholder, were punctured with niches. These niches so effectively complemented the curvature of the walls and vaults that the artists even dared to interrupt their sequence by introducing a harmonious contrast of rectangular niches with aediculae. For the rest, the whole cylinder up to the base of the dome seems to have employed the customary half-form (relief) system as articulation. The coffers lining the dome are but softened reminiscences of the crystalline straight ceiling, in the same way that beam encasements suggested the reveals of round arches. At the same time, the concentric dimensional displacement observable in the ceiling coffers proves how conscious the Romans were that an indefinitely receding vault would automatically lead to subjective planarity (here, in the observation of linear perspective). It is likewise significant that the niches inside the Pantheon make no appearance on the exterior. There they would have compromised the compact appearance of the overall form, whereas inside the building they served to diminish the impression of planarity and to augment the impression of form.

A vault, in essence, is a centralized form; as such, it is best suited to strongly centralized architectural structures such as the rotunda of the Pantheon. But it was inevitable that people would one day try to transfer the vaulted ceiling to a quadrangular room. It is surely not fortuitous that the most important surviving monuments of this kind stem from the Diocletian and Constantinian periods. Although they thus fall outside the realm of ancient art strictly defined, these buildings still manifest the fundamental postulate of nature-improving art: absolute clarity and self-containment. For this reason, and because their origins must lie in earlier times (see the Baths of Caracalla), we will consider them now.

We are dealing in these cases with oblong rooms spanned by barrel or groin vaults. Because the groin vault presented the more complicated case, we shall confine ourselves to its examination. Let us begin with the great hall of the Baths of Diocletian, which today forms the transept of Santa Maria degli Angeli. In keeping with the postulate of clarity, the mighty groin vaults rest on gigantic columns aligned in front of the wall. Certainly the earlier kind of half-rounded form, or respond, would not have sufficed to serve this buttressing function; but insofar as the supporting form detached itself from the wall, people were apparently ready to allow form and surface to split apart in much the same way as happened in the Egyptian hypostyle hall or even the Greek peripteros. We must not, however, ignore a fundamental difference: in the earlier cases, the surface was meant to be concealed by the forms placed in front of it, whereas in the vaulted Roman halls surface appeared fully exposed. Thus the wall surface finally achieved independent status alongside three-dimensional form. One needed only to discard nature-improving art's postulate of clarity, and the wall surface could flow into and merge with the vaults to create a single, unified subjective surface.

Second Period: Nature-Spiritualizing Art

The Revolution of Late Roman Art

The triumph of the monotheistic worldview swept away the last remaining obstacle to an unequivocal move from near to distant view. At the same time, this victory destroyed the motivation that pressed art made after Alexander ever closer to overcoming the near view — the contest with nature for its own sake, or art as an end in itself. Thus it happened that late Roman art after Constantine put its new freedom to use so indifferently, indeed listlessly, that modern people have been unable to accept its products for what they are, the normal continuation of Roman Imperial Antiquity. These works are instead widely regarded as symptoms of an unprecedented regression into primitive barbarity. Because the contemporaneous appearance of barbarian throngs within and outside the empire seems to support this assumption, there is scarcely any mistake so deeply entrenched in all art-historical scholarship as that of the "barbarization of late Roman art by Germanic influence." Having learned to distinguish the differences between the art produced after Alexander and that of purely "classical" Antiquity, one can now begin more compellingly to correct that error regarding late Roman and early Christian art.

ORGANIC MOTIFS

Nature-improving art in all periods has found its supreme expression in sculpture. The visible focus of the cult was not the picture but the statue of the deity. Until the last gasp of the pagan worldview, therefore, three-dimensional form was exalted as the artistic medium through which the physical essence of organic nature could reach its most perfect outward manifestation. If the new worldview proclaimed the physical realm inessential, sculpture was instantly doomed. Of course, surface was no more essential than form; but because the pagans never regarded it as such, there was no fear of misunderstanding. Meanwhile, the significance of the once-almighty form was necessarily diminished, because it potentially constituted a dangerous source of lapses into polytheistic views. This, above all, explains why sculpture plays such a minor role in late Roman art. Only in those domains where a deep-rooted cultural legacy could support its retention and where the threat of errors was minimal — for example, in sarcophagi and diptychs — do we find sculpture in late Roman art.

Late Roman and early Christian statues are characterized by two features: first, the neglect — that is, insufficient demarcation and emphasis — of surface parts; and, second, the unilateral, even exaggerated focus on individual details. These characteristics gave rise to the making ugly of late Roman figures (discussed in the chapter on motifs), though this was now transposed to the relation between form and surface. Although scholars wanted to recognize in both elements — as in that general ugliness — symptoms of barbarism, all these features signal nothing other than a singularly decisive move toward the distant view. Not only the diminution of surface parts, described earlier, points to this conclusion. The unilateral accentuation of details, particularly the eyes and the deep ridges of the hair, can likewise be explained as a move toward the distant view, for when we look at things in nature, we can apprehend everything with equal clarity only from a near viewpoint. When we observe things from a distance, only individual details appear sharp and attract the eyes' attention. Everything else is subsumed into the subjective appearance of the whole surface and must be completed imaginatively by beholders on the basis of their experience with the near view. Because this results from continuous practice, it occurs unconsciously and, so to speak, mechanically.

To do justice to late Roman statues, one must observe them from a distance. Only then will the figures lose the rigid and lifeless quality that adheres to them so disturbingly when viewed up close. This lifeless quality has been used to support the assumption that after 313 or 476 C.E. the development of visual art had to start over, as it were, from scratch. Many scholars thought to have discovered here a direct parallel with ancient Egyptian art, which likewise began with statues that appeared rigid and constrained. In fact, early Egyptian and late Roman approaches to the figure occupy two extreme, opposing poles. If one places one's eye very close to the surface of an Egyptian statue, one becomes aware of the boundless life with which the artist has imbued it; the figure loses the rigidity it had displayed when viewed from a distance. The late Roman statue, on the other hand, looks coarse and stiff when observed up close and gains ever more inner life the farther one moves away. In other words, the planarity both figures appear to share is different on each side; objective surface comes to the fore in the Egyptian figure, subjective surface in its late Roman counterpart. One will never find an ancient Egyptian statue that looks "rough." Just as we recognized the apparent "ugliness" of late Roman figures as "Organism," we find that their "roughness" is really nothing other than [a sign of their orientation toward] the "distant view."

The early Christian hostility toward three-dimensional form also applied to the half form, or relief. Whenever this medium appears, it exhibits a distinct inclination toward increased planarity. Even the carvings on the socles of the Arch of Constantine, made to honor that emperor's triumphal entry, are patently flat reliefs (figure 23). Because they instantly call to mind the low reliefs of ancient Egypt (figure 13), it is no wonder that some scholars have concluded that an eruption of barbarism had wrenched art back to a primitive stage and thus caused it to begin its whole developmental process anew. But whoever attentively compares Constantinian with Egyptian reliefs will quickly recognize the differences between them — differences that shed light on the intervening development over the course of millennia. Egyptian low reliefs consisted of partial forms perceived at close range, whose projections — which, though weak, were true to tactile experience — were quickly subsumed into the ground surface and appeared to lie on top of it like cutout pieces. Constantinian reliefs, on the other hand, look like high reliefs that have been squashed flat (if you will forgive the term), with contours that do not dissolve into the ground surface like cutout pieces but rather stand out crisply against it. This proves again that Constantinian reliefs are oriented toward the distant view. They present themselves not as part of an objective plane that can be constantly tested against the tactile senses but as part of a subjective plane, which is rooted solely in the speculative experience of our visual senses and which, when viewed from a distance, will produce the illusion of three-dimensional form. We find the same treatment of relief as flat-pressed form in late Roman ivory diptychs.

If we witness surface suddenly appear to regain supremacy during the latest phase of Roman Imperial art, we need not understand this as a regression into the objective planarity that characterized ancient Egyptian art. Rather, we should regard it as a logical advancement toward subjective planarity and thus fully in keeping with the whole preceding development.

It is instructive in this regard to consider Imperial portraits on late Roman coins. These are characterized not only by their flatness but also by the myriad lines that collectively constitute the emperor's bust. Although initially these may recall the linear style of vase painting before Alexander, one soon notices that the lines do not, as in classical art, cleanly demarcate discrete surface components such as drapery folds but merely suggest these in a sketchy way. This betrays the same movement toward subjective planarity that we perceived in Constantinian reliefs.

The same can be said about the two-dimensional arts, especially mosaics. Late Roman mosaics are characterized by a lack of
linear clarity that is obviously intentional. This phenomenon is
frequently regarded as a symptom of now-internalized barbarism.
Like any other aspect of late Roman art, however, it is a natural
product of the post-Alexander movement toward the dissolution
of solid forms into indistinct planes, as well as of the general
monotheistic hostility toward anything "beautiful" as representing physically improved nature.

As in every artistic period, in late Roman times the motivating
force of art reached its purest expression in the so-called industrial arts, especially the surface ornamentation of utilitarian objects. Bronze belt ornaments and similar items, found throughout
the western Roman Empire up to the western side of the Balkan
Peninsula, are exemplary in this regard. These display, in chip-
carved relief, tendril ornaments inherited from the Greeks. But
the old motifs are handled in such a highly refined way that, first,
it becomes difficult to distinguish pattern from ground and, second, the eye perceives not individual forms but only light and
shadow. This brings to view the equalizing, anti-"pattern" spirit
of late Roman and early Christian art no less vividly than do the
coloristic and planar tendencies.

Let us pause here to take a comparative backward glance at
our starting point in ancient Egypt. There, too, we found reliefs
wherein the ground was so densely covered with motifs that the
overall clarity suffered. Although the resultant appearance is similar on both sides, we are in fact dealing with diametric opposites.
The Egyptians did everything possible to guarantee the exclusive
domination of motifs and the complete negation of ground. The
effect was unsuccessful only because the disappearance of ground
entailed the disappearance of a weaker element, without which the
stronger could not prove its superiority. The late Romans and early

Christians, on the other hand, sought to emancipate ground and make it equal to the motif. They therefore chose for their primary motif not the human figure but other organic things such as vegetal tendrils, which they then proceeded heavily to de-Organize. They did this not so much to improve them physically as to strip them from the very outset of as much organic "meaning" (with respect to the meaningless configurations of ground) as possible. The Egyptian battle relief was intended to be viewed at close range; the farther away the beholder moves, the more tangled and indistinct the crowd of figures appears. The late Roman ornamental relief, on the other hand, was oriented toward the distant view; at close range, the eye perceives simple motifs of muddled clarity, which on their own lack any artistic appeal whatsoever.

INORGANIC MOTIFS

In a centralized structure such as the Pantheon, external form dominated so completely that the surface parts receded in comparison (figures 20 and 21). We can only surmise how these parts were handled in their details. As we saw in the Colosseum (figure 22) — and as we could conclude on the basis of the previous development — surface components as such were still (and indeed had to be) taken into consideration. In the building's interior, which was beginning to achieve greater importance than in earlier cultic buildings, artists now sought to strip away the planar character of objective surfaces at the lower level, where these surfaces were close enough to be touched, by adding niches. With regard to the exterior, then, the next step could proceed in only one direction: the surface parts would lose their objective, bounded planarity and join together as lower-order forms to constitute the larger overall form. This occurred when artists brought those niches to the exterior, which, within the Pantheon, served to make the formal articulations more readily perceptible. This was one of the most consequential steps in the entire history of three-dimensional arts, for with this the massed structure was born.

Let us consider the rotunda of the Pantheon (figure 20): its overall form will be fully apparent to anyone who approaches it, even up to just a few steps away. Now imagine the same rotunda equipped with multiple projecting niches: its overall shape could be accurately determined only when the observer moves far enough away that all the components, insofar as they are apprehensible with a single glance, have entered the visual field. Thus we can conclude that the massed structure is intrinsically suited to only the distant view. Because the distant view had no place in nature-improving art, the massed structure could fully enter art only in the late Roman and early Christian period.

When viewed from a distance, the massed structure makes an impact solely through its three-dimensional form. Because a form seen from a distance appears as a two-dimensional surface, the impression offered by a massed structure is always subjective-planar. This impression was now consciously privileged, while anything that could summon the image of an objective surface made up of individually bounded parts was avoided. The wall surfaces were left totally smooth; the pilasters, half columns, and so forth were eliminated; and the vaulted ceiling grew directly out of the weight-bearing outer wall.

This process was already carried out at least partially before Constantine, when art was conceived as an end in itself but the right of the stronger was still a dominant principle. Now this right required the subordination of partial forms to the overall form, just as it had earlier called for the subordination of surface parts. This demand reached clearest expression in the dominance of a central dome over secondary half domes. Although Byzantine artists would somewhat later invent the most perfect formulation of this type, we encounter its earliest representatives already in pre-Constantinian Rome. Indeed, people here felt so confident in their new achievement that they dared once again to break the dome-supporting cylindrical wall into a polygon in order to accommodate the niches. Artists did not worry that the now-crystalline sides would revive the objective surface parts, for they knew that the distant view would merge all surface components into a single overarching subjective surface.

Two points deserve special attention here. First, the oldest demonstrable motif of the monumental massed structure — its incorporation of projecting niches — first appeared in the interior. Such heightened attention to the interior in Roman Imperial art would necessarily shatter the traditional nature-improving system based on the near view. The objective surfaces inside the building could not be forced to submit to the overall form, because the form could never reveal itself as a whole, as something visibly bounded. No recourse remained but to transform the objective surfaces into subjective ones; this process was successfully accomplished by pulling back the surface into curving niches. After artists had thus gradually made the gaze receptive to subjective-surface impressions, it was only a matter of time before the building's exterior would begin to receive corresponding treatment.

Second, it is important to emphasize the difference of all this from our starting point in ancient Egypt — a comparison that is always supremely instructive. Again, the two kinds of art appear to be intimately related: in the centralized late Roman building, with its smooth masonry walls devoid of any structurally symbolic mural ornamentation, form and surface seem to split apart — just as in the Egyptian temple. Once again, however, we are really observing opposite approaches. We discern nothing on the Egyptian exterior but the objective surface embellished with reliefs, behind which the form emerges only when we are close enough to touch it. On the late Roman central-plan structure, we perceive nothing but the smooth form devoid of reliefs, which, when viewed from a distance, presents itself as a subjective surface.

The Roman central-plan building is the unmistakable product of an art that is considered — insofar as this was possible in Antiquity — autonomous, that is, an end in itself. Any art guided chiefly by purposeful considerations would, presumably, not have suddenly felt compelled to depart from crystalline form in favor of circular form, as in the Pantheon. What would late Roman and early Christian art do when faced with the task of inventing an architectural form for a specific new purpose? The problem posed itself in the need to create a Christian cult building; this was, indeed, an issue of such far-reaching consequence that its solution would determine the future direction of the three-dimensional arts for at least the next millennium. The late Roman early Christians were uninterested in pondering which form was most *beautiful*, but rather sought the form that was most *functional*. The first question would likely have been answered with a nod to the centralized structure; but, as our earlier discussion made plain, beauty was the last thing on which the western Romans laid any value. Thus the fateful choice fell on the side of the notoriously most practical type of structure: the forensic basilica.

Romans had long employed the basilica as a practical structure; its elevation by early Christians to the prototypical house of God makes clear their intention of humility and self-degradation. The same can be said for their renunciation of vaulting. But for the rest, the basilica reveals the same conception of form and surface observable in the late Roman centralized structure. That it was not some fundamental aversion to organically animated spatial form that led people to adopt the crystalline structure is apparent in the retention of the apse with vaulted half domes and round-arched arcades. Although the basilica is primarily a massed

249

structure, it dispenses with any single dominant feature due to the strict refusal of early Christian monotheism to recognize the right of the stronger. Even the concept of the facade was largely suppressed in the early Christian basilica, though it was retained at a very basic level. The same reasoning underlies the shifting of the tower to one side as soon as it was introduced. But the most crucial feature of the early Christian basilica was that each of its four distinct exterior sides could be observed completely independently, without the overall form ever coming clearly into view. Each side now offered the beholder's eye a subjective surface, for, as we remarked earlier, a massed structure is only perceptible from a distant viewpoint. The result can be formulated as follows: In the basilica, subjective surface gained such dominance that the underlying form receded completely. The thousand-year dominion of form over surface, like that of pattern over ground, was thereby shattered. Now windows could pierce the walls in any way at all, for the outer wall surfaces were no longer articulated by pilasters that supported the roof rafters via a cornice; the straight beamed ceiling of a basilica provided a more compelling aesthetic motivation for this than the Pantheon, in any case. Now, too, the brick wall could present itself as what it really was, the bearer of the roof.

All this had occurred countless times in utilitarian buildings since the invention of the timber storehouse, but it would not have been possible in a temple of God so long as nature-improving polytheism reigned supreme. Many scholars have attributed this phenomenon to the supposed crudeness of the partially barbarized late Romans; now that we have reached a position where we can reasonably survey the larger development of art after Alexander, it is not difficult to see just how little such a view is justified. In this case, we find the same indifference to beauty evident in contemporaneous statuary; and it is certainly significant that at the same

moment artists took the opportunity to articulate outer wall surfaces modestly with pilaster strips and blind arcades. This indifference to beauty is no sign of some alleged barbarism, but rather
represents the logical culmination of a development that unfolded
over thousands of years. Although this outcome was assuredly due
to certain substantial nonartistic influences, these did not come
from the barbarians — who, despite what people tend to believe,
remained wholly innocent in that regard. Rather, this result derived from a new, all-encompassing spiritual world-power, which,
if it wanted to emerge victorious in its battle against older forces,
had to relinquish some things that were good and beautiful.

As for the interior of the basilica, one would expect the impression of subjective planarity to present itself here even more
strongly (figure 24). In this domain, an assertion of the objective
surface constituted less of a threat, because the gaze could never
apprehend the various parts of the interior (such as the side aisles
and transept arms) at one glance, even in a single direction. For
the same reason, a clear image of the spatial configuration of the
external form, which was still present in the centralized structure,
was now impossible. What instantly attracts the gaze on entry into
a basilica is the linear-perspectival foreshortening of wall surfaces
and supports in the direction of the terminating apse. This emphatic spatial directionality guaranteed the perpetual dominance
of the subjective-planar experience in basilican structures; the side
aisles and transepts accomplished the rest.

It would be erroneous, however, to believe that late Roman
artists developed the linear-perspectival element in basilican interiors consciously. Such a view is contradicted, first, by the interruptions of the central vessel by chancels and altars and, second,
by the embellishment of the broad wall surfaces along the main
transverse arch. Being typically decorated with mosaics — that is,
emphatically two-dimensional representations rather than reliefs —

these surfaces seem directly reminiscent of ancient Egyptian mural paintings, as in the tombs at Beni Hasan (figure 12).[6] To delineate the difference between the two with sufficient clarity, I will simply point out that whereas the figures at Beni Hasan are rendered in strict profile, those in the early Christian mosaics usually turn their heads outward toward the beholder. This is the case in all Roman apse mosaics; even in the ceremonial double procession in Sant' Apollinare Nuovo in Ravenna, with its Byzantine affinity for the near view, all heads are directed in at least a three-quarter angle toward the beholder.

The basilica, as a product of the socially equalizing tendency of western Roman Christianity, enjoyed unconditional esteem only in the western half of the Roman Empire. Insofar as monumental structures were used for cultic purposes in Rome at all, the nature-improving centralized design tended, from the time of Constantine onward, to be employed for mausoleums and baptisteries; Santa Costanza holds special interest here as the foundational attempt to transform a cylindrical building into a massed structure. But the basilica, too, found widespread acceptance in the eastern caesaropapist part of the empire, at least in the years just following the triumphal advent of monotheism. It even seems to have gained the upper hand in territories such as Egypt, where the desire for liberation from the right of the stronger may have been no less intense than it was in the western Mediterranean. Only gradually did the courtly culture of Byzantium, with its absolutist forms of the state-cult, learn to assert itself — and even, under more propitious circumstances, to exercise an (at least temporary) influence on western lands.

Byzantine Art

In accordance with the general distinction between western and eastern Roman monotheism, Byzantine art grasped the relation between form and surface in a way different from its western Roman counterpart. Western artists, in keeping with their focus on the socially liberating core of Christ's teachings, combated anything in art that signified (that is, they eschewed form in favor of surface and motifs in favor of ground), while treating the contest with transitory nature with indifference, if not acceptance. By contrast, the more strictly monotheistic eastern Romans — the Semites in particular, but also the Greeks — regarded autonomous art as the most horrific atrocity; as heirs to a universal Roman monarchy founded on the right of the stronger, they viewed the equalizing tendency in art with even less sympathy. Byzantine artists had to reject the distant view because of its transitory quality. At the same time, a decisive return to the near view was out of the question because it entailed a rehabilitation of form, which did not appear compatible with a strictly monotheistic art. Hence the ambiguous or contradictory impression Byzantine art generally awakens in the beholder; the fixing of already existing forms as canonical likewise finds explanation in this circumstance. We may draw the general conclusion that the Byzantines made use of their inherited predilection for the distant view whenever they were not obliged to engage in a contest with transitory organic nature. In cases where they did have to do so, they returned to the near view, just as they reached back to inorganic motifs.

In order to substantiate this conclusion with hard facts, it is, exceptionally, more practical to treat inorganic motifs first, because in this domain the connections with Roman Imperial art manifest themselves most directly. For architectural forms, the Byzantines found no reason to stray from the path of their Roman Imperial forerunners. Because the centralized massed structure oriented toward the distant view was congruent with their belief in the right of the stronger, Byzantine artists not only preserved that form but indeed brought it to fullest perfection. They did this by adopting the Greek cross with a central dome, a design that, though not unknown to the earlier Roman Imperial period at least for interior spaces (see the second-century Praetorium in Musmieh), achieved its universally dominant position only in the East. The restoration of fragmented crystalline walls in the four arms of the cross had come to seem, by this point, completely unobjectionable; indeed, the contrasts these generated allowed the central dome fully to display its triumphal character. This was the most perfect architectural form that man had ever conceived; and it is no accident that even Western people continually returned to it later, when art once again became an end in itself.

As for organic motifs, the Byzantines shared the early Christian disdain for sculpture in the round as representing the quintessential sensual embodiment of repugnant heathen beliefs. Therefore, for any insights we must turn to two-dimensional art. This in itself reveals that Byzantine artists did not return to the near view in any substantial way. In two-dimensional arts, it was entirely characteristic for the Byzantines to avoid as much as possible portraying the nude — the very form that in the sculptural arts was the most intrinsically fruitful and appropriate of all representations of that noblest organic motif, the human figure. To apprehend clearly the relation between form and surface, we must therefore investigate the formation of draperies. Here again we encounter the foldless arrangements of late Roman diptychs, which, especially when taken in conjunction with the flat-pressed reliefs, betray a distinct concentration on subjective planarity. Somewhat later, a drapery arrangement of fine, dense folds became increasingly common, which at first glance appears to imitate Greek linear modeling prior to Alexander (mentioned with regard to ornament at p. 435, n. 2). Although, in keeping with analogies drawn elsewhere, there is certainly some correctness in this idea of imitation, the crucial point is that the Byzantines produced something completely different from what their Greek predecessors had intended. Whereas the latter used the lines of the drapery folds to splinter the overall form into easily apprehensible surface pieces, the Byzantines employed these lines to fracture as much as possible the form of the body supposedly residing beneath the draperies so as to obliterate its individual formal components. The end effect, again, is a sense of subjective planarity.

As for two-dimensional Byzantine art, this relationship is most clearly revealed in enamel works. At first glance, everything seems to indicate a return to the near view: the ground is apparently stripped of spatial significance; each figure appears to be conceived separately and independently; modeling is continually mitigated by lines; colors are once again applied solidly and without gradations. This is all done, however, for the sole purpose of stifling any direct suggestion of organic life. That the figures turn toward the beholder and that the draperies exhibit the sort of sketchiness also evident in relief figures make plain that Byzantine artists did not set out to suppress completely and unconditionally the distant-view presentation toward which their Roman Imperial heritage led them.

Islamic Art
Islamic is the only art that not only declared sculpture inessential but even, so to speak, prohibited it by law. Islam neither tolerated the three-dimensional form for organic motifs, as the late Romans did, nor proclaimed it a necessary evil, as the Byzantines did, but rather forbade it entirely. This is true for the treatment of motifs both in freestanding sculpture and reliefs as well as in two-dimensional arts. Anything that might demand or facilitate the illusion of three-dimensional form was suppressed, especially the surface parts. Nothing remained but purely subjective surface. This makes clear that Islamic art is really a logical continuation of post-

255

Alexander art — indeed, the most consequential in the whole history of art. The circle was therewith brought to completion: art returned to its starting point at pure and absolute surface. But whereas in ancient Egyptian art surface was merely the objectively tangible component of a larger formal whole, here it became the superficial subjective appearance of that whole.

The design of an Arabian palmette, with its strong contours and lack of modeling, is directly reminiscent of the ancient Egyptian lotus blossom. But its solid contours are the product of a more mature stage in the development of Islamic art, which aimed, at least in part, to achieve equal status with Byzantine art. Anyone who wishes to familiarize himself with the most basic tendencies of this art will find them most lucidly manifested in the stucco ornament of the Ibn Tulun Mosque in Cairo. Here, contours are incised very deeply into the stucco; in some cases, a single contour delineates two adjacent motifs in such a way that all ground between them vanishes. This establishes an equilibrium, akin to that found in late Roman and early Christian art, which clearly aims to rob form of its final claim — the contour line — while suppressing any ground that could serve as a foil.

The fate of Islamic art comes sharply to view in the development of inorganic motifs, especially architecture. The general hostility toward three-dimensional form required that the mosque not display any noticeable exterior shape; rather, it consisted of a plain rectangular wall enclosing a large courtyard. The building only needed to show an interior space, whose effects, as our earlier analysis suggested, had to be strictly planar. The building appears as an open hall punctuated by multiple rows of freestanding supports, as with the Egyptian hypostyle hall. Its openness, however, differentiates it markedly from its Egyptian counterpart, so that the most fundamental prerequisite of three-dimensional form — closure — falls away. The most important interior furnishing, the mihrab, stands out in neither size nor proportion but solely in its tile mosaic and inlay decoration. The column shafts (usually spolia) are the only three-dimensional element — though these continue to make a subjective-planar impression through their monotonous and directionless multiplicity.

In the latter half of the Middle Ages — obviously through the impact of mature Byzantine art, whose monuments the expanding Muslim people were constantly discovering in vanquished Eastern territories — this extremely rigid approach began to grow more flexible. Three-dimensional form reclaimed its place; not surprising, this was the centralized, subjective-planar form, that is, form lacking any fragmentation into surface pieces and containing purely flat mosaic decoration. Two basic types are discernible: the true mosque type, a domed rotunda, which had always been employed for tomb structures; and the madrasa (school), consisting of an open rectangular courtyard with four barrel-vaulted halls attached at right angles to form a Greek cross (but without a central dome). At the same time, it was characteristic that this shape was clearly visible only from within; from the outside, additional buildings obscured it. Form was not allowed to assert itself externally; meanwhile, inside the building people's eyes were drawn principally to surfaces, whose flatness was accentuated by intricate mosaic ornamentation. The open courtyard of the madrasa reinforced the sense of planarity.

The Muslims were not satisfied with this solution for long. Already the buildings of Saladin and Kalaun in Cairo betrayed a movement toward facade construction, which must have arisen from their contact with the West. Increasingly, Muslim designers and architects realized that it was predominantly the external form that gave essence and character to a structure. One can directly trace the growth of this insight in the madrasa mausoleum of Sultan Hasan and the mosque of Qait Bey. After the fall of

Constantinople, the Turks took the final step by simply transposing the Byzantine domed structure onto their mosques. If one wants to gain an overview of the Islamic shift in sensibility from the Hegira to the nineteenth century, one need only turn to two especially instructive examples in Cairo: on the one hand, the Amru Mosque, hidden by the rubble of Fostat and, from the outside, utterly unassuming in its fortresslike appearance; on the other, imposing and widely visible from its location on the citadel, the cylindrical mass of the Mehemet Ali Mosque with its double minarets. The latter's appearance alone proclaims, more forcefully than any aesthetic discourse could do, that the structure is a three-dimensional form; no coercive rules are capable of stripping it of this character so long as man's artistic activity continues, as it has always done, to take as its starting point the contest with nature.

Italian Art

Art in Italy lifted itself more slowly from the barbarism into which it had sunk after the Great Migrations than did its counterpart in the North — thus runs the conventional wisdom about the progress of Italian art before Giotto. We have recognized in this alleged barbarism — at least with regard to the relation between form and surface — an underlying presentation in the distant view. One must therefore reformulate the theorem to state that it took longer for people in Italy than for their northern peers to depart from the degree of distant viewing attained in late Roman art. The reason the North stood so far ahead of the South in this domain will become clear only once we have examined more closely the situation in the North.

Once Tuscan artists finally stepped away from the late Roman distant view, two options were possible: either a more vigorous move toward the distant view or a return to the near view. The

Tuscans opted for the latter. They had hinted much earlier that they would make this choice when they granted entry to Byzantinism — an acceptance that signaled nothing other than a return to the near view and the right of the stronger. The Tuscans thus proved themselves heirs of the ancient Italians; in subsequent periods, they wrenched other Italian groups along behind them who had meanwhile diverged further from the basic principles of Antiquity, thanks to their commingling with foreign peoples.

This led to a wider cultural opposition between Italians and Germanic peoples, which persists to the present day. With regard to nature, the Italian is still essentially a proponent of the right of the stronger: in his view, man deserves to be counted as the prime venerable creature of nature, whereas animals and plants are merely useful things. He continues to enclose his country property within walls and gates, while disdaining on principle the "nature park" and "natural flower" — despite his apparent (because lucrative) responsiveness to the cultural habits of Northern foreigners. If western Roman Christianity taught Italians one thing, it was to relinquish their submission to an abstract notion of the state and therewith slavery. For that reason, the Tuscans could never be satisfied with Byzantinism either. The individual must reach his full potential, but he must also accommodate himself to a higher unity. The law to which he must thus submit is neither as categorical as classical Antiquity's right of the stronger nor as abstract and spiritual as Germanic peoples' law of loyalty. The individual was accorded liberal room for play to a certain extent; beyond that, he was obliged to submit to the one law shared by the general population.

If one applies what has been outlined above to the visual arts of Tuscany, one arrives at the following conclusion: Generally speaking, Tuscan art returned to the near view, but not the same degree of the near view toward which classical Antiquity strove. As a result, Tuscan art took greater care to establish a balance between near and distant views, checking the distant view in places where late Roman art had gone too far (for example, in freestanding sculpture) and expanding the near view in places where ancient art, bolstered by its own governing principles, had clung to it too tenaciously (for example, in the distribution of motifs in two-dimensional arts). This process became clearly visible in the eleventh century and drew to a close at the beginning of the sixteenth.

ROMANESQUE PHASE

The essence of this transformation revealed itself first and most distinctly in the buildings of Pisa. A distinct predilection for the centralized structure is already noticeable here. Not only do the baptistery and tower conform to this system, but the system is also transposed to the basilica in the form of the crossing dome, which clearly manifests the reawakened need to condense the massed structure into a higher unity. The most important of the detail elements is the masking of exterior subjective surfaces with zones of shallow colonnades — that is, a serial alignment of individual forms. This system parallels the Greek peripteros; both systems, indeed, unmistakably express the same conditional individualism (the aristocratic state).

At the same time, we must not overlook a fundamental difference: whereas the Greek peripteros supported a roof over its cornice, the Pisan exterior colonnades bear no cornice and therefore no roof. As porches, these colonnades function as mere interruptions of the wall, whether they be surmounted by rounded arches or a flat architrave. Consequently, the columns are no longer free supports for a downward-pressing load but the shaped remnants of a wall that has, but for the horizontal connections between the columns, been eliminated. This disruption of the wall alone did not suffice to eradicate the subjective-planar impression entirely.

That was accomplished only through the infinite repetition of a single form — the easy rhythm of the column shafts, uninterrupted by even the most modest contrast (through groupings). The resultant absolute clarity appears decidedly oriented toward the near view; a viewer standing very close to any of the porch's openings perceives no less than if he were observing the same thing from a distance.

Especially noteworthy in the Duomo — the only basilican structure among Pisa's three great Romanesque buildings — is its confident articulation of the facades, a feature that had never been an issue during the early Christian period, with its equalizing tendencies. This makes explicit the differentiation of objective surface parts, a phenomenon that runs parallel to the inverted centralizing tendency of the dome and thus manifests a resolute desire for balance.

We gain a very similar picture from sculpture and reliefs of the period, such as Nicola Pisano's pulpit in Pisa. The very depth of the carving proves that this was no beginning *ab ovo*. The figures from Roman Imperial sarcophagi that served as models reveal that the last phase of classical Antiquity, with its planar tendencies, was best suited to the aims of Romanesque art in Tuscany. Compared with the late Roman figures, however, an emphatic return to the near view is evident here. Heads are modeled in clear objective planes in which previously exaggerated details modestly recede; hair lies in wavy ringlets that demand to be viewed up close. Draperies fall in long, deep, discrete folds that still, as in Byzantine art, manage to conceal the body beneath, instead of acting as a mere accompaniment that allows the body to emerge as a self-evident entity. This sort of drapery produces the same effect as the cloaking of a building with colonnades. In both cases, a fragmentation of form into surface pieces is initiated, but with no compelling harmonization of external clothing with underlying core —

that is, with no fully satisfying fusion of both components into a higher unity.

Our evidence for Romanesque approaches to two-dimensional art comes mainly from the field of manuscript illumination. In the beginning, the change was least apparent here, though in the later development this kind of work assumed a leading position. Even in Roman art, the near view prevailed so thoroughly in the depiction of groups that any art that sought to establish balance would have found some impetus to augment the distant view. Thus it happened that the most important accomplishments of Roman Imperial two-dimensional art were no longer fully appreciated — not foreshortening, not modeling through light and shadow, not even linear perspective, which would never be taken further than it had been by the Romans. Ground, even when it was made of gold, continued to be conceived as space; the selection of this most precious color proves that people imagined the sacred figures standing upon it as inhabiting a correspondingly remote and blissful space. Purposeful Christian art required no further earthly accoutrements. Even when these appeared imperative, artists easily knew how to subordinate them spatially to ground.

GIOTTESQUE ART

Giottesque art pushed what was begun in the previous period as far as a purpose-oriented Christian art would allow. Three-dimensional form again directed itself toward the near view. This change manifested itself, among other things, in the building facade's now receiving figural reliefs (as at Siena, Orvieto, the Campanile in Florence). In this context, we can also point to heightened attempts to unify the basilican structure by means of a crowning dominant element (as in the project of the Florence Cathedral dome). In organic sculpture — that is, of the human figure — one notes a gradual coalescence of body and drapery, at least above the hips. The same holds true for relief forms, insofar as one is looking at the nude body and its drapery. In the relation of figures to their spatial ground, on the other hand, a considerable swing toward the distant view is noticeable (Andrea Pisano). This conversion of the planar arts to the distant view is evident to an even greater extent, of course, in painting. Giotto and his workshop introduced innovations that pointed unambiguously toward increased distant viewing, particularly in their efforts to create a cohesive spatial context for large multi-figured compositions of conceptually purposeful content, such as hagiographic legends (figure 5). In this respect, Giottesque art may have substantially exceeded everything the Romans achieved; it went far enough, in any case, that no further advancement was possible so long as art did not seek to become an end in itself.

THE RENAISSANCE

The Renaissance brought the equalizing process to its culmination. Among organic forms, the nude human figure recovered the esteem it had not enjoyed since the time of Constantine. Even the studies necessary for this shift demanded the near view. With regard to the draped figure, we can trace three distinct stages: first, the establishment of unity between body and drapery, but with a continued employment of traditional long folds (Donatello); second, progression to a looser treatment, with shorter and transverse folds (Verrocchio); third, a completely free handling of drapery, which, however, soon led back to bulky and less distinct modeling and, with that, the distant view (Andrea Sansovino).

With regard to the most important inorganic form — the architectural structure — we must distinguish between religious and profane varieties.

The form of church architecture. Exterior. The centralized structure was now the explicit goal of artistic endeavor — even if the still-purposeful character of artistic production favored the basilica, at least at the beginning of the period (Brunelleschi). Remarkably, the aim was not a simple centralized building but a massed structure, as we find even in Bramante's Tempietto. Here the Renaissance agreed with Byzantinism, though it diverged decisively from the latter by postulating a fragmentation of form into objective-surface pieces. People did not have to search far for a means to this end; it was readily available in the architectural remains of Antiquity. People discovered that the ancient wall-masking system provided exactly what they needed in their own time. It was therefore adopted in full — not only the supporting elements (such as pilasters and responds) but also the form of the load (beams and cornices). The idea with which antique people associated this system had become essentially impossible, however, due to the inclusion of windows, which were indispensable to the basilican structure. The ancient wall-masking system allowed for no such puncturing of the wall. In the Renaissance, this in no way signified a structural-symbolic distinction between support and weight; rather, it was, more simply, an articulation of the wall surface. The pilasters (and so forth) relate to the wall surface as pattern does to ground; during the Renaissance, these terms sprang vigorously back to life. Regarding the proportional distribution of the wall, we must also, alongside the ancient wall components, factor in windows, which had disappeared in Antiquity. If proportionality was to be the supreme postulate, these alone made a thoroughgoing imitation of ancient models impossible.

   Interior. Romanesque art tried to mitigate the intrinsically subjective-planar character of the basilican interior by integrating column galleries similar to those on the exterior. In this respect, the Giottesque period closely approached the path of Northern Gothic. But as soon as people of the early Renaissance latched onto the ancient wall-masking system, they transposed it to the basilica's interior as well. By the fifteenth century, the tendency toward centralized form had become so overwhelming that the longitudinal, surface-oriented basilican system no longer presented any compelling problems in itself. This explains why no truly great or original basilican structure was erected in Florence or Rome after Brunelleschi and why every part of Saint Peter's basilica in Rome that had been built before the papacy of Julius II was demolished. New Saint Peter's, in essence, belongs to the subsequent period.

Profane architectural form. Exterior. In Italy, the roots of a monumental treatment of secular structures lie in the fourteenth century and earlier. From the very outset, these were dealt with in terms of pure surface rather than three-dimensional form. Although palaces sometimes stood independently, they appeared far more often among a line of neighboring houses. The wall was then given several rows of windows, corresponding to the number of stories. Renaissance artists divided these stories using distinct bands (not cornices) and distributed the windows on each level according to the rules of proportion. All the windows were identically framed with arches and sometimes further separated by colonnettes. (Tuscan examples continued to set the standard, but in Venice things proceeded somewhat differently.) Although the resultant uniformity appears to correspond to the near view, a basically planar character prevails. In certain instances, such as the Palazzo Rucellai, the ancient wall-masking system was attempted, but it was not widely adopted. This was probably because if the windows were arranged proportionally, they would stand too far apart; or perhaps people hesitated to simulate a three-dimensional form in a situation where the form could never come to view. Bramante was the first artist to apply the system successfully to an imposing freestanding palace structure, the Cancelleria (figure 27); the Palazzo Giraud represents a small-scale excerpt thereof.

But the finesse of a wall-masking system that aims at a more limited distant view — which people generally regard as the Song of
Songs of Renaissance harmonism — conflicts with the planar effect
of the masses. This is the case even though the simple antique
rhythm was abandoned and replaced in the massed structure by
a syncopated rhythm of contrasts (for example, with windows of
various sizes grouped together between every two pilasters):
thus Bramante chose to endow the corner masses with a sense of
movement by shaping them into projecting pavilions. Here the
master made the discovery later Baroque architects would so extensively employ: namely, that powerful masses could be effectively articulated only by means of other masses. There was little
room for such experiments in the balance-friendly Renaissance,
with its preference for moderate expression and for individual
integrity in multiplicity; Bramante undertook such an endeavor
only once, and this strictly out of necessity.

Interior. Here we will consider not individual rooms but court-
yards, for which the broken-wall system found in Pisan buildings
seems tailor-made. There was no need to fret about the lack of
correspondence to inner form, for here we find only surfaces
and no form whatsoever; the galleries were directly necessary for
communication. The repetition of columns in a simple rhythm, as
at the Cancelleria, again appears aimed at the near view — though
Bramante had also offered an example of syncopated grouping
in the courtyard of Santa Maria della Pace. This proves yet again
that the perfect equilibrium of the High Renaissance represented
but a narrow peak that all the great masters — including Raphael
and especially Michelangelo — overstepped the moment they
reached it.

Relief. In their treatment of the single figure, reliefs took part
in the retrogressive tendency of independent sculpture. With
regard to connective planar elements such as linear or aerial per-

spective, on the other hand, they competed with two-dimensional arts; this was already the case with Donatello and Ghiberti. Here we could cite numerous features mentioned in our earlier discussion of wall masking in inorganic structures.

The field of painting zealously cultivated modeling in light and shadow along with both linear and aerial perspective — though it never made any of these elements an end in itself. While these problems provoked and preoccupied the visual arts, they did not push conceptual content into the background. Color, which reveled in joyful, vivid, saturated tones most readily appealing to the near view, offers the most palpable means of gauging this phenomenon. In this domain, the higher optical unity that arises only when perception occurs at a certain distance was absent, as was the case with the other two subjective-planar elements. Such unity was essentially unavailable to the Renaissance because of the elemental desire in this period's art to establish balance between the fully optical and the fully tactile perception of nature.

Draft of the Missing Conclusion

Architecture in the Middle Ages gave rise to original productions north of the Alps, particularly in regions where the Germanic population had settled in such great numbers as to completely subsume the earlier Romance inhabitants: namely, in northern France and Germany. Where Romance peoples formed the majority — for instance, in southern France — centralized forms predominated; but victory ultimately belonged to the basilica (figure 24). Nowadays no one would claim that the Germanic element introduced anything truly innovative into basilican architecture. What is important is that this architecture was moving from the hands of people of antique artistic traditions into the hands of new groups, who were free to take fundamentally different paths from those chosen by their ancient forebears. For centuries after 476 c.e., basilicas were being erected in northern France and the Rhineland by people of Romance, not Germanic, origin. But gradually and imperceptibly, the latter grew to be not only patrons of architecture — they could already act in that capacity thanks to the material wealth that flowed into their hands — but architects as well. The sophisticated intellectual views of early Christians and Muslims toward art and science — views that ancient cultural peoples achieved only at the end of a long and complicated development — were far removed from the barbarians. The latter instinctively grasped the building for what it really was: three-dimensional form. In the beginning, to be sure, they regarded the basilican design transmitted by the Romans as sacrosanct and therefore immutable. But eventually they began to regard it with greater objectivity.

The development of medieval architecture is typically presented as the story of the vaulting of basilicas. This cannot be correct, because signs of the future development already appeared in the flat-roofed basilica, which therefore cannot have resulted from efforts to find the most perfect solution to the technical difficulties posed by vaults. Although vaulting would inarguably become normative in later times, it did not appear as the preeminent goal in itself. Rather, vaulting was merely a means to the same end toward which innovations in the flat-roofed basilica were aimed. This end was nothing other than the creation of a form for the structural mass of the basilica, which could only occur through the suppression of the previously dominant surface.

Because functional demands required the Christian temple to be, above all, an interior space, all formal experimentation began inside. People were conscious from the very outset that they were dealing with a massed structure that was, as such, incompatible with the harmonic principles of simple, cohesive architectural bodies. For this reason, the simple column or pillar had to give way to the compound pier. This formal complication of the support soon extended into the adjacent moldings of the arches; a matching articulation smoothly conjoined these arches with the supporting piers (figure 25), even if, at least initially, the horizontal abacus intervened at the impost level. Thus their plastic formation uniformly defined the piers and arches as structural elements distinct from the walls above. This system was carried over to other wall openings, namely windows and doors; the latter, with their multiple stepped jambs and archivolts, bring this innovation to view with special clarity. Nowhere was a balance with surface sought; people let surfaces stand alone, unframed and unconstrained, while lavishing attention on the three-dimensionally shaped structural members and thereby allowing form to emerge unmistakably as the privileged element.

Thus we witness a reinstatement of the right of the stronger — though in a guise quite different from the ancient version. In classical art, three-dimensional form gave the illusion of performing a structural function and thereby threw the entire wall into fetters. In Germanic medieval art, form revealed the actual inner function, for the arches were in fact genuine supports — though initially, in the rounded arch, the critical function of the load-bearing crown was not emphasized clearly enough, whereas the function of the upright supports beneath the imposts appeared unreasonably exaggerated. As a solution to these problems, the pointed arch represents the most truthful element of Germanic Christian architectural design. The genuinely supporting parts received appropriate emphasis, while the large surface masses that remained were left to themselves.

Into this underlying schema vaulting now entered. The formation of the interior continued to be the primary focus of attention throughout the Romanesque period. People sought harmony of the masses, equilibrium among the various partial masses, and cohesion among the numerous distant forces, all of which would lead to an overriding unification of the multiple parts. Connecting the formal components of the ceiling with those of the arcades proved to be Columbus's egg [a surprisingly simple solution to the problem]. The transverse ribs were, after all, nothing other than the transverse arches of the groin vaults; if one allowed the engaged shaft on the nave-facing side of the pier to surge all the way up to the springing point of the vault, the forms of the upper and lower levels would be conjoined so as to yield, at least optically, a unification of the building from floor to crown (figure 25).

As in classical Antiquity, this unity was rooted in the relation between weight-bearing supports and the load of the ceiling. There were, however, major differences in principle. First, the medieval ceiling no longer presses down from above at a right angle, as the beamed ceiling does on a columnar shaft; rather, its weight falls in a complicated outward-moving curve, so that the pressure (lateral thrust) is most efficiently countered by oblique buttressing. Second, the function of the wall supports in classical Antiquity was wholly usurped, for the weight of the straight ceiling was borne by the entire wall. In buildings that incorporated arches (such as the Colosseum), the arches relegated to aesthetically subordinate positions do the real work, while the more visually dominant wall supports are mere drones. In the Romanesque vaulted basilica, the smooth strip of wall surface between the springing of the vaults and the arcade piers is a support only in appearance; but behind it, on the exterior of the building, stand buttresses, in relation to which the interior wall merely serves as a symbol. In cases where such wall buttressing was still unknown, the area of wall delineated by this strip of stone was the portion most immediately threatened by the load pressing down from above. But the crucial point is that here, too, art did not rest until it figured out a way to distinguish clearly the actual supporting element from the solid mass of the wall. The pier shaft rose ever higher toward the ceiling, while its three-dimensional mass grew increasingly wide relative to the wall. It is only self-evident that by ancient standards, all proportionality in the individual units had to be lost in the process. Had Northern architecture adhered to considerations of harmony in individual building parts during this purpose-oriented period, it, like its Italian counterpart, would never have arrived at a new architectural style that would

enjoy centuries-long supremacy. Although the Romanesque building always demands to be observed as a whole, its advancements
come to view primarily in the interior.

Nonetheless, some attempts were made to validate considerations of three-dimensional form on the exterior as well — which
early Christian ideology had temporarily stifled but never eradi-
cated completely. We have already pointed out instances involving
individual components such as windows and portals. Pilaster strips
betray the urge to articulate the broad surface of the wall. The use
of shallow blind arcades to connect these with one another proves
that artists correctly recognized the arch to be the governing element of this style and were committed to incorporating it even
in places where its sole function was as a framing device. The corbel table was the earliest precursor of later tracery. Moreover, the
continuous series of little arches generates an impression of movement that significantly exceeds what such a modest motif would
be expected to accomplish. This applies especially to the corbel
tables on semicircular apses, which instantly recall the effect of the
Colosseum (figure 22) — though that structure was articulated by
colonnettes rather than pilaster strips.

In at least a few regions, artists strove for unity in the larger elements of the Romanesque basilican exterior. This was chiefly true
in the Rhineland. Here, people attempted to create a higher unity
by means of a single dominating motif. The crossing tower was recognized as especially useful in this regard; moreover, it was frequently attended by a number of subordinate smaller towers.
Although the resulting impression is very rich, the lower mass, as a
whole, lacks any internal motivation for the multiple towers that
crown it. For all the undeniable merits of this building type, its
physical appearance did not yet achieve the autonomous or self-
evident character of, say, the centralized domed structure in the
form of a Greek cross.

Gothic

The essence and significance of Gothic reside in this art's endowing the basilica with unified external form. This cohesiveness, however, lay not in the form as a whole but in the design of its details: the whole is reflected in the part. The French were manifestly better equipped than the Germans to arrive at this extra-artistic solution. Not only did the French invent this system; they were the only people to apply it thoroughly and consistently. It became something quite different in the hands of the Germans.

The popular definition of Gothic as a combination of pointed arches and a system of buttressing indicates the elemental concern of this art with solving the problem of the exterior. Although pointed arches are also, of course, found inside the building, buttresses have their place exclusively outside. Moreover, we are dealing not only with attached buttresses but also, and more specifically, with flying buttresses; these alone were able to create a total unification of the building from the apex of the vault to the outermost surface of the buttress base.

The pointed arch supplanted the round arch simply because it is more true; it expresses its natural function with greater accuracy. Of course, the notion of harmony must have changed substantially in the meantime; people of classical Antiquity would never have employed pointed arches, though they probably had seen them in Asia. The pointed arch is most true when both the capitals and the responds, which appear to support the arches of the vaults, are omitted, so that the span of the arch really seems to emerge from the lowest part of the base. The Germans took up this approach most concertedly, while the French, unwilling to dispense with the final remnant of illusion, stopped short of it. In this respect, too, Gothic is an organic system that cannot be squeezed to fit harmonic rules. Germanic peoples were well acquainted with symmetry but not with more refined proportionality.

The relation between form and surface in the Gothic period was again determined by the elimination of the wall (figure 26). Total elimination was impossible in a literal sense, of course; but the kind of untruth we find in the Greek temple, where the actual wall surface stood behind an illusory, non-supporting wall, would have been unacceptable in a Germanic Christian temple. In place of the once-continuous wall surface there now appeared single, discrete forms, the buttresses; but the area between these was not left open, as in the intercolumniations of the Greek temple, but filled in with tracery. This tracery is nothing other than a series of molded arches, and all the playful connections between the vertices of the arches are based no less on the arch in design. Thus we see the wall dissolving into a rhythm of massive buttresses and clusters of small arches, which frequently, through their being spanned by one or more larger arches, appear to merge into a single unit. This rhythm of simple and compound motifs (unity in multiplicity, clarity gained only through reflection) is a special characteristic of medieval art, which distinguishes it sharply from the antique.

Tracery forms were typically filled in with glass plates, which turned these forms into the massive windows that left room only for insignificant patches of solid wall surface at the edges and lowest level of the room. The wall thus does exist; but, with minor exceptions, it no longer is a lifeless surface but has become form. The last remaining openings between the wall surfaces are filled with glass; this closes the wall to the outside just as effectively as a stone wall would do, while leaving the aesthetic sense of openness intact. This plastic shaping of a raw material that does not itself display the properties of three-dimensional form — and which thereby approximates atmospheric air in its external appearance — is likewise an entirely novel phenomenon. Although ancient people did use textiles for the concealment of openings (see late Roman porches, for example at Sant' Apollinare in Ravenna), they left no doubt that these textiles were merely a temporary covering for a real opening in the wall surface. The Gothic stained-glass window, by contrast, creates the continuous illusion of an opening that is not really there. Thus even Christian medieval art did not dispense with illusion entirely; on the other hand, people took pains to show, by means of the vibrant coloration of the glass panes and the leaden rods connecting them, that they were indeed dealing with a solid envelope and not an actual open space.

Not only the rhythmic grouping of individual forms but also the way the rows of discrete forms were interconnected distinguishes the Gothic cathedral from the simple rhythms of the Greek temple. The beamed ceiling bore down on the columns of the Greek temple, binding them together into a unified entity. In a Gothic cathedral, by contrast, no horizontal load exists. What the individual forms — that is, the buttresses — support is not a horizontal lintel but a diagonally ascending vault, which is completely invisible from the outside. Again people sought unity in multiplicity, this time by introducing a common unidirectional orientation: verticality. The pinnacles of the buttresses and the pointed windows with their crowning gables all play a part in this directionality. This does not compromise the building's truth, for the function of all the externally visible forms — especially the buttresses — is to surge upward and counteract a pressure bearing down obliquely from above; hence, too, the diagonal profile of the cornices.

Such a system of infinite verticals required no dominant element. Towers were included in Gothic churches more for the sake of tradition; their indispensability to the facade is more imagined than real. At the point where a central motif would most readily have its place — over the crossing — French Gothic architecture confined itself to the practically necessary but aesthetically negligible spire. It would be mistaken, however, to think that the Gothic system was hostile to the centralized structure; on the contrary, it arose from a centralized structure, the French apse with ambulatory and radiating chapels. One need only consider the chevet of Notre Dame in Paris to recognize how a centralized Gothic structure would look. There was no room for a truly dominant element, however, in the cathedral's basilican nave. Each pinnacle forms a centralized motif unto itself, through which the larger mass of the building easily reverberates upward.

The lower buttresses protrude so imposingly from the flank of the building that they assume the appearance of walls. This is why they were masked with blind traceries; the resultant illusion already inherent in decoration was no doubt impossible to avoid here. The terminals of the buttresses' outer faces, on the other hand, included tabernacles containing figures of saints — embellishments that, taken together, were aimed at awakening associations of religious conceptual content.

In its treatment of the building's interior, Gothic did not essentially depart from Romanesque antecedents. Nothing is more indicative of the Gothic system's exclusive aim of producing a shaped exterior than the fact that French artists left their interior walls intact — even if these underwent extensive articulation by the gallery and triforium. The more rigorous Germans handled things differently. Once they decided to accept Gothic, they carried the system through to its most extreme consequences. Their choice to eliminate interior walls led to the frequent appearance of hall churches in Gothic Germany. On the exterior, they never tired of using the tower as the visible embodiment of vertical movement. The French, by contrast, who rightly feared that the towers would compete unfairly with the other vertical members of the facade, did not shrink from terminating both towers with a stark horizontal line just above the main gable. Finally, German architects integrated the indispensable roof, which the French always treated as a necessary evil, into their general tendency toward height; this led to such roofing monstrosities as we find at Saint Stephen in Vienna, a source of constant headaches for modern conservators. The piling up of immense roof surfaces over the delicate tangle of forms has something magnificently naive about it. It is a vivid demonstration of how much more elastic the sense of distinction between form and surface had become for the reflective Germanic Christians than it had been for ancient people, whose confident view of nature — and, by extension, artistic creativity — was unperturbed by either retrospective observations or transcendental scruples.

Italian Renaissance Architecture

Throughout the Middle Ages, the Italians clung to the principle that clear, thoroughgoing proportionality was indispensable for any building. Hence their reluctant engagement with the Gothic; they regarded vaulting as a necessary evil. Although for a time the Italians accustomed themselves to pointed arches, they always retained round arches alongside. So long as the functional tradition maintained its primacy, they had to adopt these foreign inventions, even if against their will. But the dawning of a new age was marked by the beginning of the fifteenth century, when art again became an end in itself. People stopped searching for the building type best sanctioned by tradition and instead sought the one that satisfied current aesthetic needs most perfectly. The path was thus clear for the Italians to grasp again the line of architectural development they had let slip in the early Christian period.

The Italian Renaissance sought to revive "good," that is, classical, architecture. But the Italians also considered the early Christian basilica classical. Thus Renaissance artists adopted the wall articulations of the early Roman Imperial period while simultane-

278

ously surmounting the columns with arches instead of masking these through a continuous order and a straight entablature, as was more in keeping with classical architecture. This circumstance in particular led inevitably to surface's attainment of far greater autonomy than had been possible in classical architecture. Even when the Renaissance employed the antique system of pilasters without arches, this system appeared more as surface decoration than as a subduing of surface by form. Architecture in the Renaissance was less close to what it had been in classical Antiquity — dominant form with subordinate surface — than the reverse: dominant surface with subordinate form. The Renaissance strove for harmony and did so with great effectiveness. But it was content to achieve this harmony within already-existing surfaces; the harmonious articulation of masses by form was initially not even attempted. On the other hand, Renaissance artists were well aware that the true ideal of architecture lay in such formal articulation, and for the most part they recognized the path that would lead most surely to its attainment — hence the ceaseless depiction of centralized structures in quattrocento pictures. Practical attempts on a large scale, however, still awaited.

Bramante's buildings represent the ripest fruit of Renaissance endeavors. The courtyard of the Cancelleria reiterates the masked arch system of the Colosseum (figures 27 and 22). It is essentially a Roman exterior structure pulled into a quadrangular courtyard; the painterly impression comes more from the courtyard than from the system itself. The wall articulation of the Cancelleria facade is executed according to the rule of the golden section — the most perfect proportional means of surface decoration, but only one of many. No one is oblivious to the contradiction between this harmonious treatment of the wall details and the chaotic effects of the overall mass of the building. Bramante knew well how to break up the building mass; to this end, he included corner pavilions, which, however, are so spindly as to barely make an impact. Although Bramante thus pointed toward future developments, the general inclination of the century that he perfectly exemplified in many respects urged him so powerfully back toward surface that he had to content himself with only modest experimentation. The tremendous consequentiality that Bramante himself ascribed to this step is evident in the very tentativeness with which he approached it. No other artist in the entire sixteenth century considered treating the palace as form; they all treated it strictly as surface, that is, as a single visible wall.

With regard to the centralized structure, Bramante's career presents us with a very similar picture. He clearly recognized that to apply this system to the massed structure while simultaneously striving for surface articulation, sophisticated feats of artistic illusion were required (San Satiro in Milan). At Saint Peter's in Rome, Bramante would finally put to use the Greek cross plan with central dome; but the connective galleries he left between the cross arms prove that he was still trying to subdue form's dominance by means of harmonically punctured surfaces. Only in the final plans for articulating the outer walls of Saint Peter's did Bramante opt unequivocally for the sole primacy of form. If this assessment is correct, it means that he also effected this crucial shift in spirit in church architecture.

Baroque Architecture

Clearly, the time was ripe for an emphasis on form in both exterior and interior structures. Combating of surface; initially through classicizing means, though this entailed surrendering the last bonds that Renaissance artists felt connected them to the classical approach. Invention of new bearers of form wherever possible — whether these were organic or inorganic was of no consequence, as long as they were not planar. Whatever was visible of the building had to be three-dimensional form, not relief on a surface or pattern on a flat ground.

Architecture's again becoming an art of form required not only a lucid recognition of what it was lacking but also a spirit of vigorous boldness, possessing both the courage to sweep away every bias in favor of the surface transmitted by the glorious Renaissance and the capacity to do so with conviction. Michelangelo was clearly the man for the job. He had already tackled the problem so vigorously in the Laurenziana that a long time would elapse before a second person would follow. In light of Bramante's indecisiveness, we have Michelangelo to thank almost exclusively for the reemergence of a period of sculptural art that would yield truly great productions; everything else made during the Renaissance was merely decorative relief art. Now Italians took up the problem that Gothic had already solved in the North. They wanted, however, to remain as faithful as possible to the ancient traditions of proportionality, on the one hand, and to clarity in the relation between load and support, on the other. Hence no uniform vertical extension of the dimensions; no separation of loads and supporting forces into elements that are perceptible only on the exterior or the interior of a building and that, as such, cohere only through a reflective process on the part of the beholder. There was yet a third way in which Italians departed from the course of Northern Gothic artists. Whereas the latter endeavored to preserve an overarching unity in basilican structures by giving all the visible components a uniform but quite drastic vertical directionality, the Italians rejected such unity in multiplicity at all costs. Because, in the end, they knew of nothing better with which to replace it, they chose to forgo genuine cohesiveness altogether and to provide the penetrating eye with the illusion of unity instead. Once this decision was reached, the centralized structure — the truly unified building — inevitably forfeited much of its significance.

Thus it was possible for even Saint Peter's to be transformed into a longitudinal building. The subsequent history of Baroque church architecture played itself out primarily in longitudinal structures. Exterior and interior were separated more starkly than ever, each forming a unified entity unto itself.

Exterior, first stage. Facade only. The long flanking walls, often reworked in Rome, were typically treated as a necessary evil. But here, too, artists sought to give the impression of a fragmentation of the larger mass through regressive stepping (profiling) of the walls. The whole wall was meant to appear as three-dimensional form; that is, the pilaster was conceived not as a separate object attached to the wall surface but as a protruding part of the wall mass itself. Not only the pilaster was meant to stand out; the entire mass should splinter apart into pilasters or other forms. In earlier periods, the wall mass seemed to be hidden behind the smooth veneer, but now it took on movement of its own; as some parts bulged outward and others sank back in, the once-cohesive surface burst apart and was supplanted by pure forms. Although antique elements — pilasters, responds, entablatures, pediments — were often employed as formal motifs, artists did not hesitate to split them in two or adjust them in other ways as needed. Nor were they reluctant to double or triple the number of pilasters, for example, even if these were superfluous from an ancient standpoint (because there was no corresponding load).

Unity was achieved by means of (1) pediments that initially remained unbroken but soon were likewise fractured; and (2) complete subordination of the flanks. The larger mass was arranged in three stacked horizontal zones. But the breakage could only be vertical; it had to run continuously from bottom to top. Thus the Baroque period arrived at verticality in the exterior as well (analogy with Gothic). First case: entrance hall of the Laurenziana. Most extreme case: Santa Maria in Campitelli.

Second stage. (*a*) The rectilinear breakage was interrupted by curving bulges in the wall mass (Sant' Agnese in the Piazza Navona). Not really that amazing! Roman art was already familiar with bulging walls; in centralized structures, these never disappeared completely. Only the way they were applied, with no relation to the center, is new. (*b*) The whole wall is made to bulge outward or inward rather than cracking into projecting or receding steps (Borromini). (*c*) Or it is simply sliced straight through (Pietro da Cortona, Galilei); this led once again to surface planarity. Cortona, whose paintings likewise returned to a bright, "plastic" manner, also instructive for painters.

Unity through artificial borders, especially the contrasting curves of the walls: Santa Maria della Pace, Bernini's Sant' Andrea. Attention thus drawn to unity through excision from surroundings (as already in Santa Susanna). Return to surface in the eighteenth century with Galilei, following Cortona's lead.

Empire style. Pilaster order with unifying pediment. Splintering of wall surface retained.

Baroque interior. First stage. Unity more important here: removal of side aisles. Ceiling: vaulted, but with barrel vaults for cohesion. Buttresses were hidden from view (placed outside, between the chapels), while inside the vaults rested on lintels surmounting double-pilastered piers between the arches of chapels. Roman system thus adopted; but now the load is borne by arches in conjunction with piers, allowing for the renewed elimination of the wall. Windows pierce the barrel vaults directly, so that the upper wall surface can be relinquished. The vaulting is an artistic form in itself. In the first stage, it is interspersed with neutral pictures borne by three-dimensional angels — mere "curtains" held by figures (Cortona). In the second stage, it opens up as a heavenly space; here, too, there are no more self-contained surfaces. Highest level of sophistication: Pozzo's painted architecture. Figures were placed on whatever wall surfaces remained visible on the piers between spandrels (as in Greek temples).

Second stage. Elaboration of floor plan through centralized or oval insertions, transepts, for more refined illumination. Breakup of unity. Addition of projecting columns, enhancement of perspectival impression. Columns destroy unity again through their placement in front of the wall mass.

Profane architecture. First stage. (1) Mass not allowed to succumb to movement. Why? Perhaps because of windows; there were already difficulties in dealing with these. (2) Avoidance of pilasters or engaged columns as overly reminiscent of the Renaissance (from Rucellai to Raphael). (3) A return to the course of Northern Romanesque architecture; those elements best suited to three-dimensional formation (such as windows) given as much independent significance as possible, so that all emphasis is placed on the wall. Such was the typical Roman Baroque palace before Bernini.

Second stage. Fracturing of the solid body of the outer wall (return to the Cancelleria) and, simultaneously, integration of pilasters (Bernini) — an early return to surface planarity? Bernini clearly believed that such openness would provide a sufficient illusion of three-dimensional form that he could shape the individual components thoroughly and in detail. Form in the whole, surface in the parts. Increasingly pronounced framing of windows; increasingly drastic emphasis on surface. Did not Bernini's paths diverge from those of Valvassori and the rest? For the typical Roman palace persevered into the eighteenth century. Bernini's fractured forms found many more imitators in the North (France, Germany). In any case, Bernini leads back to surface.

Empire style did not relinquish fragmentation into projecting pavilions.

Second Version

Lecture Notes of 1899

Introduction

One hundred and fifty years have elapsed since the discipline of
art history was born, since the structure of a history of art began
to be built. In the beginning, Aesthetics was the master builder.
She laid the foundations and sketched out the blueprints that
would lead the whole project to its future completion. From that
foundation three main sections would arise: a central building
for architecture and two secondary wings for sculpture and painting. But soon it became apparent that many works of art did not
fit into these categories. A fourth section was therefore added, a
back wing to stand behind architecture, and it was called industrial art. Then all four parts were raised with speed and vigor into
the heights.

But the higher the builders got, the more they were faced with
the uncomfortable observation that they had rushed ahead too
quickly in their initial zeal. The foundations proved weak, and
the building materials, in many cases, poorly chosen and insufficiently prepared. All the blame, of course, was placed squarely on
the master builder, Aesthetics, and she was promptly dismissed.
The building, people discovered, had to be solid. This did not
require a unified and consistent construction process; what mattered instead was to devote all attention and energy to the various

wings independently. Here began the second phase of art-historical inquiry: the strengthening of the foundations and the elaboration of the materials — in other words, the phase of specialized
investigation. Although the process of construction was not forgotten, it proceeded unevenly and without a plan, for it lacked
steady leadership. Those working on one wing paid no attention
to the progress of the others. As a result, although the four sections were indeed raised gradually into the heights, the connections between them progressively dissolved.

The problem could not remain unacknowledged for long.
Today, the building is lacking connective corners, so that, for all
its internal solidity, it still gives the impression of a ruin. It is time
to create new connections among the four sections and to endow
the fragmented whole with the impression of unity once more.
This cannot be achieved without a plan; there needs to be a broad-
sighted and consistent process of construction. Who shall be in
charge? Once set aside, Aesthetics no longer exists; she has long
been dead, and any effect she still possesses resides in the scattered auditoriums of academic philosophy. But she left behind an
heiress. Although youthful and yet unnamed, she is present nonetheless. Already she has undertaken certain endeavors that hold
much promise for the future, for they put to use the lessons of the
history of art. Whereas the old aesthetics wanted to give instruction to the discipline of art history, her heiress — modern aesthetics, if you will — eagerly lets art history teach her. She recognizes
that her very right to exist lies rooted in the history of art.

What are the most distinguished attempts to return a sense of
unity to the crumbling structure of art history? The earliest was
Gottfried Semper's effort to define the work of art as the com-
posite result of functional aims, material, and technique. We shall
later return to this attempt, which could not lead to a unified syn-
thesis of artistic activity as a whole and had relevance only for

288

industrial arts. Two other approaches held more wide-ranging significance. Both sought to encompass the underlying fourfold division with an overarching duality, and insofar as these two upper parts symmetrically completed each other, they were naturally seen to constitute a higher unity still. The older of the two sought to divide all artistic productions into two components, one idealizing and the other naturalistic. This endeavor is certainly based on an actual relationship, but no one has yet succeeded in locating the specific boundaries separating the parts. In consequence, one camp argues that all artistic production is essentially naturalistic, while the other insists that it has never been anything but idealizing. In the end, it is evident that these two concepts, despite the real relation between them, are not disposed to lead to a clear unity. Surely no construction project can proceed with such unstable elements.

The younger approach attempts to divide all artistic production into a plastic and a painterly component. Taken on its own, this distinction yields no clear solutions either. There is still no agreement as to what, exactly, is plastic and what painterly. What some call plastic, others call painterly. Thus we have endeavors, but no successes; nonetheless, we may not allow ourselves to despair over the possibility of a solution. Let us try to understand more deeply what these two attempts are seeking to do.

I begin with a concrete example. Of Attic art produced during the second half of the fifth century B.C.E., we possess works of all categories: as an architectural monument, the Parthenon (figure 15); as monuments of sculpture, the works of Phidias; as monuments of painting, countless vases. I assume you will immediately recognize these objects to be Attic works of the fifth century. Can we call such instant recognition scholarly, scientific knowledge? No — for then we would have to call even the antiques dealer a man of scholarly science. This recognition is gained through practice;

it is a form of knowledge, a learned specialty, to be sure, but not a science. The scholarly, scientific aspect begins only when we pose the question as to why the monuments of fifth-century Attica were fashioned in this way and no other. Every modern scientific endeavor rests firmly on the belief in the omnipotence of causal laws and the impossibility of the miraculous. Every phenomenon is therefore the necessary effect of some original cause. It is this cause that interests the scholarly sciences.

For as long as it has existed, art history has earnestly striven to satisfy this postulate. Not content with simply ascertaining date and provenance, it has also striven from the outset to find the causes of a given work. In the beginning, art history sought these causes in the field of aesthetics, that is, in certain laws, deter mined *a priori*, that were supposed to be equally valid for all artistic forms, whether architecture, sculpture, or painting. Winckelmann was one proponent of this viewpoint. In time, the shakiness of these *a priori* laws revealed itself; this is what we called the inability of aesthetics to oversee and direct construction of the art-historical edifice. At that point, people gave up the quest for unity and sought instead to tease out the causal forces within the various categories of art. This entailed, for instance, pursuing the history of the Greek temple backward from the Parthenon, that is, forging a chain of causes and effects, of developmental links, that would lead from Egyptian temple construction straight through to that building. This was likewise done in the field of sculpture. Today we are familiar enough with the story of sculpture's progress from Old Kingdom Egypt to Phidias. And thus it is with painting: we can survey with the utmost clarity the causal relationship between ancient Egyptian murals and fifth-century Attic vases.

Thus did art history proceed as a scholarly discipline for the last half century. Not content to discover the precise date and location of an individual work of art, it continually sought to locate origins and causes and traced these only within their respective artistic genres. That is, people strove to erect each wing independently and strenuously avoided glancing over at the other sections.

Today we are witnessing art-historical inquiry embark on a new phase. One now poses the following questions: Does the Parthenon obey the developmental laws of architecture exclusively? Do the sculptures of Phidias follow only the developmental laws of sculpture, and Attic vases solely those of painting? Is there really no transverse connection between these laws at all? Or do there exist, above them all, certain universal principles to which all works of art conform equally and without exception — underlying principles from which the laws of architecture, sculpture, and painting represent mere secondary deviations?

Today we see that all works of art, no matter how disparate and unique they seem to be, have certain elements in common. Must not the development of those common elements be shared a well? And must not the development of all artistic creation therefore represent a common progression? Let us take a concrete example. The column, the statue, and the vase have in common (1) three-dimensional form and (2) two-dimensional surfaces that coalesce thereon. Form and surface are thus basic elements of visual art. While the relation between the two may be distinct, closer examination reveals that this relation manifests itself identically in the Parthenon, in statues by Phidias, and in Attic vase paintings. The developmental laws governing these elements must be equally binding for all four artistic categories.

We are now in a better position to recognize what really matters. We should concentrate no longer on the individual work of art or on the various categories of artistic media, each for itself, but on the elements that constitute and bind them. Only by sharply distinguishing and acknowledging these will we be able to construct an appropriate crown for the academic edifice of art history. These are not a single entity, of course, but many and varied. But because they form the links between the various categories of art, they provide us with a comprehensive picture. These are the intermediary components that lead to the real summit, to the supreme ruling element of all artistic production. This seems to me the future task of art history as a scientific discipline. It does not completely deprive the older method of specialized investigation of its value. Now, as always, this kind of construction relies on solid structural materials, that is, an accurate determination of place and date. With these tools, it will be possible to carry out any investigations within the individual artistic categories with success and utility. But the actual crown of the whole, the clear recognition of the essence of the visual arts, can only become accessible through the developmental history of art's basic elements, dictated by the highest guiding factor of all artistic production.

Perhaps I can illuminate this better by referring to the close parallels between the visual arts and language. Language likewise has its proper elements, and we call the developmental history thereof the historical grammar of the language in question. Someone who merely wants to speak the language has no use for this grammar, nor does anyone who wants simply to understand it. But whoever wants to know why the language proceeded along this path and no other, whoever wants to grasp the position of the language within human culture in general — whoever, in a word, wants to comprehend the given language scientifically — cannot do without the historical grammar.

The subjects of visual art occupy an analogous position. We have long been accustomed to using the metaphor "artistic language." We say that each work of art speaks its own particular artistic language, even though the elements of visual art are naturally different from those of verbal language. But if there is such a thing as artistic language, there also exists a historical grammar of that language. This, too, is of course metaphoric; but if the one metaphor is justifiable, surely the other must be accepted as well.

A person who wants to create a work of art — the visual artist — has no need for a historical grammar of the visual arts. Nor does anyone who wants simply to enjoy the work of art as an object. But someone who seeks to comprehend the work of art scientifically will not, in the future, be able to escape it.

You will surely have come to understand by now what I intend to deliver with this historical grammar of the visual arts. One might call it elementary lessons in the visual arts.

Let me warn you from the outset of a possible misunderstanding: in no way is this meant to be an introduction to the history of art. So far is this from the case, in fact, that I would sincerely urge any novices among you to make themselves scarce. Only advanced students who already possess some knowledge of all artistic periods, and who at least have the most significant monuments of each period firmly in mind, will be able to gain something from attending these lectures. I will continually be citing particular examples and referring regularly to other monuments. It is impossible to present all my examples in reproductions, though I shall certainly try my best to do so. I am, however, limited in the materials I can use here, and, furthermore, I lack the physical potential to show you every single thing. Detailed familiarity is therefore required and assumed.

(Few hours; usefulness; only suggestions intended; first attempt.)

We will be dealing with (1) elements; (2) the developmental history thereof; (3) the factors that determined that development.

Elements.
What we shall be considering here can best be understood by
thinking of catalog cards. For example:

  1   2   3   4

*Bowl; of terra-cotta; tall base; on the cup, battle of the centaurs;
black figure.*

(1) For what purpose? Function is the primary concern, occupies
the first place, counts as most important element. One's attention is called to practical, utilitarian purposes, certain kinds of
vessel. (2) and (3) *Terra-cotta*; encompasses two elements: raw
materials and technique; made from what, and how?

On the surface, these three elements seem to be most important; they are always listed before the fourth. They are also most
material, most sensorially perceptible. These factors formed the
basis of the aesthetic system developed in the 1860s: Gottfried
Semper in *Der Stil* (Style), empirical aesthetics. Since then, every
work of art regarded as the product of practical purpose, material, and technique. Now let us see whether other elements exist.
The catalog card already gives us one in its description: (1) forms
of detail work; (2) embellishment of surfaces.

Viewed as a whole, every work of art is three-dimensional,
possessing general shape or form but bounded by planar surfaces.
Form and surface always sustain a certain relationship; and although it is true that surface can sometimes outweigh form, there
is no such thing as a non-corporeal work of art, or pure surface.
This leads us to another element: the relation between form and
surface in any work of art. Whereas Semper's aesthetic system
thought it could ignore this, more recent systems of aesthetics
have taken this relation into account and even used it as a basis for
distinguishing the plastic from the painterly.

There is yet another element latent in the word "bowl,"
which does not come fully to view, because it is concealed behind

294

the practical designation. Let us look at some other cards.

Statue of Artemis; cast bronze.

"Statue"? Does this term describe a function? Certainly not. No practical purpose implied. (Had the piece been a caryatid, purpose would have been mentioned first: for example, "table leg in the shape of Artemis.") Is the statue therefore without purpose? By no means; just no practical or utilitarian purpose. We shall discuss this in greater detail later. Immediately, in the next place, we find "of Artemis"; that is, this is the statue of a quasi-human goddess, thus the reproduction of a human figure. This provides us immediately with the "What?" — the motif of the work of art.

How does our bowl deal with this? This factor is hidden behind the word indicating function. When we hear the word "bowl," we know right away how the motif was produced. But a motif is indeed present here, no less based on nature than in the statue. The difference is that the statue's motif was drawn from organic nature and as such can be clearly defined. The motif of the bowl comes from inorganic crystalline nature and therefore requires closer description, which typically follows at a later point. As another example of industrial art, let us take *table leg in the shape of Artemis*. Because we are dealing with a model from organic nature, we can define it right away. Recent aesthetic systems have also attempted to elevate the motif to a primary principle — naturalistic versus idealizing.

Thus we have five elements:

1. Purpose: *why?* Usually this is too narrowly defined as the practical, utilitarian function meant to satisfy the needs of our five senses.

2. Raw materials: *from what?*

3. Technique: *in what way?*

4. Motif: *what?*

5. Form and surface: *how?*

People have attempted to use these five elements as the ground for a newly unified, all-encompassing approach to art and to proclaim the history of their development identical with the development of visual art in general.

Semper's empirical aesthetics. Approximates materialism most closely. Semper based his history of industrial arts only on this. Why? Let us take the "statue of Artemis" yet again. How is its style explicable on the basis of purpose, raw materials, and technique — here, where no practical function is to be seen? Such difficulties arise even in the case of architecture. Semper intended to deal with architecture but never got to that point. Surely no accident.

Now take a third card:

Oil painting; *landscape*; *on copper*.

A practical function is no more readily discernible here than in the statue; raw material and technique are even less illuminating here as motivating forces. This is why classical archaeologists and art historians snatched up Semper's thesis so eagerly when dealing with industrial arts but never applied it to so-called high art. But people also wanted to forge connections in the high arts, in architecture as well as sculpture and painting. Two elements remained: (1) motif and (2) form and surface. Although, as mentioned above, both were quickly elevated to primary principles, there is no agreement about their respective boundaries. Why? Because things are no different with these factors from how they were with the three materialist elements that Semper extolled as foundational to art-historical development. None of the five elements should be held as sole leader. They are all vehicles of development equally; but progress is really governed by another element that stands apart from, but also above, the rest. What is the principle that has guided the development of all visual art? While the five elements of the visual arts constitute a multiplicity, a higher unity must exist that transcends them all. What could this higher unity be?

Why does man create art? What is the purpose of the work of art? With these questions, we seem to have returned to the element of function, which played such a crucial role in Semper's empirical aesthetics. The kind of purpose Semper had in mind, however, was merely external. Let us examine the external functions a work of art can serve. There is no work of art without external function, but also no external function without art. Anything man creates with his hands must automatically be granted the stamp of art.

1. Practical purpose of utility. Fulfilling the needs of the five senses. Bowl, drinking vessel — serves the sense of taste. Is that a purpose of art? No. The practical purpose is thus not identical with art's purpose. Encompasses applied arts and architecture. (When this is really a sign or token — a memorial monument such as an obelisk — it is considered sculpture.)

2. Decorative purpose. Filling a void; *horror vacui*; tattooed islanders. No practical purpose for tattooing; does not serve any of the five senses. (We do not speak of the eye here; the eye is the intermediary organ that transmits external impressions to the internal senses. Nowadays we perceive all works of art with the eye. Optical needs can be satisfied by, say, glasses.) The decorative function therefore corresponds to some need of our inner senses. This brings us closer to the purpose of art, which must likewise correspond to an intrinsic human need. But the decorative purpose is still not identical with the work of art. Some works of art have nothing to do with the filling of empty space. However, the statue of Artemis was not invented simply to fill the corner of a temple, nor was the bowl fashioned merely to decorate a table. Both are works of art; yet as they were being created, no one was thinking of just filling up space. Works that serve ornamental

purposes we call "decorative." These form a bridge between in-dustrial arts and so-called high art; a fine statue, for example, can be used simply for decorative purposes.

3. Conceptual purpose. *Statue of Artemis.* Made to awaken a certain concept in the beholder, an idea of a specific divine force that makes the beholder feel protected. This purpose clearly arises from a need intrinsic to human beings and not based on the five external senses. It is therefore tempting to identify the work of art with this purpose. Works that fulfill the conceptual func-tion are typically designated "high art," as opposed to industrial or decorative arts, even though the latter sometimes overlap with their "high" counterparts; the frescoes in the Campo Santo in Pisa and the Parthenon frieze, for example, are no less "decorative" than "high" art. In many cases, such as statues of Greek gods or the Christian crucifix, these purposes do coincide. But this is only coincidence, not a full conflation of one with the other.

Thus the three external functions have not revealed the true purpose of art.

Human artistic creativity is a contest with nature.

This statement entails two things:

1. Dependence on nature in the broadest sense, the nature surrounding us as well as that within us; in other words, "the world." Man cannot transcend nature and world, because he is an integral component of both. In his artistic productions, he is inex-tricably bound to models in both organic and inorganic nature. He can concoct the most monstrous image, and yet its individual internal components will always, in some way, point back to a natural model. In this respect, those who argue that human artis-tic creation has never been anything but naturalistic are correct.

2. We are dealing with a *contest* with nature, not replication or mimicry of nature or a desire to produce the illusion of natural appearances. On the contrary: an artist who attempted such a

thing would defeat his own purpose. A truly illusionistic replication of nature is, in any case, inconceivable. Man can never imbue
organic works with life and movement. Nor can he fully imitate
an inorganic object such as a crystal in all aspects, for even if the
external form were identical with the natural model, the internal
structure — for example, the arrangement of molecules — would
still be profoundly different.

Thus the creation of art can never be — and does not seek to be
— a direct imitation of nature but rather is a contest with nature;
that is, it aims for a certain idea or conception of nature. In art,
man re-creates nature as he would like it to be and as it indeed
exists in his mind. (We will see later how this happens. For now,
general principles and traits are more important.) This will appear immediately comprehensible with regard to ancient Greek
art; as we shall see, it is no less true for the Christian Middle Ages
and for the modern age of faith in causality. It therefore makes
sense if some people insist that human artistic creativity has never
been anything but idealizing, for if man necessarily fixes his eyes
on nature, and nature alone, in his artistic endeavors, he never
tries to reproduce nature for its own sake or as it really is. From
here we can take another step back to the furthest point human
knowledge allows us to reach, and ask why man felt the urge to
improve nature through art in the first place.

This impulse, which is in fact identical with the drive to create
art, derives from man's striving for happiness. All human culture
can ultimately be explained in terms of this striving.

Man yearns incessantly for harmony. He sees this harmony
constantly disrupted and threatened by things and phenomena
of nature that exist in a state of perpetual struggle, both with
one another and with humanity. If nature were really the way it
appears in the individual human senses, man would never be able
to attain harmony. Consequently, man creates a vision of nature

in his art that frees him from nature's perpetual instability; he imagines nature to be better than it looks. He seeks to bring order to the apparent chaos, to push aside those raw random occurrences to which he is otherwise subject and vulnerable. One example: Lightning flying from the clouds can strike a man dead at any moment, just as it can a tree or an animal — this is a source of anxiety. Man therefore constructs an image that allows him to feel safe from the lightning bolt. The image or vision can assume various guises; it can manifest itself in the lightning bolt of Jupiter Tonans (with the thunderbolt), or the Christian God, or even in the domination of a causal law indirectly present in the lightning rod. In each case, man's view of nature urges him to create for himself a sense of harmonious comfort.

The comforting view of nature is something man creates in his mind. It affects man's relation to every object in the world without exception. Thus it entails not only the relation of man to extra-human nature, which we call an understanding of nature in the narrow sense, but also the relation of one person to another, which we call the understanding of morality. We can pull all this together under the single term "worldview." Just as nature paints itself in man's imagination, not in its manifold sensorially perceptible appearances but in its deepest being, so it presses man to make it appear, visible and tangible, before his eyes. This in the final analysis is the root of all artistic creativity. We may now flesh out our definition: the creation of art is a contest with nature with the aim of bringing to expression a harmonious worldview.

Herein resides the true purpose of art [Kunstzweck]. All the external functions encountered thus far are merely welcome vehicles for the activation of art's supreme purpose. The drive to create art — that is, the human need for harmony — does not let any opportunity slip by without putting it to use. Thus each object arising from an external purpose is, more or less, a work of art. Yet external purpose must nevertheless be strictly distinguished from the purpose of art. The purpose of art coincides with conceptual purpose only when the conception is aimed directly at a harmonious worldview — for example, in Greek statues of gods, such as Jupiter Tonans, or in the crucifix. One can accordingly recognize the fundamental mistake of Semper's theory, which stated that the creation of art originated with the practical purpose of utility. According to Semper, in the beginning there were only industrial arts, and through them man's sensibility for art was gradually awakened. From the very outset, practical purpose and the purpose of art have always been distinct.

Indeed, it is not at all certain that the practical function was the first to be employed in art. Perhaps it was the decorative function, as in tattooing, or maybe even the conceptual. So overwhelmingly do the most ancient monumental arts, at least in Egypt, present themselves as "high" — that is, conceptually oriented — art, and so utterly do practically purposeful arts depend on conceptual ones (for example, the lotus as an ornamental motif), that one would like to regard the latter as the older, the more primitive of the two. We shall have occasion in a different context to point out an example that suggests the conceptual purpose to be the most ancient external impetus for human artistic creativity (the fetish). Visual art, then, is but one cultural phenomenon among many. In the final analysis, its development derives from the same factor that drives the entire progress of human culture: the worldview of man, as expression of his need for comfort and contentment. Worldviews differ for different time periods and peoples; but one must always seek to know them if one wants to comprehend the art of those respective peoples and times in its deepest being. If visual art is nothing other than a vision of nature, then one must know the extent to which people of other times and places considered nature in need of — and capable of — improvement and where they looked for such improvement. The answer to these questions always lies in the then-current worldview. Before we can approach the individual elements of artistic creativity, we shall therefore have to undertake a brief survey of the three major worldview systems that have run their courses until the present. Subsequently we shall examine the development of the elements of art as these progressed under each worldview. We shall leave aside three of the five major elements prized above all others by Semper and concentrate chiefly on the two whose character is less material: motif, and form and surface. Relatively speaking, motif is the more material of these elements. On the other hand, the development of the relation between form and surface reflects the progression of visual art in general. Of the five elements, this relation is the most artistic.

Admittedly, the other elements would be interesting to examine too. We could ask, for example, why marble was used for statues in some periods and porphyry in others, why bronze casting was preferred at certain times, why enamel techniques were common here and inlaid stonework there. But all these questions can be easily answered if only one understands the history of the two main elements.

PART ONE

Worldview

The oldest apprehensible worldview is that of *anthropomorphic polytheism*: the adoration of multiple gods in a form resembling human beings. You see, from the very outset worldview and religion coincided completely, and so, naturally, did religion and art. Religion determines both natural and ethical laws. Let me just mention that this was still the case in the Christian Middle Ages. Only the modern age has freed natural law from religion. Yet not even three hundred years have passed since Galileo was thrown into prison for propounding a law of nature that contradicted a point of religious dogma. Even today, the Church, as appointed custodian of Christian revealed faith, claims the right to censor certain natural-scientific research, though this is rarely carried out in practice. Why this rift between religion and our modern worldview? Because, in the final analysis, religion — whether pagan belief in gods or Christian belief in revelation — is always based on faith, the conviction that supernatural powers exist that can freely intervene in the destiny of human beings. The modern worldview, by contrast, gives no such credence to personal intrusions of the supernatural (for example, miracles), at least within the sphere of the natural world and bodily phenomena.

In Antiquity and the Middle Ages, worldview, religion, and

art formed a single whole. Anthropomorphic polytheism is therefore the earliest human worldview we are able to recognize as a historical phenomenon. However, it was not the very first worldview. Even among the Egyptians, with whom our history of anthropomorphic polytheism — indeed, the history of mankind itself — begins, we find scattered traces of a prior animal cult, which must have preceded the pure cult of man-gods. Nor will this animal cult have represented the very primal stage. Today we can no longer recognize what that stage was. A satisfactory answer cannot be found through observation of today's so-called nature-peoples; in this regard, ethnology is abandoning itself to grossly exaggerated hopes. We can reconstruct the original state of affairs only by moving back from a later one.

As we do so, the following scenario emerges. Early man perceived himself immersed in a chaos of natural phenomena that pressed themselves on him with equal malevolence. Independent of man in both their origins and their present form, they all appeared as gods in his eyes. We call this phenomenon *infinite polytheism*. Man's need for harmony motivated him to protect himself from these powers, and he discovered a means to that end in the fetish. (We still see this in surviving primitive peoples today.) That is, by, say, carving in some way into a wooden stake, man fashioned from dead matter a protective deity. Serving this conceptual purpose, the fetish constitutes simultaneously one of the first cult objects and one of the first works of art. In this initial case, religion and art completely overlapped; the conceptual purpose and the purpose of art were one.

It is worth noting that man attributed greater potency to a work of his own hands than to himself. This need not surprise us; in fact, it will remain characteristic of polytheism even in its later manifestations. In this sense, the much-admired statues of Greek gods were true idols. We, with our modern notions of causality, are no longer capable of grasping this. A Sicilian peasant, who confronts his Madonna figure or his statue of some saint with a reverential attitude not terribly different from the early view, can probably understand it better. Amulets, whether ancient or modern, are nothing but fetishes.

We know too little about primitive fetishism and infinite polytheism to form any clear idea of the expression they found in visual art. We could certainly offer some speculation, but let us turn instead to periods more penetrable to us. As man gradually recognized his superiority over all natural things, including animals, he grew unable to envision powers superior to himself as anything other than human. In this view, all natural phenomena were brought about by human beings — but perfect humans, who were stronger than regular men and not subject to their mortality. They were omnipresent but existed beyond the grasp of the human senses. This was the essence of anthropomorphic polytheism.

CHAPTER ONE

First Period

*Antique Anthropomorphic Polytheism
to the Third Century C.E.*

Man observes all around himself a perpetual battle of natural forces. This struggle has something unsettling and unharmonious about it, especially insofar as it is threatening to man himself. But the moment a stronger party conquers and the weaker either surrenders or is beaten, the battle is over. Thus antique people came to expect regularity, the establishment of harmony by means of the stronger — the triumph of the stronger. The natural law of Antiquity, like its moral rules, was grounded in the right of the stronger — more specifically, the tangibly and materially stronger. The stronger was always right, for without it there would be no order, only chaos. Man reigned as the stronger power over all nature; among human beings, the strong person ruled over the weaker; and the gods reigned as the most powerful forces over man and nature alike.

Once man desired to see this worldview embodied in the visual arts, external contingencies gave him the opportunity to make this happen. Man began creating works that would compete with nature; these were natural works, but they presented nature not as it in fact entered into man's senses — weak, imperfect, transitory — but as the deities hidden behind nature's outward appearances: strong, perfect, enduring. Man created an improved nature, more specifically, a physically improved nature. Thus we can state: the art of anthropomorphic polytheism (that is, the art of all Antiquity) is a physical perfecting of nature. It is difficult to offer one single example that will illustrate this extremely general rule. The more sweeping the statement, the higher the categories to which we ascend, and therefore the less capable we are of demonstrating what we really mean through a single specific example. In consequence, the broadest statements can only be illustrated by surveying a whole series of cases from a distance. In each instance, the individual elements stand out most sharply and thereby dull the desired insight; the most general statements become fully clear only when we deal with specifics. But to give you at least some idea of what I am talking about, I will weave in an example right here — though, I admit, it is not necessarily a perfect one. Let us consider how the human figure was conceived in classical art of Greece. The human being appears here as a beautiful, strong being with no individual weaknesses. That such an example, taken alone, is unsatisfactory stems from its pertinence to only one phase in the history of antique art, the classical. But Antiquity encompassed nearly two thousand years of lucid historical time. This fact alone must justify our visualizing the development of the polytheistic worldview in its larger phases. We can start by distinguishing two major domains: the polytheism of ancient Near Eastern peoples and the polytheism of the Greeks and Romans.

Ancient Near Eastern Polytheism

What hides behind the outward manifestations of the material world is matter, and indeed perfect matter. For this reason, ancient Near Eastern peoples most emphatically supported the right of the stronger: only the material triumph of the strong creates harmony. One need only think of the political history of these peoples to apprehend the validity of this claim. The distinct predilection for world domination: a single strong entity should govern all. Such a worldview must demand unity in the religious sphere as well. Among divine powers, a single strongest force likewise must eventually subjugate all others. It is thus obvious that ancient Near Eastern polytheism was inclined toward monotheism from the very outset. Ancient Near Eastern peoples (with a single exception, which we shall discuss later) never arrived at true monotheism in the end, because they were unable to extricate themselves from a purely material apprehension of the divine. They succeeded in doing so more than the Greeks would, but never so thoroughly as the Jews. This will become more apparent when we examine each group on its own.

The Egyptians are most crucial here, for with them a cohesive history of art begins. This people also underwent a progression whose earliest phases are the most interesting; regrettably, we know all too little of these. It is highly significant, however, that the old regional gods always appeared as a triad: father, mother, and son — that is, three who, in a certain sense, are one. But people could not imagine the activity of the gods in any but material terms, that is, in terms of material conception. Hence the masculine and feminine principles and their fruit. The spiritual cannot have remained foreign to the Egyptians, but they despised it because it reminded them of the weak and transitory. In the visual arts, therefore, they strove to depict the material world in as perfect but at the same time as spiritless a form as possible. At the most basic level, spirit manifests itself in motion; we move in obedience to an internal impulse of the will, that is, a spiritual or mental impulse. Egyptian art suppressed movement, that most elemental manifestation of organic life, as much as possible. We can therefore say, in general, that Egyptian art in its contest with nature created works of corporeal beauty but with no indication of movement — thus lifeless works. These we shall examine more closely later. To quell any misunderstanding, I point out that a sense of movement cannot be avoided entirely in the representation of human figures; but the Egyptians (and all other early Oriental and Greek peoples until around 500 C.E.) set only the body's extremities into motion. The head and torso remained inert, as if they were inanimate crystalline masses. The later stages of the Egyptian worldview clearly aimed to shield this system from any disruption, hence the constantly increasing importance of the priestly caste in Egyptian social and state life. Both the Egyptian worldview and Egyptian art thereby thwarted any potential for further growth and advancement (a historical phenomenon that recurs rather frequently; I think immediately of the Jews and the Byzantines). For all that, the Egyptians were the only people — aside from the Jews — to have effectively staved off conquest by the Greek worldview. The Egyptian worldview and art both persevered well into the third century C.E., before collapsing all at once to make room for the Christian worldview and its art. It is no accident that Christianity — not Greek polytheism or, even earlier, Judaism, which counted many adherents in the Diaspora, especially at Alexandria — succeeded in eradicating ancient Egyptian polytheism once and for all.

Let us turn now to the second great ancient Near Eastern people, among whom some would surely want to number the ancient Egyptians: the Semites. Although we are not able to learn as much about them from their monuments as we can about the Egyptians, it is apparent that their worldview was closely related to the Egyptian. Yet the Semites never managed to entrench their worldview system so firmly as to make any further development seem laughable. Having evidently lost faith in the autocracy of the material world, most Semitic clans after Alexander the Great surrendered to the rule of Greek polytheism. Thus the ancient Semitic cults disappeared along with all Babylonian, Assyrian, and

Phoenician art, and for the next few centuries we encounter in the Semitic Orient only the Hellenistic art of the Greeks. Only one Semitic clan — and by no means the most populous — was able to achieve that toward which the polytheistic peoples of the ancient Near East had tended from the beginning: pure monotheism. I refer to the worldview of the Jews.

As numerous citations from the Bible make plain, the Jews were once polytheistic. But they had already abandoned that system before the year 1000 B.C.E. The course they chose is obvious: they had to cast off any material conceptualization of the connection between human and divine. The Jewish God is not material but pure spirit, absolute will; this is why he could only be solitary. What is spiritual cannot be subdivided. In this sense, the Judaic worldview appears to have divorced itself completely from the antique worldview many years before the birth of Christ. But in every other respect, the two views were in perfect accord. The Jews fully adhered to the right of the stronger. Every antique people was convinced that its members, and they alone, possessed the most powerful god and that this god would ultimately grant them victory. The Jews believed this, too. They never doubted the existence of other gods, such as pagan idols. But what were these material idols when compared with their immaterial God? Thus they viewed themselves as their God's chosen people and expected that eventually, following the arrival of the Messiah, he would allow them to vanquish all their enemies. The Jews had no concept of the emancipation of the weak and the oppressed. Their ethics took the form of justice (an eye for an eye, a tooth for a tooth), not the form of love, as in the Christian worldview.

We must therefore maintain that the Judaic worldview is strictly antique insofar as it seeks an individual will underlying natural phenomena, a force that can regulate these phenomena as it likes. (The sun once stopped moving in order to guarantee victory to the Hebrew army — the clearest proof that the Judaic worldview believes in miracles and thus stands diametrically opposed to our own faith in causality.) This singular power is conceived not as something material but rather as purely spiritual. The Jews' special inclination toward speculative thought was what enabled them to devise this worldview.

Now let us investigate how this Judaic worldview approached the visual arts. The Jews found harmony in the recognition that the material world in which other groups invested everything meant nothing to them. In their eyes, matter possessed no intrinsic importance whatsoever. In particular, the outward manifestations of animate life — movement and so forth — were perceived as direct effects of the spiritual power of God. Matter itself is dead and only moves through God's volition. How, then, was man to compete with nature? On its own, nature is not capable of self-improvement; the essence of things rests solely in the mind of God, and this is impossible to represent because representation can only be accomplished through material means. This led to a singular phenomenon in the history of human culture: the Jews produced no visual art. They contented themselves with pure ideas, spiritual images; they did not rely on sensual embodiments of their worldview to achieve harmony. The extreme importance of the Jews within the larger history of art is rooted not in the works they created but in the fact that they created none at all. This proves that mankind is not intrinsically compelled to produce art and that people can, under certain conditions, do without any artistic activity; this may hold significance for future developments. But now we must ask whether such a thing is really possible. If art's purpose can be circumvented, can extrinsic purposes be likewise? It is possible to circumvent the conceptual function. The decorative function is more difficult; and escaping the practical function is impossible for any higher culture. One can hardly imagine that the Jews worked up no material at all; but in light of the unavoidable consumption of artworks, they relied essentially on imports. Naturally, it is difficult to draw solid conclusions on this matter because we have no access to Jewish grave goods. (Considering the Judaic contempt for the material world, this makes perfect sense; any cult of the dead presupposes a high valuation of the material.) It is nonetheless striking that we are familiar with Babylonian, Assyrian, Phoenician, even Hittite styles but not with a Judaic one.

The Jewish worldview led to the same dead end as the Egyptian. It was inflexible and insulated, and although it has (as is well known) persevered up to our own time, it is incapable of advancing further because it accepts no enrichment from outside sources. This explains several peculiar phenomena, above all the self-imposed segregation of the Jews from other people whom they regarded as unworthy of their God's favor. This actually came as a relief to the Romans, for it made the Jews innocuous — hence the exemption of the Jews from the Imperial cult on whose behalf so many thousands of Christians were put to death. Classical people, on the other hand, found the Judaic worldview incomprehensible; from this perspective, too, the Romans could be comfortably certain that this view would stay firmly locked within the parameters of a single clan. Although their worldview doubtless represents an advancement in relation to polytheism, the Jews deprived themselves of the crucial opportunity to exploit this progress to the utmost. In Solomon's time, polytheism was not mature enough to move to a purely spiritual monotheism all at once. The spiritual element inherent in monotheism could assume decisive significance for man's cultural development only after people had tested the presumed autonomy of matter from all angles and then come to recognize through this empirical process the untenability of a strictly material conception of the divine.

The Jews' recognition thereof was gained primarily through speculation; the impact of this insight would have been entirely different had it been grounded in a practical conviction of the falseness of the earlier outlook. Any advancement beyond polytheism therefore required that one first pursue polytheism itself to the utmost detail through the personification of natural forces — a challenge ultimately taken up by the Greeks. In other words, if the mission of ancient Near Eastern peoples was to conflate their many gods into a single deity by means of a speculative approach, the Greeks were compelled, from an early stage, to multiply the number of their gods and thus more distinctly to differentiate and guide divine natural powers. If ancient Near Eastern peoples revered monarchism, Hellenic tribes pressed toward a form of individualism. This statement is confirmed when we observe the contrast in political outlook between the Greeks and ancient Near Eastern peoples, and the conception of state to which it gave rise. Although the right of the stronger also formed the basis of the Greek world order — and thus state order — certain limitations now began to appear. Slavery was still a social institution, but a new class of free sovereign citizens was emerging; that is, the multitude could now stand side by side as equals. Thus, although the stronger, in general, still held power over the life and death of the weak, this power was starting to be checked by an incipient concept of morality.

Classical Polytheism to the Hellenistic Age

Here we will be concerned with the Greek worldview in the broadest sense, namely with religion. From the outset, anthropomorphic polytheism recognized only material forces, no spiritual ones and therefore no moral ones. In contrast to its Oriental counterpart, it grasped the forces of nature individually and sought to coordinate them among themselves. Polytheism thus came to an ever sharper differentiation of natural forces and thence to an ever greater multitude of deities, each of whom enjoyed equally a certain independence and freedom of movement. The Greeks did not feel pressured to place all the gods under the domination of a single supremely strong figure. Although one highest ruler, Zeus, did exist in the heavenly sphere, there was room alongside him for the activity of countless others. One therefore did not need to turn to Zeus on every occasion but could summon other gods individually according to the natural power one needed. In this way, Greek mythology was gradually transformed into something akin to a natural-scientific universal system. For example, Aeolus is the god of the winds; today we would say the "law of air currents." That is to say, the ancients envisioned the forces of nature no less tangibly than we ourselves do; but because they conceived them solely in material rather than spiritual or abstract terms, they were unable to explain these forces with anything but a material concept of the divine. What we describe as "laws" or "principles," the Greeks could only call a "god." All their observations of nature they animated through the cult of divinity. A more specific example: one witnesses a lightning bolt spare a house at the edge of a forest over which a storm is passing. The ancient Greek assigned meaning to that natural event in the following way: this particular spot is especially pleasing to Jupiter Tonans. He spared the house because its owner had dedicated a nearby grove to him. Today we would draw on the laws of causality, arguing that electrical forces surging outward through the tips of the trees prevented the lightning bolt from striking the house.

This means that polytheism, as the Greeks understood it, led inevitably to the investigation of individual forces of nature and thus, as it continued in this direction, to our own natural sciences. But polytheism could never fully arrive at our natural sciences, because, being unable to grasp the immaterial aspect of the general principles, it could not move beyond nature's fragmentation into discrete material powers. To ancient people (not only the Greeks), the individual natural force was always personified; these groups could not imagine a power that did not arise from an individual presence — that is, from a person. Moreover, the Greeks apprehended such individual presences in strictly material terms. By realizing that natural phenomena had certain necessary causes, the Greeks paved the way for our "law." But their capacity to understand nature was constantly stunted by the fact that they always perceived a person behind the phenomenon. The Jews, who failed to acknowledge any necessary cause at all, lagged even further behind.[1] However, by removing the material person and replacing it with a spiritual being (the animate God — though he is still, to be sure, an individual), this people prepared the course for more accurate understanding.[2]

So, you see, the polytheistic worldview of the Greeks is at heart very closely related to our own. It too led to an efflorescence of natural-scientific study, especially in Alexandria during the age of the Diadochi. But this was not natural science in the modern sense, because the ancients still could not grasp the concept of causal principles. What we understand as an independently active and strictly conceptual causal law appeared to the ancients to be a personalized, material impetus. Whereas we survey large series of things from a distance and construct purely conceptual laws on the basis of such broad observation, ancient people examined each natural object at close range and as an isolated entity. This development of the polytheistic worldview into a kind of natural-scientific system could only lead, gradually but inevitably, to the collapse of polytheism. Let us return to the grove of Jupiter Tonans. People grew accustomed to the fact that the house in the grove was spared from the lightning bolt. This was initially seen as a symptom of the goodwill of Jupiter Tonans, who could very well have destroyed the house. Over time, the alternative idea had to arise that the god was compelled to refrain from destroying the house through some sacrificial act. What was once regarded as the free decision of the god in favor of the sacrificer gradually turned into a necessary compulsion; in this compulsion, we recognize a foreshadowing of our own laws of causality.

Once the Greek outlook allowed divine forces to be placed in a situation of compulsion, it implied the existence of something more powerful than those forces, something that all the deities had to obey. The Greeks' idea of the nature of the gods thus proved unsatisfactory. This not only caused their belief in the gods to be smothered, shaken, and led into absurdity; it also opened up the path toward monotheism. This was the inevitable end of Greek polytheism and its multiplication of deified natural forces: people realized that even all of them together did not sufficiently constitute the essence of the divine. But the Greeks could still not attain pure monotheism. They did so in the domain of philosophy, but this could never convince the masses. Philosophers have never been founders of religion. Philosophical systems are always impractical; they are constructed on abstruse speculations and race ahead of public consciousness. Founders of religion bring with them a simple formula that the masses comprehend easily, though the masses must be prepared long beforehand by actual events.

Thus we witness widespread philosophical monotheism among the Greeks and Romans, especially during the first two centuries of the Roman Imperial era, that is, well before the official recognition of Christianity. This represents a moment of deep significance: it signals the decline of polytheism, the preparation for Christian monotheism, the dissolution of the antique world order. But the decisive stimulus, the overturning of the formula, arose not from classical people but from the Oriental Semites. When the purely spiritual monotheism of the Semites converged with the material polytheism of the Greeks and Romans, the result was the Christian worldview, which dominated Europe beginning around the year 313. This endeavor was not immediately success-ful. The influence of Semitic speculation on classical polytheism stretches back to the age of the Diadochi; Oriental cults had infil-trated Rome since the Punic Wars. But after Septimius Severus, and even since the Antonines, we notice the eruption of a basic need to recover lost harmony by borrowing from the Semites. This has been described as the Semitization of the Roman Empire. It is an essentially religious phenomenon. People adopted cults that paved the way for the transition to monotheism; witness the Mithraic cult, which was a half-Aryan cult in any case.

Jakob Burckhardt has already called our attention to the pro-found religiosity of the third century. During the first and second centuries, people were unbelieving and consoled themselves with philosophical monotheism or with amulets (fetishes); now they yearned for solid revelations, for belief. Let us look again at the individualism of the Greeks. They imagined every force of nature — that is, every personification — to be basically autonomous, that is, endowed with an independent will. The will is a spiritual power, and this entails some acknowledgment of the spiritual. Surely more than among ancient Near Eastern people, especially the Egyptians — though this in no way implies a dominance of the spiritual. Indeed, we do not observe the Greeks' moving far be-yond ancient Near Eastern conceptions, at least outwardly, before the year 500; the first mighty jolt occurred only around the time of the Persian Wars, and from the time of Alexander the Great onward we behold an increasingly emphatic movement toward the spiritual. Clearly this movement helped pave the way for the dissolution of materialistic polytheism.

How does the development of a worldview relate to the development of visual arts in classical Antiquity? Once again, must limit myself to a few quick allusions. Point to analogies in political history first; this can be done with few words and offers revealing analogies. Referred to this earlier with regard to the golden-age Greeks. Like ancient Near Eastern people, these were most often governed by a monarchy until around 500, though the monarchies were already completely different. This was followed by a period of free civic development until the reign of Alexander the Great, then by another monarchy, this time, notably, in close conjunction with the Orient. But it was soon apparent that the Greeks could not maintain such a system over a long duration: they could no longer find the proper balance between democracy and monarchy. The people whose achievements were once so magnificent now lagged behind. The Romans initially struck a balance between democracy and monarchy, but they, too, quickly succumbed to Oriental influence, and the later Imperial age betrays the same heightened Semitization in its administration as in its worldview. Both were brought to fruition under Diocletian and Constantine; but this ultimately exhausted the capacities of the Romans. Western Rome, ancient Rome, collapsed.

A general parallel in visual arts here — derived, of course, from the human figure. In the early period, until around 500 B.C.E., the art of the Greeks, like their worldview, exhibited many traits that were identical with its ancient Near Eastern counterpart. Only in the golden age, from 500 to 330, did Greek art begin to display its own peculiar characteristics. In competing with nature, Greek artists created physical perfection. Moreover, not content with some spiritless, inanimate generality, they granted figures movement, which for the first time extended beyond the extremities to include the head and torso, that is, the portions of the body that have always been conceived as the seat of the soul. Movement is by nature already an externalization of a spiritual factor, the volitional impulse; and soon further efforts were made to summon a spiritual or emotional expression in the facial features (the mirror of the soul) as well. Neither is possible without a certain degree of individualization, which ancient Near Eastern art largely avoided because it detracted from complete bodily perfection. Greek art of the golden age was likewise restrained here; but it did move in that direction. That is, Greek art re-created works of nature in perfected (we would say "beautiful") form but simultaneously strove for the appearance of life. If ancient Near Eastern figures look beautiful, those of the Greeks appear not only beautiful but also lifelike or animated. To be sure, these qualities are only compatible if the sense of liveliness is held in check; this was the basic axiom during the golden age. Liveliness may not be so individuated that perfection suffers. This explains why classical statues of gods strike us so forcefully with their sense of necessity. Greek sculptors of the golden age did not aim to depict physical and spiritual movement so much as the physical and spiritual *capacity* for movement. Today we tend to sense a contradiction in the fact that marble figures rendered in motion do not move further; for us, this disrupts harmony. But from the time of Phidias through Praxiteles, statues were depicted not so much in motion as exuding a supreme potential for physical motion. Calm and contemplative. This is why our modern artistic sensibility since Winckelmann has almost unthinkingly deemed the sculptural art of golden-age Greece the most perfect ever. (This is also what modern painting demands: representation of capacity for movement, or movement through dynamic contours — which the medium of painting in particular allows.)

The Hellenistic Age

The balance was upset during the Hellenistic period, when a decisive turn toward the depiction of physical and spiritual movement occurred. Both art and worldview (natural sciences) now advanced toward individualization. What we call Alexandrian natural science expressed itself in art as so-called naturalism. (We shall discuss this in systematic detail in the section on elements; for the present, we must let a catchword suffice.) Hellenistic Greeks continued to render works of nature as perfect forms in their art. But although the figures still appear beautiful (as we say), they grew increasingly animated, increasingly naturalistic, increasingly individualized — and with that, their beauty suffered. The sequence of the most beautiful artworks came to an end with Lysippus; at that point, sculptural media could no longer serve well, and painting began to take over. People now desired a level of illusion that sculptural arts could not produce.

The final phase of the polytheistic worldview — its collapse in favor of the spiritual monotheism of the Semites — comes to view with special clarity in Roman works of the third century: an often-startling indifference to beauty and liveliness. Beauty had already been jolted; the same thing now happened to liveliness. People fashioned works of art in obedience to tradition but no longer took pleasure in physically improving nature. Having arrived at the insight that the true essence of things lay elsewhere than in bodily appearance, they paid that appearance no further heed. People thus continued to drag their old state gods around with them until 313 C.E., without apprehending in these anything more than a bureaucratic formula inherited from long ago. In the same way, people today who do not adhere to any form of revealed faith still mark the most important occasions in life — birth, death, marriage, and so forth — with cultic rituals. For them, such ritual activities represent nothing more than conventional formulas for documenting those events.

Second Period

Christian Monotheism, 313–1520

The boundaries of this period are hard to define. We can place its beginning at around 313; but where is its end? Officially it is still in effect today in Europe and, to a large extent, America. Running alongside are the Muslims, whom we cannot exclude from our purview because their history is so closely bound up with that of the Christian world, and, to a slightly lesser degree, the Buddhists, whom we can examine separately. But if we are to hold Christian monotheism as the definitive Western worldview since 313 C.E., it remains to be seen whether it really has been sustained into the present. Unbiased observation would conclude that Christian monotheism constituted the generally accepted worldview only until around 1520, after which a fissure opened up. Although the Christian worldview retained its primacy in the ethical domain – even today we tend to adhere to the kind of moral world order championed by Christianity – in the region of material experience the principle of causality has supplanted faith in revelation. We must therefore posit a new worldview after 1520; consequently, we shall present the second period of pure Christian monotheism as only running the span between 313 and 1520, treating it, for the most part, as a closed and autonomous unit.

Earlier we noticed how people of classical Antiquity began to falter in their polytheistic belief system as their observation of material nature — both its outward manifestations and its internal forces — gradually convinced them of its lack of divinity. We also learned why the purely spiritual monotheism of the Jews, which belongs fully to ancient history, had to remain incomprehensible to classical people. A redemptive solution could emerge only from a balance between the two. Jesus Christ was the person who discovered and expounded the redeeming formula that would make monotheism, with its insistence on the power of the spiritual over the material, palatable to classical people. The Christian conception of God entails a deep-rooted concession to polytheists. It does not rest content with God the Father, who largely corresponds to the Jewish Yahweh, but rather distinguishes, on the one side, Christ — Son of God made man, Word made flesh, spirit made human redeemer of physical matter — and, on the other, the Holy Spirit, representative of the spiritual. The implication runs as follows. Because the spiritual is the stronger force and is indivisible in its constitution of a single whole, Christianity is essentially monotheistic. At the same time, matter, though weak and transitory in its individual manifestations, is granted redemption as a whole; Christ's message explicitly calls for the emancipation of the weak and oppressed, and God's boundless love embraces all his material creations equally. Thus spirit and matter do not stand in rigid and irreconcilable opposition to each other. As in Christ, so in all organic creatures, especially human beings, the two are intimately conjoined — though spirit always remains the source of life. The cults of Mary and the saints are clearly accretions to Christianity in the material sense, but these entered only later. For our purposes, it is important that the very core of Christ's teaching entailed tolerance for the material world. This allowed for the admittance of artistic activity from the very beginning of the Christian worldview.

At this point, it may seem appropriate to ask what form artistic production took in its contest with nature under the dominion of the worldview propounded by Jesus Christ. It would, however, be rather pointless to pose this question, because the pure version of the Christian worldview, as formulated by Jesus Christ, remained intact for barely a century; furthermore, we are lacking monuments that could substantiate any *a priori* answer. We can merely acknowledge that first-century Christians were thoroughly consumed with the eschatological expectation that the Last Day would arrive in the near future. The souls of the faithful yearned for separation from matter following their union with God. People expected this to happen soon, because that is what they thought Christ had predicted. This desired withdrawal from earthly things began to wane only after the second century, as Christian communities began to set out into the world, instituting the universal Church and its hierarchy. Only after this moment can the question of the Christian attitude toward visual art have any significance. Until that point, Christians could establish no relation at all to visual art. As something material and earthly, art was useless to them — like matter itself, it was a point of utter indifference.

Even in the earliest years of Christianity, indeed since the apostolic age, so many differences are discernible in the beliefs of individual communities, especially with regard to the relation between spirit and matter, that we cannot speak of one common worldview such as Jesus Christ imagined. It is exceedingly difficult to survey the bewildering array of sects as a whole, but from the very beginning one major opposition distinguished itself within the greater mass. It had already taken shape in the first century, with the division of Jewish from pagan Christians. Having latched onto Jewish messianic expectations, the Jewish Christians were now happy to have found their redeeming Messiah. With true Oriental egoism, they declared themselves satisfied and strove to segregate themselves from the rest of the populace, as the Jews themselves had done. In essence, then, this was Judaism reformed by Christianity. Christians of pagan background, by contrast, discovered the Gospels to be aimed at the salvation of all humanity, a view that doubtless agreed more closely with Christ's intentions. It is thus only natural that Judaic Christians bound themselves so closely to the Orient, whereas pagan Christians recruited in the western lands of the empire.

I shall pass over details of the subsequent development and turn directly to the fifth century, where we confront with special clarity the deep-rooted division between the two worldviews. The Oriental worldview of the Syrians and Egyptians is known as Monophysitism. This doctrine teaches that there is one single nature in Christ; it emphasized Christ's deified humanity while pushing aside as much as possible his human, material character. Thus matter and spirit were once again rigidly separated; their union in the person of Christ, which had redeemed the material world, was dissolved. This represents nothing less than a return to the pure monotheism of the Jews. This move could not have been satisfactory to the West, for only the validation of the material world effected by Christ's human nature had won classical pagans over to Christianity. Thus the West, with the bishop of Rome at its head, defended the double nature of Christ with the utmost resolve, while the Syrian and Egyptian East argued equally vigorously for Christ's solely divine, that is, spiritual, nature.

How did the political lords of Syria and Egypt, the Byzantines, respond to this problem? They assumed the intermediary role that would remain characteristic of them and sought to mediate between West and East. Influence fluctuated in the Byzantine courts; although people never went so far as to embrace pure Monophysitism, the separation from the Latin world that would take definitive shape in the ninth century was already underway

by the fifth. After that point, we must differentiate between two
Christian worldviews: a Roman one founded on toleration of the
material world, and a Byzantine one, which, if not entirely hostile
to matter (it was still Christian, after all, and thus believed in the
Trinity), was certainly not friendly to it. The division of art into
Western and Byzantine varieties rests on this opposition of the
two basic Christian worldviews. How was the essence of each
view formed?

The Eastern Roman Christian Worldview

I am intentionally not calling this view Byzantine because everything that emanated from Byzantium at this point was pure compromise, corresponding neither to the outlook of most Eastern
Christians nor to that of most western Roman Christians. It will
behoove us, therefore, to investigate the Monophysite worldview,
for this was the view of Semitic and Egyptian Christians. For Eastern peoples, Christianity entailed a westernization, an individualization, that did not lie within their spiritual purview, and they
sought to shake it off as much as possible. As Christians, the
Monophysites had to admit some visual art, some occupation with
the material world, even while they insisted that spirit and matter
had nothing in common at heart. Our senses deceive us into
thinking that spirit and matter are fully united in natural phenomena such as human beings: that is merely an illusion. Nature,
in itself, is dead and inanimate; the spiritual is purely divine.
Whoever wants to portray nature as it really is, not just as it seems,
must therefore show it as dead and lifeless. You see, this leads
us straight to the character of ancient Near Eastern art. People
despised the spiritual in art and tried to subdue it as much as possible; but their motivation for doing so lay at the opposite pole,
and here these extremes coincided. What is dead nature? Mineral,
crystalline nature; these types were depicted in perfect form, for

in this domain perfection (that is, regularity, beauty, symmetry) can do no harm. Such art prefers to depict dead nature: that is, ornamentation with minimal organic meaning. But Christian art cannot dispense entirely with the representation of organic creatures, including human beings. Conceptual purpose: to stimulate contemplation of lofty subjects. Human beings may be depicted but only in as lifeless, as inorganic, as geometric a form as possible. Thus we see: eastern Roman Christianity strove for a beautiful but lifeless portrayal of natural things. Byzantine figures modeled on these appear rigid and stiff; but they are also solemn and appear enveloped by greater sacredness. They do not possess the rigidity of Egyptian figures. This entire art is an art of compromise. As in Eastern Antiquity, the conception of nature resides in the combination of beauty and lifelessness.

Apparent return to early Antiquity. This manifests itself in all other cultural domains. The Orient has kept its hold on Antiquity up to the present. Henceforth we encounter in the East only monarchical forms of government (analogous forms of worldview in the Byzantine and Arab worlds); the whole remaining order likewise continues to be based on the right of the stronger. This is still characteristic of all Oriental worldviews. The benefits went well beyond the moral sphere. Spirit exists not to rescue and liberate matter but to exploit it. Animals and plants in particular, but human beings as well. Loyalty is unknown. No one trusts another. Every Easterner is an egoist, even today. The ancient Eastern essence is ineradicable.

The eastern Roman Monophysites were unable to govern themselves on their own. They were dependent on Byzantium. We already noted that Byzantine court circles, composed mainly of Greeks, had no affinity for the Western outlook, which entailed a certain tolerance for matter along with spirit. This is what gave rise to the compromises — though these were not satisfactory to either side. We can conclude in general that in Byzantium in the early Byzantine period, the overwhelming tendency was to avoid corruption from the West. Such corruption would have irritated the Eastern Christian masses, who regarded Western Christianity as a kind of polytheism. This provided the impetus for a new worldview to arise at the southeastern border of the Semitic world, a worldview that would more fully conform to the sensibilities of Semitic people: Islam.

Islam returned to a spiritual Yahweh, discarding the Trinity and with it any conjunction of spirit and matter. The material world is dead, soulless. Result: the visible material symbol of the divine is a stone, the Kaaba. In contrast to Judaism, Islam opened itself to the contest with the material world, but only its dead, inanimate products — abstract ornament — not a contest with animate nature, which included plants, animals, human beings. We call this the Islamic prohibition of images. The connection between artistic activity and worldview is more vivid here than anywhere else in the previous history of mankind, except in the case of the Jews. The reversion to earlier Near Eastern Antiquity is readily apparent here. No right to self-determination; unadulterated fatalism.[1] Here we see the dead end from which ancient Near Eastern people would never escape.

The development of Islam had the most extensive effect on the Byzantine Empire. First, the entire Monophysite East surrendered itself to Arab dominion. The Monophysites felt closer in worldview to Muslims than to Western Christians. Even the Greeks were swept up powerfully in this movement. Their deep sensitivity to potential accusations of polytheism led them to Iconoclasm under the Isaurians, an imperial dynasty from Asia Minor. Here, too, the connection between the history of art and the history of culture — that is, the broader development of a worldview — is readily apparent. In the ninth century, yet another reaction occurred against the Islamic-Monophysite revolution of the eighth century, which this time was crushed by Western Christianity embodied in the Roman bishop. Only from the ninth century onward can we speak of a solid and genuine Byzantine worldview. It approximated Monophysitism very closely. People did not want to dispense with figural creation altogether, but they prevented any move toward lifelikeness by means of the familiar canon: figuration was geometrized, so to speak. This also explains how the boundaries of Byzantine and Arab-Islamic art came gradually and imperceptibly to flow over into each other by the latter half of the Middle Ages.[2]

The Western Roman Christian Worldview and
Its Relation to Art

One might simply call this art Roman because it originated in Rome. But this would lead to erroneous conclusions, in particular because Byzantine people also considered themselves Romans (and to some extent still do today). Let us therefore call it Catholic art. This designation applies to the entire Middle Ages. Catholic art emerged in pure form only among the people who gave birth to it: the progeny of classical peoples west of the Mediterranean, especially the Italians (as distinct from Germanic peoples, to whom Catholic monotheism had to be introduced). Romans in particular. We shall therefore begin by discussing the Catholic monotheism of Latin groups in the Middle Ages, most powerfully exemplified in the Italians, and specifically those from central Italy.

The essence of the Catholic worldview is most clearly recognized when one singles out the polytheistic kernel embedded deep inside it: the material world enjoyed some justification alongside the spiritual. Human beings, for example, were composed of both matter and spirit, just as the Greeks believed; but whereas in earlier times matter had been the stronger component, now spirit was more powerful. This attitude opened the door to individualism; this was most clearly expressed in the doctrine of free will, to which Catholicism has always clung with deepest determination. Great autonomy resided in matter, as the Greeks likewise supposed. We saw earlier how this notion of the autonomy of matter led the Greeks to the natural sciences. You see, Catholicism kept the door open to the natural sciences from its very inception for whenever it wanted to use them. This is why the Catholic Church today has proclaimed its agreement with most findings of natural-scientific research. It did not always do this voluntarily, to be sure; there was always some struggle involved. And so we must immediately ask why the Church did not avail itself of this option right away. Why did it not recognize the individualism of natural forces from the outset? Because this would have entailed a return to polytheism. And people did indeed realize that something existed above and beyond the various nature deities. This higher power is the spiritual Christian God. The Christian God has the power to exercise his will wherever he chooses. True, man possesses free will. But God has free will, too (unlike the polytheistic god, who can be swayed by sacrificial offerings), which is stronger than the will of human beings or any natural force. I want to live; but at any moment, God can cause me to die.

One can see, then, why classical people greeted Christianity as a relief. They were uneasy with the idea of something that was higher than their nature gods but that they, with their aversion to abstract speculation, could not grasp as a purely spiritual being. Christianity reintroduced them to this higher power and taught them to seek the divine in that supreme being alone.

We can thus describe the Catholic worldview of Latin people in the following way. Natural beings live and move according to their own free will, but the possibility of breaking the laws of nature always remains in God's hands (he can produce miracles). You see the contrast with our modern worldview, which holds that even God cannot break the laws of nature (there are no miracles in material nature). Everything must have its "natural" cause. The same contradiction exists with regard to the Greek worldview, at least in its mature phase; there, too, the gods could not disobey the conditions of sacrifice.

Thus natural phenomena are independent to a certain extent, and matter possesses some autonomous value; but spirit — that is, the will of God — stands far above both. Is it, then, worth the effort to study natural relations? People have approached this question differently in different times. Herein lies the developmental path, distinct for various groups: difference between Romans and Germanic people. Let us confine ourselves to Italy for the moment: classical people, though mixed in nationality, whose cultural life extended from Antiquity well into the Middle Ages.

Part 1, Rome from around the fourth to the sixth century. People did not think the study of nature worthwhile, because they feared a return to polytheism. One might even say that polytheism persisted among Christians. Christians did believe in a higher power resident in statues of the gods, but this was an evil, demonic power far inferior to the divine; assumed the form of the satyr. This belief in Satan or the devil lives on today. Now we must ask what people thought of artistic activity. The door stood open: people could depict animate nature, lively nature. And what about beauty? Eastern Christians accepted it in their contest with inanimate matter, and when dealing with animate things, they geometrized the lively qualities as much as possible. Western Christians admitted animate matter as such, which was potentially dangerous at a time when they were still having to contend with polytheism. Roman art avoided beauty as much as possible, even going so far as to make things ugly. This explains the remarkable phenomenon of an art that deliberately strove for ugliness. On the other hand, in this early period we see absolute indifference to liveliness. It would have been possible for people to seek out this quality; after all, nature itself possesses independent life to a certain extent. Because this was already part of the essence of natural beings, an improved nature had to be rendered in a similarly animated form. But this was not worth the effort, for material life could be obliterated by God at any moment.

Part 2, sixth to eighth century. Byzantine influence not only in the exarchate but also in Rome. Ties between East and West grew closer; definitively severed by the Schism in the mid-ninth century.

Part 3, considered the period of thoroughgoing "barbarism" in Italy. Artists abandoned both liveliness, as in Part 1, and beauty, as in Part 2. Lasted from the eighth until around the middle of the eleventh century.

Part 4, eleventh to thirteenth century. Once again people opened themselves to Byzantine influence, as Vasari already acknowledged.[3] For him, it was only with Cimabue and Giotto that Florentine art was freed from Byzantine influence.

Part 5, the fourteenth century. Age of Giotto. Here Christian-Catholic art reached the same summit as polytheistic Greek art in the golden age of 500–330 B.C.E. But whereas in the earlier period the material aspect was dominant and the spiritual-individual represented a novelty to be accepted with the utmost restraint, now the spiritual side predominated and the material was handled tentatively. Here, too, we find agreement between worldview and art. Scholasticism sharply emphasized individualism, free will, and man's self-determination while pointing out with equal insistence the hand of God directing it all. Scholasticism likewise sought to integrate at least some of the natural-scientific findings of the Greeks into Christian dogma. In the same way, Giottesque art held natural phenomena clearly in view; images grew both livelier and less geometrically beautiful. But we must not forget, first, that all artistic production, even in its external form, still existed for the glory of God and, second, that it never exceeded a rather narrow range in its truth to life. Hence that measured restraint, reminiscent of the classical golden age.

Part 6, the Renaissance. The quattrocento and beginning of the cinquecento. Now that the gates were opened, the flood could no longer be contained. Observation of nature expanded, errors were discerned, and the danger of the polytheistic kernel lingering deep within Christian doctrine manifested itself among those people who had passed through classical polytheism. Inclined to grant excessive autonomy to natural phenomena, people began to ignore the God behind them. Although they veered toward a natural-scientific manner of observation, they did not attain the conception of a higher, overarching principle, because they understood individual natural phenomena as overly autonomous; at the same time, they began to lose faith in the Christian notion of God. Moreover, the dogmatic presentation of the Christian worldview had made many claims that close observation of nature proved untrue. Hence widespread atheism. What was art to do? It grasped the material world as autonomous; it perfected it and made it beautiful. Hence the rise of the cult of beauty, which predominated even in the papal court.

With that, one developmental stage seems to draw to a conclusion. This is the development not only of Catholic monotheism but of the entire worldview of classical people after the Greeks, a worldview whose shape in the Christian era was provided by the Latins. One may therefore speak of a Greco-Roman-Latin worldview, which contained both a pagan and a Christian component but — in contrast to the ancient Near Eastern worldview — united these through a common emphasis on individualism. Animate things of nature, especially humans, are individuals composed of body and soul; for the Greeks, every man was a genuine god and, for the Christian Romans, a kind of god or daimon. But whereas the Greeks saw a compulsion presiding over everything (as discussed earlier), the Christians perceived the one spiritual God. People in the fifteenth century were aware that things in nature scorned dogmatic precepts, that they ran their own course, and that any intervention of the higher spiritual power of God seemed thus to be prohibited. This could have been the point at which our causal laws simply supplanted God. But the Romans and their Catholic monotheism were by their very nature unable to do this. Neither could move beyond individualism; they conceived of man — and therefore God — in strictly individual terms. Although faith was shaken, nothing new took its place. Thus the role of Latin people in the history of human culture — at least with regard to the formation of a worldview — comes to an end.

After 1520, Romance countries merely underwent an artificial regeneration, a damming of the unchecked drive toward natural observation (in this respect France holds an intermediary position of transition to Germanic people). Once again people were forcefully reminded of the dominance of the almighty hand of God, capable of altering the course of nature at whim, over all individual material phenomena. As a result, Italian Baroque painters never tired of painting marvels and miracles. The souls of Latin people yearned for such outpourings of harmony. But all this could not be sustained in the long run. Today Romance countries are governed more powerfully by religious indifference than any of their Germanic counterparts.

Third Period

Natural-Scientific Worldview

What does the designation "natural-scientific worldview" mean? That things in nature are entities that neither move freely and completely at will (thus, in essence, deities) nor are moved solely by the whims of a higher god; rather, they are bound together in specific ways and relate to each other as cause and effect. One can therefore say that, according to the natural-scientific worldview, the harmonic world order that people now desire resides in the law of causality. Natural things no longer besiege people blindly, nor are they steered about by quasi-human divinities; rather, things behave in obedience to an eternally fixed and immutable law. The law is inexorable (we must die) but not intentionally malevolent; once one understands this law, one can adapt oneself to it. This is the purpose of the natural sciences.

When was the law of causality discovered? It had already made an appearance in classical Antiquity: we see it clearly with Democritus, a philosopher of the fifth century B.C.E., and later with Epicurus. (We have already discussed the study of natural sciences in Greece. As we observed in Greek art, this was connected to a noticeable movement toward truth to life.) But two things prevented the law of causality from entering the general mass consciousness in Antiquity (in contrast to today, when no one believes in the possibility of miracles).

First, in trying to substantiate the law of causality, people stayed within a very narrow field. They never moved beyond individual cases. That is, whenever people came near to finding convincing empirical proof, they became absorbed in details. They did not discover the all-encompassing laws with which we are familiar today, such as the laws of Indestructibility of Matter and Conservation of Energy.

Second, recognition of the universal power of the law of causality always remained speculative and philosophical. The masses, however, are not won over with philosophy.[1]

In the Christian — specifically, the Roman Catholic — worldview, the doctrine of free will stood opposed to the law of causality. Individuals move themselves freely, and God does so most of all. Strictly speaking, then, a law of causality cannot exist. The Church eventually came to recognize such a law, but only to a limited extent; God could break it at any moment.

Only at the end of the Middle Ages did the law of causality gain some appreciation in the nominalist strain of Scholasticism. But we can speak of a distinct natural-scientific worldview only after 1520. This took shape specifically among groups of purely Germanic heritage. Naturally, its traces among these people can also be followed back before 1520.

Why 1520? Because this worldview was first articulated during the Reformation. The errors into which Catholic monotheism had fallen in Renaissance Italy convinced Germanic people that this worldview was no longer acceptable in its current form. One aspect in particular conflicted deeply with their own sensibilities, and it was Martin Luther who defined more precisely what was so objectionable: the individualism of classical and Roman people, the doctrine of free will. As Luther argued, man has no free will. What he does and how he acts — all this unfolds according to an irrevocably fixed predestination. This predestination, determined by God and eternally valid, is nothing less than a law. It defeats anything individual. Man possesses no individual volition, and no other individual stands above him, no God directing his course at will — only a law. The law, however, comes from God.

We are thinking here primarily of the moral world order (for instance, the efficacy of good works, which was swept aside after Luther), but the practical implications of a natural law are also immediately apparent. Strictly speaking, matter, too, distinguishes not individuals but only a law; this was formulated in our own century as the law of Conservation of Energy.

How does all this pertain to artistic production? Improvement of nature: our senses deceive us by showing individuals; there are no individuals. Three-dimensionality must therefore be merely illusory; natural-scientific art must be anti-sculptural. It communicates the will of things most faithfully with optical vision: hence the predominance of painting (which does not isolate objects but rather shows them within their surroundings; not isolated phenomena in nature, but extracts from nature). What differentiates such art from nature? The relations among objects come more clearly to view in the image than in nature; herein lies the improvement.[2] To create harmony, the painter portrays the impact of naturalistic causal interactions on the objects in his picture. The causal relationship is the purpose of art. One result comes sharply into focus here to reveal the essence of an art governed by the natural-scientific worldview, though, admittedly, we are now passing into the domain of art's elements. Ancient art portrayed things, quasi-human forces; the human figure ruled. The world existed solely for men; more specifically, the physically perfect and beautiful man reigned supreme. Only in the final period of decline did landscape, genre, and animal pictures emerge. Art of the Christian Middle Ages depicted things for the sake of human beings. The whole order was at heart morally grounded and oriented toward men. Once again, things of nature existed solely for human beings. Man — more specifically, the good man — likewise ruled in this art. In natural-scientific art, man counted only as much as any other natural thing. The circle of creation was not closed with the human being. Because the world cannot be grasped with human reason, it was obviously not created for mankind. Here the teleological viewpoint, wherein everything rushes toward the goal of being useful to men, falls apart. It was in Holland that, for the first time, all nature claimed equal status with human beings; for Roman and Spanish artists, man retained his primacy.

PART TWO

Elements

We shall not examine here elements of a purely material nature, such as extrinsic function, physical material, and technique.[1] We shall consider only:

1. *What* — the natural object with which man competes. Motifs. Not individual cases dictated by external functions but broad categories: how an artist chooses one over another.

2. *In what manner* man apprehends impressions of natural motifs through his external senses. Just as the composition of a work of art takes shape in the internal senses, so the beholder perceives the work internally. Although we cannot investigate how this happens, we can determine both how the artist absorbs and responds to his external, material experience of nature and how the viewer in turn absorbs and responds to the work of art. There are two possible routes: the sense of touch and the sense of sight — not, as modern art has led people to suppose, the latter alone. The tactile sense grasps motifs as three-dimensional forms, the optical sense as two-dimensional surfaces. There is a whole scale of intermediate points as well. Thus we speak of the relation between form and surface.

CHAPTER FOUR

Motifs and Purposes

The things in the world with which man can compete are divisible into two main categories: (1) inanimate, inert, inorganic motifs; (2) animate, organic motifs. The criterion is life, as manifested in movement. Inorganic beings cannot move by their own volition, cannot transport themselves from one place to another or rearrange their molecules. Organic beings can do this in either of two ways: (*a*) through growth, the internal rearrangement of molecules (as in plants and animals); (*b*) through translocation (peculiar only to animals, including human beings).

We must now discuss the relation between the two groups. Inorganic beings have no intrinsic capacity for movement, but are they truly inanimate? No, they are supremely full of movement: air, water, the earth's crust. But this movement originates in forces that work on those things from outside, forces that continuously displace and replace them and to which they are thus completely subject. These things are not entirely defenseless, of course; movement works inside them to hinder internal disruptions or the disintegration of the aggregate condition that allows them to cohere as three-dimensional entities (especially in solid bodies). Beyond this, the external pressures are counteracted by gravity. But in the end, the outside forces are strong enough to overcome such resistance. Very rarely do we confront an inorganic thing that is entirely unblemished: we can cite only the crystal. We shall therefore designate this entire category of motifs "crystalline," so as not to risk confusion with inorganic and organic. In its purest form, that of a regular polyhedron (there are also more complicated shapes, which, however, represent a clouding of the pure formal law; we will therefore stick to the so-called regular types), a crystal is an absolutely symmetrical body that yields two identical halves when sliced through its center point: right and left, upper and lower portions are always the same. It is always bounded by similarly symmetrical forms with adjoining edges. A crystal looks perfectly clear and comprehensible. While its symmetry makes it entirely self-contained — thus a discrete unit — its various facets are delineated with equal sharpness. Absolute order governs the overall arrangement. The formal law consists of: (1) absolute symmetry; (2) sharp, clear distinctions, that is, no curvature. That is, the crystalline material, in itself, lacks movement; it is thoroughly symmetrical. Symmetry is the basic principle of all crystalline matter and of all inorganic crystalline motifs. But the external forces that continuously besiege crystalline material destroy this pure formal structure, so that it often disappears without a trace. In consequence, inorganic things often appear as amorphous masses.

Organic motifs. A plant and an animal, especially when seen from the side. At first glance, these beings are not arranged symmetrically and therefore do not appear so distinct as individuals. But on closer inspection, symmetry is discernible here, too: in small parts as well as large ones, in the cells, the leaf, the annual rings of the tree; an experienced anatomist can split the entire body of an animal or a man into two symmetrical halves. This is to say that although symmetry is indeed present in large and small parts alike, it does not reveal itself clearly or openly. Why? Again, because of the forces that actively work on these things from out-side. Although the powers of resistance exercised by crystalline matter are not sufficient to hold the individual objects together, organic beings retain for a certain time (that is, for their lifetimes) an effective defensive weapon in their own power of motion, which, by counteracting external movements, stakes an at least temporary claim for the being as an individual. Once again, movement destroys the symmetry of organic things. In this case, the destruction is not so thorough as in the previous instance, because it is counteracted by internal movement: the underlying symmetry reappears during pauses and certain motions. Still, this symmetry is never found in so pure a form in the organic world as in the crystal, with the possible exception of certain very low forms of vegetal and animal life irrelevant to the visual arts.

Thus we have arrived at the following basic principles:

1. All motifs — that is, anything in organic or inorganic nature with which man can compete — were originally symmetrically formed, three-dimensional individuals (not only crystals but also plants and animals). That is, stereometric, not merely planimetric, symmetry in the various surfaces. Symmetry constitutes the first and most basic principle of all formal shaping of matter. It provides the sole norm for the formal shaping of matter. It is thus synonymous with beauty, if one sets this as the standard of physical perfection.

2. Symmetry is incessantly under attack — and, wherever possible, destroyed — by movement.

3. Symmetry and movement relate to each other as opposites. The more one side gains, the more the other must lose. (Switch to interpretation right away: symmetry is beauty, movement is organic truth to life; therefore, each must strive to banish the other.)

4. The law of symmetry is eternal and immutable. There is only *one* conceivable symmetry in any individual, because there is only a single center point around which the other parts can be

345

arranged. On the other hand, any individual is capable of innumerable motions that incessantly supplant one another, with only a fleeting, transient existence. Symmetry represents the eternal; movement, the transitory.

5. Only the crystal is perfectly symmetrical. For that reason, the crystal constitutes the only absolutely clear, self-contained, and thoroughly beautiful entity. In this respect, all animate organic matter is subordinate to the lifeless crystal.

The relation between crystalline and organic motifs may be defined as follows:

1. As individual units, such motifs are united through their originally symmetrical composition. This is common to all natural things.

2. They differ in that crystalline things either preserve this symmetry in pure form or lose their status as individuals. In these, symmetry and individuality coincide and are identical. Organic things, by contrast, retain both their individuality and, more important, their basic symmetrical structure through their partial surrender of symmetry. Here individuality and symmetry are no longer unconditionally congruent. The organic being accommodates a certain degree of asymmetry. Some of its symmetry must be relinquished, but not all. Symmetry and movement are mutually exclusive opposites, like body and soul. Symmetry is the formal law of matter, movement that of spirit. Organic motifs and the crystal are not, however, automatically opposed to each other. Visual art proves that they can tolerate each other to a certain extent. Why? Crystalline motifs are purely symmetrical, restful, while organic ones, though animated, are still not pure movement, pure spirit; they are not wholly asymmetrical. As a mixture of body and spirit, they preserve some symmetry — for example (as mentioned above), when in a state of repose. When dealing with organic matter, then, we must consider not only movement

346

but also the restful state of matter, symmetry. On the other hand, we see on closer inspection that movement also appears in inorganic motifs. Between the crystalline and the organic there exist transitional forms, which are of special interest for visual art. We shall therefore want to examine them more closely. One quickly recognizes that only the unity between both groups is absolute. The variations are graded rather than absolute, not diametrically opposed to each other as symmetry and movement are. This is significant, for it explains how the two could ever be reconciled. Let us now consider a few phenomena that bring to view the transition from crystalline to organic form. Although they are no longer strictly crystalline things, they resemble the crystalline structure in their formal laws.

First case: Symmetrical as a whole, indistinct in the parts. A regular polyhedron with an infinite number of sides is a sphere. The crystal can never be round. Its surfaces must bend so as to adjoin in sharp edges. The sphere is stereometrically symmetrical, indeed more perfectly so than any crystal. For that reason, the sphere always strikes the beholder's eyes as an individual unit. Its roundness, however, departs from crystallinity. That is, the sphere is clear as a whole but unclear in the parts; it possesses innumerable parts that slip imperceptibly into one another. Roundness results from movement. Organic things create curves for themselves through their inherent animation, their capacity for movement: in the struggle for survival, to ward off destructive outside influences (plant stems, animal limbs). The hard edges of inorganic objects must be smoothed away artificially through extrinsic forces. In reality, there is no such thing as a spherical crystal; only organic nature generates spheres — seeds, for example — and man shapes these further with his hands. This example goes beyond inorganic nature. But it shows how intimate is the relation between organic and inorganic products.

Second case: Distinct in the parts but not symmetrical as a whole. The pyramid represents an inverse disruption of the law of crystallinity. The pyramid resembles a crystal in its composition of discrete, sharp-edged surfaces. But it is not a regular polyhedron, for it displays symmetry only across the central axis, not in the upper and lower halves. Here symmetry is partial, as in organic things, rather than absolute. If I turn the pyramid on its side, even the bilateral symmetry disappears. How is this explained? The pyramid exhibits two distinct directionalities, one through which it tapers, a second through which it broadens. The broader direction represents gravity, which pulls everything toward the ground, while the narrower one signals the power of growth, which strives to draw things away from the ground. This growth force doubtless represents a movement inherent in the material. This can no longer be inorganic. The pyramid is not a crystal but an octahedron whose upward movement is halted.

We find internal movement already in the pyramid, though the essential properties of inorganic matter still cling to it. Because the pyramid dispenses with curvature despite being essentially organic, it is a transitional motif. It also departs from symmetry. But something else takes its place: the force of upward growth, counteracting gravitational pull. The pyramid's shape represents the end of that battle. If the growth force alone were present, at a certain point the pyramid would taper off into a tiny thread. The force of gravity engenders the formal beauty of the pyramid. The pyramid would appear displeasing if it were either excessively slender or excessively stout. It must exhibit balance, a proper middle between the extremes — then it has proportion. At its heart lies a sense of harmony: the two forces balance each other out. Thus we conclude: Proportion emerges where there is movement, a shifting of parts away from pure symmetry. It does not simply exist from the beginning. Although we habitually name symmetry and proportion in a single breath and tend to perceive the essence of physical beauty as residing in both, this view is neither scholarly nor scientific. Proportion does not need to be present; certainly some things are solely symmetrical (the regular polyhedron). Proportion asserts itself only where symmetry is disrupted.

A second elemental difference. There is only one form of symmetry: right and left sides must be absolutely identical. On this fact opinions cannot vary. Proportion, on the other hand, can take diverse forms. Consider the column: the Greeks employed several distinct proportional systems, which contrast markedly with Gothic and modern columns.[1] This derives from the fact that proportion is generated by movement. All movement is transitory, and therefore proportion is as well.

Proportion, then, does not constitute a fixed standard for material form. Only symmetry does. We call the standard of material form — the eternal, unconditionally valid, law-bound form — the beauty of matter. Thus the law of beauty is symmetry alone. Symmetry is beautiful, intrinsically and under all circumstances.

Although we tend to consider proportion such a norm, this is not entirely correct, as we have just observed, for proportion itself is the expression of transient motion. Sometimes, however, people equate proportion with symmetry. Why? Proportion is movement, which appears in inorganic nature and consequently resembles symmetry.[2] Thus in certain cases, art strives for proportionality even when all other movement is conscientiously excluded — for example, in ancient Egyptian figures that sit stiffly and lifelessly but whose torsos and heads display both proportion and symmetry. One can console oneself with the fact that proportion contributes to the essence of physical beauty; but, strictly speaking, it stands opposed to absolute beauty — that is, to absolute symmetry, which it disrupts. This is why, despite some variations in taste, people generally agree when it comes to proportionality. We call the sphere and the pyramid secondary crystalline forms, or transitional forms; their curvature and proportion make them tremendously important in the history of art.

How does man approach his contest with these motifs? Let us begin by asking what kind of motifs man first drew into his contest: organic or crystalline? This is closely related to the question of the earliest external purpose. We left that inquiry hanging because it is nearly impossible to answer today. My personal conviction is that human creativity originated with the conceptual purpose. But let us accept Semper's point of view and assume — as many, if not most, people do today — that the practical purpose came first. Let us imagine a primitive person who has some primitive practical need to fulfill. He has at his disposal some dead crystalline matter (in other words, some inorganic material, though it could also be something organic that had turned inorganic through deprivation of movement, such as bone or wood). One of the most ancient practical necessities was weaponry: arrowheads of stone, crude, chipped (there were no tools yet for smoothing or polishing). (It could also be a lance tip for stabbing or the blade of a scraping instrument.) We are familiar with such pointed stone weapons from prehistoric times. They are all carved into more or less regular triangular shapes. What is triangular form? It is crystalline in its display of symmetry; but this symmetry is only planimetric, not stereometric. It has a pointed tip, thus a kind of movement. It has directionality, like the pyramid, and thus proportion. It counts among the transitional forms between crystalline and organic. Now, how did man come to create this motif? Did he devise it from inorganic nature? Crystals are rare, and none possesses a purely arrowhead-like shape. What about organic nature? Organic products that can be used for piercing, such as thorns and fish bones, are considerably more slender. In reality, man did not look to any object in nature for a model, for he was

350

faced with the challenge of working up dead matter. What kind of form would nature have used under such circumstances? A crystalline one. Man — an integral component of nature himself — imparts the object with a crystalline shape. This requires no explanation: because he is a human being, that is, because he himself *is* nature, man must endow objects with natural — crystalline, symmetrical — form. Even today we can test this: a piece of paper used as a place mat will be cut symmetrically, a match is carved evenly, and so forth. In other words, where there is no motivation for giving dead matter the shape of organic motifs, man will naturally select crystalline form. The crystalline form is the most normal and self-evident for human beings because it is the most normal and self-evident for nature whenever it works with dead, inanimate matter.

But is this a pure crystal? No. The thing — in this case, the arrowhead — has a practical human purpose, and because all human activity is bound up with motion, this too must find expression in the work. Hence the triangular shape, a transitional form. While symmetrical creation is natural as an underlying basis, it is upset by directional growth; in other words, proportion mitigates symmetry.

One must hold this axiom firmly in mind: insofar as external purposes do not require a contest with organic nature, man's artistic production is essentially crystalline. And a second postulate: these are secondary rather than pure crystalline forms. That is, in their introduction of proportion, they are no longer thoroughly symmetrical. A glance at architecture and industrial arts confirms the truth of this statement. These arts have, in general, worked with symmetrical forms up to the present day — not in a purely crystalline fashion, that is, not with stereometric symmetry, but certainly with planimetric symmetry. The clear division into sharp-edged planes predominates, at least in architecture and furniture; although organic curvature occasionally makes its way into these domains, it always disappears very quickly. Even modern art, which tries to incorporate organic forms in its industrial arts, has returned in architecture to crisp rectilinear forms. At the same time, a second point holds true: man's own functional requirements — namely, movement — do not allow crystallinity to emerge in pure form; thus the seeds of organic design lie latent even in architecture and industrial arts. This is especially apparent in the applied arts; perhaps one day architecture will likewise be designed organically.

Let us now look carefully at a second point. People typically relegate architecture and industrial arts to a subordinate category. But man is most genuinely creative in these domains. Here he uses no model but rather invents forms utterly independently. If a completely unrestricted contest with nature is possible anywhere, it is here. If man transgresses a certain boundary, he submits to dependence on nature. In this respect, architecture and industrial arts constitute a higher form of art than anything else.

This explains many phenomena that might seem peculiar at first glance:

1. The presence of certain artistic purists who, even in our own century, demand the greatest possible obedience to "architectonic" laws, that is, laws of crystallinity, in sculptural arts and painting — for example, more or less symmetry in pictorial compositions. Not just classical archaeologists, in whom such one-sidedness would be understandable, but even the most profound connoisseurs of more recent art, such as the incomparable Jakob Burckhardt. Burckhardt recognized the law of crystallinity to be the formal principle underlying all art without exception.[3] In his view, man could never completely renounce this principle in his own artistic activity, this, after all, being bound to dead matter. At least not in sculptural art. But also not in painting.

2. Ideas such as Semper's that primitive artistic activity was higher and more pure than anything that followed. Semper reached this conclusion by examining the creations of uncivilized people, whose confident crystalline treatment of motifs and naive polychromatic handling of color betray a thoroughly unblemished artistic taste, as opposed to the corrupted taste of modern Europeans. At certain points, Semper takes this argument so far that he seems to believe in some original state of human perfection such as is described in the Bible. Whereas inorganic motifs possess timeless value, the organic motifs employed by modern artists have but a limited aesthetic appeal. For that reason, the works of savages are continuously pleasing, whereas modern works can please only for a certain time and under particular conditions.

How does this conclusion relate to Semper's hypothesis? Semper thought that man came to know symmetry and proportion through the industrial arts, that is, arts aimed at practical functions (1). This is correct if it means that man was originally unconscious — and only gradually became aware — of the fact that these are two distinct principles of beauty, which may well have taken a long time. Only with Platonic and Aristotelian philosophy were such generalized concepts acquired. This notion is incorrect, however, if one presumes that symmetry and proportion adhered solely to technical aspects and external purposes and that those aspects, rather than internal imperatives of human artistic creation, gave rise to these properties. In such a view, the arrowhead would be evenly triangular simply because the chipping process so demanded it: this does not really tell us anything. Or because external requirements dictated it: but an irregularly pointed shape (such as a thorn) could, under certain circumstances, have served a purpose just as well if not better. Symmetry arises neither from technique nor from practical purpose but from an internal drive that man is bound to obey: as nature himself, man works up dead matter in the same way nature does. Although man's contest with crystalline nature appears automatic, it is accompanied by a need for harmony — the same as permeates nature. The crystal itself makes clear that even dead nature possesses an innate drive toward order. Now let us suppose that the decorative purpose came first (2). In this case, we can say the same thing we did about the practical function: because the filling in of empty space likewise occurs with dead matter, man endows it with crystalline form whenever there is no impetus to shape it organically. Even if the decorative purpose (with no admixture of conceptual purpose) were utterly, completely, and intrinsically the earliest external function, human artistic production would still have originated in a contest with inorganic motifs.

Now let us take a third scenario: the conceptual purpose came first (3). What sort of notions filled primitive man? He was primarily concerned with the chaotic movements that encroached on him constantly from outside — all the more so the more lively they were. The liveliest movements are produced by animals and human beings. For that reason, these creatures would occupy the foremost place in his imagination: hence organic images. The plant, being incapable of locomotion, receded in importance from the very start. It is revealing to note that although the earliest people employed geometric patterns alongside animal and human figures, they had no foliate ornamentation. The animal figures in the Dordogne artifacts are instructive here: hunter tribes. I regard the conceptual purpose as the earliest because I see the human need for harmony, which strives to conceptualize the essence of natural forces and to develop a worldview, as the most ancient and elemental. Animals doubtless possess practical and even decorative needs, yet they have never created art. But the animal has no — or, at most, only a fleetingly fragile and basic — desire for harmony;

354

man does possess this and did come to produce art. If I am correct, then the contest with organic nature would be the earliest (Dordogne finds). But the question allows for no definitive answer.

Excursus. Egyptians too advanced to be the earliest civilized people. Prehistoric material too fragmentary. Bronze and iron artifacts often found next to stone objects. Ethnology perseveres. Scholars believe they can make a start. I am skeptical; results tend to support my suppositions. Travelers report fairly consistently that savages give organic designations to what we see as geometric ornamentation or crystalline motifs meant to fill a void. In particular the New Zealanders — this has also been noted by classical archaeologists (Conze). Rows of triangles are rows of bats. Rows of squares are flying bees. If this is true, it suggests that primitives translate organic things straight into strictly crystalline form; although this remains to be proved, it seems to me wholly plausible. But the matter falters in that we in the nineteenth century simply cannot know what those Indians [*sic*] were thinking so many centuries ago.

We know examples from the history of art in which people retrospectively imposed specific new meanings on motifs that originally signified something different; for example, pomegranate and acanthus patterns, apples in Slavic ornament. (Slavic ornament offers much illuminating material for determining the origins of such designations more generally.)

Motifs in Antiquity Under the Polytheistic Worldview
The polytheistic worldview grasps natural things as individual bodies. Its contest with nature must therefore aim at improving, perfecting, and beautifying the physical (not at improving moral or spiritual matters). We have already learned that the purest physical standard of beauty resides in crystallinity: first in symmetry, then in proportion. This crystallinity appears in pure (or

nearly pure) form only in inanimate inorganic motifs. We can therefore expect inorganic or crystalline motifs to predominate throughout Antiquity in general. But could people rest content in competing with dead matter? Clearly, they could not stay with purely crystalline inorganic motifs for long; the conceptual purpose demanded organic ones from the very outset. Even if this were not the earliest artistic purpose, it certainly existed for the Egyptians from the time there was any "worldview" to speak of. But people throughout the antique period strove to crystallize the organic motifs that were so indispensable to them — or, we might also say, to stylize them (though "style" is a multivalent term that might also refer to a painterly or naturalistic style). To stylize means to lead organic objects back to their simplest, most lucid form: crystalline form.

We must now distinguish two major categories within the antique worldview, which also happen to be chronologically discrete: (1) the older period of the ancient Near East, and (2) the younger one of Greece and Rome. Let us begin by investigating their differences.

Ancient Near Eastern Art
We are best informed about ancient Egyptian art. The early Egyptians perceived natural things as purely corporeal entities. Thus they most thoroughly exemplify the antique attitude: only changeless crystalline beauty wherever possible, with no movement whatsoever. We have already noticed how studiously these people distanced themselves from anything that called to mind spiritual functions. The same holds true for their attitude toward motion. In Egyptian eyes, movement was merely imperfect and transitory. (In comparison with crystalline symmetry, it really is utterly transitory, and the Greeks and Romans likewise recognized it as such; but it appeared especially so to the eyes of Egyptians.) These

artists suppressed it as much as possible. Organic motifs, however, are inextricably tied to motion; Egyptian artists therefore had to allow a minimum of organic movement even while maintaining the greatest possible impression of crystalline stasis. Only in this could they find harmony.

The most important organic motif is, of course, the human figure. Let us see how the Egyptians gave expression to the postulate of crystallinity here: through the so-called law of frontality, discovered in 1892 by the Danish archaeologist Julius Lange. In every ancient Egyptian statue, the expanse from the crown of the head to the sexual organs constitutes a single plane, with the head and torso being divisible into symmetrical halves. Thus the naturally symmetrical arrangement of the human body was preserved, and moments of torsion and movement were maximally suppressed. We never witness lateral inclination of the head or torso; even when the body is tilted forward or backward, the head and torso always form a straight line. The Greeks were aware of this peculiarity: Diodorus explained it in terms nearly identical with those used by Lange. Arms and legs could appear in motion, but only with the utmost restraint; at least the upper portion of the arm was always positioned parallel to the torso. The legs were posed in a calm stride. Beyond that, anything that could suggest a capacity for movement in the arms and legs was suppressed. Emphasis given to joints. This causes movement to appear mechanical, automatic (in contrast to Greek renderings). You see, then, walking and shifting about were recognized as unavoidable human characteristics, but every other movement was cut off at the root. And this in the places where one most readily seeks the residence of the spiritual or the soul: in the head and torso. Lange was correct to call this "frontality" for the obvious reason that the figure is oriented toward a strictly frontal viewpoint. People have attempted to explain these differences, which took shape in thousands of ancient Near Eastern figures, with reference to the following factors:

1. The immaturity of all primitive art, which finds it easier to conceive figures symmetrically. But is this the case in primitive art alone? We have already seen that this is not entirely correct. It is a natural imperative, not a result of incompetence, for man to begin any artistic act with symmetrical form. In any case, the technical sophistication of the Egyptians was so great that we cannot say a lack of ability compelled them to limit themselves to symmetrical forms, especially in the later phases. Some scholars have therefore suggested that this was the case initially and that it was left unchanged due to:

2. the conservatism of Oriental people, who have no desire to tamper with whatever already exists;[4] and, finally,

3. a ceremonious spirit. According to this view, the stiff and lifeless posture corresponded to the ancient Egyptians' notion of their superior human value; it has been noted that modern Orientals behave in a very solemn and measured way compared with the more animated Europeans. This is a point much cherished by recent scholars. Among well-known art historians, Wölfflin was the person to elevate this to a major factor in his explanation of artistic progress: man wants to see himself in art as he behaves, as he composes himself, in society. Although this observation is certainly correct, it offers no substantive explanation.

While each of these explanatory moments has some element of truth, none touches the core of the problem. They all merely parallel the phenomenon of frontality. Together they point to a higher common factor that necessarily encompasses not only crystallinity but also the aforementioned conservatism and ceremoniousness.

Ancient Egyptians found harmony exclusively in crystalline form because this is what their worldview demanded. It constituted a formal law: adherence to symmetry, which already inheres

in the human body and is disrupted only by momentary movements. For this reason, they strove to endow even the human figure with as much crystallinity as possible.

Such an explanation was already provided by the same person
who placed the three aforementioned causes in the foreground,
the French scholar Henri Lechat. He articulated it in a review of
Lange's principle in the *Revue des universités du Midi* (1895). He
argued that in comparison with Egyptian figures, in which the
parts take no heed of one another, the Greek statue represents an
ego (*ein Ich*), to which all the parts are subordinate. What else can
this mean but that the Greek statue reveals a spiritual cohesiveness, or individuality, that suffuses its members with life and
motion, while Egyptian statues lack this spiritual cohesiveness
entirely? The Egyptian figure exhibits a merely physical individu-
ation, which seems to arise from mechanical movement. But we
must keep in mind that the Egyptian artist *wanted* it to be so; it is
not that he was *unable* to do things differently. The Greek figure,
with its internal spiritual life, would have utterly displeased him.
Plato tells us how the starkly symmetrical posture of Egyptian
statues was dictated by priests, who would not allow livelier
configurations. This may be true (notwithstanding Lechat's skep-
ticism); the priests of the New Kingdom certainly had the power
to make such demands, and they would not have exercised it
were it not compatible with a more widespread Egyptian outlook.
Priests can only dictate what the people desire; dangers could
only enter from outside, and it was against these that the priestly
prohibitions were aimed. This resembles the case of the Jews,
whose priests continually struggled and preached against contam-
ination by Canaanite idolatry.

If antique artistic production in general had to be crystalline,
idealized, and stylized, this holds true even more for ancient
Egyptian art.

But we occasionally encounter certain phenomena in Egyptian art that seem to contradict this rule. We find figures that tempt us to call them naturalistic: portrait statues, such as the Louvre *Scribe*, whose individual features exceed strict proportionality, that is, that display more forceful movement (figure 8). We also come across depictions of rural life, hunting, and activities of manual labor that look like slices of real life, akin to genre pictures. These all appear as spontaneous accidental movements. How did they become subjects of an artistic endeavor that from its very inception aimed to visualize only the general, the eternal, and the crystalline? This seems to pose a contradiction — but only apparently. The contradiction vanishes as soon as one differentiates between the inner purpose of art and the external conceptual purpose. As we shall see, the seeming naturalism lies solely in the external conceptual function, not in the purpose of art. Art historians often confuse the two functions, all the more so to the extent that they sometimes coincide. Clarification is to be found only by separating the two purposes as sharply as possible. This point requires further elaboration.

Portraiture. It is generally assumed that a portrait is the maximally accurate reproduction in dead matter of the head of a living person. Not the same in all times. Even today the portrait does not fully correspond to that definition. If any naive people still believe that portraiture involves resemblance, the spokesmen of modern art will soon teach them differently. Paul Schultze-Naumburg informs us in black and white that a portrait need not establish the slightest likeness. That is not the task of art. Photography was invented at just the right moment; people suspected that art would soon no longer satisfy the requirements of portraiture. The portrait must exhibit full capacity for life solely in external optical appearances; that is, it must satisfy the conditions of causal relations with surrounding elements such as space, atmosphere, light, and color. Whether the individual person is captured — that is, whether the immutable physical presence of the head is reproduced precisely and accurately — is of secondary importance. When a person insists that his portrait display an individual *habitus* — his own individual *habitus* — this is merely an echo of the now-obsolete notion that a person is truly an individual entity. Such an idea was fine for the antique era, when every person was also a daimon, and for the Catholic Middle Ages, when people likewise had certain (albeit limited) daimonic conceptions about human individuality, but today art has other objectives. It must depict not the individual, who no longer exists — or, more precisely, is a set of molecules too tiny to be depicted — but the universal connectedness of all natural phenomena. This art presents its subject not as a physically unified individual but as a complex of optical appearances that strike the beholder's eye instantaneously.

You might be thinking that this is just the exaggerated theory of a crazed hypermodern man. But you will see things differently if you trace the history of portrait painting back a few centuries. The precursors of modern Impressionism were the Dutch painters of the seventeenth century. How did they understand the portrait? Here Rembrandt is most instructive. For all his optical and coloristic experiments, in *The Anatomy Lesson of Dr. Tulp* he still worked up the heads sharply and clearly, so that each would be instantly recognizable as an individual. In *The Night Watch*, he largely sacrificed individuality to optical appearances, to the effects of light and shadow. Here Rembrandt was ahead of his time; his patrons were dissatisfied, and this marks the beginning of the decline of his esteem in public opinion. But it distinctly proves that art that essentially aims to depict natural things in their causal context — as did Dutch art — must suppress the material and individual. What the most modern painters are trying to do thus fully conforms to the trajectory of normal development.

It is only natural if this progress does not run smoothly but meets with bumps and digressions, for the old cannot be conquered all at once. But the progression from Dutch painting to our own day proves that the demand for individualization in portraiture is steadily declining.

Now we must ask: What is the external purpose of a modern portrait? Portrayal of individuality; the patron, at least, still desires this. What is art's purpose? Portrayal of causal relationships in nature. Extrinsic purpose and art's purpose are thus two separate things; not only do they not correspond, but they even contradict each other. Today, the purpose of art predominates. One can predict the final result: art's purpose will completely subsume the external purpose, and people will cease having their portraits made.

Let us return to Egyptian portraits. Here, too, we need to distinguish between external purposes and the purpose of art. Art's purpose is obvious in ancient Egyptian art: it strove against personalization. What, then, was the external purpose of Egyptian portraits? Stemming from tombs, the portraits were rooted in ideas about life after death: the *ka*. Conceptually they were closely aligned with the paintings and reliefs on tomb walls displaying gift-bearing figures, hunting trophies, and the like. The idea was that in the afterlife, the person in question — that is, whoever was depicted — would really enjoy all the goods presented to him in the pictures. Considerable weight was therefore placed on the individual persona, and the visual arts had likewise to take it into account. The accidental qualities, the personality, the transient features thus arose from the external purpose, not the purpose of art.

We encounter such drastic kinds of portrait likeness only in Old Kingdom art. New Kingdom portraits have a more generalized beauty; here we find only kings, as many as there were gods.

A movement from the individual to the general must have occurred in Egyptian art. (The Jews established the highest level of generalization.) That is, the idea of the afterlife that gave rise to portraiture came first: here, too, the conceptual purpose appeared earlier, and the ultimately victorious purpose of art later.[5] The Greeks underwent the opposite progression: they arrived at portraits only at a late stage, and these grew increasingly individualized rather than generalized.[6] Now it becomes clear what these snippets from nature mean. These are neither landscapes nor genre scenes (in the modern sense) that attract us with their artistic conveyance of causal relationships. Rather, the beholder's pleasure rests in conceptually oriented effects alone: gifts must be brought to the portrayed person pictorially, for this alone guarantees the act of offering after death. (Occasionally the physiognomic aspect extends to the torso as well, providing important proof that we are not dealing with spiritual concepts of personality. See, for example, the chest of the *Scribe*, the rounded belly of the *Sheikh el-Beled* [figures 8 and 9].) The clearest evidence of the exceptional position of these portraits lies in the fact that they represent a tiny minority of all statues. When reproducing the human figure, people always obeyed art's demands for crystallinity whenever external purposes did not require otherwise.

The same phenomenon manifests itself more radically in the following case. Egyptian art treated objects as individual corporeal units, each autonomous and self-contained ("individual" must not be confused with "personality"; relate to each other as body and soul). What happened when a conceptual purpose demanded several individuals standing together in a connected relationship, that is, a group? The purpose of art in ancient Egypt had to oppose the group; Egyptian artists could never find harmony in the group as such. Conceptual purposes nonetheless often compelled them to combine multiple figures into a group. We must therefore inquire how ancient Egyptian art treated group compositions. You see, here lies a crucial seed of all subsequent development, which led to the freeing of the individual from isolation, and thence to modern art based on causality.

First case. Man and woman were already arranged in groups during the Old Kingdom. The composition was purely mechanical. She typically wraps her arm around him (the unavoidable overlapping itself disturbs the clear sense of individuality), thereby asserting that she belongs to him. The law of frontality governs the rest. Each figure remains a discrete unit; no spiritual closeness binds them together.

Second case. Three figures in one relief: the king between two goddesses. Thus three individuals. The problem: they must form a single entity. A corporeal one, of course. Crystallinity must step in. The figures stand thus: goddess king goddess

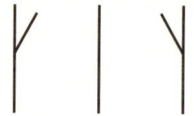

All three figures the same height (that is, no dominant directionality, no exceeding of the law of crystallinity, the utmost restfulness). What dominates are (1) alignment of elements of the same height; (2) a symmetry of contrasts, as with the octahedron. The goddesses are composed of the same shapes and gestures, but inverted: this gives rise to the organic aspect. This is not the pure symmetry of a cube, where right and left sides can be exchanged and yet look exactly the same, but a symmetry of contrasts. Order and regularity also reside in contrasts. Only when completely unequal things are brought together does order cease to exist.

Curvature, proportion, contrast are semicrystalline elements. Contrast thus joined what was already established.

Here composition entered the scene. By composition, we understand the arrangement of figures in a certain order so as to form a higher entity: composition thus also represents an improvement of nature. Figures are not thrown together haphazardly but are organized by the artist's will in such a way that they arouse in the beholder a harmonic — that is, a unified and solid — impression. In Egyptian art, only crystallization could achieve this effect. Each figure was conceived as an individual and designed in crystalline fashion — all contrary to organic nature. But the figures were still drawn together in at least individual relationships; this gap opened the way for all subsequent innovations.

Definition: Composition is the crystallization of the group.

Third case. More figures still. Tombs introduced another necessity: the slaves' presentation of gifts to the deceased person had to be shown in relief or painting. The deceased, large, seated to one side. Slaves, small, approaching him in a row, all the same height (isocephaly):

$$|\ |\ |\ |\ |\ |\ |\ |$$

Once again we find the principle of symmetry, but it is broken, disrupted by the main figure. This figure stands out through its size alone, not its placement within the composition. Subsequent art avoided this disruptive arrangement whenever possible. We would expect the main figure to be shifted to the center and the secondary figures to be distributed symmetrically to the right and left. But here we reach the limits of Egyptian style. Its reliefs can only show figures in profile (we will understand the reasons for this when we discuss the relation between form and surface). It can therefore depict the primary figure from only one side, and any others that approach him must do so from the opposite side. At this point, the Egyptians could no longer sustain the law of

365

crystallinity, though surely they must have wanted to. This would have entailed canceling out the conceptual purpose: the slaves would not be able to approach the figure, and he would not notice them. You see, then, art's purpose could no longer accompany the conceptual purpose so closely, because a fissure had opened between them. The Egyptian artist dispensed with absolutely crystalline composition. He nonetheless clung to it as tightly as possible — hence the serial alignment of identical elements.

The problem deepened whenever a larger assembly of figures was necessary, as in hunting and battle scenes — see the battle of Ramses II against the Hittites (figure 10). Here the conceptual purpose completely overpowered the Egyptian artist. Because his own means did not suffice, he had to sacrifice art's purpose. Composition ceased to exist. Only the main figure, the victorious Ramses, had to be prominently visible, and for that reason he alone was presented in large scale. Herein lies the singular harmony: the triumph of the stronger emerges clearly and unmistakably. As a result, naturalistic or painterly elements appear that would otherwise have been unthinkable: individualized features in the heads of the foes, thus naturalism; concealment of figures until only a contour remains visible, a painterly motif. Greek and Roman artists never went so far in these areas — which proves that the elements the Egyptian had to conquer in the battle picture lay so far from him that he was willing to surrender any effort to create harmony. This is the same phenomenon we noticed in those naturalistic portraits and apparently genre snippets of nature. The Egyptian probably regarded the battle picture as a necessary evil. This may be why such images come only from a relatively short span of time (Tuthmosside and Ramesside periods). Erman was right to state that the naturalistic current broke through every so often, only to fall into dust.

Of special interest is the monotheistic revolution that occurred

366

under Amenhotep IV, who recognized the sun as the sole divinity. Even Erman was struck by certain peculiarities in the visual arts that ran parallel with this change in outlook. But in both realms, these were only fleeting episodes.

Enough with the human figure. We can draw the same conclusions for the depiction of plants. Only two plants were portrayed repeatedly: the lotus and the papyrus. Of these, the lotus was more important. Why this selection and no other? Because of its conceptual significance (connection to cult). This was subsequently transposed to the practical and decorative domains. Thus conceptual needs introduced organic motifs into works of practical or decorative purpose once those motifs were made inorganic. Indeed, in a few projections (as a profile calyx, a rosette, a palmette), the lotus was so strongly crystallized that one would not recognize it without the aid of explanatory inscriptions. At the same time, we do find scattered "naturalistic" renderings of the lotus, which appear in conjunction with a specific conceptual purpose. (As with portrait figures, these are isolated exceptions. Examples of naturalistically designed trees, such as the date palm, emerge in the same way.)

Thus we see that conceptual needs sometimes involve tasks that conflict with the purpose of art and thereby urge its destruction. In Egyptian art, personality was the goal toward which conceptual purposes pressed; Greek and Roman art would later pursue this direction. We can therefore conclude that the conceptual purpose introduces new objectives, whereas practical and decorative functions are conservative. This still applies today: industrial arts, decorative arts, and architecture are supremely conservative and still tend to generate types. Rebellion against this currently; but eventually will revert to types. Sculptural arts and painting seek out fresh paths.

In ornament, individual plants also established connections

with one another. Because conceptual purposes did not compel them to do so, they could obey fully the law of crystalline composition. Because we can observe how this transpired most easily by comparison with the Greeks' employment of the same foliate motifs, we will defer this topic until we reach Greek art.

It remains to investigate how Egyptians treated inorganic motifs where these did appear (namely, in architecture and industrial arts). We are especially interested in the extent to which Egyptian artists made concessions to the organic.

Architecture. The oldest structures are the pyramids (not all the same shape); typical examples are the three in Giza: four-sided pyramids. Here the influence of crystallinity is particularly clear: the bisected octahedron, because upward growth was unnecessary. Bilateral symmetry; clear divisions by sharp edges. These are strictly individuals that surge up from the desert floor. Although no temples have survived from the earliest times (the significance of the so-called Temple of the Sphinx is still uncertain, though this building was hardly unknown to later temple design), we do have tombs: so-called mastaba tombs. What is most interesting is that externally these took the form of today's fellah houses; this has rightly led to the conclusion that ancient Egyptian dwellings had the same shape as the modern clay houses of the fellahin. The basic form of these houses is the pyramidal base. This form, evidently derived from the pyramids, is at once an individual entity and genuinely crystalline. Hence the artificial appearance of fellah villages, with their islands of houses nestled behind palm trees. The absence of a roof or other exterior articulation is characteristic and contributes to the impression of absolute individuality. The elimination of a pointed crown signals another forward step, for now extension in width receives an emphasis equal to extension in height. The cause of this is, again, movement — that is, the human need to take shelter within something, to which purpose a pointed top could only be a hindrance.

As temples sprang up, they likewise took the shape of houses. We need only note that even when single houses or temples were combined, they still appeared as individual units. Only two elements departed from this general tendency toward movement. (1) The horizontal termination of the upper wall with a cavetto. The plan of the pyramidal support looked brutal in a monumental work. It is not easy to explain the choice of the cavetto; it seems to imitate the feathered crowns we often find worn as headdresses in pictures. Perhaps people wanted to declare the absence of a surmounting roof and therefore presented the upper part of the building as a person wearing a crown of feathers. Once again, we see a case where the Egyptians were unable to master the conceptual purpose and consequently let organic form emerge unhindered, certainly more than the Greeks would ever do. (2) Pylons (also in the shape of houses) that stood in front of the main temple, reached far above it, and thereby prepared the way for the merging of parts into a higher unity. Such cohesion indicates a deviation from strict individuality. But Egyptian artists never attained the true complexity of parts that would have yielded a higher form of individuality, as happened later in the central-plan building. Merely hints at this; progress in this direction did not continue; indeed, everything in the Egyptians fought against it. Thus in all Egyptian architecture, the exterior would preserve its character of crystalline individuality.

The relation between form and surface can be investigated more fruitfully with regard to architectural interiors, because here the problem of space arises. The question of motifs may also be posed with regard to the freestanding supports: pillars and columns (figure 14). The pillar is more strongly crystalline, the column more organic and mobile. It is therefore important to note that the earliest known free supports in Egyptian buildings (from the Fourth Dynasty) are not columns but pillars. Quadrangular pillars are found in the Old Kingdom mastaba tombs at Saqqara, for instance, as well as in the so-called Temple of the Sphinx at Giza. Although columns did appear at Beni Hasan (Middle Kingdom, Twelfth Dynasty), pillars continued to predominate. There were now eight- and sixteen-sided examples (crystalline formations); sometimes even twenty-four-sided. Occasionally the sides were cut into concave grooves = fluting: indicates a movement toward Organism. The Egyptians carried this no further than the Greeks would do. At Beni Hasan, we also find cylindrical columns in the guise of plants: thus the conceptual purpose engendered the round column. Columns became normative only during the New Kingdom. Significantly, the earliest columns imitated organic things, namely plants — more specifically, the lotus stalk. This allows us to conclude that, once again, conceptual purposes introduced organic motifs to an inorganic function. Here again, Egyptian artists could not master the conceptual purpose.

It is only logical that the industrial arts drew on Organism to a much greater degree. Given that the practical function of industrial objects required their being in continuous motion (in the human hand), it makes sense that curvature had long prevailed in this domain. We also observe the direct application of organic motifs to utilitarian ends — for example, human figures as tool handles, animal bodies as vessels.

It would be interesting to examine other ancient Near Eastern arts, especially Semitic, as a transitional stage on the way to Greek art. But for our current purposes, it is more pressing to highlight only the main stations of development: (1) Egyptian; (2) classical Greek; (3) Hellenistic and Roman. Let me call your attention to just a few points about Assyrian art, to prove that we are not leaving open any substantial gaps by skipping over it. As Lange has

shown, the law of frontality also applied to Assyrian art. The symmetrical compositional technique of the Assyrian heraldic style —
for example, two griffins flanking a central so-called Sacred Tree
— is well known. I would add that in their ornament, too, Assyrian artists obeyed the same laws as their Egyptian counterparts.

The Summit of Antique Art with the Greeks
The Greeks conceived all organic natural things in strictly corporeal terms; individuals were always embodied individuals. At the
same time, they also granted validity to the spiritual. A cleft did
not divide them so starkly from the divine; there was no veiled
image to Sais whose peplos these people feared to raise. Accordingly, they possessed a philosophy that competed with religion,
indeed that tackled it with great force; the Egyptians did not.
Heinrich Brunn explained how this approach to the spiritual constituted the very essence of Greek art, though, unfortunately, he
corrupted his own argument by clinging to Semper's views. At
first, the Greeks did not regard the spiritual as fundamentally different from the corporeal. In the philosophical realm, this expressed itself in Democritus's notion of the materiality of the soul
— exceptionally fine stuff, to be sure, but real material. While the
concrete and three-dimensional remained essential, a spiritual
component to the three-dimensional body was now explicitly
acknowledged.

It would be mistaken to believe that the Greek worldview was
elementally different from the ancient Egyptian; in their main
points, they are really at one. Their art makes this instantly apparent. We did discern naturalistic qualities and genre elements in
Egyptian art. If the Greeks were so deeply inclined to regard spiritual activity as essential, they would have had to go substantially
beyond Egyptian art in naturalistic and genre elements. But what
we see is in fact the opposite. We find no portraits so personalized

and no barbarian faces so caricatured in classical Greek art as in Egyptian; no such painterly surfaces or loose compositions were devised in Greek art as in Egyptian battle pictures; nor were any such naturalistic renderings of plants or foliate columns produced in Greece as are found in Egypt. In all these cases, Greek art was more strictly crystalline. This confirms that physical individualism, crystallinity, and stylization formed the principal goals of Greek artists from the beginning. But by making certain concessions to spiritual movement, to natural accuracy, and to the organic world, they succeeded in submitting organic motifs to the artistic principle of crystallinity for the first time. For the Egyptians, these elements related to each other as oil and water: they were irreconcilable opposites. The Greeks found the proper balance; by Organizing the crystalline through moderate curvature and movement, they were better equipped to crystallize the organic. Crystal = beauty; Organism = truth to nature. Classical-age Greeks struck a balance between beauty and truth to nature. This, the so-called classical period, was but a narrow peak. We must now cast a glance at the surrounding foothills, early Greek art.

Early Greek Art

As is well known, the Greeks were able to build further by standing on the shoulders of their ancient Near Eastern counterparts. From the latter, they acquired the basic tools for attaining a higher level of artistic activity; the Greeks could thus bypass initial experimentation and proceed directly to a higher stage.[7] The *Apollo of Tenea*, a sixth-century statue, expresses the relation between ancient Egyptian and early Greek art most clearly. Thoroughly crystalline as a whole, no less than any Egyptian statue. Law of frontality: arms arranged symmetrically, whereas numerous Egyptian figures have one arm lifted — thus a regression in terms of external movement. But look at the legs: ankles, knees. Joints

372

sharply emphasized — these exhibit the capacity for movement. Thus from the very outset, the purpose of Greek art aimed not so much at external movement as at the internal capacity for movement; that is, an internal volition is present that moves the body at will. At the same time, all fleeting external movement is shunned as unharmonious. The capacity for movement can be described as the struggle for truth to nature. This, however, imposes restrictions on beauty. Ancient Egyptian figures were not as angular and bland, though in cases where Egyptian works were naturalistic, they strike us as even more angular and caricatured.

This is a work of the sixth century. Did this tendency really arise so late? It is already visible in older works, the earliest coming from so-called Mycenaean culture. Here we are dealing primarily with ornament. We find in the treatment of foliate ornament the same qualities that appear in the *Apollo of Tenea*. Most motifs, at least those that persevered longest, stemmed from Egypt. But their manner of conjunction is different, tighter. Invention of the undulating tendril. Here an internal compulsion asserts itself, along with clear directionality. The Egyptians presented the motif as externally constrained, as merely existing, being. A simple sequence:

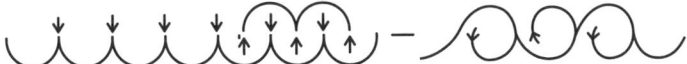

The tendril solved the problem of the combination and disposition of motifs. How did early Greek art deal with figural groupings? Here, too, early Greek art avoided extremes. It left no battle pictures that rendered the chaotic action of battle in a single scene. It knew only friezelike arrangements — for example, in the François Vase, where rows of figures move about on solid ground (figure 28):   ⌐ | | | | | ¬

Here already is the classical separation of parts. On the other hand, the main figure is no longer highlighted externally through larger scale: all figures, unless they are children, have approximately the same height. Some overlapping is evident — for example, in two persons positioned one behind the other — but that is all. This manifests an Egyptianizing tendency that will later disappear. In figural vase paintings of conceptually significant content, we do not find the striving for closed, cohesive compositions that would later emerge. The Greeks did not reach this point before the year 500, though the seeds were already well in place: witness the Calydonian hunt scene on the François Vase, where the primary motif, the boar, occupies the exact center, with five rows of people approaching from the right and the left. Interesting, the way the horses are grouped in pairs. No systematic conceptual purpose; portrayal of the fate of Troilus in distinct episodes without interruption, connected only through internal significance. The Greek ideal had not yet been discovered but was swiftly being approached.

Inorganic motifs. Intermediary position here too. Neither angled pillars nor partially naturalistic foliate columns; with few exceptions, only entirely fluted columns. Nothing strictly crystalline, though the organic is extensively crystallized. The treatment of the capital (echinus, which betrays inner tension) again aims to display an inner capacity for movement in the joints. Still, the columns appear restful = frontal.

Classical Art

Utmost brevity here, because period already well known. Again we will investigate individuality and crystallization, grouping and composition.

Individuality and crystallization. Some scholars claim that the law of frontality was definitively abandoned after 500. This holds true only under certain conditions. Frontality was upset in that torso and head were no longer disposed entirely symmetrically but were permitted to shift to the side. But the overall frontality — the frontal orientation — was preserved: that is, the figure was positioned so that one side alone, the broad side (which was not necessarily the front), would be seen. We will discuss this in greater depth when we deal with the relation between form and surface. We must mention it here, however, because it demonstrates that people still insisted on the individuality of human beings (or natural things in general). The frontal view signifies the negation of space; it is the prerequisite for the juxtaposition of things or their belonging together. At the same time, we find an avoidance of shadows, which give rise to indistinctness and thereby eradicate individual self-containment. This rule continued to resonate but was increasingly disobeyed. Polyclitus and Myron, Phidias and Praxiteles still adhered to it. With Lysippus, the first artist to depart from this tendency, the classical period came to an end.

Artists had already broken from strict symmetry around 500, when they began to introduce lateral movements.[8] These were swiftly amplified: lateral motions appear almost mannered in the works of Praxiteles — though this was because only sidelong movement was available to that master. Crystallinity was shattered, but what replaced it? Artists did what nature does with organic things: they offered an occasional glimpse of symmetry, in both the details and the whole.

Symmetry in the whole. Although right and left sides are no longer starkly symmetrical, the contours must maintain balance. Contrast expands into contrapposto: contrast through diagonal correspondences. Movements of extremities are diagonally opposed. The head is also important here. Thus, in theory, movement is free, but it clearly conforms to a specific organizational principle,

and that principle generates harmony. Wherever the law of contrapposto was broken in the classical period, one must assume the
presence of a second figure standing next to and balancing out the
first, as with the *Aristogeiton and Harmodios* (figure 30). Polyclitus's *Doryphorus* invented the relaxed and weight-bearing legs,
which form the root of the contrast.

If harmony no longer resides in symmetry, if the various components can no longer be identical, then they must be completely
opposed: only then is symmetry possible. This schema persisted
throughout all Antiquity (*Augustus of Prima Porta*, Constantine's
Lateran, the Christian reliefs on sarcophagi). Only in later mosaics did artists depart from this schema, proving the emergence
of a new art. But it was resuscitated in the High Renaissance. Lateran *Sophocles*: example of the perfected style even after Lysippus.
No more frontal orientation. Idealized Greek portrayal: supreme
capacity for physical movement in a body that appears completely
free and in control of its members. Diagonal correspondence in
the curves. Utmost capacity for spiritual animation in the head:
displays nothing momentary. At the same time, the head harks
back to the old frontal view, with its direct outward gaze. One
can even say it lacks character completely, for character is specific
and personal.

Symmetry in the parts. As we will soon see, although organic
movement asserts itself here, crystallinity is maintained as much
as possible. Regular facial features, regular torso. Crystallinity reveals itself further in the smaller components: clear division of
parts. This is not accomplished by means of sharply angled edges,

to be sure; curves predominate. But the individual smaller planes making up the torso and head settle themselves next to each other very distinctly; this is facilitated through a complete avoidance of shadows, that is, through the greatest possible planarity. But remember why this disruption of crystalline frontality occurred in the first place: to bring to view the spiritual element, the animation, of the human being by means of movement. Movement in the whole was tempered through contrapposto and frontality. Furthermore, the display of momentary movement, or any momentary quality at all, was avoided, at least in principle. Anything transitory had to express itself chiefly in the smaller parts; thus the parts are designed to appear capable of any movement whatsoever. Artists accomplished this by giving emphasis to the connecting points, that is, the joints. These display much stronger modeling, which, by nature, possesses an accidental and personal character and casts shadows. You see how those elements meant to awaken the impression of truth to life produce their effects most readily in a naturalistic and painterly sense. But the basic rule remains: classical art is governed by the perfectly harmonious balance between crystalline beauty and organic truth to life. With regard to spiritual aspects, anything momentary is suppressed. Although heads appear capable of the loftiest spiritual and intellectual life, they tend to stare indifferently outward, betraying no affect. This art, then, still denies both space (adheres tightly to a single plane) and time (the momentary).

What about the arrangement of multiple figures? The basic approach of classical art likewise struggled against grouping, that is, the combination of numerous figures into a higher entity, for the following reasons. (1) The very presence of multiple figures disrupts strict individuality; (2) connections between the figures would inevitably take shape, which would automatically introduce spiritual motivations; (3) the presence of multiple individuals entails sequential alignments and thus space, and conceptual demands often require the placement of figures directly in front of one another (even if only partially — for example, in the linking of arms); (4) interrelationships between persons almost always involve a momentary quality and hence the concept of time.

The Egyptians could not resolve this contradiction. The Greeks were able to do so thanks to their very concessions to truth to life, that is, to space and time: greater capacity for movement. The Greeks were aware of the contradiction but knew how to make it less palpable. They exercised the greatest restraint in independent sculpture, because there spatial and temporal relations — that is, the disruption of individuality — were most concretely apparent and therefore most disturbing. Statue groups, such as the *Aristogeiton and Harmodios*, were always exceptions; as we have seen, they were symmetrically arranged (figure 30).

Only the figures in temple pediments remain to be considered (figure 11). Their individuality is likewise not heavily emphasized. The figures often stand wholly isolated, directing themselves exclusively toward the beholder. In rare instances, two or, even more exceptionally, three will stand together in a mutual relationship; but this is mere posturing, for the figures are not bound by any genuine connection. The law of crystallization organizing these groups is most clearly developed in temple pediments, where practical and artistic functions coincided. Nearly pure symmetry of contrasts: the main figure (for example, Athena) stands in the center as dominant element; those to the left and right respond, displaying not only external bodily responses but also, wherever possible, internal spiritual ones. Once again, manifestation of internal connections! Thus both elements: body and spirit, though spirit is confined within physical laws.

The movement of classical composition is freest on two-dimensional surfaces: reliefs and paintings. Figures are still distributed across a single plane (as in Egyptian art), and modeling is still restricted to the barest necessity. But, compared with the Egyptians, Greek artists had the advantage of being able to show the body *en face*, that is, from any angle they chose — so long as they stayed within a single plane. Generally speaking, they employed the same type of composition we observed in sculpture in the round: based on either symmetry or contrapposto. Overall balance was established; although emphasis was typically placed on the center, this was not pulled upward to form a crown as in temple pediments. That would have granted too much importance to directionality, which the Greeks tolerated only when the diagonal frame of the pediment compelled them to do so. This rule also applies to Greek sarcophagi. For example, the Alexander sarcophagus from Sidon: both long sides; the color, which must reinforce this, is polychromatic rather than coloristic. But vase paintings constitute our chief examples in this domain (Theodor Schreiber has recently presented the major stages of this development). Example: the *Aldobrandini Wedding* already includes suggestions of space, but no doors between chambers — still repeated in Roman times (figure 29)!

In other instances, even the Greeks were unable to master the conceptual purpose. We refer to the frieze: continuous scene, which, by definition, must struggle against individual compartmentalization. With that, time and space seeped in. These could no longer be suppressed. What emerges is a serial procession consisting of numerous momentary episodes. There is no room for crystallized individuality of the whole. Witness the Panathenaic procession on the Parthenon. The beholder must examine — and find harmony in — each figure for itself while constantly explaining away movement as arising from the conceptual purpose. When one observes the whole, one finds harmony solely in the serial arrangement (isocephaly), just as in Egyptian art; but here it is wholly inadequate. The frieze thus represents a subversive element in Greek art. It led to painterly composition. Were it not for the isocephaly, this would already have happened in the Parthenon. Other differences from Egyptian art include:

1. the Egyptians depicted contemporary battles (Ramses [figure 10]), the Greeks heroic ones;

2. the Greeks characterized foreign races (Aegina sculptures [figure 11]) with less exaggeration than the Egyptians;

3. the Greeks reduced the number of fighters, aimed to give the impression not of a melee but of individual combats.

All this is "idealistic" when compared with Egyptian art. The "naturalistic" element of Greek art lies in its treatment of the single figure.

Classical Greek art constantly reveals itself as an art of balance, of mediation between the extremes of crystallinity and Organism. The Greeks avoided both the muddled chaos of the Ramses battle (figure 10) and the starkly symmetrical compositional type of the king flanked by goddesses.

Inorganic motifs. Here, too, space and time were denied on principle. The temple was an individual, self-contained entity, closed on all sides. It was incapable of accommodating any enlargement through additions, as in the Egyptian temple; the interior did not rely on spatial effects. Anything that might indicate momentary movement — as, for example, in the Baroque style — was zealously avoided. But the demand for the capacity for movement increased: the Ionic column, with its base, assumed a place alongside the Doric.

Late Antique Art

With Alexander the Great began the decline of the antique worldview and antique art. But one must not forget that this worldview, and its art, continued to persevere. It expressed itself externally in the following ways. The deity types that emerged during the Greek classical period were repeated ceaselessly until the time of Constantine.[9] Not only the gods and goddesses but also many other classical types. Heroic battles from the fifth century B.C.E. appeared on sarcophagi of the third century C.E. This has long been noticed; until recently, scholars even thought that all late antique art did was copy what had been produced during the fifth and fourth centuries before Christ. As a result, they regarded the six centuries between Alexander and Constantine as the downfall of ancient art. In recent years, people have finally come to understand that this art also pursued an ascendant path. A few even seem inclined to forget about the decline in favor of this ascent and want to erect an insurmountable barricade between classical and Roman art. The old view still has its proponents, however, especially among classical archaeologists. It is correct that Lysippus was the decisive pioneer of the new developments in art. But the truth lies somewhere in the middle. This last great period of antique art belongs as much to pagan polytheism as to monotheism. Pagan Antiquity had the upper hand at the beginning, of course, and the new monotheistic art at the end. The question remains as to when the latter began to predominate, for at that point the boundary for any subdivision has to be drawn. Such subdivision is imperative for that long stretch from Alexander to Constantine. Until now, scholars have differentiated Greek-Hellenistic art in the age of the Diadochi from Roman Imperial art. I cannot condone this distinction. I find the art of the Roman Empire up to the Antonines to possess an overwhelmingly antique character. It retains the Hellenistic inclination toward heightened truth to life. Only after the Antonines did the monotheistic-Semitic side begin to claim dominance. We can therefore locate the divisions thus: (1) Hellenistic art from Alexander the Great to Marcus Aurelius; (2) late Roman art from Marcus Aurelius to Constantine. I do not think it necessary to regard the birth of Christ as marking any fundamental division. Beauty and truth to nature continued to be elemental, primary objectives both before and after that event. This is not to deny that such a subdivision may have been important to people at the time.

We recognized the balance between crystallinity and Organism, beauty and truth to life to constitute the essence of classical art. The more prominent was obviously truth to life — that is, movement, the spiritual, the personal. Throughout the period, art sought to perfect the embodied individual, but the spiritual element residing within was brought to expression with increasing clarity. The spiritual, however, cannot be grasped individually; herein lies the root of all subsequent disruptions of individual cohesion. Things — especially the human figure — now assumed relationships with one another openly, not simply because they were compelled to do so by outside forces: thus artistic consideration for space and time was born. This paved the way for modern art, which is also an art of space and time.[10] First, numerous works of art, especially statues of deities, still strove to appear spaceless, timeless, eternal. Second, never in Antiquity did artists devote deep and serious attention to space and time. These factors were never elevated to an artistic problem in the way that linear perspective would be for quattrocento artists. The linear perspective of Roman Imperial art can never satisfy modern demands, for it resulted solely from concessions. This will become clearer when we turn to the relation between form and surface. How did this new consideration for space and time, for the relative and momentary, manifest itself in Hellenistic art?

Individuality and crystallization. Lysippus removed the frontal view from frontality: now the three-dimensional body moved freely in space. This could only suppress crystallinity further. A whole series of symptoms bear witness to this: portraits in marble. Also crop up in Greek art; scattered forerunners in the classical phase. More specifically, portrait heads. Sometimes, to be sure, we find full statues, for example, the Lateran *Sophocles*; but he is clothed in such a way that his arms and legs are invisible. The majority are simply heads. This implies that the head was no longer regarded as one member among many, as in Egyptian art, but seen as a privileged part. This must be because the spiritual finds particularly strong expression there.

1. Personalized physical characteristics with minimization of proportion and thus crystallinity. There are certainly some ugly heads among Greek portraits (Socrates, Demosthenes), but physical ugliness was always softened by spiritual nobility. In other words, the harmony destroyed by bodily movement was compensated for by spiritual repose. The Egyptians would have found this incomprehensible.

2. Spiritual characterization was also a goal; indeed, spiritual qualities were so greatly emphasized that they often strike us as the primary feature — for example, in portraits of philosophers.

These are all innovations: a movement toward transitory veristic appearances at the expense of timeless beauty. But much was retained on the other side:

1. Who was portrayed? Only famous men. Thus conceptual purposes prevailed, as with the Egyptians. The portrait was not, as we would say, an end in itself. It was the *man* who was of interest.

2. In terms of body: rhythmic flow of contours — roundness (half crystalline), avoidance of disruptive corners, rising and falling curves. No pronounced lateral movement.

3. In terms of spirit: avoidance of the momentary. Although the eyes suggest some internal activity, they do not yet focus on any particular point in space (Caracalla). This is especially evident in the general lack of accentuation of the pupils. In Egyptian art, at least in the early phases, the conceptual purpose demanded that

these receive some emphasis. This no longer held true for later periods, as the Ramesside statues demonstrate. In the majority of Greek busts, the eyes were probably left unpainted. For good reason: painting them would have given them too transient an expression of inner life.

Thus the Greek portrait still clung to the postulate of restrained movement even after Alexander the Great. To put it more accurately, this movement was more potential than actual (Roman portraits, such as that of Caracalla, display lively bodily movement). This is important, because we find very lively momentary movements in other early Hellenistic works. But only where these were motivated by conceptual demands. Classical artists exercised restraint even in such cases; this is why their creations appear so compelling, so necessary. Artists of the Hellenistic period allowed spiritual movement to run its own course and the reby wrest the upper hand from its physical counterpart.

This manifested itself in two ways. (1) In the lively momentary movements of the body. For quite some time, artists had problems mastering all movements and reproducing all foreshortenings on the plane. (2) In emotional movements when the body is at rest, as in the *Farnese Hercules*. Massive body, but tired and collapsing; almost melancholy expression of exhaustion in the face. Pathos wholly new; recalls Michelangelo's problem in the Medici tombs. This is why people often compare Hellenistic art with the Italian Baroque; the two really do exhibit some common features. I need only remind you of the *Laocoön* (figure 1). Bernini, the preeminent master of Italian Baroque, discovered in the *Laocoön* the closest cousin of his own art, as did Michelangelo, the true father of the Baroque style, before him. The more animated the single figure was, the less clear it became. As the sense of the absolute necessity of individual integrity diminished, the need for group composition grew.

Composition. This explains why the arrangement of groups played a greater role in Hellenistic art than ever before. It even infiltrated sculpture in the round; in the *Laocoön*, as in Egyptian art, three discrete figures combined to yield one unified entity. But this was a higher unity with a dominant central element (also sought consistently in Italian Baroque art). Thus we find the pyramidal structure, which would attain such significance for planar composition only during the Renaissance.

So: supreme crystalline repose in the composition as a whole and — in starkest contrast — the most vigorous movement in the three figures individually. Physically: superhuman strain to fend off the snakes. Spiritually: utter anguish. By virtue of its very contradictions, the *Laocoön* has recently inspired a substantial literature of aesthetics.

Whereas the figures of the *Laocoön* group still inhabited a single plane, the *Farnese Bull* abandoned even that. One is compelled to walk around it: complete destruction of the frontal view (figure 19).

If it was necessary to establish a higher individual unity in independent statuary, people took this further in the two surface arts, relief and painting. Here they determined to dissolve compositional crystallinity even more. We have already learned how this art began to deal with space and time. Rather than standing juxtaposed on a single plane, figures were now dispersed along several spatially distinct planes: foreground and background. What was exceptional in sculpture (*Farnese Bull*) became the rule in relief and painting. In other words, thoroughgoing crystallinity could not be strictly maintained even in softened form, as in the *Aldobrandini Wedding* (figure 29). A pronounced movement toward painterly composition began to appear. This is most readily observed in a concrete example: *Alexander Mosaic* (figure 4). Pompeian mosaic from the second century B.C.E. The old elements of crystalline composition are still evident: symmetry, contrasts. But these are very much loosened and embellished with accessories: not empty ground but space. Transition to a coloristic treatment that no longer acknowledged ground. Another point worth mentioning: the interaction among figures on different planes, their causal relationship from the beholder's perspective. Although they stand in front of or behind one another instead of occupying a single plane, they are discrete individuals who pay no heed to one another. The picture is still artificially composed of distinct figures for the sake of the beholder, who would otherwise not find it pleasing. Once this distinction was also abandoned and figures were joined with light, air, and coloristic reflections so as to form a cohesive whole, pure painterly composition would be achieved. Antiquity never reached this point, even in the Roman Imperial age.

Alexander battle versus Ramses battle (figures 4 and 10): (1) battle scene in which the main figure is no larger than the others; (2) figures placed behind, not on top of, one another (an advancement beyond Greek vase painting). Isocephaly; above, sparse air with lances crossed at the tips and a bare, leafless tree; crowding, overlapping, foreshortening.

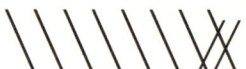

In front, four things displayed in full. From left to right: Alexander, the satrap, the supply horse, the chariot of Darius. All symmetrically arranged, all oriented toward the right; only the supply horse causes a halt. Darius and Alexander the chief figures. Only their heads rise freely against the background. Darius's more fully visible, as pathetic main subject. Victorious Alexander less imposing. Space and time.

Painterly composition in the whole. The crystalline component resides in the isocephaly, in the two fixed points that divide the plane into three parts (the head of Darius and the bare tree), in the four primary figures in the foreground, in the directional contrasts, and so forth. On the other hand, organic innovations cannot be overlooked: this is not just any heroic conflict but the actual, physical battle against the Persians. Costume precisely observed. Thus the transitory is no longer elevated to something eternal and generic but portrayed as transitory. The horse, turning neither right nor left, forms the true center of the composition.

Considerations of composition and individual unity were never fully abandoned in favor of pure optical appearances, that is, the unembellished causal relations of things. No one ever took linear perspective so far as to conceal significant things or to aim for a one-sided composition.

But neither did artists come to a standstill with the *Alexander Mosaic.* They went a few steps further during the first century of the Imperial age. Let us now turn to the progress of composition in this second subperiod of Hellenistic art, the early Imperial age. What Schreiber called Hellenistic relief images form the transition.[11] The Grimani reliefs were still designed symmetrically (figure 2); likewise the relief with farmer and cow. Today people tend to cite the Arch of Titus, specifically the relief with the booty-bearing soldiers, as the extreme example of the loosening tendency of Roman relief composition (figure 18). The figures are divided into three groups, each with a crowning head. The uniform directionality is mitigated by a raised military standard thrust in the opposite direction, and again by the half arch, whose non-contrasting half is obscured (one assumes that this was painted on; but it is doubtful that painting played so extensive a role here). The participants in front do not walk through the arch but move past it. Why? Because the artist did not want to show them

from behind: truth to nature, or causality, had to give way if individuality was to be preserved. Lorenzo Ghiberti broke from this
schema. Although his compositions are airier, more painterly, the
movements therein appear less true to life; that is, his figures lack
a higher capacity for movement.

What we have said about reliefs also applies to painting (examples from Pompeii). Painting veered toward Impressionism in the
early stages of the Roman Imperial age, but only in small details,
individual parts — just as the recognition of natural laws remained
confined to individual details.

But one thing was new in late antique art. Because it conceived
objects no longer in strictly individual terms but also, to a certain
degree, in their causal relationships, this art had to summon more
things than ever into its contest; in other words, it expanded its
circle of motifs. Earlier we noted that Egyptian and classical artists
did not concern themselves with distinct species of nature; artistic
treatment was paramount. Now everything seemed to change as
artists snatched up natural subjects that had earlier been ignored.
They depicted animals, for example, with great natural accuracy
(*Sala degli Animali* [figure 3]). Of course, we do not know the
extent to which some conceptual purpose may have been involved.
Landscapes also began to emerge (Esquiline landscapes [figure
16]). Admittedly, this, too, was largely for conceptual reasons:
these were not autonomous landscapes but history paintings. It
appears that the motif was significant for its own sake — but this is
only apparently true. Still, even though the selection remained
quite limited and the whole trend barely lasted a century, the
range of motifs could never again be as narrow as it had been previously. The realm of ornament confirms this. Whereas formerly
people were satisfied with ancient Egyptian lotus blossoms and
palmettes and employed the acanthus as the highest embellishment, now they introduced into their ornament numerous plant

species that held special appeal. These included favorite garden flowers and fruits, especially vines with clusters of grapes, which persevered well into the Christian Middle Ages. Evidently these were connected to conceptual purposes.

Inorganic realm. An equally significant change seems to have occurred during the age of the Diadochi, though we have no material evidence for it. The achievements were analogous to those of the *Laocoön*. Conjunction of numerous individuals, as in Egyptian art, one of whom predominates.

1. Massed structure, central-plan structure. The Serapeion in Alexandria. These point straight to Roman monuments. The beginnings probably lie in Hellenism.

2. Creation of a conception of interior space.

3. Probable introduction of curves to architecture.[12]

Pliny and other ancient writers were aware that Lysippus fashioned rounded rather than quadrangular bodies. Therefore, we need not be surprised that curvature also found its way into architecture.[13] The Pantheon bears witness to this (figures 20 and 21; we do not count theaters here, because they did not create an enclosed space). Its formation at the time of Hadrian is now certain. Although Agrippa probably also built a rotunda, it is unclear whether he vaulted it or simply surmounted it with a wooden canopy-roof; columns added to the renovated structure further unified the spatial core.[14] But the Hadrianic building did not contain the porch we see today; this stems, at earliest, from the Antonine period, probably around the time of Septimius Severus. Most important for our purposes: externally an individual; windowless (openings for the galleries beneath the dome do not count as windows); single light source from above. Not a massed structure, but a centralized one. Thoroughly symmetrical, but also thoroughly curved: absolute clarity not in the parts but in the whole. The curved vaulting, in comparison with the clear beamed ceiling, likewise represents a suppression of clarity. Thus everywhere, even in architecture, crystallinity softens and retreats. Most important here is the conception of space, which we shall discuss in relation to form and surface.

In this context, we must also point out the exedrae that crop up everywhere in Roman floor plans.

Organic forms also seeped increasingly into industrial arts. We already mentioned the new "naturalistic" motifs in decorative ornament. As for sculptural treatments of industrial art, we point out the great Roman silver finds with their naturalistic embellishment: Hildesheim, Boscoreale.

Late Roman Art

In the relatively short span of time between 150 and 350 c.e., two ages split apart. The polytheistic age, which encompassed all the centuries of Antiquity, retreated, and a new age exploded onto the scene to dominate the coming millennia. How strange that the art of this period has been almost totally disregarded until now. Its monuments still stand, and one therefore has to notice its existence, but the artistry of these has not been deemed worthy of investigation. Why? Because people have seen in them only the old antique element, and this in a state of collapse. Indeed, one of the defining characteristics of these works is their indifference to the primary objectives of antique art: beauty and truth to nature. Traces of both remain (indeed, this is what makes these recognizable as antique works at all) — enough for the works to be judged according to what has been lost. But alongside this negative there must be a positive: after all, art seeks to create harmony, and this can only be accomplished through positive efforts. Medieval art history could also be called on in this context; but the connective links have hitherto been absent. In addition, the aesthetic system of that time differs exceedingly from the modern one, and we can therefore have just as little sympathy for late Roman art as we do for the superstitious views of late Roman cults.

We observe two trends: (1) The inherited polytheistic movement, which fuses body and soul into a single individual and was common to all Antiquity, led to heightened verisimilitude, especially after Alexander the Great. (2) A new monotheistic movement, which sought a strict separation of body and soul and proclaimed the body transitory and thus contemptible.

We can trace the polytheistic tendency — heightened truth to nature — back to the middle of the third century, particularly in official artworks such as imperial portraits: Decius. The monotheistic tendency revealed itself concurrently, especially in private works such as sarcophagi: sarcophagus of Alexander Severus and Mamaea in the Capitoline Museum.

This trend escalated abruptly after the year 250. We are unable to see clearly into the fearsome battles of the Illyric emperors; calm settled again only under Diocletian and Constantine, and thenceforth art assumed the following appearance. Portrait of Magnus Decentius and the so-called Constantine (Louvre). Arch of Constantine (pagan) neither beautiful nor lively in its parts, but displays crystalline composition as a whole (figure 23); sarcophagus in Santa Costanza (Christian). What are the most striking characteristics of these monuments? (1) Spiritual expression is abolished, and art confines itself exclusively to the material (blank, material gazes; stiff, lifeless stances; heads positioned straight ahead: return to frontality). (2) Art has suppressed any organic personalization, thereby allowing crystallinity to reclaim its place (sharply chiseled lips; clear arches of eyebrows; smooth foreheads; fully rounded cheeks). In the sarcophagus of Constantina, this comes to view in the preponderance of decorative detail, in the crystalline construction of individual natural motifs (flowers, animals). Beauty is crystalline. Whereas the foliate ornament on

Constantina's sarcophagus impresses us as beautiful, the putti and animal do not, because in them the rules of proportion were not observed. Artists strove for crystallinity in inorganic but not organic motifs; they sought crystallinity in the group.

These aspects immediately call to mind ancient Near Eastern approaches. They were a concomitant of monotheism, with its sharp divide between spirit and body. We thus appear to have come full circle. But we have not arrived completely at the starting point. The split between body and spirit in Christianity was not as pronounced as in ancient Egyptian or Judaic thought. Its effects were therefore not as far-reaching; art achieved neither full frontality nor beauty. Herein lies the character of Christian art during this period; this is why it does not appeal to us. Its character was too weakly defined. But this is precisely what allowed Christian art to develop further. Its potential for progress was actualized later, during the Middle Ages, in contrast to ancient Near Eastern art (both Arabic and Byzantine), which remained static.

Inorganic motifs in late Roman art. Architecture.

1. Expansion of earlier antique tendencies through the development of the central-plan building.

2. Development of a new direction through the monumental reshaping of the longitudinal structure as a basilica.

At this point, the centralized structure became a massed structure. First, stories stacked on top of one another (theater), then individual elements grouped side by side or clustered together, but always symmetrically and with a clear dominant focus: the antique compositional principle.[15] What was new was the additive arrangement of components: addition of exedrae around the circumference of a round structure, as in the Minerva Medica. The conception of the individual unit remained the same, but a higher form of individuality now took shape. The basilica, on the other hand, was completely novel in several respects. First, it was an exclusively utilitarian building — practical purpose as well as artistic — for which established aesthetic rules possessed no unconditional validity (similar to the way the Egyptians vaulted their utilitarian buildings but deemed vaulting inappropriate for monumental structures).[16] Something hitherto shunned was now validated as a monumental artistic motif. Second, it was a massed structure but not a centralized structure — that is, it allowed no single element to dominate the whole. The overall composition does not reveal itself at a glance; composition is lacking in the individual entity. This is a sign of progress, a loosening and relinquishing of an antique postulate. Third, it stripped away all curvature (except in the apse) and made the walls completely straight again — that is, crystalline in the parts. Crystallinity, then, was surrendered in the whole but revived in details. We thus witness an advancement in the whole: division into extremes, even more emphatic in postclassical Antiquity. In this respect, it is correct to claim that medieval art brought about the most decisive rejection of classical Antiquity: whereas antique art strove for balance, Christian art split into extremes. The same phenomenon as in religion and philosophy: whereas the Greeks merged spirit and body to form a whole individual, the Christians separated them.

Ornamentation: abolished naturalistic motifs, returned to stark crystallinity.

CHAPTER FIVE

Form and Surface

All things of nature extend themselves in the three dimensions of
height, width, and depth. Today we take for granted, as the Greeks
already did, that bodies in nature are composed of atoms and
molecules. Molecules are essentially three-dimensional but are so
minuscule as to be imperceptible to the human eye. Natural things
confront our senses not as atoms but as atomic complexes. Insofar
as we are dealing with solid bodies, these complexes appear to be
persistent, that is, at least temporarily immutable. We can thus
conclude that every object of nature occupies three dimensions.
This three-dimensional extension, common to all natural things,
we call "form."

How do we obtain any impression of natural things external to
ourselves? Through our senses. The sense of sight, or optical sense,
plays the leading role in this process. But the optical sense alone
does not suffice to provide us with a true sense of form. The sense
of sight is unable to penetrate objects; it apprehends in a given
thing merely the one surface that happens to be turned toward the
viewer. That is to say, the eye perceives not a three-dimensional
form but a two-dimensional surface; it sees height and width but
not depth. To convince ourselves of the actuality of depth, we
must call on another sense, the sense of touch, or tactile sense.
The optical sense merely reveals the existence of an object; the

tactile sense presents its form. Today we need only a single glance to recognize that, say, a man is standing before us. But our optical sense alone does not inform us of this; rather, we draw on our past experience in the domain of touch. Thus we would have something essential, form, given us by the tactile sense, and something illusory, surface, which the optical sense deceptively dangles before us. This we call the "optical" or "subjective surface."

What does the sense of touch tell us? It informs us not only that the body is self-contained in three dimensions but also that this sense of integrity is itself effected through surfaces. The tactile sense cannot penetrate objects; but it can grasp the object from various sides simultaneously, whereas the sense of sight apprehends the object only from a single side. Thus the sense of touch also gives us information about the bounding surface of a given thing; let us call this the "tactile" or "objective surface." It may seem that the optical and tactile surfaces are identical. But in the study of art history, it is crucial to realize that these surfaces are distinct. The work of art will look fundamentally different according to which surface the artist depends on. How are the two differentiated?

In reality, the optical surface is always strictly two-dimensional. The image unfolds before our eyes in only two dimensions; we must not be deceived by our awareness that objects appearing in two dimensions actually signify three-dimensional forms. Our internal consciousness teaches us this on the basis of accumulated experience. But to our external sense of sight, objects consist exclusively of two-dimensional surfaces, absolute planes. The molecules we observe in things lie side by side on a single plane.

What about the tactile surface? It is certainly feasible that the tactile surface could also constitute an absolute plane, in other words, that tactile and optical surfaces could coincide, as in a cube. If you hold a cube before your eyes in such a way that you perceive just one side, your eye sees the molecules lying on a single plane. But the tactile sense likewise apprehends a smooth surface with no convexities or concavities. Thus in this case, the tactile surface is similarly two-dimensional. Such examples, however, are rare (moreover, when I hold the cube in my hand I feel its three-dimensionality directly). Now let us consider another kind of crystal, a polyhedron containing more than six faces. Unless the crystal were unusually large and you were holding it directly in front of your nose, you would never see just one side. But if you examined it from far enough away that it remained recognizable in its broader contours, you would perceive more than one side. Whereas our optical sense perceives this multiplicity of faces as occupying a single plane, the tactile sense infers that the sides abut one another at angles and recede into depth. Thus the tactile surface is no longer two-dimensional but three-dimensional. Let us now replace the crystal with an organic thing such as a human figure. Although this strikes the eyes as a single plane, a two-dimensional surface, the moment one touches this surface it assumes what we call volumes or modeling.

Tactile and optical surfaces are thus two separate things: the optical is always planar, the tactile is typically irregular, three-dimensional, volumetric; only exceptionally is it regular.

We have just stated that man does not normally put the sense of touch to use first when seeking to comprehend the three-dimensional configuration of a natural object. The prior experience of the tactile sense, recalled by the sense of sight, suffices. Consequently, the optical sense is crucial for apprehending the tactile surface. We must therefore inquire how the sense of sight relates to perception of tactile surfaces.

We learn from experience at a very early age — already in childhood, inasmuch as experience is not inherited — that wherever the tactile sense alerts us to the interruption of an even surface by some projection or recess, the optical sense apprehends a shadow (and ultimately, of course, a light for which the shadow serves as a foil). Whenever our eyes catch sight of a shadow, we therefore do not need the tactile sense to convince us that there is volume, a rising or sinking of the surface in depth. The shadow is an index of form. It does not, however, possess the substance of a three-dimensional projection or relief. Shadows change not only according to the object's illumination or the beholder's angle of vision but also, and even more important, according to the distance at which the object is observed. Among the innumerable variations of this phenomenon, three broader cases of special significance can be singled out.

1. If you examine the object in closest proximity, holding it, as it were, before your nose so that you apprehend only a partial surface of the overall form, shadows will appear minimal. The surface itself is not large, and the smaller it is, the smoother and more regular it looks. In this *near view*, the tactile surface approximates the plane, that is, the optical surface, because any discernible shadows appear very weak.

2. If we move far enough away from the object to survey its contours fully in height and width, we can recognize the object easily as a three-dimensional form. Now the effect of shadows on the surface is much greater (try holding a finger very close and then farther away); the shadows also grow perceptible on the contours, allowing us to infer the recession of surfaces into depth, a modeling toward the back — and thus self-containment in the depth dimension. The distance at which, by drawing on prior experience with shadows, we are able to recognize the thing as unified and self-contained while distinctly apprehending the relief-like configuration of its outer surface is the *normal view*. In the normal view, the object's volumetric character strikes the imperfect sense of sight with the greatest relative accuracy.

3. Removing ourselves still farther from the observed object, the finer shadows begin to blur; illuminated and shaded sections flow together to create a uniform median tone, thereby gaining a chromatic value that consistently appears planar (optic). Only the thickest, blackest shadows might still make their presence known. In the *distant view*, then, the optical experience that otherwise ran parallel to the tactile breaks away. The eye perceives only an optical surface, a plane. Whatever shadows remain visible possess only the value of a color, of black — a purely planar value.

We have now differentiated near, normal, and distant views. The near view grasps only bits and pieces; one must look at one part of the form at a time and recombine these mentally. The normal view takes up the whole and the parts (as much as can be seen at once) simultaneously. The distant view sees only the whole and not the parts.

The respective distance naturally changes for any given object. The wall of a house remains planar even when viewed from several paces away, whereas I see a polyhedron as a whole even if it's directly in front of my nose. The smaller the object, the more the normal view approximates the near view. The distant view, by contrast, is always far removed from both. The tiniest thing, when observed from afar, looks different when seen up close.

How does visual art contend with this issue? If art really strove to imitate nature, the matter would be quite simple. The artist would merely cast the object in plaster, and paint its outer surfaces to correspond to nature. A person could then view the object in the closest proximity or from a distance, however he wished, and he would receive a plastic or a painterly impression. However, visual art is not an imitation of nature but a contest with it. The artist wants to present only those aspects of a natural thing that will be pleasing to us. These have changed dramatically through various times and cultures. In some times, people preferred to see

399

things at close range, in others — today, for example — from a distance. This development constitutes a substantial chapter in the history of art, one no less significant than the development of motifs. In the end, the former depends just as heavily as the latter on the sequence of man's worldviews.

We must dispose of one possible misunderstanding from the outset. It is well known that there exist both an art of form and an art of surface. The art of form is freestanding sculpture, wherein objects are rendered in three dimensions as tactile surfaces. The art of surface is painting, wherein objects are portrayed in two dimensions as optical surfaces. Relief stands directly between these. One might imagine sculpture to be geared toward the near view and painting toward the distant. This is correct insofar as it is difficult for a statue to be fully effective from a great distance and a painting to be so at very close range. In this respect, sculpture does correspond better to the near view and painting to the distant. The terms "plastic" and "painterly" are therefore synonymous with "oriented toward the near view" and "oriented toward the distant view." Nevertheless, there are such things as painterly, or distance-oriented, statues, and sculptural paintings best viewed at close range. In other words, statues, reliefs, and paintings have always coexisted in the history of visual art, regardless of people's general affinity for close or distant viewing. This means that there should be no more talk of "stylistic laws" specifically applicable to sculpture or painting, which scholars so tirelessly posit. Those who wish to prescribe distinct laws for materials and techniques have also tried to do so for forms and surfaces. This is an arbitrary endeavor, grounded firmly in a modern perspective. Every worldview produces its own stylistic laws. Absolute stylistic laws have just as little existence as an absolute aesthetic system.

Origins

(Insofar as these are discernible in Egyptian art.)

Peering out at the world around him, primitive man found himself confronted by chaos. Into that chaos he sought to bring order. The first step was to pull forward the things that held special attraction, so that in place of a muddled, chaotic mass he had before him individual entities. Here we return to the basic outlook of all ancient people: natural things are embodied individuals. (This becomes clearest by comparison with our current view. No chaos shocks us, because we know that a natural-scientific law is present to sustain order within and among things; today we conceive objects as units within larger cohesive categories. We are capable of conceptualizing a given thing solely in terms of causes and effects. For that reason, we paint things in dynamic reciprocal contexts. Our modern pictures would strike ancient Egyptians as nothing less than a glorification of chaos. Whereas the Egyptians yearned above all for isolation and clarity of individual objects, we desire connections, mixtures, equalization.) It is thus easy to answer the question as to whether primitive man comprehended objects in a tactile or an optical manner. The optical approach showed him chaos; the tactile offered him sufficient conviction of the individual integrity of things. Visual art therefore had to begin with the tactile surface. From this point, we can reconstruct the whole development *a priori*. The earliest period was governed by tactile perception in the near view. Today, as we all know, optical perception in the distant view prevails. These represent opposing extremes. Normal-view perception must therefore reside in the middle, during periods of balance. Indeed, we encounter the normal view most readily in classical Greek art and in the Italian High Renaissance.

What do we mean by tactile perception?

1. This entails the individual modeling of each part and the

subsequent reassembly of these based on one's prior experience of the whole. It has long been noted that the individual surface parts of Egyptian statues are rendered quite accurately and naturally, that only their proper cohesion is lacking. This is of course spoken from the standpoint of modern aesthetics; *we* apprehend the human figure optically, as a whole, and pay more attention to the cohesion of parts — to the whole — than to the parts themselves. This in itself presupposes optical perception. The Egyptians, by contrast, fundamentally shunned optical perception. They sought only the tactile surface. This basic attitude persisted well into the classical art of the Greeks. Lysippus was the first artist to perceive and present the human figure optically, as a whole — a move not lost on the ancients. Pliny mentioned it explicitly, though people have generally not understood what he meant: Lysippus, as he put it, portrayed figures not as they are but as they are seen. In short, one still looked for the whole over the parts.

2. The tactile surface is characterized by its display of only weak shadows; it presents the eye with the impression of smooth planarity. It is well known that Egyptian figures are planar, so much so that they approximate the optical surface in smooth regularity. This seems to pose a contradiction: people sought individual unity so as to escape optical chaos, and at the same time they moved toward the optical surface, which distorts individual unity and leads back to chaos. But the flatness registers only from the normal or distant view. Whoever wants to examine Egyptian figures correctly must touch their surfaces with his fingertips. He will then discover not an even surface but the finest modeling, a fluid outward and inward movement, which is nonetheless subdued enough to cast only the weakest shadows. This is discernible only from the closest proximity and is thus directed exclusively toward the near view. Viewed from close up, the parts look completely faithful to nature; only the whole comes across as stiff and

lifeless. Shadows are patently avoided. Why? Because shadows suggest three-dimensionality and thus space. And this people eschewed space at all costs. Chaos dwells in space, clarity and order in spaceless individuality (for the Greeks, space was synonymous with chaos; witness Hesiod's *Theogony*).

We can now make the following claim: the earliest art, from ancient Egypt, grasped objects as individually bounded, but only in height and width. It refrained as much as possible from depicting any boundaries in depth, for these can never fully reveal themselves to man — not to his sense of touch and even less to his sense of sight — and they would therefore always retain an indistinct quality. Better to have no delimitation in depth at all than unclear delimitation. Egyptian art is thus at once individualistic and surface-oriented. Herein lies the root of many misunderstandings. People call the character of Egyptian art plastic or sculptural, which is accurate insofar as Egyptian art conceives things as individuals. But works of Egyptian art are also flat and planar. How does that correspond to its plasticity? By "plastic," one typically understands "formed," or modeled in three dimensions. But the "formed" aspect of Egyptian art seems to be maximally suppressed. If "plastic" denotes something individually formed in three dimensions, this only applies fully to art after Lysippus. Ancient Egyptian art cannot be called plastic in this sense, because it does not strive for three-dimensional formation. Nor is it strictly painterly. Rather, it is both surface-bound and concerned with individual cohesiveness. The type of three-dimensional figure devised by Lysippus would not have appealed to Egyptians; it would have struck them as chaotic nature, as optical deception. The Egyptian artist believed he was rendering figures as they *are*, not as they appear to the eyes through spatial illusions. The following schema thus emerges. All ancient art is concerned with individual unity:

first period, up to Lysippus: surface-bound and oriented toward the near view (tactile surfaces);

second period, Lysippus to Marcus Aurelius: things formed individually (oriented toward the normal view);

third period, Marcus Aurelius to Constantine: surface-bound and oriented toward the distant view (optical surface).

Toward the end, the individual struggled against the general until we seem to be dealing strictly with the general, a kind of impressionism (we have already demonstrated that individualism nonetheless maintained its predominance).

Statuary

Egyptian artists worked up all four sides in a planar fashion (in keeping with the crystalline model, they saw the human body as four-sided: quadratic design of the Greeks until Lysippus). But one side still constituted the main face, the frontal view, and the whole was essentially confined to this. Why? Because of the desire for absolute symmetry (frontality), which can be enjoyed exclusively in the frontal view.

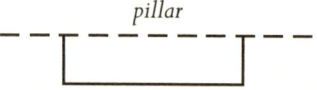

pillar

The side opposite the front was often either worked into a pillar or leaned against a separate support.[1] This plainly shows that space was meant to be abolished; nothing existed behind the statue. This tactile surface orientation is easy to generate in flesh; the nude retained a preeminent position in Egyptian art, and indeed throughout all Antiquity. This reveals most clearly the difference between antique art and Christian Byzantine art, with its preference for the fully clothed body. The history of costume reveals the same distinction: attire that is wrapped around the body versus that which is pulled on. As in that case, other elements also interrupt the surface. These include: (1) among bodily elements, hair; (2) among extrinsic things, drapery.

Hair formation is always fundamentally important; indeed, it frequently forms the surest criterion for determining style. The hair itself was represented not as a series of individual units but as an unclear mass, often markedly sculptural in form (crimped strands). Egyptian artists changed this. They turned the hair into a tactile surface by merging them into a rounded mass and articulating this larger surface in a tactile way through the addition of fine grooves, which, when viewed from close up, revealed thin shadows on the surface. The then-current hairstyle allowed for this, though it was also surely the outgrowth of an artistic need. People wore their hair *in natura* just as they preferred to see it; this applied all the more to art.

The formation of drapery is even more important. It automatically involves a break from the overriding law of harmony that demands absolute individual integrity and clarity, for the garment envelops the individual body as something foreign, at least partially concealing it and making it indistinct. Egyptian artists worked to avoid this as much as they could.

First, they extensively minimized draperies, especially in the earlier period (surely the climate helped, but here, as everywhere else, cause and effect are closely interlinked).

Second, they lay the drapery tight against the body, so as to conceal the form of the body as little as possible. In other words, they fundamentally rejected folds: folds suggest three-dimensionally formed garments, and Egyptians despised the formed. There could never be true drapery, that is, garments with folds, in Egyptian art. We occasionally find in Old Kingdom art a broad garment that does not lie on the body (in the *Ti* figure, it resembles crinoline), but this lacks folds entirely, like a rounded cone.

405

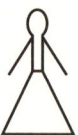

Of special interest are those cases where folds had to be incorporated because the actual costume demanded them. People of the Old Kingdom must have worn finely pleated skirts for at least some time; these were portrayed, but always with exceedingly weak shadows. Noble women of the New Kingdom wore broad garments that stood out from the body; a seated Ramses figure demonstrates how sculpture handled this. Painting had it easier, for there the naked body could shine forth through very thin material.

Color. Every natural object has a colored outer surface; that is, it exerts a certain stimulus on the human eye that we call coloration. This stimulus is perceived not by the tactile sense but by the sense of sight alone; it is strictly optical and surface-bound. The word "color" therefore makes us think instantly of painting: conventional wisdom holds color and painting to be one and the same. But color is also inextricable from form, in the same way that the tactile surface is inextricable from form. Both sculpture and painting have employed color from the very beginning. Of course we are aware that our modern sculpture is for the most part achromatic and that coloration was the rule in other artistic periods, especially in Antiquity and then the quattrocento. At this point, the question arises: If color is optical and surface-bound, why did Egyptian art, which aimed for concrete, tangible individuality, introduce it at all? The problem resolves itself when we realize that to incorporate color or not was not a matter of choice for the Egyptian artist. Color, as an integral part of dead matter, was indelibly present. Art could only mitigate that necessary evil, subjugating it to its own special purposes. Here we must clear up a misunderstanding. Are our modern statues really colorless? They do bear in themselves the natural color of the material. If hewn from marble, they are white. Our eyes perceive that very well; they would be affected much differently if the statue were painted in various bright colors. Our taste, as we call it, craves white, that is, light-colored statues; this is not the proper place to discuss why. The question, then, is not whether we should compose the work with colors but whether we should leave it with its natural coloration or give it a new one, and, if so, which. The matter was no different for the Egyptians. They, too, had no choice, so that despite their deep-rooted avoidance of anything purely optical, they still had to accept colored sculpture — all the while with an orientation toward the tactile, not the optical, surface.

There are three possibilities for the application of color in the visual arts:

1. One can leave the dead material its natural color, as is the rule today.

2. One can remove the natural color from the dead material and replace it with that of the natural model with which the work of art competes, as, for instance, in a clay statue of a human figure painted with flesh tones: natural coloration.

3. One can remove the natural color from the dead material and replace it not with the corresponding color of the model but with some other: so, for example, one paints a statue of a human figure with a blue pigment (for instance, in so-called Egyptian porcelain). Here the motivation is purely decorative: the blue color exerts a more powerful attraction on the eyes than the natural color of the clay. Conventional or decorative painting.

All three cases already appear in Egyptian art, just as they are still evident today. Thus we see that coloration is not a decisive criterion in itself. Of course, people preferred to paint statues in some times and to leave them unpainted in others, but never did one choice entail the complete exclusion of the other. We always have to deal with the treatment of color in individual cases. Once again we recognize that what is important is not the material aspect itself (as noted earlier with respect to motifs) but the way it is handled. Deep misunderstandings continue to prevail in this domain too (the painting of statues and reliefs), most of which are traceable to Semper. His essays always begin with the words: "In the beginning, there was textile art." Everywhere he saw only the material functions of covering and binding (we see in these the shifting relations between the overall form and its surface parts). He conceived color as a covering, and because his axiom held that every work of ancient art had to have some covering, he concluded that every work of art was either colorfully painted or coated with beaten metal — in other words, that it was never allowed to display its natural color. In his view, every antique statue, every relief, every remotely important architectural component must once have been polychromed. Wherever we do not see this, the original coloring must simply have faded away; it had to have been there at one point.

Today we have recovered so many unpainted works from ancient Egyptian tombs, which have been protected from the destructive impact of weathering and so on, as to leave no doubt: painted and unpainted works of art existed side by side in Old Kingdom Egypt. In some cases, people were content with the natural color, in others they felt the need to introduce another — we will deal with this shortly. Semper undoubtedly overshot the mark with regard to Greek art as well.

How did Egyptian artists treat color? As noted, Egyptian art sought clarity in internal parts. Each component therefore had to possess its own uniform coloration; for each distinct part, the near view had to apprehend only one color. Multiple colors that blended into one another would have effaced that clarity, disrupted the self-containment of the surface parts, and brought about indistinctness, disorder, and thus uneasiness. The same holds true for shading, which in some respects is no different from color itself. A surface part in shadow looks different from an unshaded one, even if the underlying hue is identical. This again explains the hostility of Egyptian art to shadows. We call this piecemeal coloration of parts "polychromy." Although it prevailed in Antiquity more generally, this approach permeated Egyptian art particularly thoroughly and to the exclusion of all else.

We can best comprehend how deeply polychromy is linked to the near view by envisioning an inverse relationship. Let us look to paintings rather than statues, because these are more appropriate here (the same principles apply to statues). In Egyptian art, human figures display a single flesh tone from head to feet. Modern portraits, on the other hand, exhibit, even in the smallest area (for example, the cheek), a wide array of diverse colors placed directly next to each other. When viewed up close, these look quite unnatural and seem to make no sense; only when viewed from a distance do the flecks coalesce to form a unified tone. We call this method of producing higher chromatic unity through the combination of diverse hues "colorism." We can thus differentiate two distinct ways of handling color in visual art: polychromy and colorism.

The difference is as follows:

1. Polychromy is most effective in the near view and only conditionally so in the normal view.

2. Colorism is most effective in the distant view and only conditionally so in the normal view.

3. Polychromy seeks individual unity and sharp distinctions of parts.

4. Colorism seeks general unity and connections among individual parts. (This is why it could not achieve predominance in
Antiquity, an era that, in principle, was intrinsically inclined toward individualism; it gained some ascendancy only in the latest
phase of Antiquity but got stuck halfway.)

Let us return to statuary. A few examples of the use of polychromy:

Old Kingdom portrait statues. Those of limestone were almost always painted. Example: *Rahotep*. Brown skin, white loin-
cloth. Black hair and pupils. Jewelry painted on.

Wooden statues, by contrast, were often left unpainted; see
the *Sheikh el-Beled*, where only the pupils, made of a colored
substance, were inserted separately (figure 9). We already find
unpainted statues of deities in the Old Kingdom. This makes plain
that the "naturalistic" painting of portrait statues was intimately
tied to their conceptual significance. From the New Kingdom, we
primarily have statues of kings and gods. These were fashioned
from precious materials such as pink granite, syenite, and basalt
but were never painted, even on the pupils; see the Ramesside
figures. When conceptual purposes did not demand otherwise,
people relished the natural appeal of the raw material; they certainly had little thought for the necessity of the covering that
Semper regards as so indispensable. If the so-called porcelain figures were painted, this was only because the plain clay did not
sufficiently excite the eyes. In such cases, people displayed an
affinity for complementary colors: green and red, violet and yellow. This was hardly an inviolable law, however, for we frequently
find combinations of red and blue, yellow and white. (Complementary — harmony, higher chromatic unity; already points toward colorism.) Contrasting — sharper distinction of parts.

Relief

We have noted that Egyptian statues often stand against a pillar so that the figure is detached from the three-dimensional space beyond. This tendency also characterizes reliefs. The relief aims to create a tactile surface while breaking away from the three-dimensional extension of space and the resultant lack of visual clarity. For that reason, the subject of a relief — for example, a human figure — will be rendered with a certain degree of modeling but, in keeping with the near view, will be maximally planar, devoid of shadow, and oriented toward a primary face. The three remaining sides (back, right, and left) remain subsumed within the smooth and polished crystalline material. This creates the sense of ground. Ground and space were originally irreconcilable opposites; ground was introduced so that space might be evaded. But ground is also a necessary evil. In it, the seeds of future space lie latent that would later emerge in fact. But ground was initially treated in such a way as to suggest space as little as possible.

The basic question remains: Why did people produce reliefs in the first place? Why did they not stay content with the frontally oriented, planar statue standing against a pillar? Relief was necessary from the moment the figure could no longer stand autonomously — when, for instance, an accompanying inscription was required. Inscription and figure had to be brought together, placed into conjunction. This already represents a disruption of strict individuality and begins to lead to space. Relief is the first step on the path toward an art of space. At first, of course, people worked to suppress any suggestion of space and to present everything on the ground as discrete, independent individuals.

The earliest relief type was probably sunken relief, with the figures carved into the raw material:

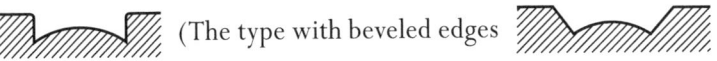 (The type with beveled edges

may have come first.) Here the figures were incised into the raw material. With this technique, the material ground divides rather than connects, and, consequently, the juxtaposed figures appear most independent. But at the same time, even in Old Kingdom art, reliefs emerged with receding ground (figure 13) — the type that would prevail in all subsequent periods up to the present. This likewise represents a step toward an art of space, for it is evident here that the figures all inhabit a single plane, whereas this was not apparent earlier. But here, with this single plane, the Egyptians stopped. No further progress was possible, for that would have led to the presence of multiple grounds at various levels, to differentiation between foreground and background, and hence to the depiction of real space.

The relation between figure and ground — or, as it is called in decorative art, between pattern and ground — is therefore of fundamental importance. A basic principle of Egyptian art was that ground would never, under any circumstances, receive consideration. (This makes more sense if we cast a glance at Greek art, which endeavored to bring figures and ground into a harmonious relationship by filling the ground appropriately, so that it looked neither too empty nor too full. In Egyptian art, we find only extremes: either broad surfaces of the ground remained blank, or they were recklessly filled up, as in battle scenes.) Ground, like shadows, is merely a nothing, a void; artists knew that any concessions they made to it would lead to space.

So much for the relation between ground and figure. As far as the figure itself is concerned, its treatment is essentially the same as that of the statue: as flat as possible, splayed out wide. Although figures appear schematic when viewed from a distance, at close range we often marvel at their supremely fine modeling. Color appears again and again: either people were satisfied with the natural color, or they replaced it with another.

On the stances of relief figures (should have been discussed in the section on motifs). Although a frontal presentation would also naturally have been the most desirable option in reliefs, here it would have made absolute conformity to the surface impossible. The legs had to be shown striding forward, which would have entailed their occupying two planes, while facial projections, especially the nose, would have been squashed flat. The foreshortening of whole limbs had to be avoided at all costs due to its disruption of clarity. Figures in Egyptian reliefs are therefore always rendered in profile wherever this was imperative: that is, in the head and legs. The chest was always turned outward, for it could — indeed ought to — appear frontal. Hence the curious contortion of Egyptian bodies, which was only seldom modified.

Two-Dimensional Art (Painting, Drawing, Inlay Work)
Painting (and other two-dimensional art) is based on the optical surface. It therefore seems likely that it would be absent from Egyptian art, with its predilection for the tactile surface. The main objective, however, was the tactile delimitation of height and width, which could be effected in two-dimensional arts through sharp, clear, unambiguous outlines. As a result, all Egyptian painting is contour drawing, absolutely solid and crisp (modern painting, in contrast, dispenses with outlines, allowing objects to spill over into space as fluidly as possible). On the other hand, Egyptian painting eschews the delimitation of objects in depth, that is, modeling. Egyptian painting is silhouette painting; its essence never really changed (figure 12). Within the outlines of a human figure, we find no modeling; only those parts were accentuated that were already distinguished by color: hair, eyes, ornament.

Thus there is a difference between relief and painting. Reliefs include some modeling of the tactile surface, even if this remains maximally flat and shadowless. Painting allows for no modeling, for this would involve strictly optical foreshortenings, which in turn would cause indistinctness. Painting, in other words, could not provide tactile modeling in depth or tolerate optical foreshortening.

Architecture
Schmarsow recently declared the formation of space to be the primary purpose of all architecture. If this were true, the Egyptians would never have developed architecture at all, because they fundamentally rejected space. But in fact the Egyptians laid the groundwork for all monumental architecture. This makes plain that architecture and the formation of space were not originally identical. An architecture of space did exist, but it arose only in a later stage of development, as people prepared to make the transition from normal to distant viewing.

Architecture initially set out to create an individual entity with distinct, unshaded surface parts. The oldest kind of architecture is thus the commemorative monument. Pyramids were tomb markers whose exteriors always consisted of smooth triangular surfaces divided into tall steps. No spatial effects whatsoever were intended in the interior. This consisted merely of a small grave chamber and a corridor leading to it: both necessary evils. Although the mastaba tombs, which were designed as houses, do contain rooms, these were always fragmented by pillars so that any sense of cohesive space was studiously destroyed.

Temple. Here, too, the exterior displays a regular tectonic surface that coincides with the optical surface, with no projections or recesses and specifically no windows. The interior does not reveal itself to the outside at all: it seems nonexistent, with only a door breaking through as a necessary evil. But these many exterior surfaces come across as empty and bare; they demanded to be filled and were therefore covered with figural reliefs dedicated to the greater glory of the god and the royal patron figure 14). Their composition took no account of the layout of the ground surfaces, for that would have meant acknowledging the ground. Greek artists would have found this imperative; the Egyptians zealously avoided it.

Two components must be distinguished inside: the courtyard; and the main hall.

1. The courtyard. Not entirely closed, no true space because open at the top. Even the side walls were disquieting to the Egyptian artist, for they seemed together to form a square room. He therefore masked the walls with pillars and columns, that is, individual forms with tactile surfaces.

2. The main hall. Could not always be circumvented, as at Karnak; certain ceremonies required complete enclosure. Therefore covered by a flat roof. But then space was certain to creep in. The Egyptian warded it off by filling the entire room with many three-dimensional forms: columns, which break up not only the floor and ceiling but also the lateral surfaces and never allow the eyes to confront a cohesive optical surface.[2]

What about illumination? A light source was needed, and this demanded the puncturing of any absolute closure. Windows in the side walls were out of the question, because they would have interrupted the tactile surface. A hypaethral arrangement, on the other hand, would have yielded excessive openness. A system of illumination was devised that would unite light entering from the sides and from above: this was taken up again most successfully later, in the basilica.

(clerestory)

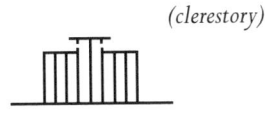

Form and Surface Among the Greeks

Here we must examine more closely the earlier stages, which have been recognized since Schliemann. We must see that the great accomplishments of the classical Greeks were imminent from the very start.

What does this mean?

a. The Egyptians got mired in the tactile treatment of parts (for example, in the human figure); now the concern was to produce an organically cohesive whole.

b. The Egyptians were objectivist, regarding all things as independent bodies; now people reached the insight that all observation is subjective.

c. In consequence, they had to accept space and time, for these, too, are subjective.

d. All this was possible only once people renounced, at least in part, uniformly tactile perception and moved toward the optical.

Mycenaean Art

Terra-cotta whorls with engraved (incised) lines have been found in Troy that may date to even earlier times.

a. The composition, in keeping with rotating, whirling motion, is not rigidly crystalline, radiating. This is a surface work. Is it relief or strictly two-dimensional art?

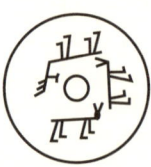

b. Not painted but incised. Technically, this should recall sunken relief. Engraved figures stand between relief and two-dimensional art; also crop up in Egyptian art, if only, characteris-

416

tically, seldom. But it is not sunken relief. Why? Because it lacks physical presence. So it seems we are dealing with a graphic art after all. The body is certainly not spatially bounded at the front, as with sunken reliefs. But neither is it bounded in height or depth; in every dimension, it is only a line, a delimitation of almost purely mathematical value. What does this imply? Tactile perception? Surely not. Not only is the deer not rendered in the near view, but also it is a strictly optical memory image. The engraved line works solely through shadows, often colored ones, and nothing else: black on red, for example.[3] The Eskimo pictograph still relies on this system today. It is tempting to speculate that the earliest origins of art are located here. One thing, however, is certain: if the Greeks had stopped there, they would have remained at the level of the Eskimo. It is therefore of the utmost significance that they moved on to reproduce actual physical dimensions. Did they accomplish this step by their own power? We cannot determine this with any certainty. But we do observe:

1. the widespread penetration of Oriental influence and, with it, corporality;

2. regressive movements in early Greek art (Dipylon) where the Oriental features — and alongside them corporality — recede. This allows us to conclude with some probability that Greek artists were spurred on to corporeal representation by Oriental works of art.

We must linger for a moment over the engraved animal figures. What does linear representation signify? A tendency against any sense of dimensionality whatsoever. It is mere appearance. It simply suggests not only depth but also width and height, thus demanding that one draw on prior experience. This is not a worldview that grasps things as three-dimensional, embodied individuals; it is, rather, a fantasy-laden outlook.

Let us take note of one more thing. The ancient Near Eastern, particularly the Semitic, worldview is characterized by clear, sharp, precise ways of thinking — hence its overwhelming predilection for the practical, the useful, the material. All Indo-Germanic worldviews we have studied thus far are characterized by an affinity for the fantastic or imaginary. These views were less lucid, but for that more flexible and thus capable of further growth. We must maintain, then, that we encounter in the Greeks the earliest apprehensible tendency toward the imaginative reproduction of optically perceived memory images.

There are no such linear projections in Egyptian art. Even in geometric ornament, we find only colored surfaces, not engraved lines. (Where we do see such cutting of the surface, it is always as sunken relief; the grooves form the contours containing the body, not the body itself.) A short sharp line would have struck Egyptians as incomprehensible, even preposterous. This also manifests an elemental difference between Egyptian-Semitic and Indo-Germanic art.

We should like to introduce here a few works that have long been regarded as typical examples of Mycenaean art.

1. Tomb stele with both spiral ornament and figural representations. These remain in low relief; they no longer are lines but exhibit characteristics of bodies in height and width. They are apparently based on Egyptian models (though never sunken reliefs), but with receding ground:

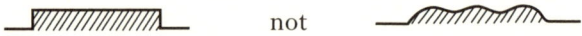

In other words, vertically anchored and with no modeling. No dynamic tactile surface, but rather a strictly two-dimensional optical surface (we never encounter such surface treatment in ancient Near Eastern art, though we do very often in Byzantine, especially among the Monophysite Copts, and Muslim art, which is likewise grounded in the optical surface). Ground and pattern: the ground is covered with spiral ornament and no figures. *Horror vacui*! Acknowledgment of ground, which over time inevitably leads to acceptance of space.

2. Lion Gate at Mycenae. The lions are no longer carved in the strict low relief of Egyptian art; their outer legs protrude freely, as is often the case with Assyrian gate guardians. This time the modeling is of tactile surfaces (very weak modeling). Ancient Near Eastern influence here, too, less Egyptian than Mesopotamian. The heraldic style likewise attests to this! But a progression beyond Oriental models is observable in the fact that a column occupies the center and the lions rest their front paws on a pedestal; this establishes a tighter connection among the parts while calling greater attention to the dominant element than in Assyrian and certainly Egyptian art. Also a translation of the Oriental into Greek.

3. With regard to painting, we refer to the Warrior Vase. Frieze with a row of marching soldiers; simple serial arrangement as in Egyptian art.

a. The figures occupy the entire height of the register (no air above; seems to be a negation of the ground, but is an acknowledgment thereof).

b. The figures are arrayed so that a minimal amount of space remains between each pair; relation between figure and ground, but no filler ornament.

c. Equal distance between figures; regular dispersal of ground.

Individual formation of bodies: contour drawing, without modeling; round profiles as in Egyptian art, but the left arm is hidden from view. Whereas the Egyptians would have regarded this as a lack of clarity and finish, the Greeks insisted on subjective optical presentations.

At least as reconstructed, the figure in the scene of the capture of the bull (mural from Tiryns) includes a linear suggestion of thigh and calf muscles. This, exceptionally, would have gone beyond Egyptian achievements.

The Vapheio Cups
The Vapheio cups caused considerable bewilderment when they were discovered. They seemed anachronistic. At the same time, they had so much in common with other monuments of Mycenaean art that their contemporaneity cannot be doubted.

Here one can clearly observe what prejudice is all about. Brunn, who regarded the Dipylon vases as exemplary of true proto-Hellenistic art and saw in Mycenaean art only outside influences, was forced either to surrender his prior views or to inflict violence on the art-historical language the cups actually speak. He chose the latter course, arguing that the cups lacked genuine composition, specifically, tectonic composition. The Dipylon vases were the first, he thought, to exhibit composition, and a strictly symmetrical composition at that. Brunn did not even approach the relation between form and surface.

Let us look closely at the composition of the two cups.

1. Center: a trapped bull, curled up. To the right, a fleeing bull that leaps downward. Left: an escaped bull that springs upward. This is composition — indeed, the loosened contrapposto compositional type of the classical age, not the stiff and static kind displayed in the Dipylon vase. That piece, when held up against the Vapheio cups (which surpass it by far), lingers at the level of the Egyptians. Moreover, Brunn buys into the prejudice that art must always represent religious themes. This aspect, however, recedes considerably in Mycenaean art. The scenes of the bull capture probably are not conceptually meaningful in the manner of Egyptian images, but rather are pictures intended to suggest a "mood" (*Stimmungsbilder*).

2. Center: opposition from the very start: restfulness and activity; contrast is sought everywhere. Two bulls (center: two kings, two consuls, *Aldobrandini Wedding*) side by side, overlapping, mutually concealing each other and displaying a reciprocal and dynamic relationship (both are full-grown bulls and not, say, a mother and calf). Single striding bulls to either side, that on the right raising his head (bellowing), that on the left lowering his (grazing). Contrappostal structure and secondary accessories are wisely employed so as to remove any stiffness or rigidity. In addition, a suggestion of terrain with plants and flowers (precursor of landscape images) and, at the same time, common ground for all: clear sense of space; no more strict isolation. But *horror vacui!* Clouds surge onto the scene. Some natural formation is depicted above the main subjects, in any case, and it could be clouds. Or perhaps mountains delimiting the horizon. Occlusion by a tree in the first cup (we also find occlusion in Egyptian art, but in marsh scenes, conditioned by concepts).

And now the relation between form and surface:

High instead of low relief, exceeding by far anything in Assyrian art. No conjoining of diverse tactile surfaces, but rather an optical appearance of wholeness; normal view; bunching together of certain folds; surface often fragmented by heavy shadows, not merely partial shadows. The latter characteristic was unheard of even in later Greek art, at least until Lysippus. The same goes for the musculature of the men. Hence the thoroughly lively design. But still a memory image: see the human figures, who stand on the ground with insufficient stability and whose thin bodies recall the Dipylon figures; indeed the linear stylization itself.

The human figures are all shown in profile. But the design of the falling figure, with its moments of overlapping, has no equivalent in Egyptian art; even less so the bulls, who turn their whole heads outward: direct and daring foreshortening.

Brunn accused the Vapheio cups of losing grasp of the "tec-tonic." But it was in this realm that Mycenaean artists achieved the most decisive gains, even earlier (as far as we know) than their Assyrian counterparts.

Division into an inner field and borders of purely ornamental surface. Only the figural elements required no border. The Vapheio cups signal an advancement in so-called naturalism (the most modern tendency in industrial arts), surpassing anything else in Antiquity.

The Dipylon Vases

The art of the Vapheio cups signals a step in a direction that artists would not approach again until much later, in the fourth century. We do not know the circumstances that led to a regression after this point. The old linear tendency prevailed for a while, though it was now heavily dependent on Egyptian design principles. This situation determined the whole subsequent development. We find predominantly human figures, which no longer are strictly linear but display a slight expansion of the broader parts, though they are pure silhouettes with no distinct outlines. Only the head is outlined separately on account of the eyes. Forerunners of black-figure vase painting; clearly memory images, not near-view pre-sentations. This contrasts with Egyptian art, which did not em-ploy such representational practices. What does this imply? The Egyptians were principally concerned with establishing bound-aries — hence isolation — in height and width. It did not matter what lay between; artists simply filled the area with color. The Greeks reproduced a memory image and conceded it one single dimension. Did they reach this stage independently? Probably with Egyptian assistance; the combination of profile head and frontal torso is Egyptian. Sepulchral function, religious essence move dis-tinctly to the foreground in the Dipylon vase paintings.

The various categories of vases — early Attic, proto-Corinthian, Corinthian, and so on — exhibit further stages of development. Here the modeling of the nude body was gradually perfected; surface components such as calf muscles and knees were defined by separate lines. This process had been initiated many centuries earlier in the painting of the bull capture from Tiryns. Drapery came last; it tended to be shown condensed into solid masses as late as the sixth century.

Sculpture likewise lagged far behind Vapheio. It worked with tactile surfaces.

1. Statues in the round: *Apollo of Tenea*. Nonetheless an advancement beyond the planarity of Egyptian sculpture.

2. Relief: Attic tomb stele from the pre-classical period. Profile treatment and tactile surfaces. Of special interest are cases where a foot had to appear foreshortened; the artist simply bent it at a right angle.

Artists went far beyond the Egyptians, however, in their rendering of internal articulations. Although this was still low relief, it was far more plastically formed, with much stronger shadows. In some instances, people even pushed toward high relief (especially in marginal locations: Selinunte metopes); but there the handling of details suffered.

Here, too, innovations are most tangible in architecture and industrial arts.

Architecture. The Greek temple is unique with respect to its Egyptian counterpart. Its basic features were already well in place before 500 B.C.E. The details were perfected between 500 and 300 and never changed thereafter. The peripteral temples of the third century C.E. are no different in layout from those built before Alexander.

The Greek temple, like the Egyptian, is an individual unit. Like the Egyptian, it developed from the house and stretched out the ground plan longitudinally (not centralized, evidently so as to accommodate unidirectional movement). But the Egyptian temple was no more than an inclined wall (because of the growth movement) terminated by a crowning cavetto. The roof was flat, hidden from view. The interior did not reveal itself to the outside: spiritlessness. The Greek temple has straight walls — is thus more purely crystalline — and the growth movement betrays itself in one part alone, the roof, which, being pitched, reveals externally the presence of the interior.

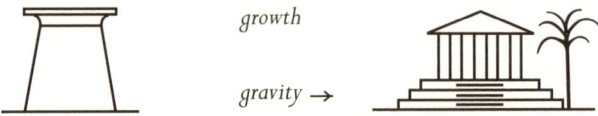

growth

gravity →

Finally, a pronounced base was inserted at the bottom. Thus stark separation and, at the same time, cohesion of parts: everything is motivated. A unified entity emerges. The roof is beautiful only in the pediment; from the sides, it is unattractive. But by exposing the interior to the outside, the roof stimulates fantasy. Windows were not yet included; the principal impression was still determined by the exterior. With this, we come to the most striking innovation: the columns surrounding the main structure. Peripteros. Whereas the Egyptian temple had shown the bare tactile surfaces of the walls, the Greek structure was three-dimensionally formed, with no penetration of the inner core.

Wherein lies the archaic quality of Greek temples prior to 500?

1. Massive diameter of the columns. Gigantic constructions consistently belong to periods that favor surfaces, so as either to appear oriented toward the near view even from a distance or to exert the impression of great volume (optical surface). We find colossi in ancient Egypt and later Antiquity but not in the classical age, which was more concerned with three-dimensional form.

2. Connections are not everywhere complete. The Doric column did not include a base; only the Ionic would do so. Capital: Doric is blockier; torus; foliage painted onto the surface. Ionic capital: actually stands beyond these lines. The Corinthian capital is based on the Doric but gives plasticity, three-dimensional form, to the foliage. The normal view reveals itself.

Treatment of interior. The Greek temple did not aim to be an interior space (even less so than the Egyptian, which occasionally had to be such; this was considered a necessary evil). Rather, it was simply a residence for the deity who dwelled in the statue. No windows. Light was still required from time to time: hypaethral arrangements for overhead light (probably not basilican, Egyptian; but this is uncertain, because no constructions of this kind have survived intact). In any event, there was never any thought of expanding the space laterally; this was also opposed by the structures' hypaethral design. As we see in the temples at Paestum, this did not involve a small opening; rather, the entire central vessel lay open to the sky.

The Classical Age

This period completes the transition from near to normal viewing and from objective to subjective perception of nature: man, not art, was now the measure of all things. In consequence, both space and time gained recognition. But the process came to its conclusion only at the end of the period. The man who achieved this, Lysippus, is in fact the same person who introduced the post-classical age, the Hellenistic period in art.

What did Lysippus do? He definitively released the body from quadratic construction (the frontal view) and thereby discarded the last remnant of flatness, the attachment to a single plane. Instead of ☐ there is now ⬭ ; I am, of course, exaggerating both. He also brought the surfaces of the various parts closer to

three-dimensional form. Earlier profile so: ⌒⌒⌒
with broad but weak shadows (partial shadows). New profile:
⌒⌒⌒⌒ , with narrow (linear) but sharper, more striking
shadows. Shadows were formerly a necessary evil; they now
became an artistic medium to be expressly sought out. Earlier,
weak, unenergetic partial shadows overlay the body; now a whole
network of linear shadows inscribed themselves thereon.

Kekulé noted this change already in 1870 with regard to the
Doryphorus and *Apoxyomenos*. He used these works to explicate a
passage from Pliny: whereas earlier artists formed human figures as
they *are*, Lysippus formed them as they *appear*, as they are perceived.
This articulates what we have just found. Kekulé translated it the
same way (he was probably uncertain at first, because he could not
explain the "being" aspect of earlier art). He was later led astray by
a passage from Aristotle that asserted something similar but was
doubtless meant metaphorically. In the 1893 *Jahrbuch des deutschen
archäologischen Instituts*, he rescinded his initial explanation and
posited a new one that brought into play the question of idealism in
antique art. There is no doubt that his initial interpretation was the
correct one: we have become acquainted with this progression first-
hand and recognize that not only the *Doryphorus* but all pre-Lysippic
art in general represented the "being" as opposed to the "being
seen." We also now know what "being" means: objective, autonomous being, the "thing in itself." The "being seen," in contrast, signifies the thing as perceived by the human faculties.

To this we must add one more point: in the Pliny passage, the
Lysippic manner is described as "nova intactaque ratio [new and
untried method]."[4] What does *intacta* mean? Until now, people
have generally assumed it to be synonymous with *nova* (new), as
in "adhuc inusitata [unusual before that point]." But this metaphor
is highly unusual. Ought *intacta* not also be taken literally, as "the
untouched manner," that which does not rely on the tactile sense?

All the more so because Pliny would later explicitly present the optical sense as the defining factor of the new style? True, philologists have argued that such a usage would have been no less peculiar. But it is worth investigating whether the field of textual criticism might still have a solution at hand.

Survey of statues, reliefs, paintings of the classical period.

Hellenistic Art

Normal view: the whole as three-dimensional form, and the parts. The depth dimension was admitted: shadows, space. The further development witnessed a heightening of the three-dimensional impression. Parts were articulated with increasing complexity; as they conjoin more tightly or jump out more forcefully at the eye, the viewer must move ever farther away to gain a comprehensive view of the whole. This tendency leads from normal to distant viewing. Let us begin with sculpture in the round.

Greek Hellenistic art. *Laocoön* (figure 1). Compressed muscles; exaggerated; in no real person do they protrude so much. Precisely this allows us to recognize the proper balance of classical art. Graphically rendered: ⌒⌒⌒ The *Farnese Hercules*. Often called Baroque. What must the end result be? There are now so many surface parts that they are no longer individually distinguishable; only the whole remains intact, subsuming the discrete components. The infinite polygon becomes a circle, the formed-ness becomes surface, specifically optical surface. This occurred at the beginning of the Roman Imperial period. Externally, it seemed to present an essential affinity with classical art. The whole reveals itself as a whole; the parts do not proclaim themselves so brashly; Augustan statues often remind viewers of classical ones. The parts, however, are more restrained than in classical art when observed up close but jump out when seen from a distance. This characterizes Roman statuary well into the middle of the second century. The monuments of Trajan still possessed this character. In this unclassical movement toward the distant view, the Indo-Germanic character of a comparatively unmixed people made itself felt. But it was not the first time. Although standing in opposition to Semitic people, the Greeks gradually became "Semitized"; the Romans had nothing against this either.

Relief. High relief is obviously Hellenistic, as the Pergamon Altar teaches us. The figures no longer occupy a single plane; rather, some stand farther forward and some farther back: space. This also gave rise to landscape imagery — for example, in the smaller Pergamon frieze (here again we encounter what we saw much earlier in the Vapheio cups). It is always useful to recall the limitations of these novelties, however; ancient artists never achieved the spatial effects we find in works of Lorenzo Ghiberti (landscape) and Donatello (architecture). They conceived space as existing only between scattered objects, not as something universal, as we do today.

Roman relief prior to Marcus Aurelius became more restrained, less protrusive. Here we witness the first harbingers of the new planarity that would later develop; but at this point, the proclivity toward flatness is only relative. Relief, in itself, is still high relief.

Painting. This domain underwent the least amount of development during the classical period: in essence, it stayed at the level of Tiryns. The most important issue was how to depict shadow, which, after all, was something incorporeal. Shadows arose naturally in statues and reliefs. But the intrinsically planar medium of painting must render shadows artificially, by means of color. This difficulty hindered vase painters from representing shadows throughout the whole classical period. Now it finally happened. At first, people envisioned shadows as lines and simply clumped them together: shading. See the engraved Ficoroni Cist. Then they took darker colors and smoothed them in, as in Etruscan paintings. They supplemented the local color with light or shadows according to need. Here we have the deliberate optical illusions of subjectivist art, which earlier objectivist art shunned on principle. Cast shadows were also introduced: the "unswept floor" (figure 17).

This intensified during the Imperial period with progressively distant viewing. The fastidious modeling of parts in light and shadow loosened, and light and shadow appeared in ever stronger contrasts: broader volumes — which again, as in Augustan sculpture, entailed a certain planarity. Coloration emerged as an increasingly definitive factor. The final consequence was for the whole to be perceived simply as a momentary complex of colors. But Antiquity never arrived at this decidedly modern solution. Light and shadow remained essential elements of painting to the end.

Architecture. Here the crucial point involves the interior: interior space finally made its appearance. It was already suggested earlier, in the temple roof. We are, regrettably, ill informed about the very first stages. The oldest extant example stems from the second century, just before the inception of the late Roman period: the Pantheon (figure 21). The space is centralized! Indeed, the oldest interior spaces were centralized. Why? Because this endowed them with maximum clarity. Same measurements in each direction. An oblong room introduces tension, hence greater indistinctness. But the Pantheon already took this design further: the room was articulated by niches. This in itself offered rich modulations. The surface was broken. But still no windows to communicate with the outside!

The exterior demanded the same treatment as in classical Greek art: a three-dimensional form should replace the tactile surface. But because the distant view now prevailed, people had no need to accentuate the forms; it sufficed to attach them to the wall in partial depth: engaged columns or responds, pilasters.

429

Thus arose the familiar system of wall articulation with socles, pilasters, and beams. The Hellenistic age invented that too. Pseudo peripteros.

Arches and vaults were another innovation of the Roman period (probably even the Hellenistic). How do these express the relation between form and surface? Both were employed for utilitarian purposes since the ancient Near Eastern era. The question is when they were incorporated into monumental architecture.

The arch is a valuable structural element, indispensable in any massed structure. Today, arches are visible on the Pantheon's exterior. They are relieving arches set into the wall. Formerly overlaid with a marble veneer (which probably followed a pseudo-peripteral system), they were not meant to be seen. But one observation is interesting here: on noticing these arches on the drum today, you might take them to be window frames. This very fact helps us recognize the close inner kinship of the arch with the wall opening (door and window). But at the time the Pantheon was built, any actual opening (door) had to be framed by a straight lintel.

In practice, arches emerged only where the great wall masses opened themselves to the outside. They were initially designed so as not to enclose any interior space: theaters (Marcellus, Colosseum [figure 22]), whose interiors lay open to the sky. In these cases, arches were integrated into the wall-masking system. They were not meant to be windows. Taken together, they give the impression of porches: the formed element again supplanted the closed wall. For us moderns, however, they look more like windows than porches. Although the transition was clearly at hand, people of the early Imperial age dared proceed no further; they would not acknowledge the window in monumental buildings.

One could say that recognition of the window in monumental form (as mediator between interior and exterior space) would have brought Antiquity to a close. It could happen only in the late

Roman period, which belongs just as much to the Middle Ages as to Antiquity.

In the Hellenistic age, space was acknowledged in the interior; on the exterior, it did not yet exist.

Vaulting had to be accepted from the moment walls assumed curvature. Vaulting entails no greater lack of clarity in the ceiling than in the walls, either for the interior space or for the exterior appearance. Only the floor had to remain straight.

Late Roman Art
Characteristic of motifs: in place of earlier classical balance, a radical divergence of beauty and truth to life. Beauty moves again toward stark crystallinity, truth to life toward the most fleeting and transitory appearances. This finds expression in the relation between part and whole. The whole is beautiful, and the parts are not (Arch of Constantine [figure 23]). The whole is true, and the parts are not (we often do not recognize this, because we are accustomed to apprehending the parts simultaneously). We observe the same phenomenon with respect to form and surface. The whole is given in the near view, the parts in the distant: departure from the equalizing normal view. The figural group provides the best example. Compositionally, the figures all occupy a single plane; the scene behind them disappears, and the landscape gradually falls away: near-view presentation. The individual figures, on the other hand, are shown in a supremely distant view. We have arrived fully at the optical surface. Late Roman art, like Egyptian, is again flat and planar; but now it is the optical, not the tactile, surface that is desired. Shadows are not broad and weak but linear, narrow, and deeply black.

Sequence of development:

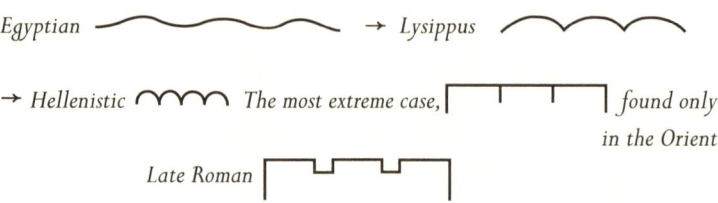

How, we might ask, does this bring to view the contrast between the ancient Near Eastern and the Indo-Germanic essence? We have observed how the penetration of Orientalism came to characterize the late Roman period. We detected a "Semitization" of the public's intellectual outlook. This makes plain: the tactile — Oriental — element is encroaching, hence the near view.

Now let us start with reliefs: ... (*not written down*) ...

Painting. Characteristic: predominance of mosaic, a medium intrinsically geared toward the distant view because its effectiveness relies on the cohesion of individual tesserae. In the late Roman period, the stones became increasingly large and therefore the effect more distance-oriented. Linear drawing such as we saw in antique vase painting returns in mosaics: white on black and vice versa. Baths of Caracalla (never completely obsolete but only now became a desirable artistic medium).

Architecture. Windows in central-plan structures. This means the interior also governs the outer view and more distance-oriented effects: a great "borehole." Richer articulation of space by niches, inside and outside alike. Introduction of the oblong interior. Baths of Caracalla. But people also incorporated forms (columns) meant to catch and hold the eyes (Baths of Diocletian). Reversion to Egyptian forms, at first as vault supports. These forms then broke away from the wall and moved toward the center. This was the basilica.

432

Caracalla   Diocletian   Basilica

The wall-masking system fell away; the bare wall took full effect; pilasters would not work from so far away. The pattern was provided by the shadow-producing borehole, the window. Now it was arched. In other words, the building no longer required the aesthetic defense effected by the antique wall-masking system (as in the Colosseum). The wall was set directly on top. We witness this in the palace of Diocletian at Spoleto.

Notes

1. Note on ethnographic research and its shortcomings; the need for its replacement by *a priori* study (?), the lessons of Egyptology (?), and so forth. Observations on natural peoples are difficult to test and not to be given much weight.

2. Mesopotamian art as we know it — more specifically, Assyrian art — ran parallel with early Greek art in its essential characteristics.

3. The exception represented by Amenhotep IV is instructive precisely because it paralleled a forceful shift in cultural views during that king's reign. So far as I am aware, this exception had neither specific nor general repercussions; as a singular episode, it retains enduring symptomatic value for the discipline of art history. Such individualization as we see, for example, in the Louvre *Scribe* has a cause much different from an artistic one; we will address this in the chapter on motifs.

4. To formulate a clear distinction between the accomplishments of the age of the Diadochi and the Roman Imperial age is perhaps the single most important task of the discipline of art history today. Some light has already been shed on the problem, by Franz Wickhoff's *Die Wiener Genesis* (The Vienna Genesis) in particular. There is much to support the idea that the Hellenistic period represents the mature conclusion of what had unfolded during the Attic golden age and that the moment of decay assumed larger dimensions only later, during the

435

Imperial age. But if the *Laocoön* does indeed belong to the period of the Diadochi, that would provide sufficient support for those who would like to move the origins of decline further back into the Hellenistic age.

FIRST VERSION CHAPTER TWO: SECOND PERIOD

1. *Editors' note*: Throughout the book, Riegl uses the term "Form" to refer to sculpture in the round. Compare below, pp. 187–89. See also Translator's Preface.

2. This can be supported with very striking examples, for the Byzantines directly copied Greek ornamental patterns from the fourth and fifth centuries B.C.E. We will return to this curious phenomenon of a Greek renaissance in the chapter on motifs and again at a later point.

3. It is well known that the Russian Empire is considered the only genuine surviving representative of Byzantium. In reality, we can find as many remnants of the abstract Byzantine concept of state in today's caesaropapism, with its right of the stronger built on a powerful administrative hierarchy and blindly obedient masses, its rigid regimentation of all public and many private styles of life, its immense premium on ceremonial rituals, and so on. However, that we are witnessing its final phases is proved by the fact that Russian Byzantinism is, as its attitude toward visual art demonstrates, more deeply rooted in paganism, with whose (probably very remote) disappearance all abstract forms of state (not necessarily the Russian imperial system as such) will likewise have to vanish. In ancient Byzantium, religious art was, of course, the only kind; there existed just as little profane art as before the dissolution of classical Antiquity. Of course, some works of art were made for profane uses, but the contest with nature did not yet disrupt the boundaries defined by objects used in religious contexts. Things are completely different in contemporary Russia. Cultivated men now perform religious ceremonial rites alongside the pagan masses, but they also consume works of art that engage in the contest with material nature for its own sake. On one side, then, we see an embarrassing fulfillment of ceremonial duties prescribed by the monotheistic state-cult, on the other a luxurious enjoyment of pantheistically oriented art: exactly the same inner contradiction we observed in the Roman Imperial age prior to Constantine. Sooner or later, this conflict will

436

demand to be resolved; and once the number of cultivated people in Russia exceeds that of the common folk, the bell will toll for fifteen-hundred-year-old Byzantine art as well.

4. While Islam does not officially recognize the right of the weak to stand on equal footing with the powerful, it does acknowledge a private obligation to tolerate the weak, who in turn voluntarily subordinate themselves to the stronger. Hence the organization of beggary in the Orient into a legitimate source of employment. It is highly revealing, for example, that the fellahin children who today beg from European travelers in a quasi-English gibberish appeal not to the giver's goodness or sense of justice but to physical qualities that allow the latter to appear as the stronger: "rich man," "beautiful man." This makes plain, more eloquently than many words could do, the deep-rooted respect Oriental people still have for the right of the stronger (not the spiritually superior).

First Version Chapter Three: Third Period: Art as Reproduction of Transitory Nature

1. This was also the case in the first century of the Roman Imperial era.

2. *Editors' note*: By "Baroque art" Riegl means art from the High Renaissance until around 1800 and, more specifically (as will be clear from his ensuing discussion), what the current definition of post-Renaissance styles would call Mannerism and Baroque.

First Version Chapter Four: Purpose

1. Under certain circumstances, even the conceptual purpose slides into the domain of practical needs. All religious art serves a quite concrete purpose: to obtain material benefits from superhuman powers. Christianity is no exception. Although the joys of heaven may be fantasized as spiritual, the pains of hell are fierce and physically palpable torments, which the human being seeks to avoid through his artistic cultivation of religious ideas.

2. For the sake of a clear and systematic discussion, we are restricting the number of arguments in support of individual points here, so as not to intrude on the later chapter about motifs.

3. In its approach to narrative content, Persian miniature painting constitutes an artistic sphere of its own, even formulating its own peculiar style. Further examination of this area would be important for the close relations it reveals to East Asian art.

4. The lower wall surfaces, long regarded as suitable for church paintings, were substantially retained even in Gothic buildings.

5. This assertion is to be taken more literally than people today are generally accustomed to doing. Roman Imperial portraits represent the true appearance of transitory nature more closely than Impressionists' momentary shots. People today think they can reproduce heads with natural accuracy only when these are viewed from a greater distance. But antique heads, as well as those made by most of the great sixteenth- and seventeenth-century portraitists, were intended for close viewing; one ought to accept this approach without prejudice and consider it at least equally valid.

6. Almost without exception, grotesques — practical objects that, for reasons having to do with decorative or conceptual functions, are given unusual shape — emerge in periods when functional aspects predominate, not when art is an end in itself.

FIRST VERSION CHAPTER FIVE: MOTIFS

1. *Deleted in the manuscript*: The prehistoric carved bones from the Dordogne caves reveal that knife handles were shaped as reindeer and other such things. The significance these animals must have possessed for a hunting people suffices to prove that it was the conceptual function that introduced these animals to art.

2. The development of Greek vegetal ornament as a step-by-step process of perfecting Egyptian models through curvature and proportion can be traced up to the time of Pericles. Even in the rough form outlined in *"Stilfragen"* (1893), this point, in general, has been disputed by no one. It is therefore incomprehensible to me how people can persist in believing that the Greeks suddenly began to portray the acanthus weed in organic form around 430 B.C.E. In this respect, German classical archaeology seems inclined to place more

438

faith in the highbrow fancies of modern artists than in its own unimpaired senses.

3. Etruscan portrait heads, whose accidental and transitory character has aroused such admiration that some people believe them to stem from a special inclination of ancient Etruscan art toward naturalism, can also be explained through their analogy to early Egyptian portrait figures, which were certainly not created by any Western race. That is to say, they can be understood as a supremely meticulous attempt to fashion an alter ego for burial purposes, during which process the need for the utmost similarity between the individual and his likeness demanded both the inclusion of accidentals and a faithfulness to natural models. It is otherwise incomprehensible why the naturalism of Etruscan art, like that of Egyptian art, would have been limited to only one kind of portrait head.

4. Of course, no such postulate could be obeyed consistently in historical Dutch art. Even in Rembrandt's work, we encounter contrapposto figures modeled on Italian prototypes. Faced with such cases, one must always bear in mind that there is an exception to every rule but that the rule does not therefore cease to be a rule.

5. This is most readily seen in ecclesiastical art. Modern pictures of religious subjects are either straightforward copies of older works or purely ends in themselves. Any conceptual purpose they possess consists of propaganda for modern interests — for example, socialism, with which the life and teachings of Christ furnish fruitful points of connection. Here we are faced with an interesting parallel. The Roman Imperial age likewise witnessed the emergence of both an understanding of art as an end in itself and the social lessons of Christianity. The result was the annihilation of art as an end in itself by the Christian message. Although one would be tempted to project this outcome onto our own immediate future and to predict an abrupt reversion to the opposite extreme, one must beware of overlooking the differences between then and now. Whereas Christian socialism was full of despair and contempt for everything worldly (which included any conception of art as a contest with earthly nature), modern socialism, at least in its serious forms, strides forward with confident aspirations to improve the world.

FIRST VERSION CHAPTER SIX: FORM AND SURFACE

1. Exactly how close the eye must come to an object in order to obtain the impression of pure flatness depends on the size of the object. If one is looking at the wall of a house, for example, a distance of one step, or even several, would be sufficient; the smaller the object, the more closely the eye must approach it.

2. The designation of something as relief or half form is based, of course, only on an average measurement. In reliefs, the extent of the form's three-dimensional projection beyond the surface fluctuates from around one-eighth of the actual body size to nearly complete roundness. In Antiquity, the earliest (ancient Egyptian) reliefs are also the flattest. They grow progressively more raised until, in the end, fully rounded forms appear simply stuck onto the ground, as in the porphyry sarcophagi in the Vatican; admittedly, there was at the same time an inverse movement toward the opposite extreme.

By two-dimensional arts, we mean painting in the broadest sense; along with painting narrowly defined (colored linear media), the term also encompasses drawing, intarsia, mosaic, textile arts, and so on. These are not, to be sure, necessarily strictly linear arts, which would entail motif and ground actually lying on the same plane. Although this is the case with intarsia and mosaic, it does not apply completely to embroidery or even hand drawings. In those instances, however, the projection of motif from ground is so minimal as to be safely exempted from consideration. Exceptional cases such as raised embroidery in textiles are, of course, to be viewed as relief.

3. See note 2 above. An exception can be found in the rows of kneeling 3. See note 2 above. An exception can be found in the rows of kneeling prisoners in Ramesside battle reliefs; here, only the figure in the nearest foreground is visible as a complete and fully closed silhouette, while those behind him tend to be occluded and to assert themselves as merely narrow strips (figure 10). This exceptional case is art-historically significant for two reasons. First, it violates the postulate that every figure must remain self-contained and distinctly visible; second, it represents a step toward the illusion of three-dimensional depth. These are, of course, mere symptoms, which are further mitigated and overpowered by a definite harmonism (the equal level of projection of all the figures

and the lack of any perspectival foreshortening toward the back). Nevertheless, they suggest the direction that art would later take, even if by that point the Egyptians had stopped being capable of pursuing it with any conviction.

4. The so-called Pavilion of Ramses III at Medinet Habu does not tell us enough; moreover, it stands inside a temple, which raises doubts even as to its original function.

5. A brick cylinder left smooth and unembellished seems to have been inconceivable during the reigns of Agrippa and Hadrian. Only after Constantine were people able to suppress the objective-surface parts thoroughly in favor of overall form, which entailed the full aesthetic negation of the former. Moreover, we sense the current absence of the Pantheon's original veneer especially acutely when trying to gain an accurate assessment of its place in the development of the three-dimensional arts.

6. Scattered exceptions such as the Baptistery of the Orthodox in Ravenna tend, on closer observation, to confirm the rule.

SECOND VERSION CHAPTER ONE: FIRST PERIOD: ANTIQUE ANTHROPOMORPHIC POLYTHEISM TO THE THIRD CENTURY C.E.

1. The Greek could coerce his deities through sacrifice; Yahweh cannot be so coerced, even through sacrificial offerings.

2. Our law too is a spiritual, not an individual, one.

SECOND VERSION CHAPTER TWO: SECOND PERIOD: CHRISTIAN MONOTHEISM, 313–1520

1. Predestination is the exact opposite. One can construct a system of causal relationships on that basis; that law alone speaks for predestination.

2. We must wait to see whether anything new and fruitful comes from the union of the Byzantine worldview with that of Slavic peoples. In religious art, the Russians are conservative; at the same time, they make use of profane works that propound the modern notion of causality.

3. Germanic influences are likewise apparent here.

SECOND VERSION CHAPTER THREE: THIRD PERIOD: NATURAL-SCIENTIFIC WORLDVIEW

1. Art and philosophy do not coincide the way art and religion do, which both create harmony for mankind. Philosophy always runs slightly ahead; being critical, it does not create harmony, but rather destroys it. It is certainly capable of creating harmony — but only at a later point, after its lessons have become common property. It is useful for our understanding of art-historical progress to keep an eye on the twists and turns of philosophy, for philosophical systems likewise grew out of the attitudes of their time and their people and therefore *must* display a close relation to the prevailing worldview. However, this parallel is not so immediately given and is therefore not so illuminating.

2. The painter brings forth highlights, shadows, and coloristic reflections not readily perceptible in nature.

SECOND VERSION PART TWO: ELEMENTS

1. Note that decorative purpose and conceptual purpose are not material — they are rooted in the internal senses — but join, externally, with the purpose of art.

SECOND VERSION CHAPTER FOUR: MOTIFS AND PURPOSES

1. Beautiful head (*Schöner Kopf*), an unclear term: here, too, beauty consists not of regularity alone but of the relation between the forces of gravity and the forces of growth. Size relationships of individual parts: "taste" is varied. There is no taste with respect to symmetry. Why is proportionality relative, not absolute? Proportion is the balanced relationship between the forces of gravity and the forces of growth. It depends mostly on the movement of the growth force. One can imagine this to be stronger or weaker. If it is conceived as stronger, then the column (for example) will naturally have to be more slender, and its balance will be retained. Hence the variation of definitions across time.

2. If not in an entire crystalline body, then certainly in parts. This makes clear that even crystals are not individuals and that during their formation from molecules forces of motion must be at work.

3. Symmetry is the single absolute formal law of matter. But man remains

inextricably bound to matter in his production of visual art.

4. The Orient itself is not, however, completely static; it, too, has its own developmental history. There is even such progression within Egyptian art.

5. In the relation between the conceptual purpose and the purpose of art, there are three conceivable scenarios:

1. An older conceptual purpose is clung to conservatively even while a newer one, fundamentally incompatible with the other, already claims dominance (for example, our modern portraits, and just as apparently those of Egyptian art: Book of the Dead, from the Twelfth Dynasty. These personalized conceptions grow increasingly pale over time).

2. Conceptual purpose and the purpose of art harmonize. They coincide in the statues of Greek gods from the classical age, but no longer in the Imperial era, when the conceptual purposes involved were already overcome, even though people continued to produce statues of Zeus for political reasons.

3. New conceptual purposes crop up that are ahead of their time, and the purpose of art cannot catch up to them right away. This was the case in Egypt, for example, with the battle paintings, indeed, with all group images containing an extensive array of figures.

6. In this way, we can also explain realistic portraits; the frontality, immobility, and absence of individualized spiritual or mental expression remain intact. (Adolf Erman already observed that a naturalistic Egyptian art appeared alongside the idealized, though this could never make any real advancement, evidently because it had no solid ground.)

7. The situation may be similar with regard to the progress of Latin and Germanic peoples, who likewise stood at a low level but, because they were familiar early on with more sophisticated art, were able to surpass it relatively quickly.

8. If there was also forward and backward movement, the figure had to be viewed from the side.

9. The Greeks still called pagans "Hellenes" in the fourth century C.E.

10. The origins of this development lie with the Greeks, not the Romans.

But note that these are just the earliest origins.

11. Still debate as to whether Hellenistic-Alexandrian or produced in Rome under the emperor Augustus; for us, a question of secondary importance.

12. (1) Massed structure (centralized structure); (2) space; (3) rounded building. Parallels with sculpture and painting to (1) additive composition; (2) spatial arts in general; (3) the canon of Lysippus.

13. The quadrangular temple with its columnar facade persisted alongside this, likewise the veneration of Hellenic statues of gods.

14. People think that this, along with Agrippa's Pantheon, burned down during the rule of Trajan at the end of the first century.

15. The increasingly frequent replacement of round with polygonal plans indicates a return to strict crystallinity.

16. This can also be demonstrated in the Monophysite worldview.

SECOND VERSION CHAPTER FIVE: FORM AND SURFACE

1. One attributes this to the "wood style." Here, too, one can recognize the inner connection between planarity and crystallinity. (The crystal is bounded by absolutely regular faces.)

2. At Medinet Habu, there is an interior with four walls; but it is turned into four corridors because the central portion is filled with stones.

3. This makes plain that it was not necessary for artistic activity to *begin* with the tactile line. Perhaps even the Egyptians passed through a stage in which they employed optical memory images.

4. See Pliny the Elder, *Natural History: A Selection*, trans. and intro. John F. Healy (London: Penguin, 1991), book 34, par. 65, p. 316. — TRANS.

Illustrations

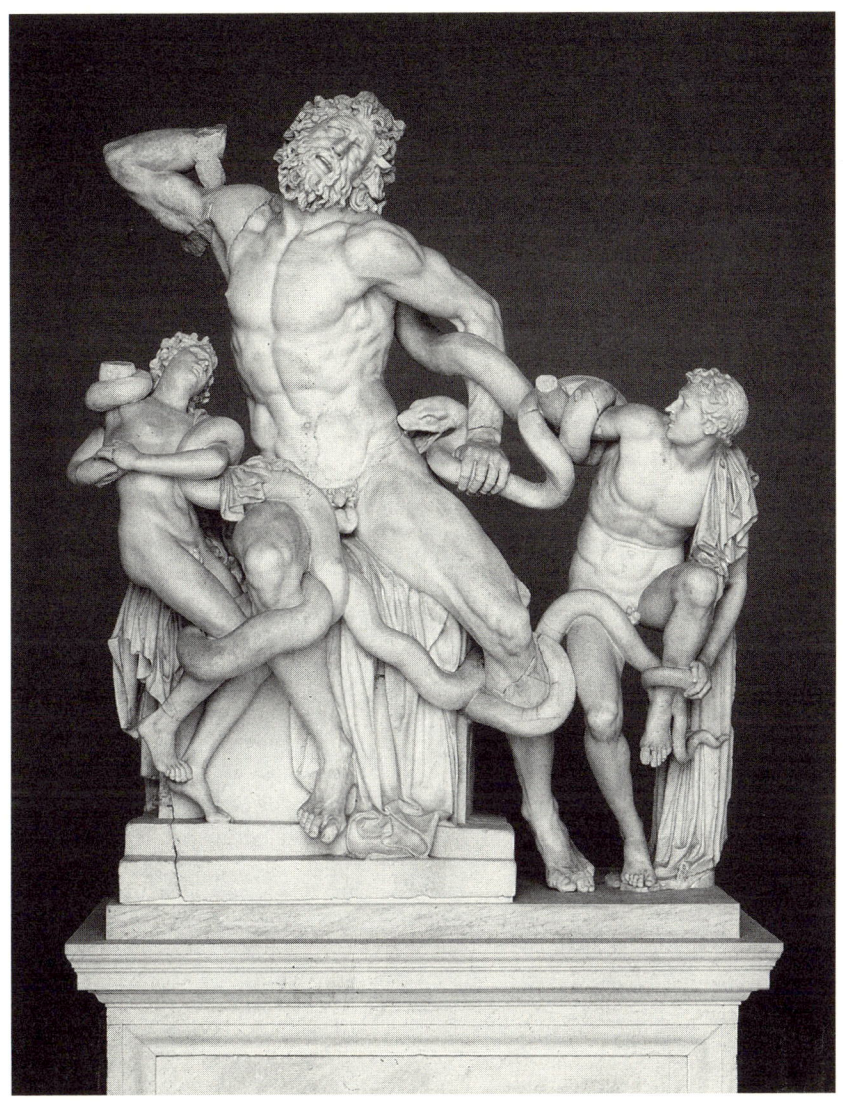

Figure 1. *Laocoön and His Sons*. Marble, 1st century BCE). Museo Pio Clementino, Vatican
Museums, Rome. (Nimatallah/Art Resource, NY.)

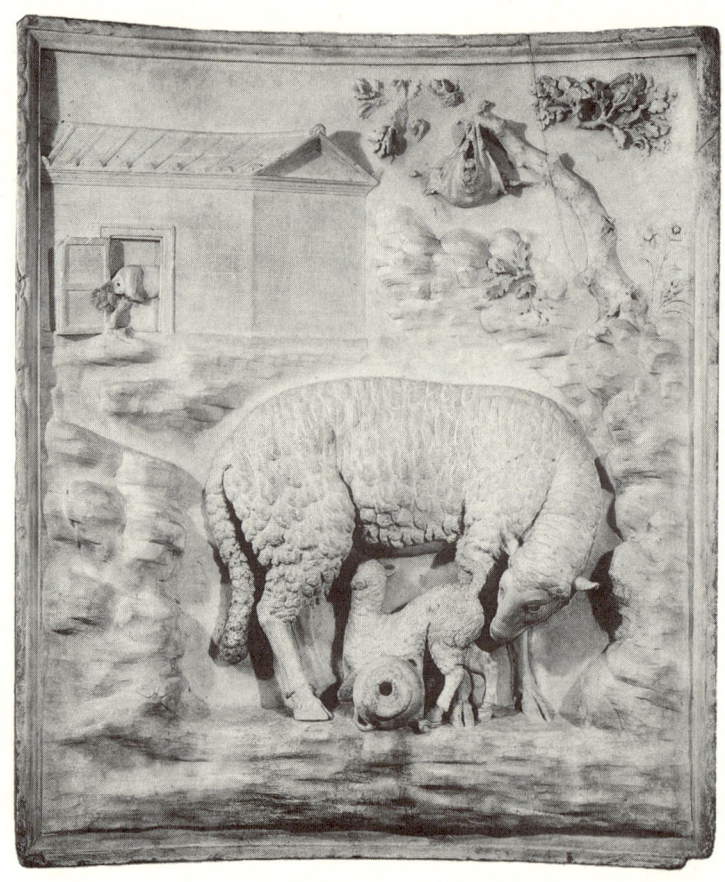

Figure 2. Grimani fountain relief, originally from Praeneste, near Rome. Marble, Mid-1st century CE. Kunsthistorisches Museum, Vienna. (Erich Lessing/Art Resource, NY.)

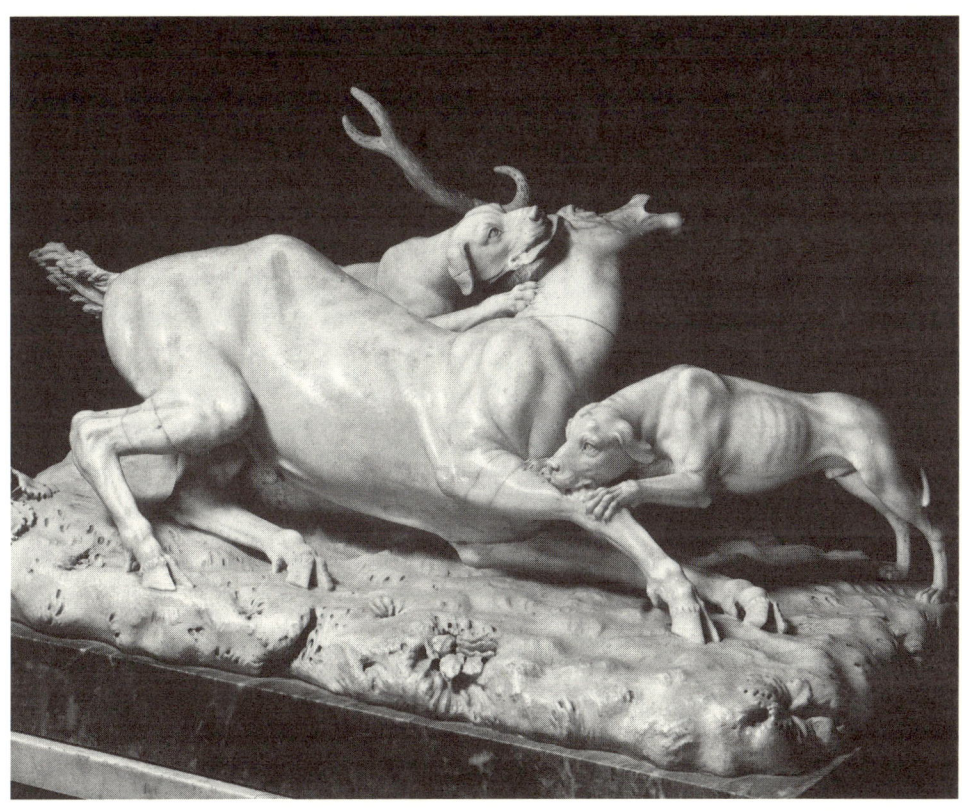

Figure 3. Stag attacked by two dogs. Marble, 1st century BCE. Sala degli Animali, Vatican Palace, Rome. (Alinari/Art Resource, NY.)

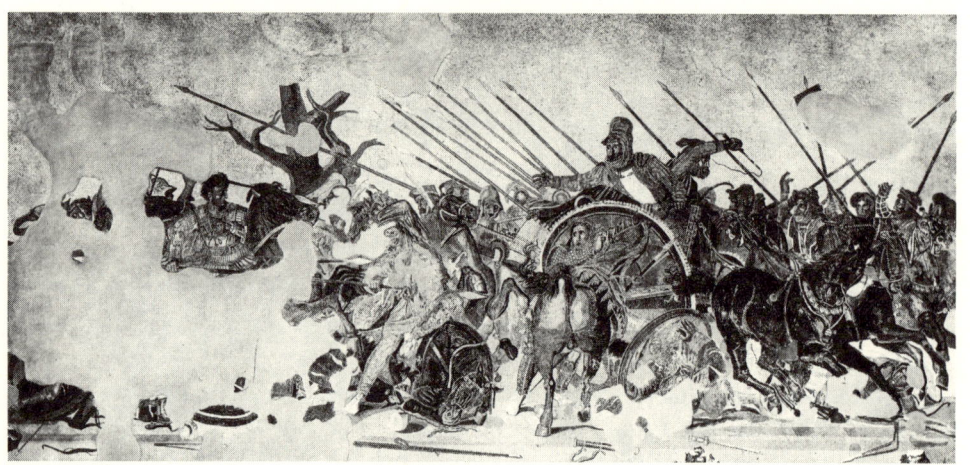

Figure 4. *Alexander Mosaic*, showing the battle of Alexander the Great and Darius III. Roman copy of an original of the early 3rd century BCE painting. Museo Archeologico Nazionale, Naples. (Alinari/Art Resource, NY.)

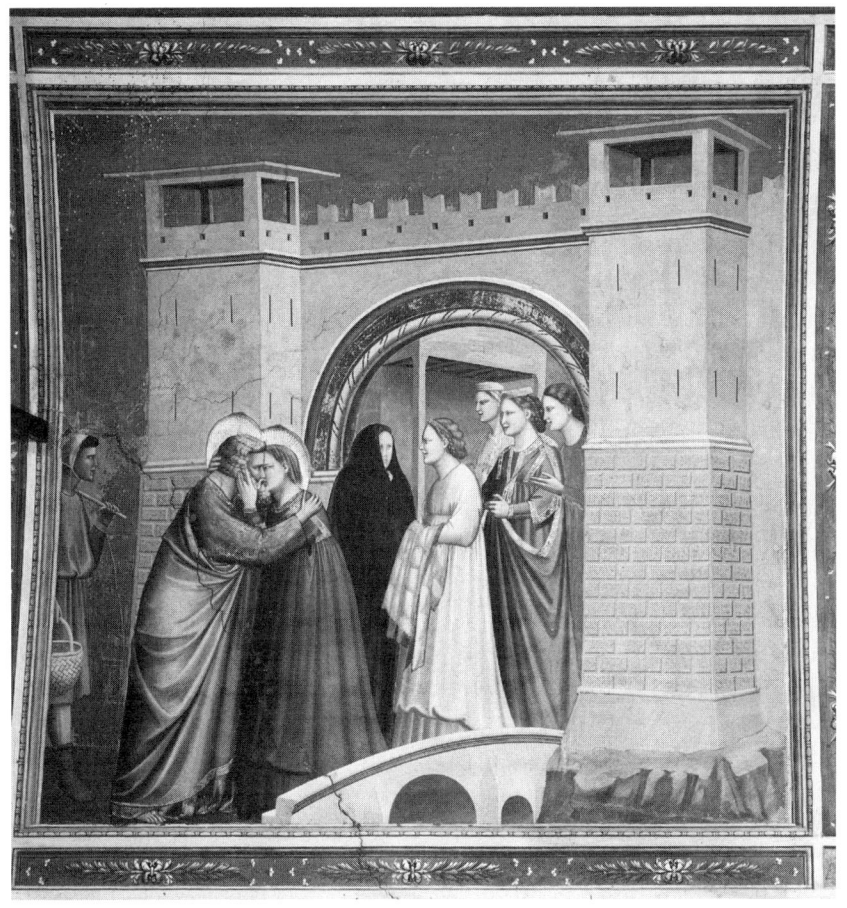

Figure 5. Giotto di Bondone (1266–1336). Meeting of Joachim and Anna at the Golden Gate. Fresco in Scrovegni Chapel, Padua. (Scala/Art Resource, NY.)

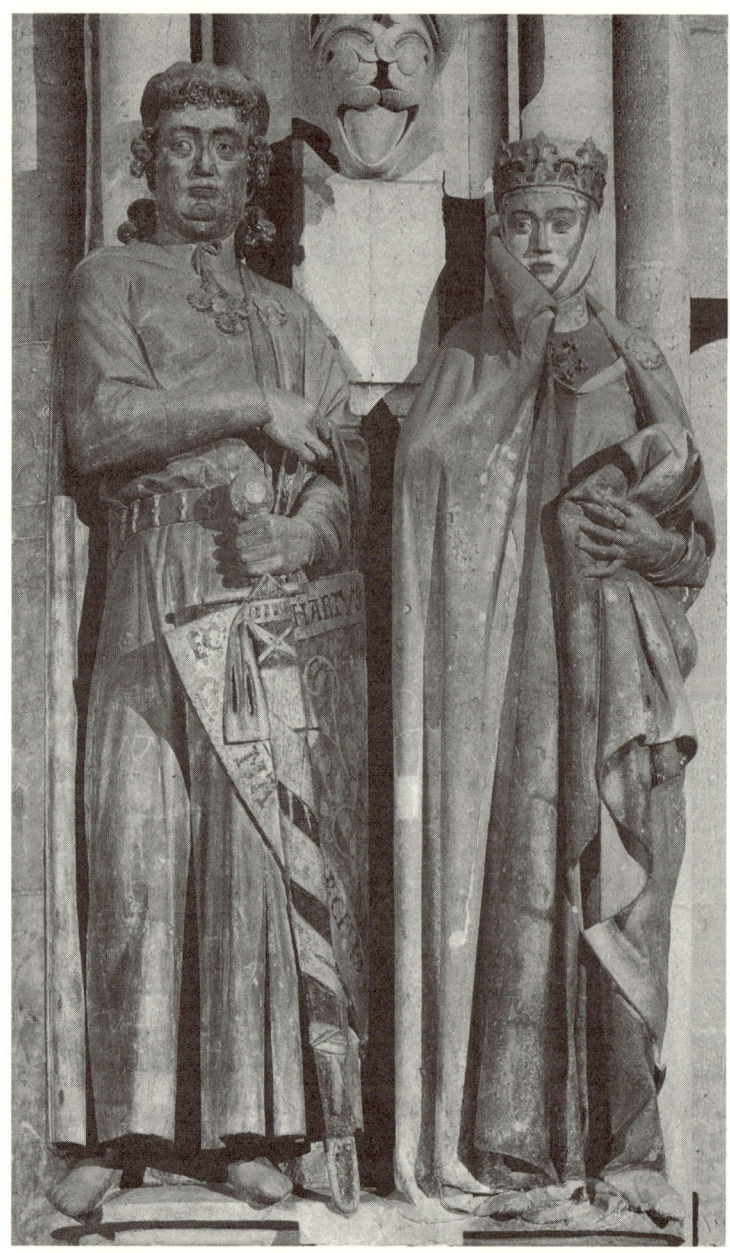

Figure 6. Donor statues of Margrave Eckehard II of Meissen and Uta, in west choir of Cathedral of Sts. Peter and Paul, Naumburg. Painted limestone, ca. 1250. (Erich Lessing/Art Resource, NY.)

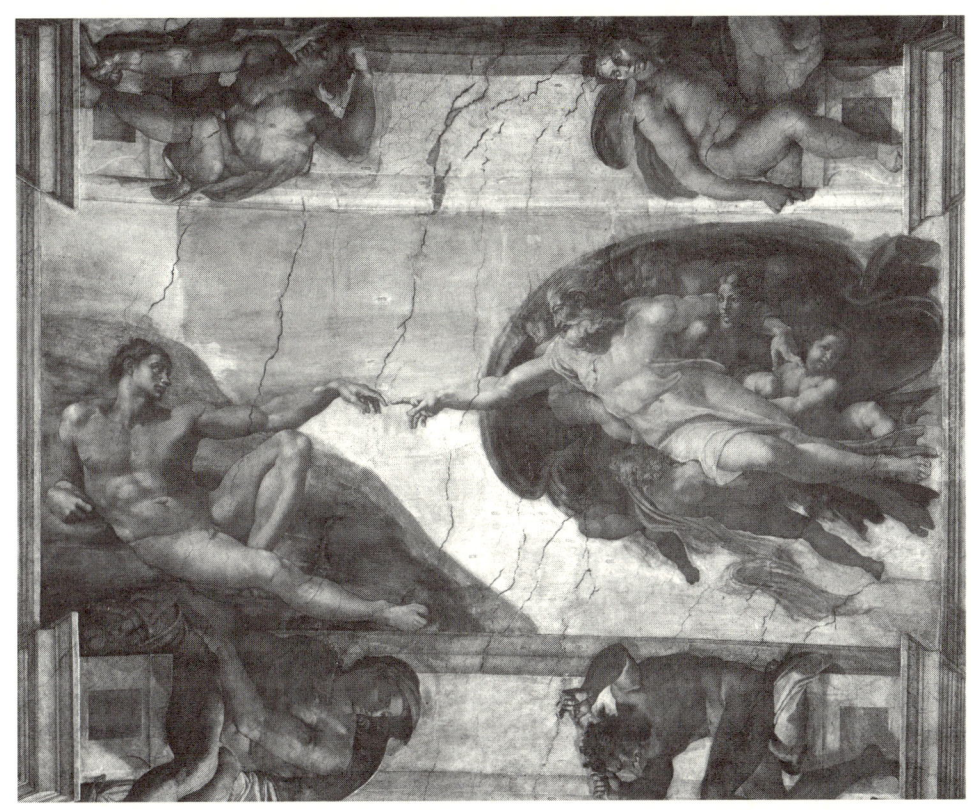

Figure 7. Michelangelo (1475–1564). Creation of Adam. Detail of ceiling fresco in Sistine Chapel, Vatican Palace, Rome. (Scala/Art Resource, NY.)

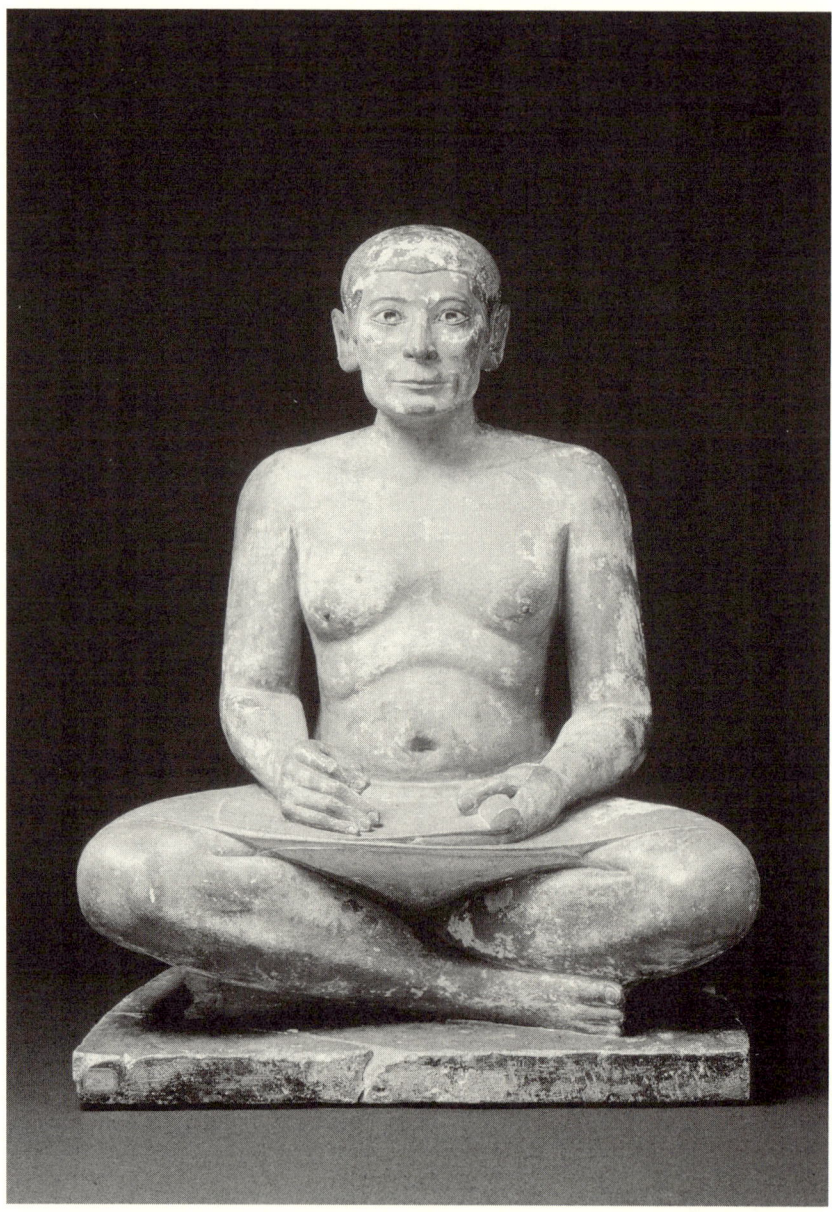

Figure 8. *Seated Scribe*, from the tomb of Kai, Saqqara. Dynasty 5, 2494–2345 BCE. Painted limestone. Photo by RMN – Herve Lewandowski. Musée du Louvre, Paris. (Réunion des Musées Nationaux/Art Resource, NY.)

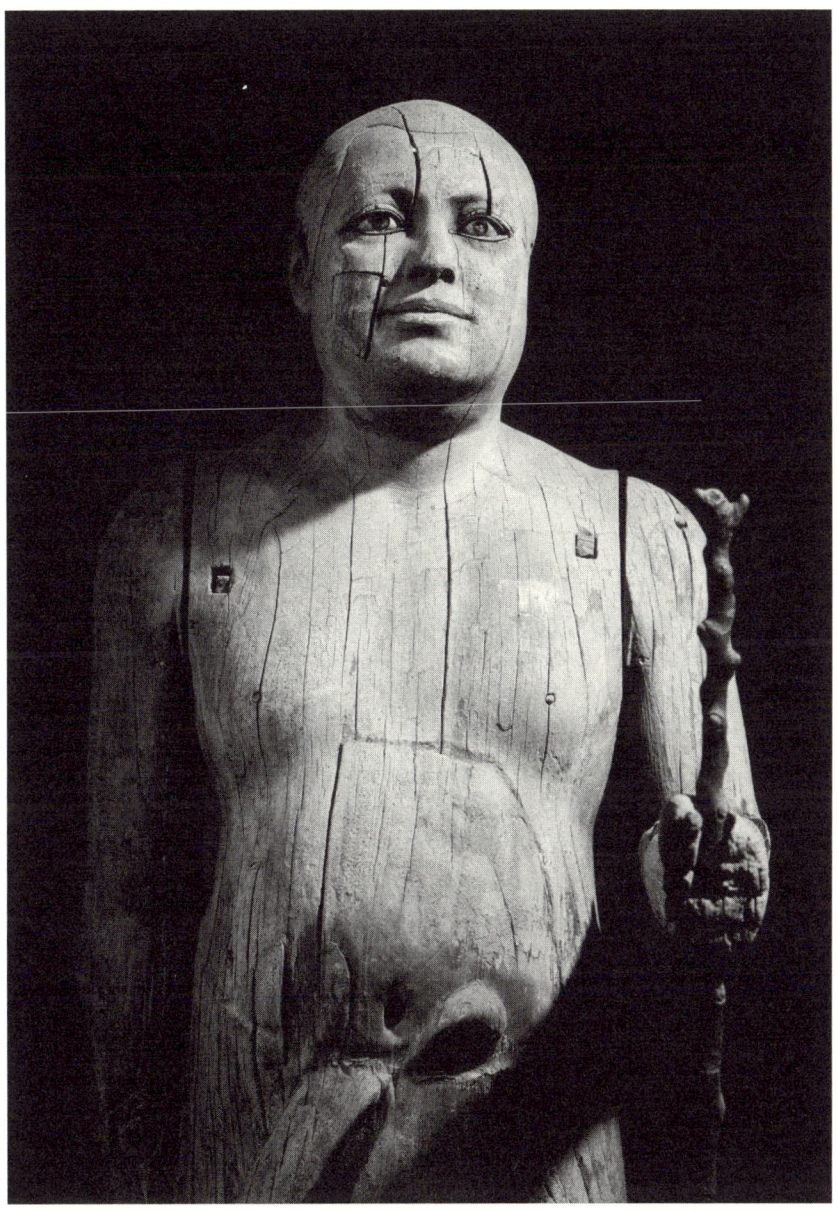

Figure 9. Painted wooden statue of Ka-Aper, known as "Sheikh el-Beled" (Village Headman).
Dynasty 5, 2494–2345 BCE. Egyptian Museum, Cairo. (Werner Forman/Art Resource, NY.)

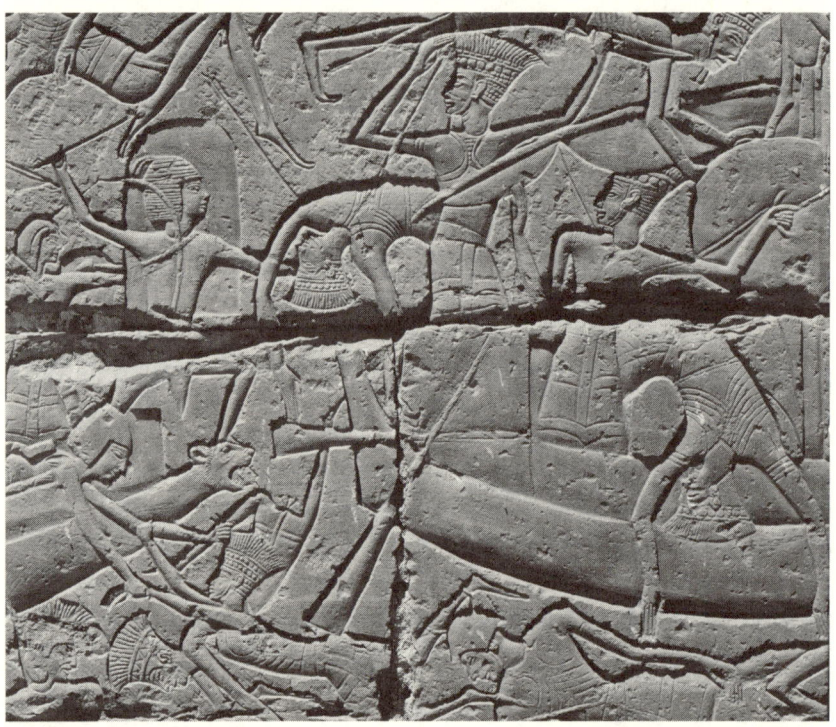

Figure 10. Naval battle of Egyptian troops against the Sea People. Relief from outer wall of the main temple of Ramses III, Medinet Habu, Thebes. Dynasty 20, 1187–1156 BCE. (Erich Lessing/ Art Resource, NY.)

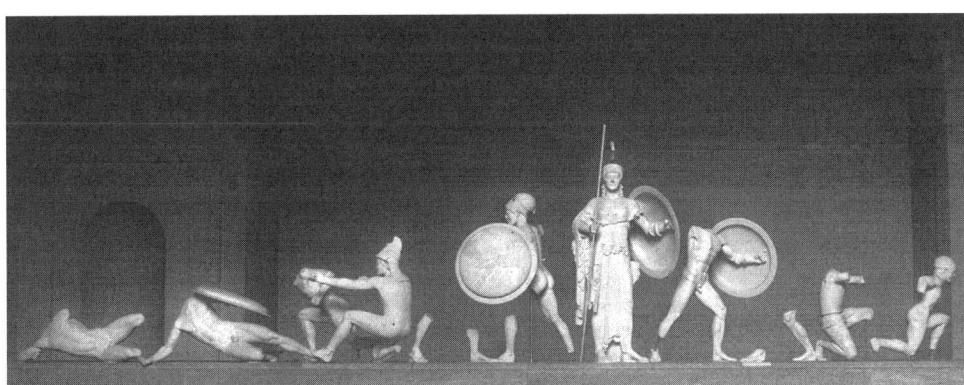

Figure 11. Marble sculptures from west pediment of Temple of Aphaia at Aegina, ca. 500–480 BCE. Glyptothek, Staatliche Antikensammlung, Munich. (Vanni/Art Resource, NY.)

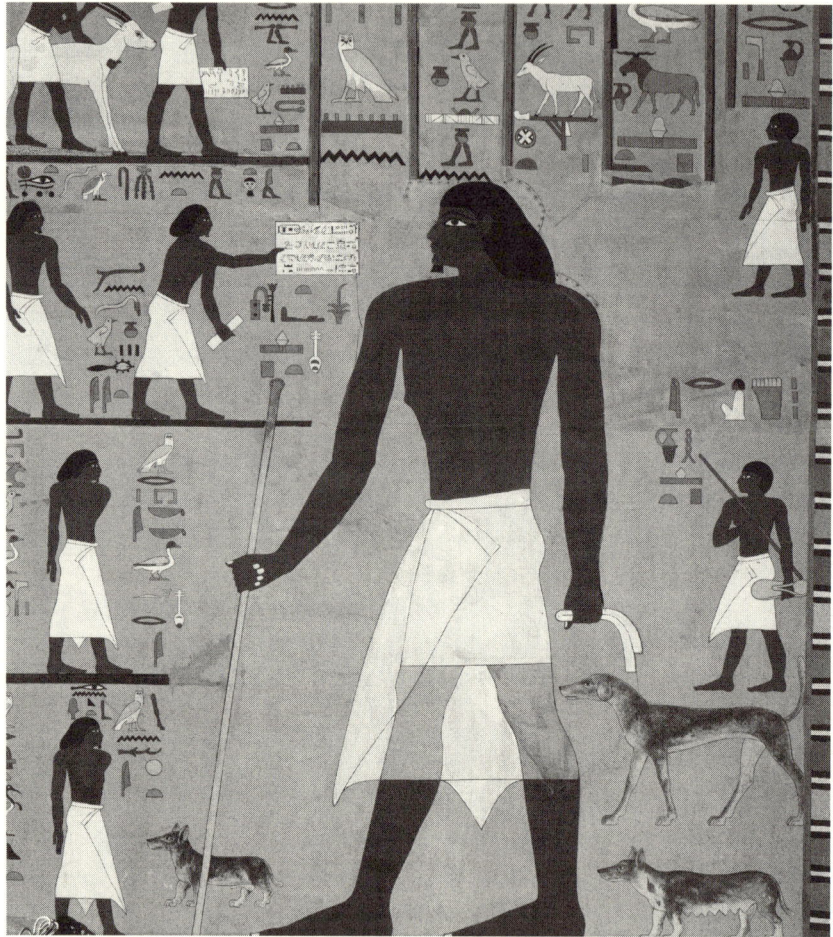

Figure 12. Mural of Egyptian dignitary, from tomb of Khnum-hotep II at Beni Hasan. Dynasty 12, ca. 1890 BCE. Watercolor copy by Ernst Weidenbach, 1873. Kunsthistorisches Museum, Vienna. (Erich Lessing/Art Resource, NY.)

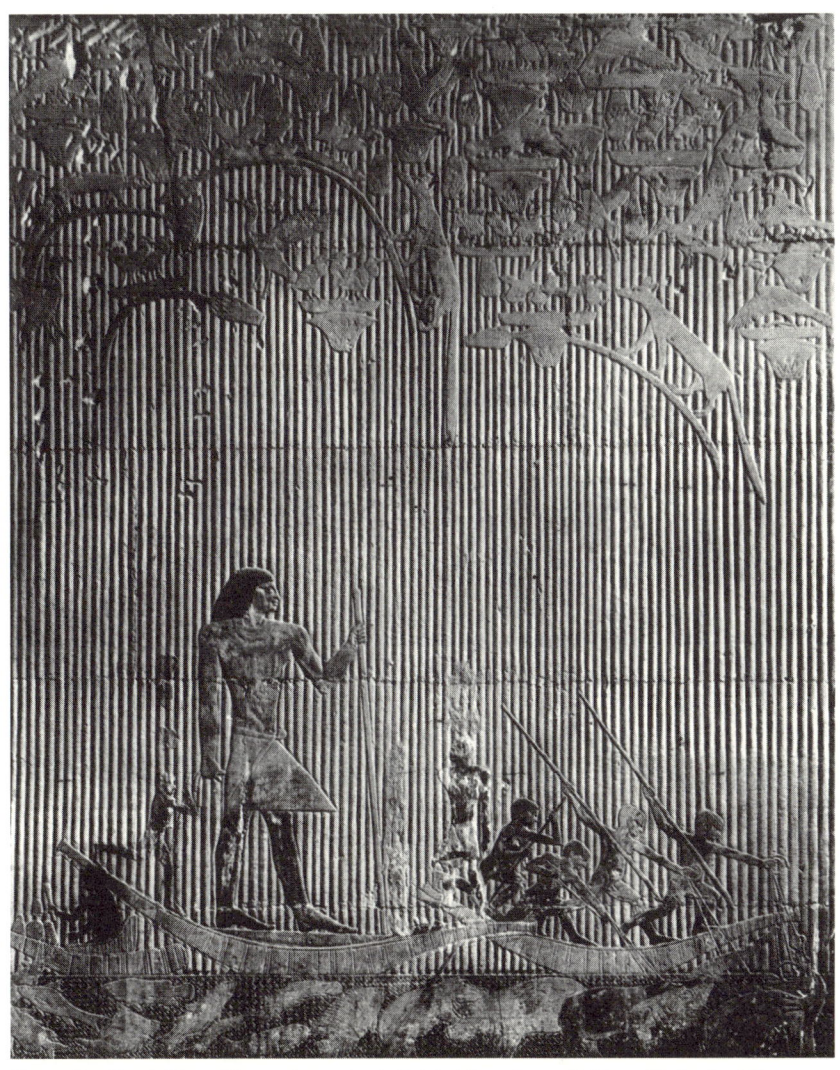

Figure 13. Ti watching a hippopotamus hunt. Painted limestone relief from the tomb of Ti, Saqqara. Dynasty 5, ca. 2450. BCE. (Foto Marburg/Art Resource, NY.)

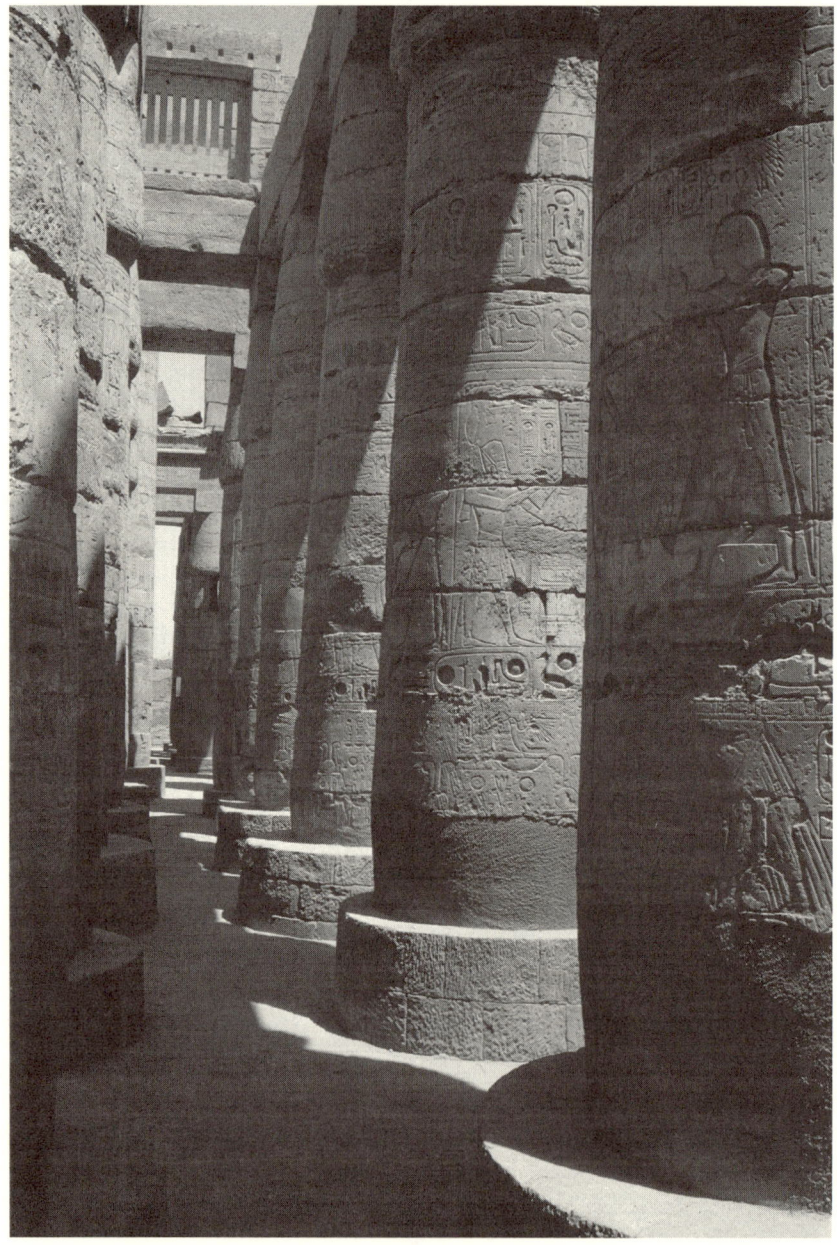

Figure 14. Great Temple of Amun, Karnak, Thebes. Carved relief columns in hypostyle hall. Dynasty 19, ca. 1280 BCE. (Erich Lessing/Art Resource, NY.)

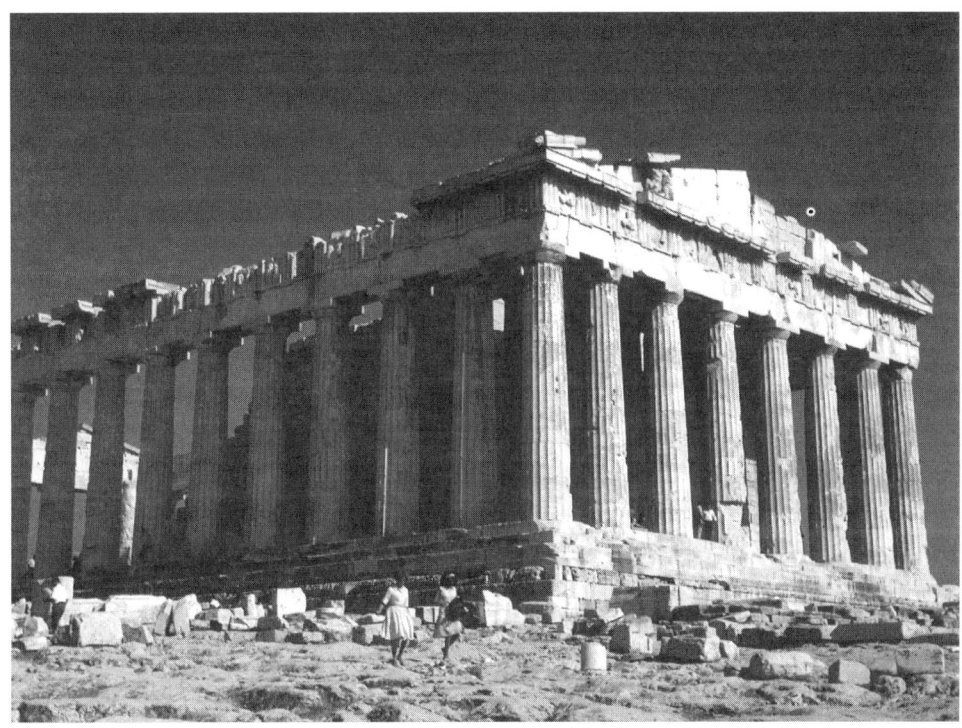

Figure 15. Parthenon, Acropolis, Athens. 447–432 BCE. (Art Resource, NY.)

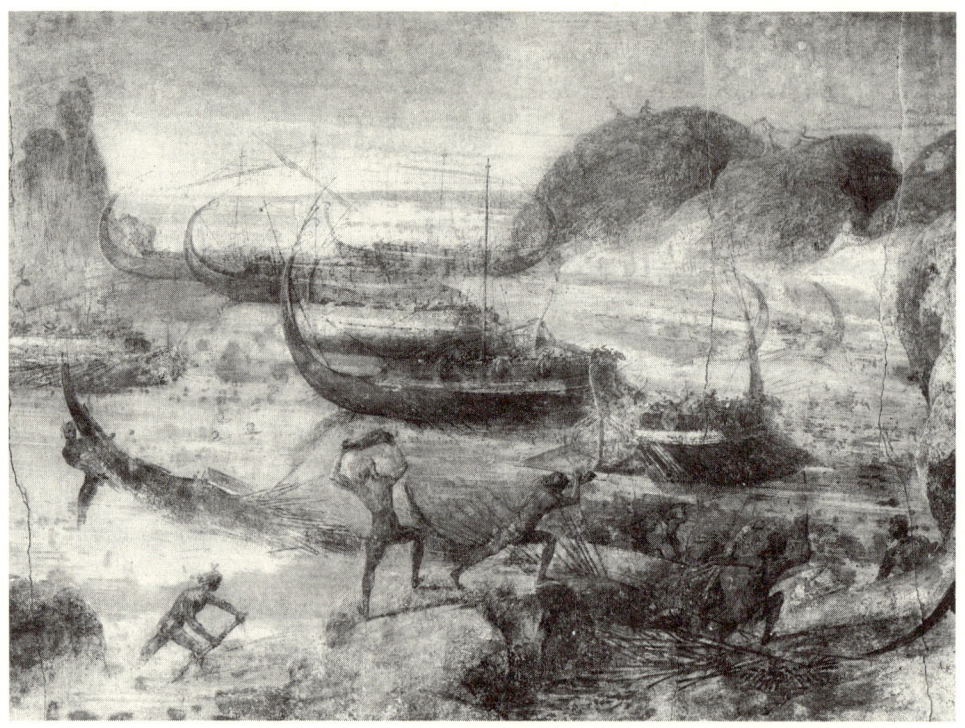

Figure 16. *The Laestrygonians Hurling Rocks at the Fleet of Ulysses*. Wall painting from a house on the Esquiline Hill, Rome. 1st century BCE. Museo Gregoriano Profano, Vatican Museums, Rome. (Alinari/Art Resource, NY.)

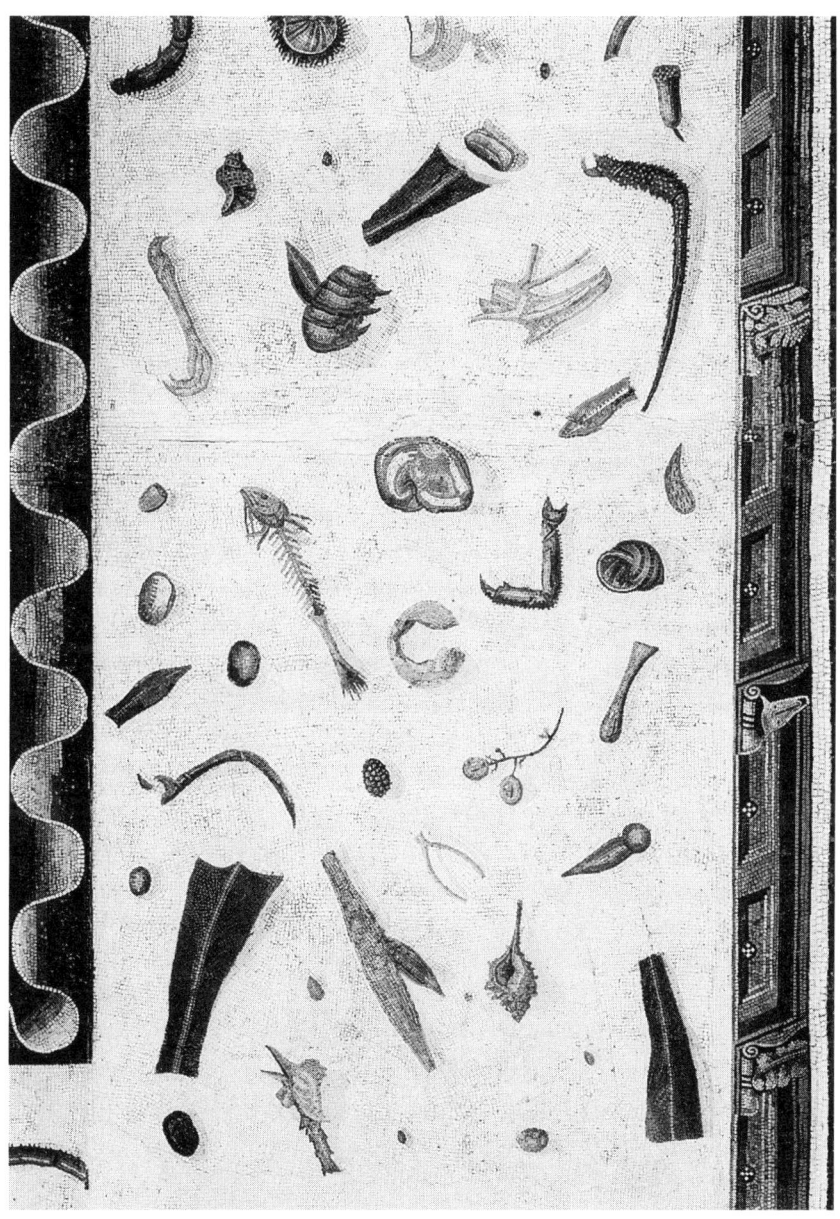

Figure 17. *Unswept Floor*. Mosaic variant by Herakleitos of a 2nd-century BCE painting by Sosos of Pergamon. 2nd century CE. Museo Gregoriano Profano, ex Lateranese, Vatican, Rome. (Scala/Art Resource, NY.)

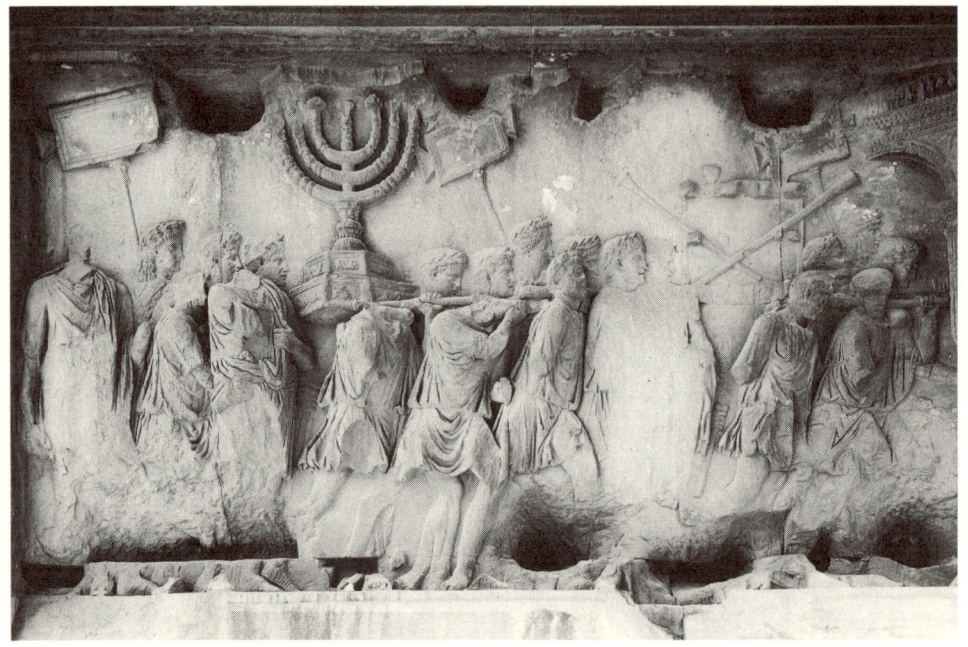

Figure 18. Removal of spoils from the Temple of Solomon in Jerusalem. Marble relief in passageway of the Arch of Titus, Rome, ca. 81 CE. (Erich Lessing/Art Resource, NY.)

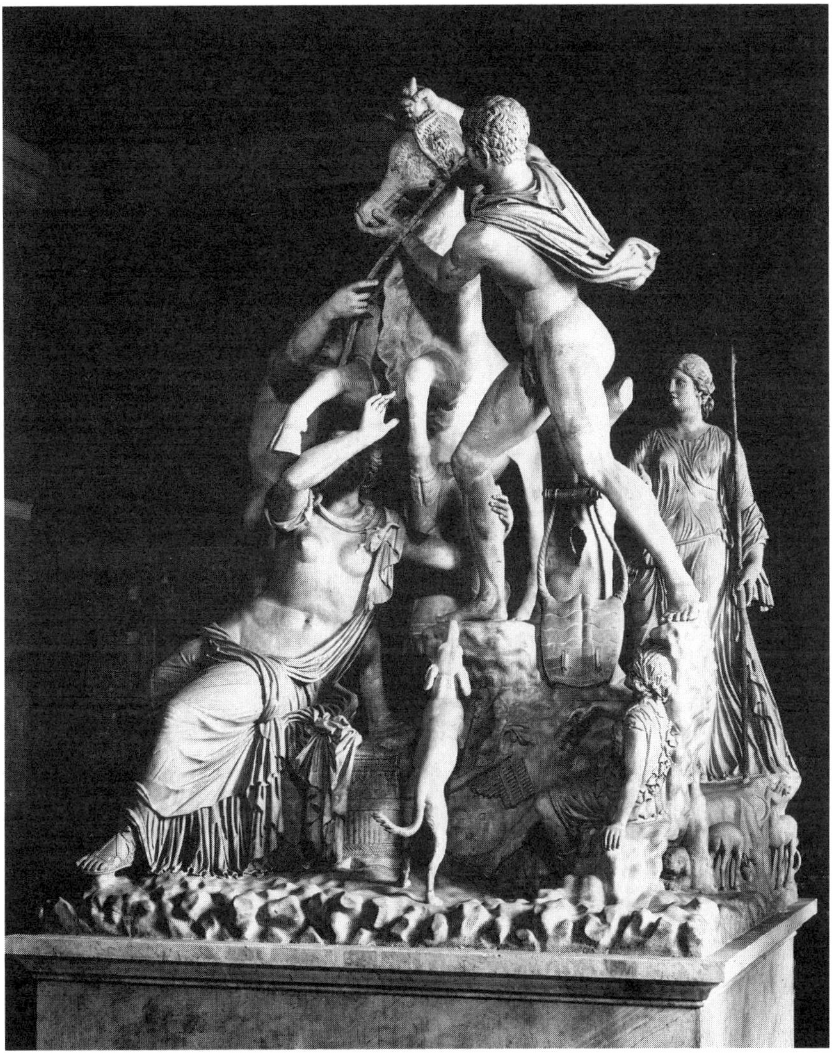

Figure 19. Farnese Bull. Roman adaptation of Greek sculpture by Apollonios and Tauriskos. Marble, 3rd century CE.

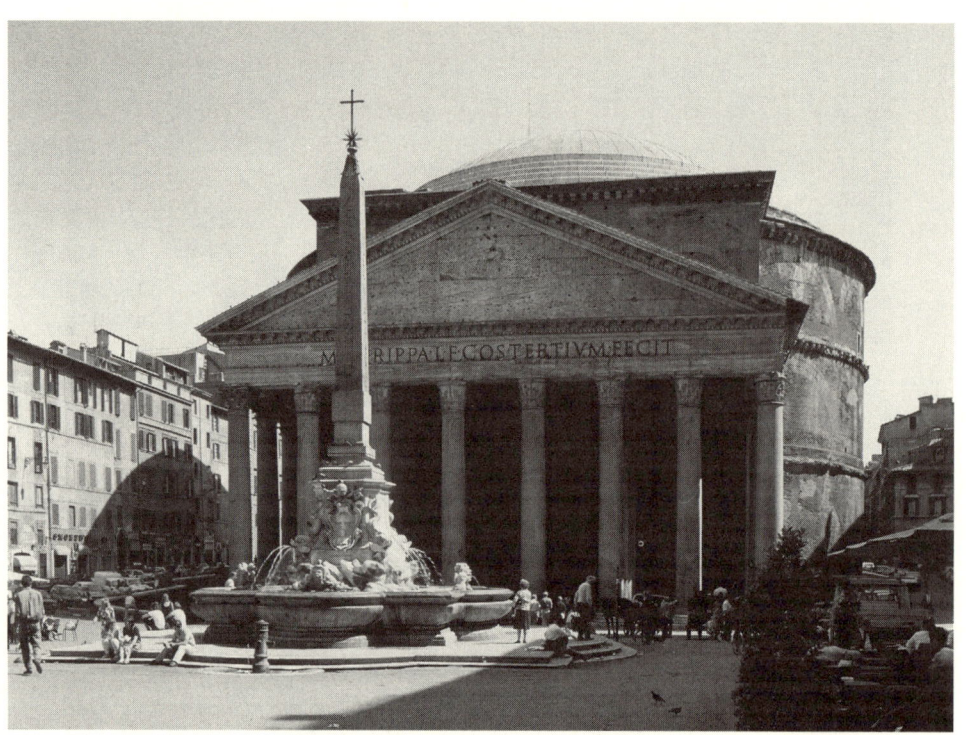

Figure 20. Pantheon, Rome, 125–28 CE. Exterior view. (Scala/Art Resource, NY.)

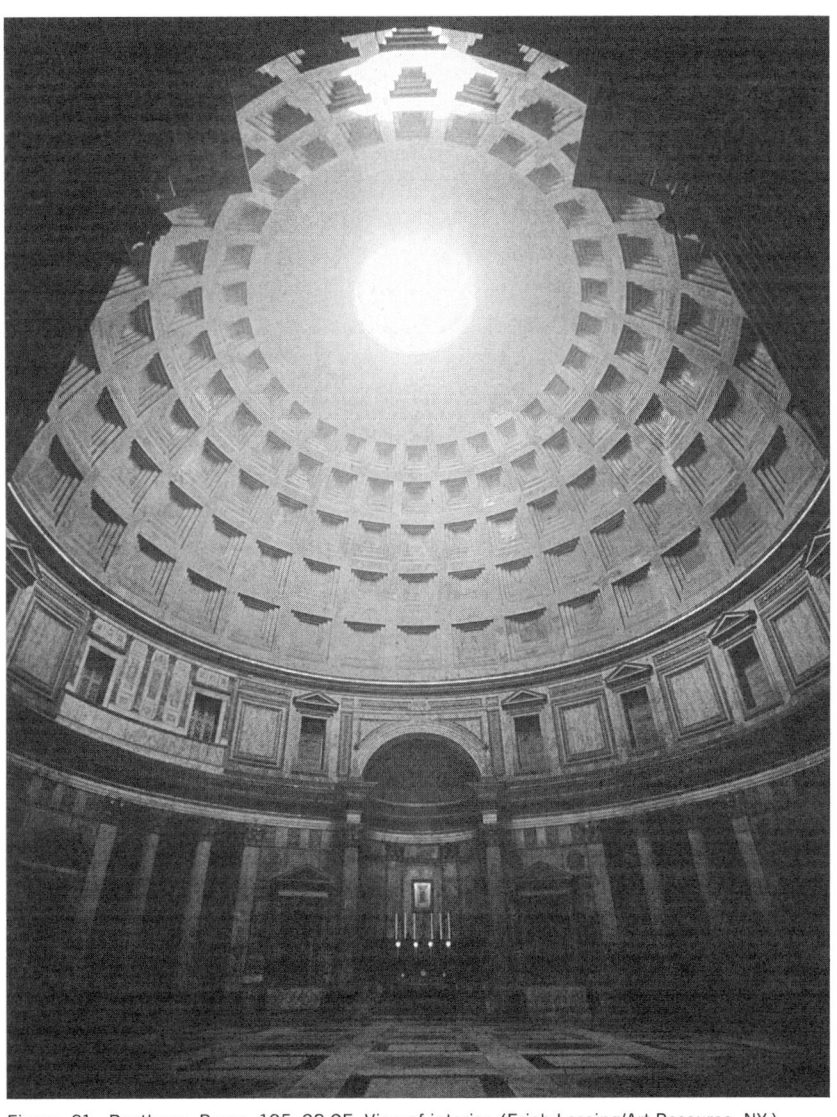

Figure. 21. Pantheon, Rome, 125–28 CE. View of interior. (Erich Lessing/Art Resource, NY.)

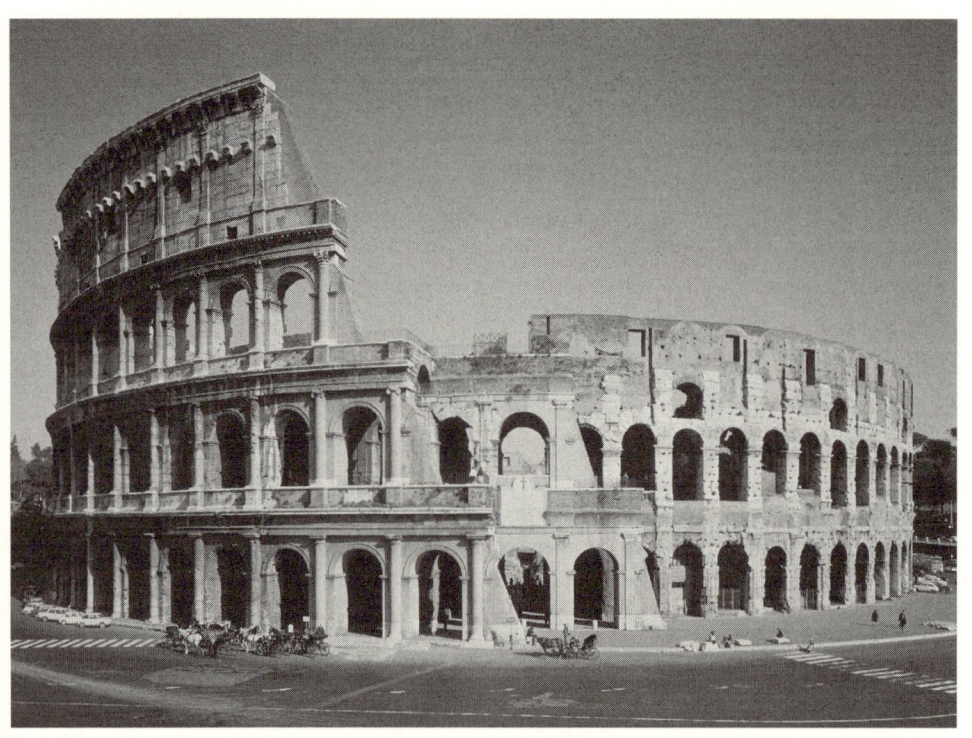

Figure 22. Colosseum, Rome, 72–80 CE. Exterior view. (Scala/Art Resource, NY.).

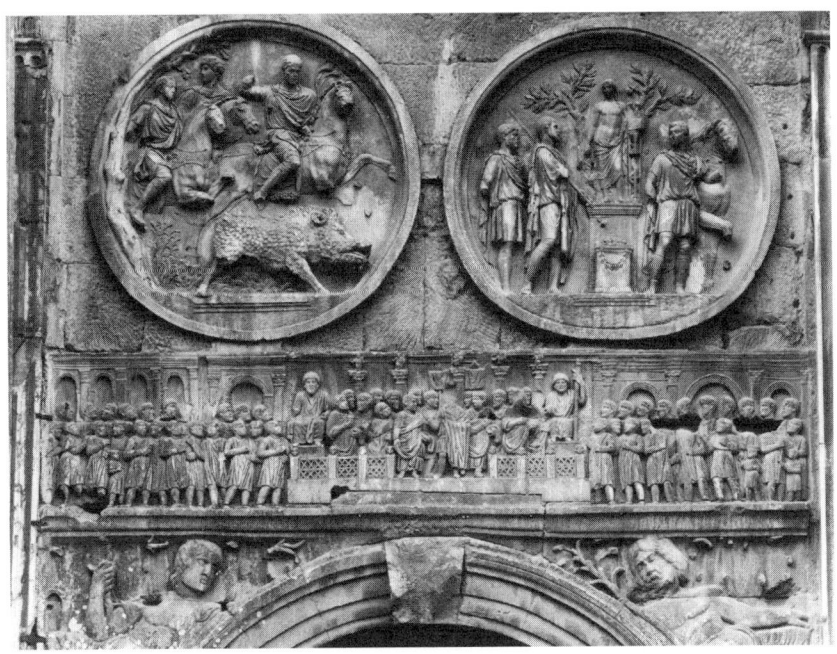

Figure 23. Arch of Constantine, Rome, 312–15 CE. Detail of Constantinian frieze, below (312–15 CE) and Hadrianic roundels, above (ca. 130–38 CE). (Alinari/Art Resource, NY.)

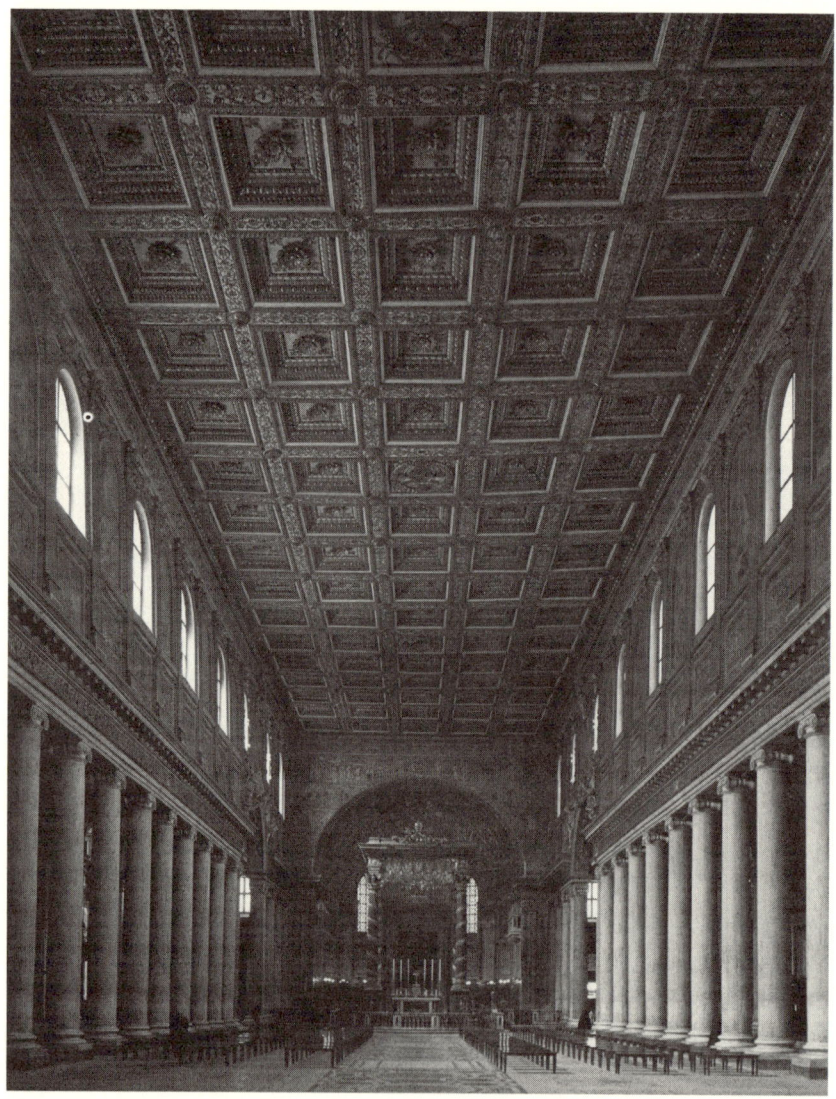

Figure 24. Sta. Maria Maggiore, Rome, 432–40. Interior view of nave toward apse. (Erich Lessing/ Art Resource, NY.)

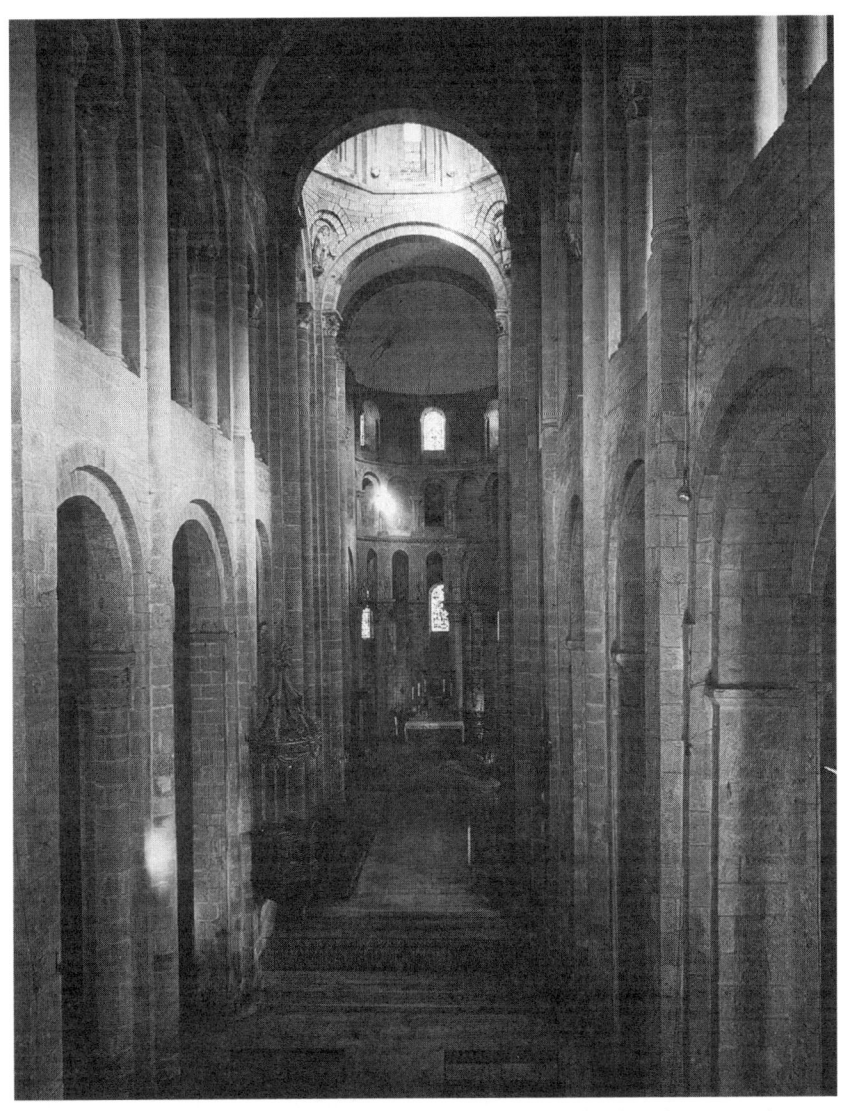

Figure 25. Abbey church of St. Foy, Conques, ca. 1050–1120. Interior view of nave toward apse. (Scala/Art Resource, NY.)

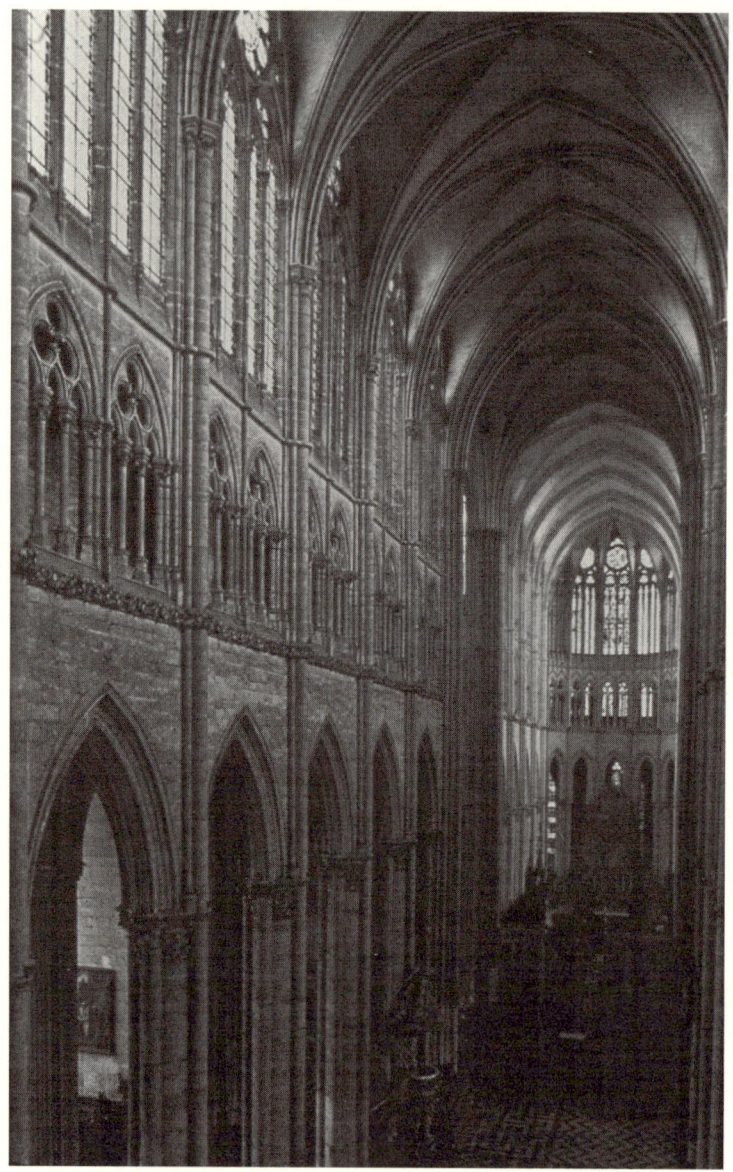

Figure 26. Cathedral of Notre-Dame, Amiens, 1220–69. Interior view of nave toward east. (Anthony Scibilia/Art Resource, NY.)

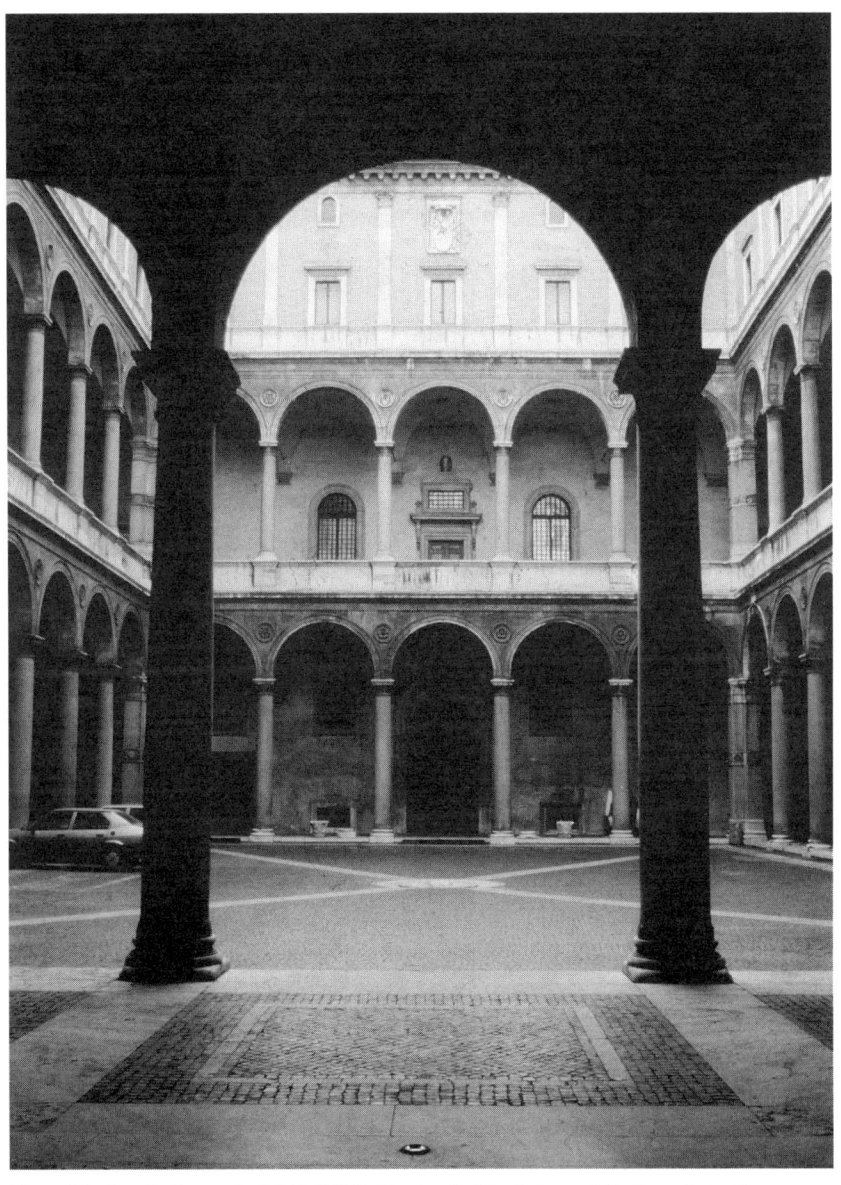

Figure 27. Donato Bramante (1444–1514). Courtyard of the Palazzo della Cancellaria, Rome. (Vanni/Art Resource, NY.)

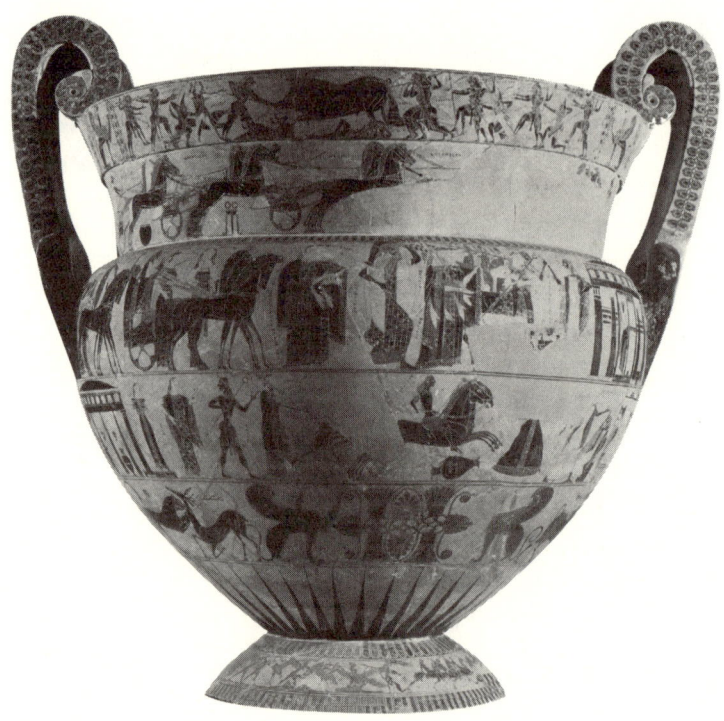

Figure 28. Ergotimos (6th century BCE, potter) and Kleitias (575–560 BCE, vase painter). François Vase. Attic black-figure volute krater, from Chiusi, ca. 570 BCE. Museo Archeologico, Florence. (Scala/Art Resource, NY.)

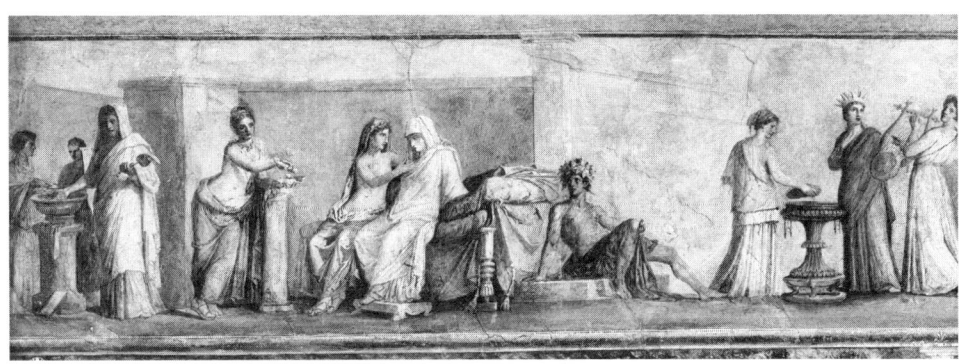

Figure 29. Aldobrandini Wedding. Wall painting from a house on the Esquiline Hill, Rome. 1st century BCE.
(Alinari/Art Resource, NY.)

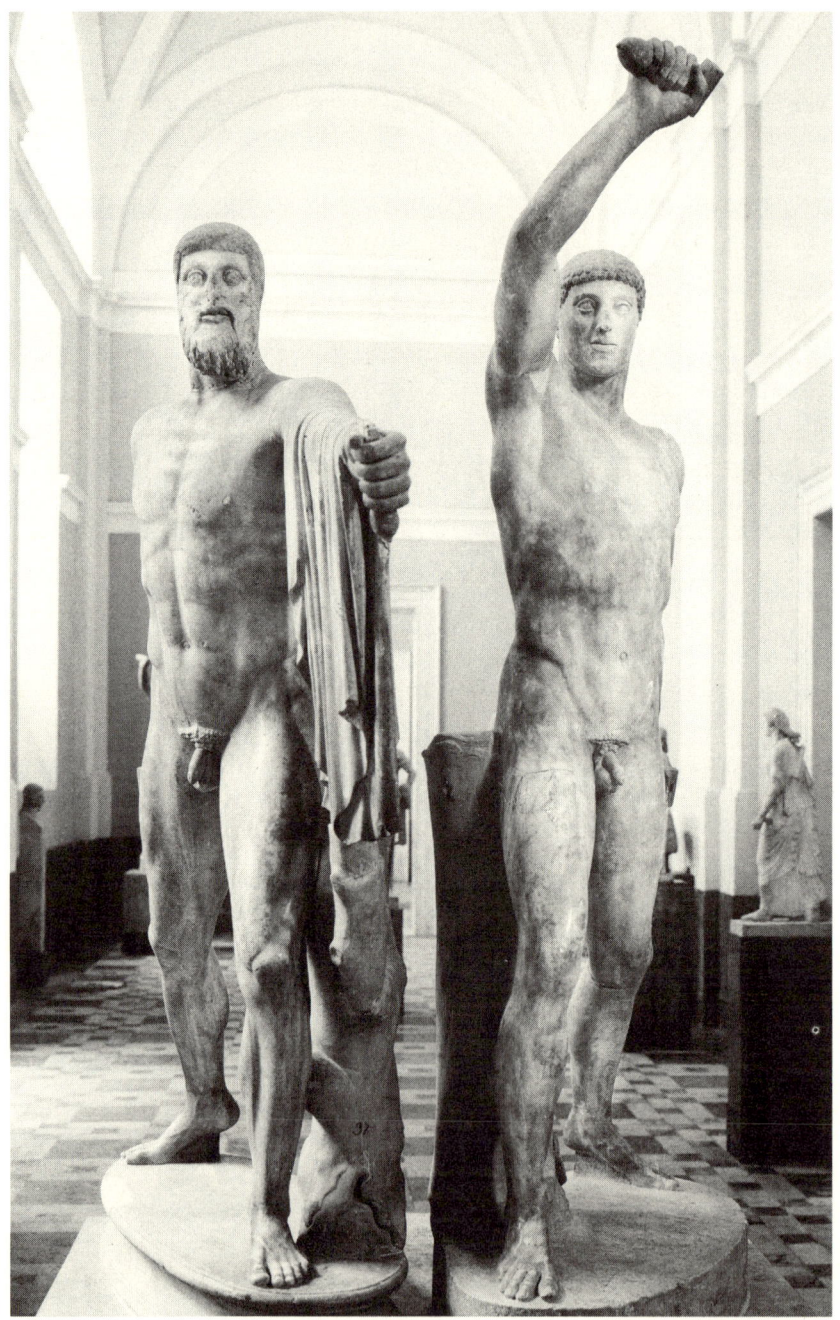

Figure 30. *Aristogeiton and Harmodios (The Tyrranicides)*. Marble copies after originals by Kritios and Nesiotes, ca. 477 BCE. Museo Archeologico Nazionale, Naples. (Alinari/Art Resource, NY.)

Index

190, 204–11, 241–46, 255, 343, 344–45, 353; in polytheistic worldview, 355–56; in Roman Imperial art, 147–49, 391, 431; Second Period (313–1520), 241–60; Third Period (post-1520), 167–86.

Movement, organic forms and, 123, 127–28, 132, 177, 200; in Egyptian art, 205, 356–57; in Greek art (pre-Alexander), 205, 320, 373, 375–76, 380; illusionism, 133; modern art and, 183; movement of inorganic nature, 343; suppression of, 309; symmetry and, 345, 346–47.

Muhammad (Prophet of Islam), 96, 158.

Murals, 148, 214, 221, 252, 290.

Murillo, Barolomé Esteban, 104–105.

Museum for Art and Industry of Vienna, 12.

Music, 99–100, 110.

Mycenaean age, 135, 204, 373, 416–22.

Myron, 375.

NATURALISM, 13, 17, 78, 139, 289; in Egyptian art, 366, 373, 443 n.6; in Greek art (pre-Alexander), 422; in Hellenistic Age, 321. *See also* Illusionism.

Nature: autonomous will of, 58; beautification of, 140–49; Byzantine art and, 69–72; causal relationships in, 18; Germanic view of, 86, 87–89, 163; human relation to, 57, 132; illusion or counterfeit of, 52; improvements of, 58, 59, 65, 69–74, 91, 131; inorganic, 123, 124, 128, 295; modern culture and, 185;

monotheistic view of, 67; motifs taken from, 123; organic, 131, 163, 165, 167, 184, 241, 350; perfected, 82; Renaissance view of, 95, 97; in Roman Imperial art, 38, 39–40; spiritualization of, 74, 112–14; transitory, 83, 88, 95, 97; viewed by Eastern Christianity, 328; viewed by Western Christianity, 331–32; Western culture and, 74–75.

Nature, artistic competition with, 16, 43–44, 51–53, 182, 298–302; Byzantine art, 70; color and, 407; distance of observation and, 399–400; Greek art (pre-Alexander), 319–20; harmony and, 205; Islamic prohibition of, 112, 158; Judaic worldview and, 312; limits of, 230; Northern (Germanic) art, 94; Reformation and, 166.

Nature, improvement of: aerial perspective and, 223–24; anthropomorphic polytheism and, 307–308; architecture and, 237; composition and, 365; distant view and, 247; light and shadow in, 220; near view and, 248; organic forms preferred, 138; profane art and, 161; surface and, 189–90.

Nazis, 23.

Near Eastern art, 136, 144, 145, 320; anthropomorphic polytheism and, 308–21, 356–71; Eastern Christianity and, 327; influence on early Greek art, 419; stasis of, 392. *See also* Byzantine art; Egyptian art; Islamic art.

Near view, 188, 192, 217, 242, 267, 398; in Egyptian art, 194, 409; in Italian art, 259–60, 262; monotheism and, 241; in Roman Imperial art, 215, 431; sculpture and, 400.

495

Zone Books series design by Bruce Mau Design
Type composed by Archetype
Image placement & production by Julie Fry
Printed and bound by Maple Press